Comparative European Party Systems

Contemporary Issues in European Politics
Volume 5
Garland Reference Library of Social Science
Volume 1175

Comparative European Party Systems

An Analysis of Parliamentary Elections Since 1945

Alan Siaroff

Garland Publishing, Inc.
A Member of the Taylor & Francis Group
New York and London
2000

Published in 2000 by
Garland Publishing Inc.
A member of the Taylor & Francis Group
29 West 35th Street
New York, NY 10001

10 9 8 7 6 5 4 3 2 1

Library of Congress Cataloging-in-Publication Data

Siaroff, Alan.
Comparative European party systems / Alan Siaroff.
p. cm.—(Garland reference library of social science ; vol. 1175. Contemporary issues in European politics ; v. 5)
Includes index.
ISBN 0-8153-2930-X (alk. paper)
1. Political parties—Europe. 2. Europe—Politics and government—1945– I. Title. II. Series: Garland reference library of social science ; v. 1175. III. Series: Garland reference library of social science. Contemporary issues in European politics ; v. 5.
JN50.S57 2000
324.2'094—dc21 99-31727
CIP

Printed on acid-free, 250-year-life paper
Manufactured in the United States of America

Contents

List of Tables

Acknowledgments

This book began when I was teaching at the University of British Columbia, and it could not have been finished without the hard work and commitment of my research assistants there: Ariane Farrell, Nicos Fassler, and John Merer. At Garland Publishing, I wish to thank Leo Balk, Mia Zamora, and Andrea Johnson. Thanks also to the people at Stratford Publishing Services, and last but certainly not least, the series editor, Carl Hodge, for getting everything into publishable form.

Although this book project has taken a few years, it is really the result of two decades of interest in and study of European politics. Over my long academic career my parents have been fully supportive of my endeavors, and it is to them that I dedicate this work.

Alan Siaroff
The University of Lethbridge
Lethbridge, Alberta, Canada
15 December 1999

Series Editor's Preface

It is an especially gratifying experience to be able to contribute a preface for Alan Siaroff's great book on elections in Europe. There is no political science more fundamental than that which concerns itself with how people exercise the most basic of democratic rights—the choice of a government through the ballot box. Long before the end of the Cold War, Western Europe was already the world's best laboratory for comparative electoral studies. It offered a degree of politico-cultural homogeneity and variation meaningful enough to make it a particularly fertile ground for comparative work. Ever since the historic changes of 1989–1991 the former Soviet sphere in the East has been home to revolutionary democratic change on a scale that puts many of the most venerated assumptions concerning democratic governance to the test. For that reason above all, Siaroff's work will stand for some time to come as the most sweeping comparative analysis of Western and Eastern Europe's decade of radical transitions.

That is no small achievement. In order to complete a study so broadly comparative as this one—and to mold the facts into a format and prose digestible to the undergraduate and graduate legions of European political studies—the author must be a confident master of his material. Judgements and generalizations made across political contexts and cultural borders also require a hefty dollop of professional courage. In this book Siaroff has demonstrated an enviable combination of steady commitment to his craft and a vision of Europe expansive enough to imagine great possibilities for the democratic future. The organization and content of the book speak volumes about its author's dedication to the heuristic calling of all sound political science. Over the coming years the book's inherent usefulness to all serious students of electoral affairs will in turn testify to the debt we owe to Siaroff's scholarship.

As series editor, I would like to thank him personally for publishing his book with Garland. Working with him has been an education; getting to know him as a friend and colleague has been a privilege.

Carl Cavanagh Hodge

Nonparty Acronyms

Benelux	Belgium, Netherlands, and Luxembourg
#M	number of (cabinet) ministers
#MON	number of months
#P	number of parties
#S	number of seats
%V	percentage of the vote (that is, of valid votes)
2PSC	two-party seat concentration
2PVC	two-party vote concentration
CAB DOM	cabinet dominance
CIS	Commonwealth of Independent States
CL	civil liberties score *(Freedom House)*
DISP	disproportionality
EC	European Community
ED	electoral decisiveness
EEA	European Economic Area
EFRG	electoral fragmentation
EFTA	European Free Trade Association
EM	earned majority
ENEP	effective number of electoral parties
ENPP	effective number of parliamentary parties
EU	European Union
FP	formation period
GC	grand coalition
gov't	government
HP	hung parliament

I	independents (in a cabinet)*
MAJ	majority
MIN	minority
MM	manufactured majority
MP	multi-party
MPs	members of parliament
MWC	minimal winning coalition
MWGC	minimal winning grand coalition
NATO	North Atlantic Treaty Organization
OVC	oversized coalition
OVGC	oversized grand coalition
P3%S	parties with 3 percent of the seats
PARL BASE	parliamentary base
pe	postelections
PFRG	parliamentary fragmentation
PR	political rights score *(Freedom House)*
PR	proportional representation
SBL	seat bias of leading party
SBT2	seat bias of the top two parties
SMP	single-member plurality
SP	single party
SR1:2	seat ratio of first to second party
SR2:3	seat ratio of second to third party
STV	single transferable vote
TO	turnout
TRNC	Turkish Republic of Northern Cyprus
TVOL	total volatility
WV	wasted votes

*Ind is used to designate an independent as prime minister.

PART I

Comparative Analysis

CHAPTER 1

Introduction and Context

WHERE IS EUROPE?

This work seeks to be a comprehensive analysis of European party systems. In terms of what and where Europe is, however, debate persists. Geographers would tend to define it broadly, up to the Ural Mountains at the start of Siberia. In contrast, historically such areas as Russia and Spain have at times not been included (Wallace 1990). In the current context one may be tempted to begin with the European Union; however, this contains only fifteen members, almost all in Western and Southern Europe. A better place to start is in fact with the Strasbourg-based Council of Europe (see Table 1.1).

Table 1.1 Council of Europe Membership as of December 1999

Albania	member since 13/07/1995
Andorra	member since 10/10/1994
Austria	member since 16/04/1956
Belgium	member since 05/05/1949
Bulgaria	member since 07/05/1992
Croatia	member since 06/11/1996
Cyprus	member since 24/05/1961
Czech Republic	member since 30/06/1993
Denmark	member since 05/05/1949
Estonia	member since 14/05/1993

continued

Table 1.1 *Continued*

Finland	member since 05/05/1989
France	member since 05/05/1949
Georgia	member since 27/04/1999
Germany	member since 09/08/1949
Greece	member since 09/08/1949
Hungary	member since 06/11/1990
Iceland	member since 09/03/1950
Ireland	member since 05/05/1949
Italy	member since 05/05/1949
Latvia	member since 01/02/1995
Liechtenstein	member since 23/11/1978
Lithuania	member since 14/05/1993
Luxembourg	member since 05/05/1949
the "former Yugoslav Republic of Macedonia"	member since 09/11/1995
Malta	member since 29/04/1965
Moldova	member since 13/07/1995
Netherlands	member since 05/05/1949
Norway	member since 05/05/1949
Poland	member since 29/11/1991
Portugal	member since 22/09/1976
Romania	member since 07/10/1993
Russian Federation	member since 28/02/1996
San Marino	member since 16/11/1988
Slovakia	member since 30/06/1993
Slovenia	member since 14/05/1993
Spain	member since 24/11/1977
Sweden	member since 05/05/1949
Switzerland	member since 06/05/1963
Turkey	member since 13/04/1950
Ukraine	member since 09/11/1995
United Kingdom	member since 05/05/1949

The Council of Europe was established in 1949 by ten European countries. Its stated purpose is to promote democracy and human rights throughout the continent. It also is involved in social, cultural, and legal matters—loosely, everything but defense. However, it did not turn out to be the incipient European government desired by some of its founders. Nevertheless, compared to the European Union or NATO, it is "easy" to join, in that no barriers are placed or vetoes made on worthy applicants. Membership in the Council of Europe thus serves as confirmation of at least modest human rights, and also implicitly of one's "Europeanness." Although this latter point may be of relevance for would-be members of the European Union, it also gives a sense of Europe to this analysis.

From its original ten members it spread into the rest of Western (and Mediterranean) Europe. From 1990 to 1999, various Central and Eastern European countries joined, bringing the membership up to forty-one. The newest member is Georgia. Since 1996, the other two Transcaucasian countries (Armenia and Azerbaijan) have had "special guest" status pending full membership. For its part, Bosnia-Herzegovina had observer status.

Thus it seems that Europe goes as far east as the Urals, and as far southeast as Turkey and Transcaucasia. Europe also contain several microstates—Andorra, Liechtenstein, Monaco, San Marino, and Vatican City. Of these, only Liechtenstein will be analyzed, since it is a separate member of the European Free Trade Association (EFTA). Furthermore, this analysis recognizes (without passing any judgment) that Cyprus is de facto a divided island, and that the Turkish government of the north of the island does control a de facto state. Finally, for simplicity's sake, the Russian Federation will henceforth be referred to as Russia, and the "former Yugoslav Republic of Macedonia" simply as Macedonia.

What of subnational governments and regions? There are many of these, as several European nations are either federal or have entrenched regional governments (Austria, Belgium, France, Germany, Italy, Russia, Spain, Sweden, Ukraine, and now the United Kingdom). Of these many regions, five particularly newsworthy ones have been chosen for separate analysis: the Basque Country and Catalonia in Spain, and Northern Ireland, Scotland, and Wales in the United Kingdom. The party systems in these regions will thus be analyzed like any national one, although of course the Basque Country and Catalonia also contribute to the overall Spanish party system, as do the three Celtic regions vis-à-vis the United Kingdom as a whole.

Although being part of Europe is a necessary condition for this analysis, it is not a sufficient one. A polity must also be reasonably competitive and democratic, since the notion of a party system normally implies two or more parties and the differences and relations among these. The most common source for worldwide levels of democratization are the annual reports prepared by the New York–based Freedom House survey team; their 1998 rankings of European countries and territories are given in Table 1.2.

Freedom House measures each country on political rights (PR) and civil liberties (CL) using a seven-point scale, with one being the most free and seven being the least free. *Political rights* refers to such things as responsible government, free and fair elections, freedom to form new political parties, the ability of the opposition to have a chance at power, and minority rights. *Civil liberties* refers to such things as freedom of assembly, freedom of association, freedom of discussion, freedom of religion, freedom of the press, the rule of law, and the absence of extreme corruption. On the basis of both of these scores, nations are thus classified as free, partly free, or not free. More specifically, Freedom House also uses the dichotomous category of electoral democracies (or not), in which electoral democracies are defined "as countries in which there are reasonably free and fair elections characterized by significant choices for voters in a context of free political organization, reasonable access to the media and secret ballot elections" (Karatnycky 1998: 7–8). A polity thus may be only partly free but still be an electoral democracy.

It seems reasonable that at a minimum a polity must be an electoral democracy for its party politics to have relevance and for its party system to be comparable to those of other electoral democracies. Consequently, Armenia, Azerbaijan, Belarus, and Yugoslavia will be dropped from further analysis. For a different reason, so too will Albania and Bosnia-Herzegovina: although both are technically partly free electoral democracies, both of them exist in a precarious, post–civil war reality that hinders definitive analysis. What remains, then, are forty-four different polities (including Northern Cyprus, the Basque Country, Catalonia, Northern Ireland, Scotland, and Wales).

Table 1.2 Freedom House Rankings, end 1998

Country	PR	CL	Freedom Rating	Electoral Democracy
Albania	4	5	partly free	yes
Armenia	4	4	partly free	no
Austria	1	1	free	yes
Azerbaijan	6	4	partly free	no

Country	PR	CL	Freedom Rating	Electoral Democracy
Belarus	6	6	not free	no
Belgium	1	2	free	yes
Bosnia-Herzegovina	5	5	partly free	yes
Bulgaria	2	3	free	yes
Croatia	4	4	partly free	yes
Cyprus (Greek)	1	1	free	yes
TRNC	4	2	partly free	yes
Czech Republic	1	2	free	yes
Denmark	1	1	free	yes
Estonia	1	2	free	yes
Finland	1	1	free	yes
France	1	2	free	yes
Georgia	3	4	partly free	yes
Germany	1	2	free	yes
Greece	1	3	free	yes
Hungary	1	2	free	yes
Iceland	1	1	free	yes
Ireland	1	1	free	yes
Italy	1	2	free	yes
Latvia	1	2	free	yes
Liechtenstein	1	1	free	yes
Lithuania	1	2	free	yes
Luxembourg	1	1	free	yes
Macedonia	3	3	partly free	yes
Malta	1	1	free	yes
Moldova	2	4	partly free	yes
Netherlands	1	1	free	yes
Norway	1	1	free	yes
Poland	1	2	free	yes
Portugal	1	1	free	yes

continued

Table 1.2 *Continued*

Country	PR	CL	Freedom Rating	Electoral Democracy
Romania	2	2	free	yes
Russia	4	4	partly free	yes
Slovakia	2	2	free	yes
Slovenia	1	2	free	yes
Spain	1	2	free	yes
Sweden	1	1	free	yes
Switzerland	1	1	free	yes
Turkey	4	5	partly free	yes
Ukraine	3	4	partly free	yes
United Kingdom	1	2	free	yes
Northern Ireland	3	3	partly free	yes
Yugoslavia	6	6	not free	no

Sources: Freedom House, *Freedom in the World 1997–1998, Freedom in the World 1998–1999.*

NATIONAL PARLIAMENTARY VERSUS OTHER ELECTIONS

This analysis will cover all postwar (or postdemocratization) parliamentary elections for the aforementioned forty-four polities. Although there is nowhere that one would want to call a parliamentary election completely irrelevant, in some places they are not as relevant for politics, inasmuch as there are other forums for political expression. In the cases of Liechtenstein and Switzerland, the requirements of direct democracy mean that parliaments are not ultimately sovereign. Phrased differently, even if one's parliamentary party of choice is not that successful, one can still affect specific policies through initiatives and referenda. Liechtenstein and Switzerland are of course rather idiosyncratic in this regard. What is more common, however, is a political role—perhaps even the main political role—for the head of state.

HEADS OF STATE AND GOVERNMENT

Almost all European countries have a head of state who is separate from the head of government (although the former may control the latter). There are only three exceptions here. The first is Switzerland, the seven cabinet ministers of which are all formally equal, with each taking a one-year turn serving as head of state and government. The second exception is (Greek) Cyprus, which is the only formal presidential system in Europe. In other words, the Cypriot president is both head of state and head of government. The third exception is Georgia, which as of its 1995 constitution effectively has a presidential system as well.

The remaining thirty-six *national* systems thus have both a head of state and a head of government. (In contrast, subnational governments in Europe do not have "heads of state," as one finds in Australia and Canada.) These can be initially divided into monarchies and republics. Constitutional monarchies are found in the Low Countries (Belgium, Luxembourg, the Netherlands), Liechtenstein, Scandinavia (Denmark, Norway, Sweden), Spain, and the United Kingdom. Generally these monarchs are largely figureheads, although they may play a role in government formation (in Sweden even this role has been transferred to the speaker). In Liechtenstein, however, the prince does have some say in policy. By definition, in all of these cases the position of head of state is achieved through birth and heredity.

In the remaining twenty-seven cases the head of state is a president. These presidents can either be elected by the population or selected by the parliament (in Germany and Italy by the parliament and regional delegates). These presidents also vary enormously in terms of their powers. For the sake of simplicity, let us distinguish between very strong presidents, moderately strong presidents, and weak presidents. A very strong president is the most important and powerful person in her or his country, to the point where he or she runs the country, at least in terms of foreign policy and overall domestic policy. Such presidents normally handpick their prime ministers and perhaps the rest of the cabinet as well. Thus, even if the prime minister is the formal head of government, she or he must actually defer to the president. Many strong presidents have powers of decree as well as veto. Finally, strong presidents often have the power to dissolve parliament, either at will or in certain situations. In short, the composition of parliament may be no more than a hindrance to a very strong president.

A moderately strong president, in contrast, only shares in the running of her or his country. He or she has some influence in the choice of prime minister and perhaps other ministers but does not have a free hand. There is often a division of labor involved here in that a moderately strong president is on the one hand the central (but not necessarily overwhelming) figure in foreign policy, but on the other hand only plays a modest role in domestic policy. His or her effect on domestic policy tends to come through modest veto powers. Domestic policy is thus the purview of the prime minister and cabinet, who are much more concerned with the responses of parliament than of the president.

Finally, a weak president is either a complete figurehead or has very limited powers of veto and at most a limited role in selecting the prime minister, who is the sole and clear head of government. A weak president can be an effective national symbol, popular personally, and even well known internationally, as is Václav Havel of the Czech Republic, but in no sense does he or she run the country.

Putting the method of selection together with their general powers gives six potential combinations of European presidents, five of which exist in actuality (see Table 1.3). All very strong presidents and almost all moderately strong presidents are elected; this obviously reflects in part the need for democratic legitimacy. Of course, many weak presidents are also chosen by election.

What does all of this mean for party politics, broadly defined? Three points are worth stressing here. First, where a very strong president is elected, this presidential election is in fact the most important election in the country, more so than the parliamentary one. The parliamentary election will still provide the basis for our comparative analysis, but the politicians, the media, and certainly the voters may not be as obsessed with it. A lesser variant of this scenario might occur with moderately strong presidents. Second, where the government exists largely at the whim of the president, the effects of parliamentary elections on government formation and stability (see Chapter 5) tend to be moot. Such is the situation with most strong presidents (France excepted) and also, of course, with the fully presidential system in Cyprus. Third and finally, a presidential or effectively presidential system is hypothesized to lead to less institutionalized party politics than a parliamentary system, since presidential candidates can campaign as independents or have only loose party ties.

Table 1.3 Presidents in Europe Today (Non-Presidential Systems)

	Directly Elected	**Selected by Parliament**
Very Strong Presidents	Croatia	
	France	
	Russia	
	Ukraine	

	Directly Elected	Selected by Parliament
Moderately Strong Presidents	Bulgaria	Turkey
	TRNC	
	Finland	
	Macedonia	
	Moldova	
	Poland	
	Portugal	
	Romania	
Weak Presidents	Austria	Czech Republic
	Iceland	Estonia
	Ireland	Germany
	Lithuania	Greece
	Slovakia*	Hungary
	Slovenia	Italy
		Latvia
		Malta

*From 1999

PAN-EUROPEAN ELECTIONS

Fifteen of the countries examined are also now members of the European Union, which has had since 1979 a directly elected European Parliament. European Parliament elections are held every five years. These cannot be examined in the same way as the forty-four cases in this book, however, because they are conducted essentially by national parties, often on national rather than European issues, and using national electoral systems rather than one European Union system. After the elections the various deputies do however sit in transnational party groups. European Parliament elections are thus not examined in this study, but the interested reader is directed to Bardi (1996), Gaffney (1996), Hix and Lord (1997), and Lodge (1996).

POLITICAL PARTIES AND KEY AXES OF COMPETITION

Klaus von Beyme (1985) has noted nine main types of parties or "spiritual families" found in Western Europe, all of which can also now be found in Eastern Europe. In a basic chronological order of formation, these are as follows: First, there are **liberal** or **radical parties**. These arose to struggle for responsible government, the separation of church and state, and free market economics. They are also internationalist and, in the postwar context, committed to European integration. Their historic support came from the secular middle class, and that is still the group most likely to support these parties. However, liberal and radical parties are now rather small and certainly are not the main party of the middle classes.

In many countries, the main middle-class party is thus now a **conservative party**. Originally rather elitist, paternalistic, and suspicious of unrestrained capitalism, conservatives today (with the exception of certain French Gaullists) share the liberal commitment to free markets. They are usually more nationalistic than liberals, especially where a polity has separate liberal and conservative parties, as is the case in Britain (the Conservatives, France (the Gaullists), and Italy (Berlusconi's Forza Italia). However, the conservative parties of Scandinavia and the Mediterranean (Greece, Malta, Portugal, Spain) are not significantly nationalistic and are strongly committed to European integration. The Mediterranean countries, for their part, do not have liberal parties, and in Finland and Norway the liberals have basically disappeared over time; in these places, the conservatives cover a broader spectrum; A further way in which conservatives often can be distinguished from liberals is that whereas liberals are strongly secular, conservatives tend to be moderately religious and supportive of "family values," even if their religiosity is more implicit than explicit. Here too, however, the secular Nordic conservatives are exceptions to this general pattern.

Next there are **socialist** or **social democratic parties**. These were formed to represent the working class and to push for socioeconomic change. Most of these parties have long shed their explicit socialism and are leftist more in their commitment to social programs than in their support for state ownership. Since the 1960s, at least, these parties tend to be quite in favor of European integration. Their support base has broadened from the working class to include elements of the middle class, especially in the public sector. Indeed, the French Socialists' core supporters have always been middle rather than working class. Rivaling the socialists for the support of the working class (and some intellectuals) have been **communist parties.** These have been clearly more left wing in their economics and in their foreign policy and also more skeptical of European integration. With the ending of the Cold War, there are very few parties that still call themselves "communist"—mainly the parties of France, a rump group in Italy, and those of post-Soviet countries such as Moldova, Russia, and Ukraine. Everywhere else, including east-central Europe, the communist parties that used to exist have transformed themselves, usually into social democratic parties (e.g., in Italy and Poland) but sometimes into what will be called new-left parties (e.g., in Sweden).

In most Catholic or mixed Catholic-Protestant countries in Europe, there is a **Christian democratic party**. These parties are obviously explicit in their religiosity and seek to represent all Christians. Nevertheless, they tend to do better among Catholics than among Protestants, and are weaker (Scandinavia) or nonexistent in Protestant nations. Christian democrats are explicitly cross-class in their orientation and are strong supporters of the welfare state. The major Christian democratic parties have also been the most ardent supporters of European integration right from its beginnings in the 1950s.

Separate **agrarian parties** have always existed in Nordic Europe and now exist in many Eastern European systems as well. With the decline in the rural population, the Nordic agrarian parties in the 1960s and 1970s renamed themselves **center parties**. They tend to be fairly environmentalist and sometimes skeptical of European integration, especially if this seems to hurt national farmers.

In countries where there is a cohesive, geographically concentrated, and self-conscious national minority (based on language or religion or on both of these factors), one tends to find **regional** or **ethnic parties**. In Italy there is now a regional party, the Northern League, based essentially on regional economic differences. The support for regional or ethnic parties tends to cut across class lines, but usually they are moderately conservative on left-right issues (as in Belgium [Flanders], Finland, Hungary, Romania, and Spain). In the United Kingdom, however, the Scottish and Welsh nationalists are left of center.

Right-wing extremist parties are certainly not new; witness the fascist and Nazi parties of interwar Europe. However, in the 1950s and 1960s (not coincidentally, decades of prosperity) the far right was quite marginal. Since the 1970s, however, right-wing extremist parties have grown in support, capitalizing on unemployment, immigration, and populist opposition to the "political class." In Scandinavia, such parties also have campaigned against high levels of taxation. The core supporters of right-wing extremist parties are young, poorly educated males, but these parties also appeal to disaffected conservatives.

Various **new-left parties** arose in the 1960s in prosperous Northern European nations such as Denmark and the Netherlands. Although left of center on socioeconomic affairs, they stressed greater citizen input and other "postmaterialist" issues. Their supporters have been young, well educated, and secular. Since the 1970s, in a wider group of nations, various **ecology** or **Green** parties have arisen. Although they often arose in opposition to nuclear power, and sometimes refused to place themselves on the traditional left-right axis, these green parties are now really variants (or, if one prefers, subgroups) of new-left parties, in that they share the same broader themes and bases of support. Moreover, Green parties now place themselves on the left and are more than willing to be part of social-democratic-led governments (as in France, Germany, and Italy).

All of the parties described here occur throughout Europe, as the country analyses in Part II show. However, there is a further type of party found in some East-Central Europe cases (Croatia, Romania, and Slovakia). In these cases, the party is a major one, so it is worth noting. These parties are postcommunist and thus are left of center. However, they are not very far to the left of center, and what is key for them is not economics per se but nationalism or even xenophobia. They thus have points in common with far-right parties, but they are much broader in their support base in part because they are more successfully populist. Let us thus call such parties **left-center national populist parties**.

Table 1.4 indicates for the European polities the presence today of each of these types of parties, with the criterion for inclusion being that such a party has won at least 3 percent of the seats in recent elections. A small (x) indicates a party within a bigger grouping as opposed to a clearly autonomous party.

Table 1.4 Parties in Europe Today

1. Liberal or radical party
2. Conservative party
3. Socialist or social-democratic party
4. Communist party
5. Christian-democratic party
6. Agrarian or center party
7. Regional or ethnic party
8. Right-wing extremist party
9. Ecology or new-left party
10. Left-center national populist party

	1.	**2.**	**3.**	**4.**	**5.**	**6.**	**7.**	**8.**	**9.**	**10.**
Austria	X		X		X			X	X	
Belgium	X		X		X		X	X	X	
Bulgaria	X		X				X			

	1.	2.	3.	4.	5.	6.	7.	8.	9.	10.
Croatia	X							X		X
Cyprus	X	X	X	X						
TRNC		X	X	X						
Czech Republic	X		X		X	X		X		
Denmark	X	X	X		X	X		X	X	
Estonia	X	X	X			X		X		
Finland		X	X			X	X		X	
France	X	X	X	X	(x)			X	X	
Georgia		X		(x)			(x)			
Germany	X		X	X	X		(x)		X	
Greece		X	X	X						
Hungary		X	X		X	X		X		
Iceland		X	X	X		X			X	
Ireland	X	X	X							
Italy		X	X	X	X		X	X		
Latvia		X	X		X	X		X		
Liechtenstein	X				X				X	
Lithuania	X	X	X		X	X				
Luxembourg	X		X		X				X	
Macedonia	X	X	X				X			
Malta			X		X					
Moldova		X	X			X				
Netherlands	X		X		X				X	
Norway		X	X		X	X		X	X	
Poland	X		X		X	X				
Portugal		X	X	X	X					
Romania	X				(x)		X			X
Russia	X			X		X		X		
Slovakia	X		X		X		X			X
Slovenia	X		X		X				X	

continued

Table 1.4 *Continued*

	1.	2.	3.	4.	5.	6.	7.	8.	9.	10.
Spain		X	X	X			X			
Basque Country		X	X	X			X			
Catalonia		X	X				X			
Sweden	X	X	X		X	X			X	
Switzerland	X		X		X	X		X	X	
Turkey	X		X (Islamic party)					X		
Ukraine		X	X	X		X			X	
United Kingdom	X	X	X							
Northern Ireland							X			
Scotland	X	X	X				X			
Wales	X	X	X				X			

As can be seen, social democratic parties exist almost everywhere. However, other types of parties are more limited. In particular, it is rare to have both a conservative and a Christian democratic party, and basically impossible to have both a large conservative and a large Christian democratic party. Indeed, if rather than talking about all the parties and cleavages or ideologies in a system we focus on the major ones, we can suggest perhaps six main patterns in Europe.

The first of these is essentially unidimensional, involving a social democratic party on the left and a conservative party on the right. There may be other smaller parties, but the social democrats and the conservatives are the main ones, and the key competition is between these two. This pattern is found in the Czech Republic, Greece, Malta, Portugal, Spain, and the United Kingdom. In the Maltese and Spanish cases, the conservatives are quite religious, but there is not a separate liberal pole; thus, we would still want to place these with the others in this group.

Pattern One:

Socio-economic Left ······ Social Democrats ······ Conservatives ······ Socio-economic Right

In the second pattern, competition is centered around two axes, left-right issues and a religiosity cleavage. There is no clear center but, rather,

Christian democrats on the religious center right and liberals on the secular center right. Consequently, there are points of commonality between the social democrats and the Christian democrats (e.g., union rights and welfare state spending), between the social democrats and the liberals (civil liberties and, usually, foreign policy), and between the Christian democrats and the liberals (private ownership and limiting the size of government). This pattern is at the core of party politics in Austria, the Benelux countries (Belgium, Luxembourg, Netherlands), Germany, Switzerland to a large extent, Italy until recently, and now Poland and Slovenia. Of course, in all of these systems there are additional parties, but these are the core dimensions.

Pattern Two:

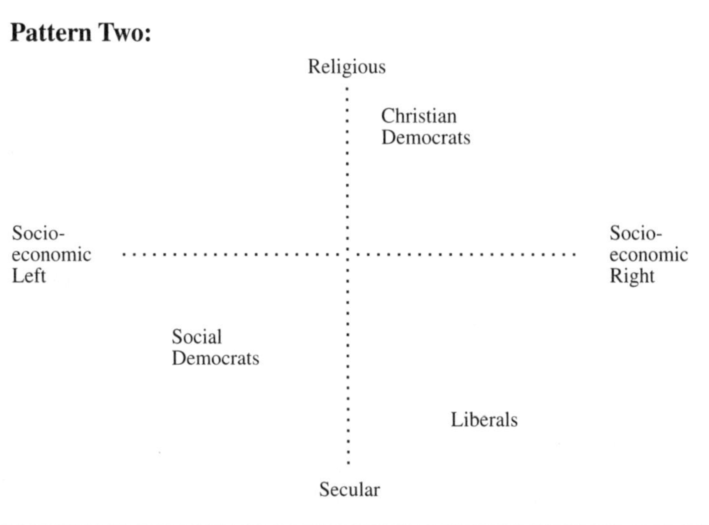

In the third pattern, the division on the center right is not religiosity but, rather, the rural-versus-urban cleavage. That is, there is a right-of-center urban (or more precisely suburban) party—the conservatives, and there is a right-of-center rural party. This pattern is found in Denmark, Finland since the 1970s, Iceland, and to some extent Switzerland. Incidentally, in each case the right-of-center rural party has a different name: Liberals in Denmark, Center Party in Finland (which was quite centrist between the world wars and after World War II but moved right in the 1970s), Progressive Party in Iceland, and People's Party in Switzerland.

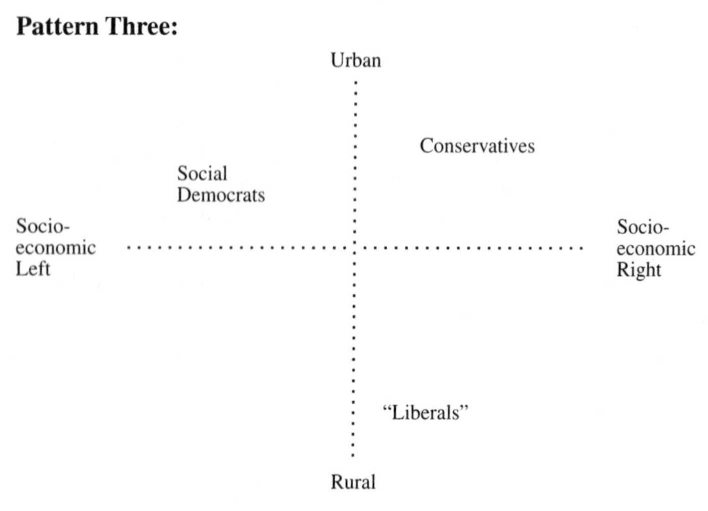

In the fourth pattern, the axes remain the same as in the third pattern, but the (main) rural party is clearly in the center on left-right matters, and thus open to cooperation with the social democrats. This pattern existed in Norway and Sweden (each with additional parties) until the 1970s. It now seems to exist in Estonia, although Estonia is more a system of fluid alliances than freestanding parties. Perhaps not coincidentally, since the 1970s Norway and Sweden have exhibited a fifth pattern, wherein the urban-rural cleavage has been subsumed into a broader growth-versus-environmentalism division, with support for European Union membership paralleling this division. In this fifth pattern, a new left party has drawn away support from the social democrats.

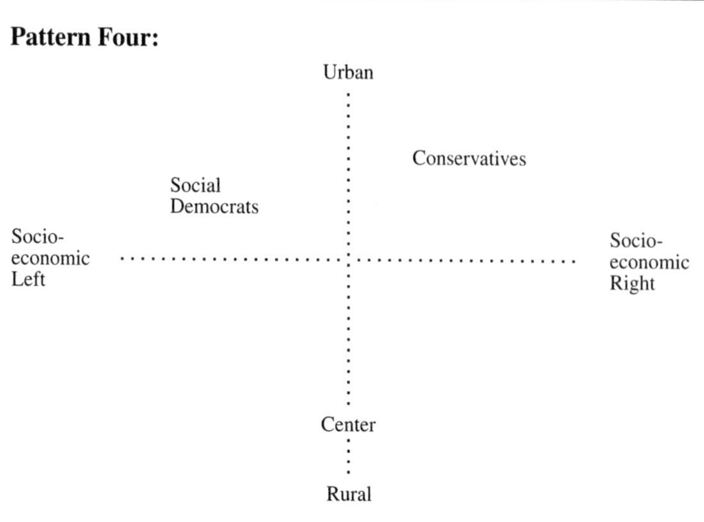
Pattern Four:
Urban
Conservatives
Social
Democrats
Socio-
economic
Left
Socio-
economic
Right
Center
Rural

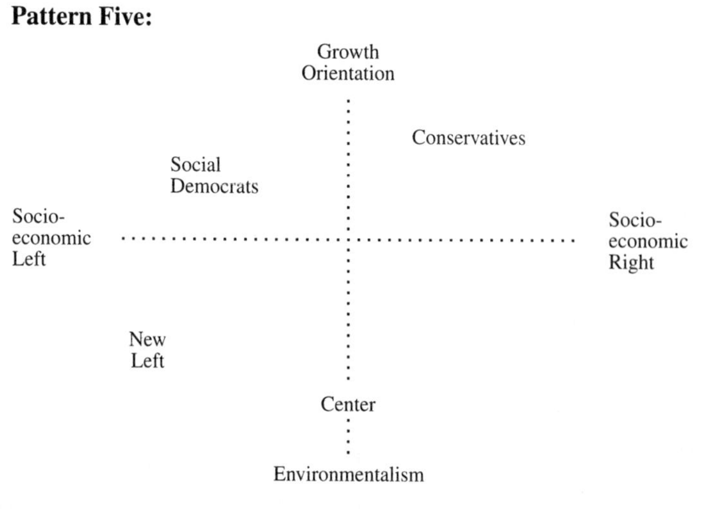
Pattern Five:
Growth
Orientation
Conservatives
Social
Democrats
Socio-
economic
Left
Socio-
economic
Right
New
Left
Center
Environmentalism

Finally, in the sixth pattern the second axis of competition is nationalism/xenophobia versus cosmopolitanism/tolerance. Although some scholars see this as a central axis everywhere, we would limit its key role to a few cases. In this pattern the social democrats are on the cosmopolitan left and the liberals are on the cosmopolitan right. A far-right party occupies the right xenophobic extreme. There is a major middle-of-the-road party (in the left-right sense) that ranges from moderately nationalistic (conservatives, but not as free market as most) to quite nationalistic (a left-center national populist party). This pattern is found in France since the 1980s, Hungary, Romania, and Slovakia. It also existed in the mid-1990s in Latvia. In Hungary, it should be noted, the conservative MDF has become much weaker, and the dominant moderate nationalist party is the right-of-center FIDESZ (Young Democrats).

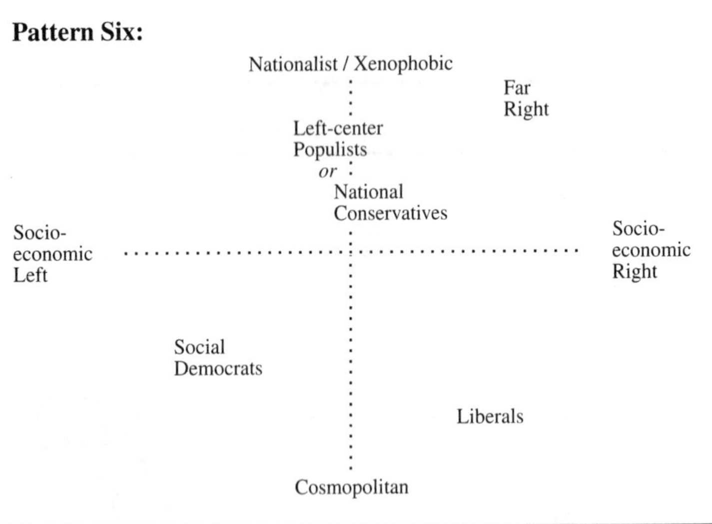

THE FULL RANGE OF POLITICAL DIVISIONS

The polities under examination differ in two further contextual ways. The first of these is the range of issue dimensions, as opposed to the main one or two. Table 1.5, modified and expanded from the postwar analysis of Lijphart (1999: 78–87), suggests nine issues over which a population may divide. Issues noted are either highly salient (H) or moderately salient (M).

We can presuppose as a hypothesis that the more issue dimensions there are, the more parties there will be to speak to these. However, one party—or, more precisely, two opposing parties—could speak to two or more issue dimensions if these are overlapping. This being said, if, following Lijphart, we score high salience as a 1.0 and moderate salience as a 0.5, then Switzerland clearly has the most issue dimensions (5.0), followed by Belgium, Finland, and Sweden (4.0). The fewest issue dimensions (2.0) are found in Bulgaria, Croatia, Liechtenstein, Spain, and the United Kingdom. In terms of the dimensions themselves, left-right socioeconomic issues are far and away the most important issue dimension in Europe, followed by religiosity and nationalism/xenophobia. Religion, as opposed to religiosity, is only relevant in the religiously divided polities, but in one of these—Northern Ireland—it is extremely salient.

Table 1.5 Issue Dimensions in the 1990s

1. Religion
2. Regional/cultural/ethnic
3. Religiosity
4. Urban–rural
5. Regime support
6. Nationalism/xenophobia
7. Socio-economic
8. Foreign policy
9. Postmaterialism

	1.	**2.**	**3.**	**4.**	**5.**	**6.**	**7.**	**8.**	**9.**
Austria			M			H	H		M
Belgium		H	H			M	H		M
Bulgaria	M	M					H		
Croatia						H	H	M	
Cyprus				M		M	M		
TRNC				M		H	H		
Czech Republic		M					H		
Denmark				H			H	M	M
Estonia		M		M?		M	H		
Finland		M	M	H			H	M	M
France			M			H	H	M	M
Georgia						M	M	H	M
Germany	M	M	H			M	H		M
Greece							H	M	

continued

Table 1.5 *Continued*

	1.	**2.**	**3.**	**4.**	**5.**	**6.**	**7.**	**8.**	**9.**
Hungary			H	M		H	H		
Iceland				H			H	M	
Ireland						H	H	M	
Italy		M	M			M	H		M
Latvia				M?		M	H		
Liechtenstein			H				M		M
Lithuania				M?			H		
Luxembourg			H				H		M
Macedonia		H				M	M	M	
Malta			H				H	H	
Moldova		M		M	M		H		
Netherlands			H				H		M
Norway			H	H		M	H	H	M
Poland			H	H			H		
Portugal			M			M	H		
Romania		M				H	H		
Russia				M	H	M	H	M	
Slovakia		M	M			H	H	M	
Slovenia			H	M?			H		M
Spain		M	M				H		
Basque Country		H	M		H		M		
Catalonia		H	M	H			H		
Sweden			M	M			H	H	H
Switzerland	H	M		H		M	H	M	M
Turkey		H	H	H			H		
Ukraine		H		M	M	H	H	M	
United Kingdom		M					H	M	
Northern Ireland	H				H		H		
Scotland					H		H		M
Wales		H		M			H		
TOTALS	3.0	13.0	16.0	14.0	5.0	14.5	41.5	10.5	8.0

If we go back a generation, to the 1960s, what was different? As Table 1.6 shows, the socioeconomic issue dimension was still the most important one, followed by religiosity. At the other end, postmaterialism had only just begun to appear. Of the seventeen cases so analyzed, those with the most issue dimensions (3.5) were Germany, Italy, the Netherlands, and Turkey. The countries with the least issue dimensions were Liechtenstein and the United Kingdom (1.5), followed by Austria, Luxembourg, and Sweden (2.0). Sweden is thus an illustrative case of evolution to greater complexity: in the 1960s it had no appreciable divisions on religiosity, foreign policy, or postmaterialism, but now it has these.

Table 1.6 Issue Dimensions in the 1960s

1. Religion
2. Regional/cultural/ethnic
3. Religiosity
4. Urban–rural
5. Regime support
6. Nationalism/xenophobia
7. Socio-economic
8. Foreign policy
9. Postmaterialism

	1.	**2.**	**3.**	**4.**	**5.**	**6.**	**7.**	**8.**	**9.**
Austria			H				H		
Belgium		H	H				H		
Denmark				H			H	M	
Finland		M		H	M		H	M	
France			M		M	M	H	M	
Germany	M	M	H				H	M	
Iceland				H			H	H	
Ireland						H	M	M	
Italy			H		M	M	H	M	
Liechtenstein			H				M		
Luxembourg			H				H		
Netherlands	H		H				H		M
Norway			M	H			H		
Sweden				H			H		
Switzerland	M	M		H			H		
Turkey		H	M	M		M	H		
United Kingdom		M					H		
TOTALS	2.0	4.0	8.5	6.5	1.5	2.5	16.0	4.0	0.5

POLITICAL PARTICIPATION

The final overall way in which these polities differ is in terms of political participation. This is measured in two ways for the 1990s. The first is party membership, calculated as a percentage of the electorate, with the raw data taken from the *Europa Yearbook*. Because accurate data are not available for all places, particularly in Eastern Europe, a five-point scale has been used in which total membership above 20 percent of the electorate scores a "5," membership between 15 and 20 percent scores a "4," membership between 10 and 15 percent scores a "3," membership between 5 and 10 percent scores a "2," and membership less than 5 percent scores a "1." Countries do seem to fit clearly into one of these five categories. The second measurement of political participation is voter turnout, averaged for all elections in the 1990s (from the data in Chapter 2). The actual data are given in Table 1.7, but to compare with the party membership scales, a similar five-point scale is used in which turnout above 90 percent of the electorate scores a "5," turnout between 80 and 90 percent scores a "4," turnout between 70 and 80 percent scores a "3," turnout between 60 and 70 percent scores a "2," and turnout less than 60 percent scores a "1." Of course, this measure is biased in favor of polities with compulsory voting, these being Belgium, Cyprus (Greek), Greece, Italy, Liechtenstein, Luxembourg, and Turkey. However, in Italy the sanction is not even a fine, merely a "negative" stamp on one's identification, whereas in Greece the supposed jail sentences do not seem to be enforced! Thus the bias is limited in these two cases. On the other hand, even without compulsory voting one would likely get high turnout in Cyprus. In short, using voter turnout is truly biased only as concerns Belgium, Luxembourg, and (especially, it seems) Liechtenstein (given the Swiss figures).

As Table 1.7 shows, political participation is highest in Nordic and especially Mediterranean Europe, and lowest in Eastern Europe (although Bulgaria and Romania stand out from that region). Political participation is also higher in smaller rather than larger countries, at least in Western Europe. Finally, as hypothesized earlier, political participation in parliamentary elections is lower where there is a powerful, directly elected president (France, Georgia, Poland, Russia).

Table 1.7 Political Participation in the 1990s (five-point scale)

Country	Party Membership	Voter Turnout	Combined Rank
Malta	5	5 (95.9 %)	5.0
TRNC	5	5 (90.3 %)	5.0
Austria	5	4 (81.8 %)	4.5
Cyprus (Greek)	4	5 (93.6 %)	4.5
Iceland	5	4 (86.2 %)	4.5
Sweden	5	4 (84.7 %)	4.5
Belgium	2	5 (91.4 %)	3.5
Bulgaria	3	4 (81.0 %)	3.5
Luxembourg	3	4 (87.1 %)	3.5
Denmark	2	4 (83.9 %)	3.0
Finland	3	3 (70.8 %)	3.0
Italy	2	4 (85.4 %)	3.0
Liechtenstein	2*	4 (86.5 %)	3.0
Norway	3	3 (76.9 %)	3.0
Romania	3	3 (76.2 %)	3.0
Turkey	2*	4 (85.3 %)	3.0
Czech Republic	1	4 (83.0 %)	2.5
Slovakia	1	4 (84.9 %)	2.5
Slovenia	2	3 (74.9 %)	2.5
Croatia	1	3 (73.4 %)	2.0
Georgia	2	2 (68.7 %)	2.0
Germany	1	3 (79.7 %)	2.0
Greece	1	3 (77.1 %)	2.0
Ireland	2	2 (67.2 %)	2.0
Latvia	1	3 (77.9 %)	2.0
Macedonia	1*	3 (77.3 %)	2.0
Moldova	1	3 (75.8 %)	2.0
Netherlands	1	3 (75.8 %)	2.0
Spain	1	3 (77.2 %)	2.0
Ukraine	1	3 (72.8 %)	2.0
United Kingdom	1	3 (74.6 %)	2.0

continued

Table 1.7 *Continued*

Country	Party Membership	Voter Turnout	Combined Rank
Estonia	1	2 (64.1 %)	1.5
France	1	2 (68.4 %)	1.5
Hungary	1	2 (63.4 %)	1.5
Lithuania	1	2 (64.1 %)	1.5
Portugal	1	2 (65.6 %)	1.5
Switzerland	2	1 (43.8 %)	1.5
Poland	1	1 (47.7 %)	1.0
Russia	1	1 (59.6 %)	1.0

*Rough estimates

REFERENCES

Bardi, Luciano (1996). "Transnational Trends in European Parties and the 1994 Elections of the European Parliament." *Party Politics,* Vol. 2, No. 1, pp. 99–114.

Freedom House (annual). *Freedom in the World: The Annual Survey of Political Rights and Civil Liberties.* New Brunswick, N.J.: Transaction Publishers.

Gaffney, John, ed. (1996). *Political Parties and the European Union.* London and New York: Routledge.

Hix, Simon, and Christopher Lord (1997). *Political Parties in the European Union.* New York: St. Martin's Press.

Karatnycky, Adrian (1998). "The Comparative Survey of Freedom 1997–1998: Freedom in the 'Democratic Age,'" in Freedom House, *Freedom in the World: The Annual Survey of Political Rights and Civil Liberties 1997–1998.* New Brunswick, N.J.: Transaction Publishers.

Lijphart, Arend (1999). *Patterns of Democracy: Government Forms and Performance in Thirty-six Countries.* New Haven: Yale University Press.

Lodge, Juliet, ed. (1996). *The 1994 Elections to the European Parliament.* London: Pinter.

von Beyne, Klaus (1985). *Political Parties in Western Democracies.* New York: St. Martin's Press.

Wallace, William (1990). *The Transformation of Western Europe.* London: Royal Institute for International Affairs and Pinter Publishers.

CHAPTER 2

Data on Elections

This chapter provides a comprehensive data set on the hitherto 372 postwar elections in the forty-four cases examined. In terms of the number of elections held, Denmark clearly stands out with the most, at twenty-two. In contrast, for Eastern and Central European countries only two to four post-democratization elections have occurred so far. Information is given case by case. The variables given, and their lowest and highest values in specific elections, are as follows:

Elections. Election dates are given in the form day(s)/month(s)/year. When more than a single date is given, this reflects the fact that there were multiple rounds of voting on the given dates. However, if, for example, problems in a tiny number of constituencies led to new elections in these and only these, then just the original election date is given.

TO—Turnout. Unless otherwise noted, turnout is the total number of votes cast, whether valid or invalid, as a share of the electorate. For elections in which multiple rounds of voting occur, the first ballot turnout is given. The lowest turnout values are those of Switzerland 1995 (42.2 percent), Poland 1991 (43.2 percent), and Switzerland 1999 (43.3 percent). The highest turnout values are those of Austria 1949 (96.8 percent), Liechtenstein 1958 (96.4 percent), and Malta from 1987 to 1996 (average of 96.1 percent across three elections).

EFRG—Electoral Fragmentation. This figure weights parties by size and is obtained by first taking the vote share of each party as a decimal (for example, 42.2 percent = 0.427), squaring this value, and summing these values for all parties. Independents are ignored. The figure obtained is then subtracted from 1 to produce the figure for electoral fragmentation. Consequently, the higher the value, the more fragmented electorally the elections. The lowest EFRG scores are those of Liechtenstein in 1945 and 1958 (0.496 each time). The highest EFRG scores are those of Ukraine 1994 (0.978) and Poland 1991 (0.928).

PFRG—Parliamentary Fragmentation. This figure is obtained in the same way as EFRG, except that the percentage of filled seats won is used instead of percentage of votes. Likewise, then, the higher the value, the more fragmented the parliament. The lowest PFRG scores are those of Turkey 1954 (0.128) and Turkey 1950 (0.240). The highest PFRG scores are those of Russia 1993 (0.930), Ukraine 1994 (0.926), and Poland 1991 (0.908).

ENEP—Effective Number of Electoral Parties. This figure weights parties by size by first taking the vote share of each party as a decimal (for example, 42.2 percent = 0.427), squaring this value, and summing these values for all parties. Independents are ignored. The figure obtained is then inverted (that is, 1/X) to produce the figure for effective number of electoral parties. The correlation between EFRG and ENEP is always perfect, but the latter measure is perhaps more intuitively understandable. The lowest ENEP scores, that is, the lowest effective number of electoral parties are, again, those of Liechtenstein in 1945 and 1958 (1.98 each time). The highest ENEP scores are those of Ukraine 1994 (an amazing 46.20) and Poland 1991 (13.83).

ENPP—Effective Number of Parliamentary Parties. This figure is obtained in the same way as ENEP, except that the percentage of filled seats won is used instead of percentage of votes. The lowest ENPP scores, that is, the lowest effective number of parliamentary parties, are those of Turkey 1954 (1.15) and Turkey 1950 (1.32). Again, since parties are weighted by size this did not mean that Turkey had literally less than two parties, but that it had one predominant one (and in fact there were two parties). The highest ENPP scores are those of Russia 1993 (14.41), Ukraine 1994 (13.50), and Poland 1991 (10.85).

P3%S—Parties with 3 Percent of the Seats. This figure, popularized by Ware (1996), is simply the number of parties winning 3 percent or more of the filled seats. There is no weighting of the parties herein. This figure is always an integer value (two, three, four, et cetera). Note that the calculation is always made as a result of the elections, not what may happen "down the road" when parties may split or independents may join a tiny party. Although it is mathematically possible for there to be no party, or just one party, with more than 3 percent of the seats, in reality the smallest value for P3%S is two. This occurs in Austria 1945, Turkey 1950–57, TRNC 1990, in every election in Liechtenstein from 1945 through 1989, in every (post-independence) election in Malta (1966 through 1998 inclusive), and in every election in the United Kingdom from 1945 through 1979. Conversely, the highest value for P3%S is ten, found in Belgium 1991 through 1999, Denmark 1977, and Poland 1991. These cases are followed by P3%S values of nine in Denmark 1973, Latvia 1995, and the Netherlands 1972.

ED—Electoral Decisiveness. This is not a numerical value, but rather a two-letter code indicating how decisive the particular elections were. One of the following results is given: HP = hung parliament (no party with a majority of seats); EM = earned majority (a party with a majority of both seats and votes); or MM = manufactured majority (a party with a majority of seats but not a majority of votes).

FP—Formation Period. This value is the number of days after the elections until a new cabinet fully takes office. As discussed in Chapter 5, under a system of positive parliamentarianism a government must first be confirmed by the legislature before it can actually assume power, even if it has already been sworn in by the head of state. Consequently, this latter date is used for the calculation, whenever it has been obtained. The lowest FP value is 1, wherein a cabinet is appointed "immediately" (that is, the next day), presumably reappointing a cabinet without change, or else with an extremely quick formation. To the best of my knowledge, FP scores of 1 are found in Austria 1979; Denmark 1984; Malta 1966; Norway 1949, 1953, and 1957; Sweden 1952, 1956, and 1958; and the United Kingdom 1964 and 1970. The highest FP values, that is, the longest formation periods, are found in the Netherlands: 208 (days) in 1977, and 163 in 1972.

DISP—Disproportionality. Disproportionality refers to the difference between the vote totals and the seat totals. There are alternative ways to calculate disproportionality. In this analysis we shall use the Loosemore-Haneby Index. That is, one takes the absolute difference between the percentage of votes and the percentage of seats won by a particular party (or the "others") and sums this value for all parties (and others). Finally, since one assumes that one party's gains are another's loss, the figure is divided by 2 to give DISP. Consequently, the higher the value the more disproportionate the result, in other words the more biased is the electoral system. Conversely, a disproportionality score of 0.0 would indicate that each party received exactly the share of seats to match its share of votes. This "perfect" outcome has never occurred precisely in Europe, but it has essentially happened in Liechtenstein (DISP of 0.2 in 1982, and 0.4 in 1949). Disproportionality of less than 1.0 also occurs in Denmark (DISP of 0.6 in 1950, and 0.8 in 1998). In contrast, the highest DISP scores are found in France 1993 (40.4) and Georgia 1995 (33.5).

WV—Wasted Votes. This is the total percentage of votes cast for parties that did not receive any parliamentary representation. In electoral systems with various "parts" (that is, single member and proportional seats, or multitiered districts), it is sufficient to achieve representation *somewhere* to be excluded from the value. That is, wasted votes only measure the votes for parties who did not receive any seats in any way. Of course, a given party may not have received a "fair" number of seats, but that is assessed by DISP. There have been many elections where there were no discernible votes wasted, that is, WV = 0.0. This occurs in Denmark 1945; Iceland 1949; Liechtenstein on many occasions (1945, 1949, 1953, 1957, 1958, 1978, 1982, February 1993, October 1993, and 1997); Luxembourg 1964; Malta 1976 and 1981; Norway 1953; and Sweden 1958. In contrast, the highest number of wasted votes occurs in Georgia 1995 (41.6 percent) and Poland 1993 (34.6 percent).

SBL—Seat Bias of Leading Party. This is the value obtained by subtracting the percentage of votes won from the percentage of seats won by the party winning the most seats. It reflects the extent to which the electoral system is biased either in favor of or against the plurality or leading party (in terms of seats). In the vast majority of cases this value is positive, indicating that the leading party received more seats that strictly merited proportional to its votes. However, there have been cases where the value is negative: Italy 1994 (–2.3 percent); France 1951 (–2.0 percent); Denmark 1947 (–1.5 percent) and 1945 (–0.4 percent); and Cyprus 1991 (–0.1 percent). In the case of France 1951, this outcome was certainly "intentional," in that the bonuses given to (centrist) alliances outside of Paris were intended to lessen the strength of the Communists and Gaullists. The Gaullists still won the most seats, but not their proportionate amount. France in its Fifth Republic also provides the opposite phenomena—very high SBL in 1968 (29.9 percent in favor of the Gaullists), 1993 (22.4 percent in favor of the Gaullists), 1958 (22.1 percent in favor of the Gaullists), and 1981 (21.5 percent in favor of the Socialists. However, the most extreme positive values of SBL have occurred in Turkey: 36.6 percent in 1954 and 32.9 percent in 1950 (both in favor of the DP), as well as 28.6 percent in 1987 (in favor of ANAP).

SBT2—Seat Bias of Top Two Parties. This is the same measure as SBL, except for the top two parties. That is, this value is obtained by subtracting the combined percentage of votes won from the combined percentage of seats won by the two parties winning the most seats. SBT2 is simply the difference between the next two variables, 2PVC and 2PSC. SBT2 reflects the extent to which the electoral system is biased either in favor of or against the top two parties (in terms of seats). In the vast majority of cases this value is positive, indicating that the top two parties received more seats that strictly merited proportional to their votes, thus potentially creating a manufactured "two-partyness." However, for France 1951 this value is -10.9, as the system of bonuses given to (centrist) alliances outside of Paris was intended to lessen the strength of the Communists and Gaullists. The French Communists were clearly the leading party in terms of votes (25.9 percent), but only came second in terms of seats (17.8 percent). A clearly negative SBT2 also occurs in Russia 1993 (-8.6 percent), where the Liberal Democrats won only five of the single-member seats. In contrast, the highest SBT2 values are those of France 1993 (40.2 percent), Poland 1993 (30.1 percent), France 1958 (28.5 percent), and Georgia 1995 (28.0 percent).

2PVC—Two-Party Vote Concentration. This is the sum of the percentage of votes for the two parties obtaining the most *seats* in parliament. The lowest values here are found in Poland 1991 (24.3 percent), Belgium 1999 (28.4 percent), and Italy 1994 (28.8 percent). Very low values are also found in Latvia 1995 (30.0 percent) and Belgium 1991 and 1995 (30.3 percent in each case). The highest possible value, 100.0 percent, occurs at various times in Liechtenstein (1945, 1949, 1953, 1957, 1958, 1978, and 1982).

2PSC—Two-Party Seat Concentration. This is the sum of the percentage of seats for the two parties obtaining the most seats in parliament. The lowest values here are found in Poland 1991 (26.5 percent), Russia 1993 (29.8 percent), and Belgium 1999 (30.0 percent).

The highest possible value, 100.0 percent, occurs in every election in Liechtenstein from 1945 through 1989, in every (postindependence) election in Malta (1966 through 1998 inclusive), and in the TRNC 1990.

SR1:2—Seat Ratio First to Second Party. This is the ratio obtained by comparing the seats of the party with the largest number of seats to the seats of the party with the second-largest number of seats. If the top two parties win exactly the same number of seats, then the SR1:2 is 1.00. This equality occurs in the Netherlands 1952, Switzerland 1959 and 1979, and the TRNC 1993. Otherwise, the greater the gap the larger the value. The highest SR1:2 values are those of Turkey 1954 (16.29) and 1950 (6.67). Very high values also occur in Croatia 1992 (6.07), France 1968 (6.07), and the TRNC 1976 (5.00).

SR2:3—Seat Ratio Second to Third Party. This is the ratio obtained by comparing the seats of the party with the second largest number of seats to the seats of the party with the third largest number of seats. If the second and third parties win exactly the same number of seats, then the SR1:2 is 1.00. This equality occurs in Austria 1999, Belgium 1995, Denmark 1979, and thrice in Finland (1945, 1958, 1970). Conversely, if only two parties win all the seats and there is no third party in parliament, then this value is infinity (or if there is no third party at all then this measure is inapplicable). Such outcomes occur in all the cases where the 2PSC is 100.0, that is, in every election in Liechtenstein from 1945 through 1989, in every (postindependence) election in Malta (1966 through 1998 inclusive), and in the TRNC 1990.

TVOL—Total Volatility. This value is the only one to compare an election with the previous elections. It is thus not given for the first elections in a polity. Total volatility is calculated by first taking the absolute difference between the percentage of votes won in the elections and the percentage won in the previous elections by a particular party (or any "others") and summing this value for all parties (and others). This value is then divided by 2 to yield TVOL. If TVOL is 0.0, then there is no aggregate vote change from the previous elections. This essentially occurs in Malta 1987 (0.3 percent) and Austria 1975 (0.5 percent). The highest volatility scores are found in Turkey 1983 (98.1 percent, when the previous parties had been banned) and Turkey 1987 (61.0 percent). Very high volatility scores are also found in certain East European elections: Poland 1998 (63.9 percent), Russia 1995 (53.7 percent), Slovakia 1992

(52.8 percent), and Latvia 1995 (51.4 percent). Note the elections data in the case analyses of Part II will not normally yield precisely the same amount as here, since in Part II tables tiny and/or fleeting parties are usually put into "others" to save space. In this part, however, the calculations are based on the total number of parties for which separate data exist.

REFERENCE

Ware, Alan (1996). *Political Parties and Party Systems.* Oxford: Oxford University Press.

ELECTORAL DATA

Austria

Elections:	TO	EFRG	PFRG	ENEP	ENPP	P3%S	ED
25/10/45	94.3	0.550	0.522	2.22	2.09	2	MM
09/10/49	96.8	0.640	0.607	2.78	2.54	4	HP
22/02/53	95.8	0.638	0.596	2.76	2.48	3	HP
13/05/56	96.0	0.597	0.551	2.48	2.23	3	HP
10/05/59	94.2	0.597	0.545	2.48	2.20	3	HP
18/11/62	93.8	0.594	0.591	2.47	2.44	3	HP
06/03/66	93.8	0.581	0.533	2.39	2.14	3	MM
01/03/70	91.8	0.653	0.529	2.29	2.12	3	HP
10/10/71	92.4	0.561	0.529	2.28	2.12	3	EM
05/10/75	92.9	0.559	0.548	2.27	2.21	3	EM
06/05/79	92.2	0.561	0.550	2.28	2.22	3	EM
24/04/83	90.6	0.584	0.557	2.40	2.26	3	HP
23/11/86	88.9	0.632	0.620	2.72	2.63	4	HP
07/10/90	86.1	0.684	0.666	3.16	2.99	4	HP
09/10/94	78.1	0.742	0.732	3.87	3.73	5	HP
17/12/95	82.7	0.721	0.712	3.59	3.47	5	HP
03/10/99	80.4	0.738	0.707	3.82	3.41	4	HP

Belgium

Elections:	TO	EFRG	PFRG	ENEP	ENPP	P3%S	ED
17/02/46	90.3	0.695	0.656	3.28	2.91	4	HP
25/06/49	94.4	0.693	0.636	3.26	2.75	4	HP
04/06/50	92.6	0.638	0.599	2.76	2.50	4	MM
11/04/54	93.2	0.675	0.620	3.08	2.63	3	HP
01/06/58	93.6	0.642	0.592	2.79	2.45	3	HP
26/03/61	92.3	0.676	0.628	3.08	2.69	3	HP
23/05/65	91.6	0.749	0.722	3.98	3.59	4	HP
31/03/68	90.0	0.805	0.797	5.13	4.93	6	HP

FP	DISP	WV	SBL	SBT2	2PVC	2PSC	SR1:2	SR2:3	TVOL
54	3.2	0.2	1.7	3.2	94.4	97.6	1.12	19.00	—
29	4.6	0.5	2.7	4.6	82.7	87.3	1.15	4.19	12.0
38	5.7	0.4	3.5	5.6	83.4	89.0	1.01	5.21	3.6
40	5.6	0.1	3.7	5.5	89.0	94.5	1.11	12.33	5.8
67	6.3	3.4	3.7	6.2	89.0	95.2	1.01	9.75	3.0
129	4.6	3.5	2.1	0.8	89.4	90.2	1.07	9.50	1.7
44	5.5	3.7	3.2	5.4	90.9	96.3	1.15	12.33	4.8
50	3.9	1.4	0.7	3.9	93.1	97.0	1.03	15.80	6.9
25	1.4	1.4	0.8	1.4	93.1	94.5	1.16	8.00	2.0
23	1.3	1.2	0.4	1.2	93.3	94.5	1.16	8.00	0.5
1	1.1	1.0	0.9	1.9	92.9	94.0	1.23	7.00	1.3
30	4.7	4.1	1.6	2.7	90.8	93.5	1.11	6.75	4.6
59	1.5	1.0	0.6	1.4	84.4	85.8	1.04	4.28	9.7
71	3.8	3.8	0.9	1.6	74.9	76.5	1.33	1.82	9.6
47	1.8	1.6	0.6	1.3	62.6	63.9	1.25	1.24	14.1
86	2.0	1.4	0.7	1.4	66.4	67.8	1.34	1.33	3.8
—	5.6	5.6	2.3	3.8	60.1	63.9	1.25	1.00	8.1

FP	DISP	WV	SBL	SBT2	2PVC	2PSC	SR1:2	SR2:3	TVOL
46	5.6	2.1	3.0	5.6	74.1	79.7	1.33	3.00	—
38	7.4	4.0	6.0	7.4	73.2	80.6	1.59	2.28	10.1
24	5.1	1.8	3.2	5.0	82.2	87.2	1.40	3.85	9.9
25	6.9	2.8	3.7	7.0	78.4	85.4	1.10	3.44	7.6
32	6.5	2.8	2.6	6.4	82.3	88.7	1.24	4.00	5.4
40	6.7	1.4	3.8	6.7	78.2	84.9	1.14	4.20	7.1
69	5.0	2.5	1.9	3.9	62.6	66.5	1.20	1.33	16.1
89	2.0	0.3	–0.2	1.1	50.3	51.4	1.18	1.07	7.4

continued

Belgium *Continued*

Elections:	TO	EFRG	PFRG	ENEP	ENPP	P3%S	ED
07/11/71	91.5	0.838	0.824	6.16	5.69	7	HP
10/03/74	89.5	0.836	0.827	6.11	5.79	7	HP
17/04/77	95.1	0.824	0.810	5.70	5.26	7	HP
17/12/78	94.8	0.867	0.853	7.53	6.80	8	HP
08/11/81	94.6	0.889	0.869	9.00	7.63	8	HP
13/10/85	93.6	0.877	0.857	8.14	7.01	7	HP
13/12/87	93.4	0.877	0.860	8.12	7.13	7	HP
24/11/91	92.3	0.898	0.881	9.81	8.41	10	HP
21/05/95	91.2	0.894	0.892	9.46	9.29	10	HP
13/06/99	90.7	0.903	0.890	10.32	9.05	10	HP

Bulgaria

Elections:	TO	EFRG	PFRG	ENEP	ENPP	P3%S	ED
10/06/90	90.6	0.624	0.587	2.66	2.42	4	MM
13/10/91	83.9	0.762	0.585	4.19	2.41	3	HP
18/12/94	75.2	0.740	0.633	3.85	2.73	5	MM
19/04/97	74.2	0.668	0.603	3.01	2.52	5	EM

Croatia

Elections:	TO	EFRG	PFRG	ENEP	ENPP	P3%S	ED
02/08/92	75.6	0.765	0.600	4.26	2.50	3	MM
29/10/95	68.8	0.737	0.613	3.81	2.59	4	MM

Cyprus

Elections:	TO	EFRG	PFRG	ENEP	ENPP	P3%S	ED
05/09/76	85.3	?	0.561	?	2.28	3	?
24/05/81	95.7	0.740	0.705	3.85	3.39	4	HP
08/12/85	94.6	0.723	0.720	3.61	3.57	4	HP
19/05/91	94.3	0.728	0.715	3.67	3.51	4	HP
26/05/96	92.9	0.737	0.716	3.81	3.53	5	HP

FP	DISP	WV	SBL	SBT2	2PVC	2PSC	SR1:2	SR2:3	TVOL
82	3.2	0.9	2.4	2.6	48.3	50.9	1.30	1.96	7.3
55	3.8	1.5	1.1	1.4	50.0	51.4	1.18	2.00	4.3
53	5.1	2.2	2.1	2.3	53.3	55.6	1.11	2.33	4.8
115	7.4	2.6	0.8	0.7	38.5	39.2	2.19	1.04	4.7
43	9.5	2.1	1.0	4.8	32.0	36.8	1.23	1.25	16.4
46	7.8	3.7	1.8	4.4	35.2	39.6	1.40	1.09	8.8
146	7.2	2.8	0.8	4.0	35.2	39.2	1.08	1.25	4.9
104	8.1	1.5	1.7	4.6	30.3	34.9	1.11	1.25	11.4
33	7.19	4.0	2.1	3.0	30.3	33.3	1.38	1.00	9.7
33	6.9	4.6	1.0	1.6	28.4	30.0	1.05	1.16	10.1

FP	DISP	WV	SBL	SBT2	2PVC	2PSC	SR1:2	SR2:3	TVOL
102	7.1	0.9	5.6	3.8	85.0	88.8	1.47	6.26	—
30	25.0	25.0	11.5	22.5	67.5	90.0	1.05	4.42	21.6
39	15.6	15.6	8.6	13.2	67.7	80.9	1.81	3.83	26.3
32	7.7	7.7	4.9	7.1	74.2	81.3	2.36	3.22	25.5

FP	DISP	WV	SBL	SBT2	2PVC	2PSC	SR1:2	SR2:3	TVOL
37	26.5	11.8	17.9	10.7	61.0	71.7	6.07	1.27	—
9	18.1	11.0	13.9	9.7	63.5	73.2	4.17	1.50	7.6

FP	DISP	WV	SBL	SBT2	2PVC	2PSC	SR1:2	SR2:3	TVOL
n.a.	?	?	?	?	?	85.7	2.33	2.25	—
n.a.	7.7	7.6	1.5	3.9	64.7	68.6	1.00	1.50	?
n.a.	1.3	0.3	0.3	1.3	61.2	62.5	1.19	1.07	12.7
n.a.	3.3	3.2	–0.1	1.4	66.4	67.8	1.11	1.64	?
n.a.	4.4	4.3	1.2	2.1	67.5	69.6	1.05	1.90	?

TRNC

Elections:	TO	EFRG	PRFG	ENEP	ENPP	P3%S	ED
20/06/76	74.3	0.640	0.410	2.78	1.69	4	EM
28/06/81	88.6	0.706	0.666	3.40	3.00	4	HP
23/06/85	87.4	0.776	0.666	4.47	2.99	4	HP
06/05/90	91.5	0.503	0.435	2.01	1.77	2	EM
12/12/93	92.9	0.748	0.718	3.97	3.54	4	HP
06/12/98	86.5	0.742	0.668	3.88	3.01	4	HP

Czech Republic

Elections:	TO	EFRG	PRFG	ENEP	ENPP	P3%S	ED
08–09/06/90	96.7	0.715	0.550	3.50	2.22	4	MM
05–06/06/92	85.1	0.863	0.792	7.29	4.80	8	HP
31/05–01/06/96	76.4	0.815	0.759	5.41	4.15	6	HP
19–20/06/98	74.0	0.784	0.730	4.63	3.71	5	HP

Note: The 1990 and 1992 elections were to the Czech National Council within then-Czechoslovakia.

Denmark

Elections:	TO	EFRG	PFRG	ENEP	ENPP	P3%S	ED
30/10/45	86.3	0.781	0.777	4.56	4.47	5	HP
28/10/47	85.8	0.737	0.719	3.80	3.56	6	HP
05/09/50	81.9	0.751	0.749	4.01	3.98	6	HP
21/04/53	80.8	0.745	0.740	3.92	3.85	6	HP
22/09/53	80.6	0.737	0.725	3.80	3.63	6	HP
14/05/57	83.7	0.744	0.735	3.90	3.77	6	HP
15/11/60	85.8	0.737	0.722	3.81	3.60	6	HP
22/09/64	85.5	0.734	0.715	3.75	3.51	5	HP
22/11/66	88.6	0.763	0.748	4.22	3.97	5	HP
23/01/68	89.3	0.781	0.764	4.56	4.24	5	HP
21/09/71	87.2	0.779	0.746	4.52	3.94	5	HP
04/12/73	87.7	0.859	0.855	7.11	6.90	9	HP

FP	DISP	WV	SBL	SBT2	2PVC	2PSC	SR1:2	SR2:3	TVOL
15	21.3	1.5	21.3	16.1	73.9	90.0	5.00	3.00	—
37	6.3	0.3	2.5	6.5	71.0	77.5	1.38	2.17	24.5
37	18.1	17.3	11.3	13.9	58.1	72.0	2.00	1.20	25.0
55	13.3	0.8	13.3	0.8	99.2	100.0	2.13	∞	10.2
31	6.8	3.5	2.1	4.9	59.1	64.0	1.00	1.23	31.8
36	11.1	8.4	7.7	11.1	62.9	74.0	1.85	1.86	17.5

FP	DISP	WV	SBL	SBT2	2PVC	2PSC	SR1:2	SR2:3	TVOL
—	18.9	18.9	14.0	16.8	62.7	79.5	3.97	1.45	—
27	19.1	19.1	8.3	11.7	43.8	55.5	2.17	2.19	20.2
4	11.2	11.2	4.4	8.5	56.0	64.5	1.11	2.77	24.2
32	11.3	11.3	4.7	8.5	60.0	68.5	1.17	2.63	16.1

FP	DISP	WV	SBL	SBT2	2PVC	2PSC	SR1:2	SR2:3	TVOL
9	2.5	0.0	–0.4	1.9	56.2	58.1	1.26	1.46	—
34	5.5	1.8	–1.5	4.0	67.6	71.6	1.16	2.88	14.7
10	0.6	0.3	0.0	0.2	60.9	61.1	1.84	1.19	10.4
14	1.2	1.2	0.5	0.5	62.5	63.0	1.85	1.27	3.2
8	3.1	2.7	1.0	1.9	64.4	66.3	1.76	1.40	4.7
13	2.5	2.3	0.6	1.2	64.5	65.7	1.56	1.50	3.8
3	3.3	3.3	1.3	1.9	63.2	65.1	2.00	1.19	11.1
4	3.7	3.3	1.5	2.4	62.7	65.1	2.00	1.06	3.1
6	3.2	3.1	1.1	1.8	57.6	59.4	1.97	1.03	9.6
10	3.7	3.7	1.3	2.0	54.5	56.5	1.68	1.09	10.9
19	6.9	6.9	2.7	3.7	54.0	57.7	2.26	1.03	9.6
14	2.2	1.5	0.7	0.8	41.5	42.3	1.64	1.40	21.2

continued

Denmark *Continued*

Elections:	TO	EFRG	PFRG	ENEP	ENPP	P3%S	ED
09/01/75	88.2	0.821	0.815	5.60	5.42	8	HP
15/02/77	87.9	0.809	0.808	5.23	5.20	10	HP
23/10/79	85.6	0.799	0.793	4.99	4.82	8	HP
08/12/81	83.2	0.826	0.817	5.75	5.47	7	HP
10/01/84	88.4	0.809	0.802	5.25	5.04	7	HP
08/09/87	86.7	0.829	0.812	5.83	5.31	7	HP
10/05/88	85.7	0.829	0.812	5.84	5.32	7	HP
12/12/90	81.4	0.794	0.771	4.86	4.37	7	HP
21/09/94	84.3	0.790	0.780	4.77	4.54	7	HP
11/03/98	85.9	0.789	0.788	4.73	4.72	7	HP

Estonia

Elections:	TO	EFRG	PFRG	ENEP	ENPP	P3%S	ED
20/09/92	67.8	0.848	0.772	6.60	4.39	6	HP
05/03/95	69.6	0.834	0.763	6.03	4.22	7	HP
07/03/99	54.9	0.855	0.818	6.88	5.50	7	HP

Finland

Elections:	TO	EFRG	PFRG	ENEP	ENPP	P3%S	ED
17–18/03/45	74.9	0.804	0.790	5.09	4.77	6	HP
01–02/07/48	78.2	0.796	0.780	4.90	4.54	5	HP
02–03/07/51	74.6	0.798	0.791	4.96	4.78	6	HP
07–08/03/54	79.9	0.799	0.788	4.98	4.71	6	HP
06–07/07/58	75.0	0.807	0.795	5.19	4.87	6	HP
04–05/02/62	85.1	0.829	0.804	5.86	S.09	6	HP
20–21/03/66	84.9	0.808	0.799	5.22	4.96	7	HP
15–16/03/70	82.2	0.838	0.821	6.17	5.58	7	HP
02–03/01/72	81.4	0.832	0.818	S.9S	5.51	7	HP
21–22/09/75	79.7	0.830	0.812	5.89	5.31	7	HP
12–13/03/79	81.2	0.826	0.808	5.74	5.21	7	HP

FP	DISP	WV	SBL	SBT2	2PVC	2PSC	SR1:2	SR2:3	TVOL
35	3.1	1.8	0.4	1.1	53.2	54.3	1.26	1.75	17.8
10	1.7	0.9	0.1	0.4	51.6	52.0	2.50	1.24	18.3
3	2.7	2.3	0.6	0.7	50.8	51.5	3.09	1.00	10.6
22	2.8	2.8	0.8	0.9	47.7	48.6	2.27	1.24	12.5
1	2.6	2.3	0.4	1.0	55.0	56.0	1.33	1.91	10.8
2	4.5	4.5	1.6	2.5	50.1	52.6	1.42	1.41	9.2
24	4.8	4.8	1.6	2.3	49.1	51.4	1.57	1.46	6.2
5	5.2	5.2	2.0	3.1	53.4	56.5	2.30	1.03	13.9
5	2.4	1.8	0.8	1.5	57.9	59.4	1.48	1.56	10.1
12	0.8	0.5	0.0	0.0	60.0	60.0	1.50	2.63	11.8

FP	DISP	WV	SBL	SBT2	2PVC	2PSC	SR1:2	SR2:3	TVOL
31	17.6	8.0	7.9	11.1	44.3	55.4	2.29	1.13	—
43	12.8	12.8	7.9	10.6	48.4	59.0	2.16	1.19	47.7
18	9.6	8.4	4.3	6.0	39.5	45.5	1.56	1.00	26.9

FP	DISP	WV	SBL	SBT2	2PVC	2PSC	SR1:2	SR2:3	TVOL
30	4.2	1.5	0.1	0.9	48.6	49.5	1.02	1.00	—
27	4.5	0.8	3.8	4.5	50.5	55.0	1.04	1.42	6.3
79	2.3	0.6	0.0	2.2	49.8	52.0	1.04	1.19	3.8
58	3.2	0.1	0.8	3.2	50.3	53.5	1.02	1.23	3.1
53	3.9	1.0	1.8	2.6	46.4	49.0	1.04	1.00	6.3
67	7.9	3.7	3.5	S.0	45.0	50.0	1.13	1.24	5.6
67	4.5	0.4	0.3	3.6	48.4	52.0	1.12	1.20	8.4
60	5.7	1.6	2.1	3.6	41.4	44.0	1.38	1.00	14.6
49	4.4	1.0	1.7	3.2	42.8	46.0	1.49	1.06	4.1
69	6.6	0.8	2.1	3.2	43.8	47.0	1.35	1.03	7.2
74	5.1	1.7	2.2	3.9	45.6	49.5	1.11	1.34	5.8

continued

Finland *Continued*

Elections:	TO	EFRG	PFRG	ENEP	ENPP	P3%S	ED
20–21/03/83	81.0	0.816	0.813	5.45	5.34	S	HP
15–16/03/87	76.4	0.837	0.797	6.15	4.93	6	HP
17/03/91	72.1	0.831	0.809	5.92	5.23	8	HP
19/03/95	71.9	0.827	0.795	5.78	4.88	7	HP
21/03/99	68.3	0.830	0.806	S.90	S.1S	7	HP

Note: Starting in 1975, turnout figures are based only on the Finnish electorate resident in Finland.

France—Fourth Republic

Elections:	TO	EFRG	PFRG	ENEP	ENPP	P3%S	ED
21/10/45*	79.8	0.783	0.762	4.61	4.20	5	HP
02/06/46	81.9	0.778	0.759	4.51	4.15	S	HP
10/11/46	78.1	0.785	0.769	4.65	4.32	S	HP
17/06/51	80.2	0.815	0.831	5.42	5.92	6	HP
02/01/56	82.2	0.836	0.825	6.09	5.73	7	HP

*Elections for constituent assembly.

France—Fifth Republic

Elections:	TO	EFRG	PFRG	ENEP	ENPP	P3%S	ED
23–30/11/58	77.0	0.830	0.710	5.87	3.44	5	HP
18–25/11/62	68.8	0.809	0.767	5.25	4.29	7	HP
05–12/03/67	80.9	0.792	0.734	4.81	3.76	5	HP
23–30/06/68	80.0	0.728	0.435	3.68	1.77	5	MM
04–11/03/73	81.2	0.831	0.775	5.91	4.44	7	HP
12–19/03/78	83.3	0.795	0.753	4.87	4.05	4	HP
14–21/06/81	70.9	0.750	0.594	3.99	2.46	5	MM
16/03/86	78.5	0.785	0.743	4.66	3.90	5	HP
05–12/06/88	66.2	0.772	0.675	4.38	4.38	4	HP
21–28/03/93	68.9	0.860	0.668	7.14	3.01	5	HP
25/05–01/06/97	67.9	0.708	0.601	3.43	2.51	5	HP

FP	DISP	WV	SBL	SBT2	2PVC	2PSC	SR1:2	SR2:3	TVOL
46	3.9	0.2	1.8	1.7	48.8	SO.S	1.30	1.16	10.3
45	10.5	3.6	3.9	7.3	47.2	54.5	1.06	1.33	11.3
40	6.7	2.3	2.7	4.6	46.9	Sl.5	1.15	1.20	10.9
25	8.5	3.7	3.2	5.3	48.2	53.5	1.43	1.13	10.6
23	7.4	3.8	2.6	4.2	45.3	49.5	1.06	1.04	8.8

FP	DISP	WV	SBL	SBT2	2PVC	2PSC	SR1:2	SR2:3	TVOL
—	6.3	0.5	2.3	4.4	51.0	55.4	1.05	1.05	—
17	5.3	0.4	2.6	4.4	54.3	58.7	1.10	1.27	5.4
36	4.7	0.3	1.9	4.6	54.9	59.5	1.05	1.76	6.0
52	11.6	0.7	–2.0	–10.9	48.4	37.5	1.10	1.03	20.0
29	6.3	1.1	1.1	3.3	41.2	44.5	1.55	1.08	20.2

FP	DISP	WV	SBL	SBT2	2PVC	2PSC	SR1:2	SR2:3	TVOL
46	29.5	3.9	22.1	28.5	42.7	71.2	1.49	2.33	26.7
26	16.8	0.7	10.0	11.3	44.6	55.9	3.00	1.35	19.2
32	17.8	2.3	9.0	15.2	50.5	65.7	1.62	1.64	4.0
19	29.9	5.3	29.9	25.5	60.2	85.7	6.07	1.73	11.4
32	17.3	2.2	13.1	15.0	43.1	58.1	1.75	1.37	10.9
23	12.7	8.2	7.3	11.9	44.2	56.1	1.13	1.14	6.7
9	21.5	3.1	21.5	17.6	58.6	76.2	3.51	1.27	13.5
4	12.6	3.4	4.3	3.8	58.1	61.9	1.36	1.14	16.7
23	18.7	1.0	10.2	15.0	55.2	70.2	2.00	1.06	10.4
8	40.4	26.4	22.4	40.2	39.5	79.7	1.16	3.94	19.2
3	31;8	2.6	18.4	25.9	39.1	65.0	1.80	1.24	13.8

Georgia

Elections:	TO	EFRG	PFRG	ENEP	ENPP	P3%S	ED
11/10/92	74.3	?	–0.900	?	~10.00	6	HP
05–19/11/95	64.0	0.913	0.745	11.46	3.92	3	HP
31/10–14/11/99	67.9	0.715	0.581	3.51	2.38	3	MM

Germany

Elections:	TO	EFRG	PFRG	ENEP	ENPP	P3%S	ED
14/08/49	78.5	0.796	0.751	4.90	4.01	7	HP
06/09/53	85.8	0.698	0.641	3.31	2.79	5	HP
15/09/57	87.8	0.637	0.582	2.76	2.39	4	EM
17/09/61	87.7	0.646	0.602	2.83	2.51	3	HP
19/09/65	86.8	0.609	0.581	2.56	2.38	3	HP
28/09/69	86.7	0.600	0.554	2.50	2.24	3	HP
19/11/72	91.1	0.582	0.572	2.39	2.33	3	HP
30/10/76	90.7	0.576	0.568	2.36	2.31	3	HP
09/10/80	88.6	0.606	0.589	2.54	2.43	3	HP
06/03/83	89.1	0.608	0.602	2.55	2.51	4	HP
25/01/87	84.3	0.652	0.643	2.87	2.80	4	HP
02/12/90	77.8	0.681	0.622	3.14	2.65	3	HP
16/10/94	79.1	0.683	0.655	3.15	2.90	5	HP
27/09/98	82.2	0.698	0.656	3.31	2.91	5	HP

Note: The CDU/CSU is always counted as one party.

Greece

Elections:	TO	EFRG	PFRG	ENEP	ENPP	P3%S	ED
17/11/74	79.5	0.635	0.420	2.74	1.73	3	EM
20/11/77	81.1	0.733	0.569	3.74	2.32	4	MM
18/10/81	78.6	0.627	0.523	2.68	2.10	3	MM
02/06/85	83.8	0.614	0.534	2.59	2.14	3	MM
18/06/89	84.5	0.634	0.584	2.73	2.40	3	HP
05/11/89	78.7	0.609	0.570	2.56	2.32	3	HP

FP	DISP	WV	SBL	SBT2	2PVC	2PSC	SR1:2	SR2:3	TVOL
28	?	?	?	?	?	31.3	1.61	1.29	—
n.a.	33.5	41.6	21.5	28.0	33.4	61.4	3.12	1.17	?
n.a.	14.6	21.2	14.6	13.2	71.3	84.5	2.32	3.50	~38

FP	DISP	WV	SBL	SBT2	2PVC	2PSC	SR1:2	SR2:3	TVOL
37	6.2	5.2	3.6	7.0	60.2	67.2	1.06	2.52	—
44	7.3	7.5	4.7	6.9	74.0	80.9	1.61	3.15	21.2
43	6.9	7.0	4.1	6.3	82.0	88.3	1.60	4.12	9.2
58	5.7	5.7	3.2	5.1	81.5	86.6	1.27	2.84	11.5
37	3.6	3.6	1.8	3.2	86.9	90.1	1.21	4.12	7.6
23	5.4	5.4	2.7	5.2	88.8	94.0	1.08	7.47	6.0
26	1.1	1.0	0.6	1.1	90.7	91.8	1.02	5.61	6.0
47	0.9	0.8	0.4	0.9	91.2	92.1	1.14	5.49	3.9
31	2.1	2.0	1.0	2.0	87.4	89.4	1.04	4.11	4.5
24	0.8	0.4	0.2	0.8	87.0	87.8	1.26	5.68	8.4
45	1.4	1.3	0.6	1.0	81.3	82.3	1.20	4.04	5.7
46	8.1	8.1	4.4	7.0	77.3	84.3	1.33	3.03	8.4
32	3.6	3.5	2.3	3.4	77.9	81.3	1.17	5.36	8.3
30	6.0	6.0	3.6	5.1	76.0	81.1	1.22	5.21	7.8

FP	DISP	WV	SBL	SBT2	2PVC	2PSC	SR1:2	SR2:3	TVOL
4	19.0	2.2	18.9	18.5	74.8	93.3	3.67	5.00	—
8	21.3	0.9	15.9	21.3	67.1	88.4	1.88	8.36	35.9
3	11.7	5.1	9.2	11.6	84.0	95.6	1.50	8.85	27.0
3	9.1	1.6	7.9	9.1	86.6	95.7	1.28	10.50	5.6
14	6.6	1.9	4.0	6.6	83.4	90.0	1.i6	4.46	8.6
17	5.1	?	3.1	5.1	86.9	92.0	1.16	6.10	4.2

continued

Greece *Continued*

Elections:	TO	EFRG	PFRG	ENEP	ENPP	P3%S	ED
08/04/90	77.0	0.621	0.580	2.64	2.37	3	MM
10/10/93	78.2	0.620	0.540	2.63	2.17	4	MM
22/09/96	76.3	0.674	0.575	3.07	2.36	5	MM

Hungary

Elections:	TO	EFRG	PFRG	ENEP	ENPP	P3%S	ED
25/03–08/04/90	65.1	0.851	0.737	6.71	3.80	6	HP
08–29/05/94	68.9	0.818	0.655	5.49	2.90	6	MM
10–24/05/98	56.3	0.785	0.710	4.64	3.45	6	HP

Iceland

Elections:	TO	EFRG	PFRG	ENEP	ENPP	P3%S	ED
30/06/46	87.4	0.721	0.722	3.58	3.60	4	HP
23/10/49	89.0	0.719	0.712	3.55	3.47	4	HP
28/06/53	89.9	0.760	0.709	4.16	3.44	5	HP
24/06/56	92.1	0.724	0.712	3.62	3.48	4	HP
28/06/59	90.6	0.706	0.687	3.40	3.20	4	HP
25/10/59	90.4	0.726	0.710	3.66	3.44	5	HP
06/06/63	91.1	0.703	0.699	3.37	3.33	4	HP
11/06/67	91.4	0.735	0.718	3.77	3.55	4	HP
13/06/71	90.4	0.756	0.740	4.10	3.85	5	HP
30/06/74	91.4	0.712	0.705	3.47	3.38	5	HP
25/06/78	90.3	0.763	0.741	4.21	3.85	4	HP
02/12/79	89.3	0.744	0.736	3.90	3.79	4	HP
23/04/83	88.6	0.765	0.754	4.26	4.07	6	HP
25/04/87	90.1	0.827	0.813	5.77	5.35	6	HP
20/04/91	87.6	0.763	0.735	4.23	3.77	5	HP
08/04/95	87.0	0.767	0.747	4.29	3.95	6	HP
08/05/99	84.1	0.718	0.711	3.55	3.45	5	HP

FP	DISP	WV	SBL	SBT2	2PVC	2PSC	SR1:2	SR2:3	TVOL
3	5.6	?	3.1	5.5	85.5	91.0	1.22	6.47	3.8
3	9.8	4.4	9.8	7.5	86.2	93.7	1.53	11.10	10.8
2	12.5	5.3	12.5	10.4	79.6	90.0	1.50	9.80	8.6

FP	DISP	WV	SBL	SBT2	2PVC	2PSC	SR1:2	SR2:3	TVOL
45	22.0	15.8	2.1	20.7	45.6	66.3	1.78	2.09	—
27	21.1	12.7	21.1	19.4	52.8	72.2	2.99	1.89	21.8
45	14.0	9.2	10.1	12.5	60.5	73.0	1.10	2.79	31.0

FP	DISP	WV	SBL	SBT2	2PVC	2PSC	SR1:2	SR2:3	TVOL
?	1.9	0.1	–1.0	0.9	62.6	63.5	1.54	1.30	—
45	8.2	0.0	–3.0	5.2	64.0	69.2	1.12	1.89	1.4
77	12.2	3.3	3.3	12.2	59.0	71.2	1.31	2.29	9.4
30	17.1	4.5	–5.9	11.2	58.0	69.2	1.12	2.13	11.2
8	9.3	2.5	–4.0	5.3	69.7	75.0	1.05	2.71	11.8
26	3.6	3.4	0.3	2.9	65.4	68.3	1.41	1.70	4.4
161	3.5	0.2	–1.4	2.1	69.6	71.7	1.26	2.11	4.4
1	3.8	1.1	0.8	2.7	65.6	68.3	1.28	2.00	6.3
31	3.5	2.0	0.5	3.5	61.5	65.0	1.29	1.70	10.4
60	3.5	0.4	–1.0	2.4	67.6	70.0	1.47	1.55	8.1
67	5.5	5.5	0.6	0.0	55.6	55.6	1.43	1.00	19.3
68	3.4	0.9	–0.4	3.0	60.3	63.3	1.24	1.55	11.1
33	4.9	1.1	–0.2	4.6	57.0	61.6	1.64	1.40	16.1
74	4.4	3.1	1.4	3.1	46.1	49.2	1.38	1.30	23.7
10	4.8	4.3	2.7	4.4	57.5	61.9	2.00	1.30	13.3
22	3.1	1.8	2.6	3.1	60.4	63.5	1.67	1.67	11.6
20	1.7	0.7	0.6	0.8	67.5	68.3	1.53	1.42	16.9

Ireland

Elections:	TO	EFRG	PFRG	ENEP	ENPP	P3%S	ED
04/02/48	74.2	0.756	0.724	4.10	3.62	6	HP
30/05/51	75.3	0.704	0.692	3.37	3.25	4	HP
18/04/54	76.4	0.692	0.671	3.25	3.04	4	HP
05/03/57	71.3	0.684	0.636	3.16	2.75	3	MM
04/10/61	70.6	0.690	0.645	3.23	2.82	3	HP
07/04/65	75.1	0.632	0.620	2.72	2.63	3	MM
16/06/69	76.9	0.646	0.592	2.82	2.45	3	MM
28/02/73	76.6	0.644	0.613	2.81	2.58	3	HP
16/06/77	76.3	0.637	0.579	2.76	2.38	3	EM
11/06/81	76.2	0.651	0.617	2.86	2.61	3	HP
18/02/82	73.8	0.628	0.609	2.69	2.56	3	HP
24/11/82	72.9	0.632	0.608	2.72	2.55	3	HP
17/02/87	73.3	0.712	0.655	3.48	2.89	4	HP
15/06/89	68.5	0.704	0.664	3.38	2.98	5	HP
25/11/92	68.5	0.746	0.711	3.94	3.46	4	HP
06/06/97	65.9	0.752	0.667	4.03	3.00	3	HP

Italy

Elections:	TO	EFRG	PFRG	ENEP	ENPP	P3%S	ED
02/06/46*	89.1	0.787	0.772	4.71	4.39	6	HP
18–19/04/48	92.2	0.660	0.611	2.94	2.57	5	MM
07/06/53	93.9	0.761	0.718	4.18	3.54	6	HP
25–26/05/58	93.7	0.741	0.710	3.87	3.45	5	HP
28–29/04/63	92.9	0.759	0.733	4.15	3.74	6	HP
19–20/05/68	92.8	0.747	0.717	3.95	3.53	6	HP
07–08/05/72	93.1	0.754	0.719	4.07	3.55	6	HP
20–21/06/76	93.3	0.716	0.684	3.52	3.16	4	HP
03–04/06/79	90.4	0.744	0.713	3.91	3.48	5	HP
26–27/06/83	89.0	0.778	0.751	4.51	4.01	6	HP
14–15/06/87	90.5	0.783	0.755	4.61	4.08	5	HP

FP	DISP	WV	SBL	SBT2	2PVC	2PSC	SR1:2	SR2:3	TVOL
14	7.3	0.1	4.4	5.7	61.7	67.4	2.19	2.21	—
14	3.3	0.1	0.6	2.0	72.1	74.1	1.73	2.50	12.3
44	4.1	2.3	0.8	2.8	75.4	78.2	1.30	2.63	7.3
15	5.4	0.5	4.8	5.4	74.9	80.3	1.95	3.33	11.2
7	5.8	1.2	4.8	5.4	75.8	81.2	1.49	2.94	9.9
14	2.4	0.7	2.3	0.8	81.8	82.6	1.53	2.14	8.3
18	7.0	2.5	6.4	7.0	79.8	86.8	1.50	2.78	2.8
14	4.1	2.5	1.7	4.1	81.3	85.4	1.28	2.84	3.8
19	6.2	2.9	6.2	4.8	81.1	85.9	1.95	2.53	7.6
19	4.5	1.2	1.7	4.4	81.8	86.2	1.15	4.33	9.1
19	2.2	1.7	1.5	2.2	84.6	86.8	1.29	4.20	3.5
19	3.2	1.1	0.0	3.0	84.4	87.4	1.07	4.38	3.8
21	9.3	4.5	4.7	8.3	71.2	79.5	1.59	3.64	16.2
27	6.2	2.3	2.2	6.0	73.5	79.5	1.40	3.67	7.8
48	6.5	2.5	1.9	4.5	63.6	68.1	1.51	1.36	15.1
20	11.7	2.0	7.1	11.7	67.2	78.9	1.43	3.18	9.9

FP	DISP	WV	SBL	SBT2	2PVC	2PSC	SR1:2	SR2:3	TVOL
44	3.3	2.1	2.0	2.0	55.9	57.9	1.80	1.11	—
35	5.6	1.4	4.6	5.5	79.5	85.0	1.67	5.55	23.0
39	6.1	2.3	4.5	6.1	62.7	68.8	1.84	1.91	14.1
38	4.4	0.5	3.4	4.2	65.1	69.3	1.95	1.67	5.2
73	4.3	0.9	3.1	4.1	63.5	67.6	1.57	1.91	8.5
'52	4.3	1.0	3.2	4.4	65.9	70.3	1.50	1.95	7.8
60	5.3	3.6	3.7	4.9	65.9	70.8	1.49	2.93	5.3
50	4.6	0.1	3.0	4.6	73.1	77.7	1.16	3.98	9.1
68	5.8	1.8	3.1	4.6	68.7	73.3	1.30	3.24	5.3
45	4.5	2.0	2.8	4.4	62.8	67.2	1.14	2.71	8.3
51	5.0	1.9	2.8	4.3	60.9	65.2	1.32	1.88	16.2

continued

Italy *Continued*

Elections:	TO	EFRG	PFRG	ENEP	ENPP	P3%S	ED
05–06/04/92	87.3	0.849	0.825	6.62	5.73	7	HP
26–27/03/94	86.1	0.868	0.862	7.58	7.26	7	HP
21/04/96	82.9	0.860	0.838	7.14	6.17	8	HP

*Elections for constituent assembly.

Latvia

Elections:	TO	EFRG	PFRG	ENEP	ENPP	P3%S	ED
05–06/06/93	89.9	0.840	0.802	6.26	5.05	8	HP
30/09–01/10/95	71.9	0.900	0.868	9.96	7.59	9	HP
03–04/10/98	71.9	0.858	0.818	7.03	5.49	6	HP

Liechtenstein

Elections:	TO	EFRG	PFRG	ENEP	ENPP	P3%S	ED
29/04/45	93.3	0.496	0.498	1.98	1.99	2	EM
06/02/49	91.9	0.499	0.498	2.00	1.99	2	EM
15/02/53	90.7	0.560	0.498	2.27	1.99	2	EM
14/06/53	93.3	0.501	0.498	2.00	1.99	2	EM
01/09/57	93.4	0.500	0.498	2.00	1.99	2	EM
23/03/58	96.4	0.496	0.480	1.98	1.92	2	EM
24/03/62	94.9	0.585	0.498	2.41	1.99	2	MM
06/02/66	95.6	0.576	0.498	2.36	1.99	2	MM
01/02/70	94.9	0.516	0.498	2.06	1.99	2	MM
03/02/74	95.5	0.528	0.498	2.12	1.99	2	MM
03/02/78	95.7	0.501	0.498	2.00	1.99	2	MM
07/02/82	95.3	0.498	0.498	1.99	1.99	2	EM
02/02/86	93.3	0.562	0.498	2.28	1.99	2	EM
03–05/03/89	90.9	0.593	0.499	2.46	2.00	2	MM
07/02/93	87.5	0.588	0.570	2.43	2.32	3	HP
21/10/93	85.3	0.571	0.534	2.33	2.15	3	EM
31/01–02/02/97	86.8	0.591	0.563	2.44	2.29	3	MM

Note: Women were not granted the right to vote in or stand for elections in Liechtenstein until 01/07/1984.

FP	DISP	WV	SBL	SBT2	2PVC	2PSC	SR1:2	SR2:3	TVOL
89	5.0	3.7	3.0	3.8	45.8	49.6	1.93	1.16	13.7
54	21.0	2.7	–2.3	7.2	28.8	36.0	1.01	1.01	41.4
40	10.7	?	6.0	5.0	41.7	46.7	1.39	1.32	21.0

FP	DISP	WV	SBL	SBT2	2PVC	2PSC	SR1:2	SR2:3	TVOL
44	10.8	10.7	3.6	5.2	45.8	51.0	2.40	1.15	—
4	13.4	12.5	2.7	5.0	30.0	35.0	1.06	1.06	51.4
54	11.9	11.9	2.8	5.7	39.3	45.0	1.14	1.24	32.5

FP	DISP	WV	SBL	SBT2	2PVC	2PSC	SR1:2	SR2:3	TVOL
?	1.5	0.0	1.4	0.0	100.0	100.0	1.14	n.a.	—
?	0.4	0.0	0.4	0.0	100.0	100.0	1.14	n.a.	1.8
?	6.9	6.8	2.8	7.0	93.0	100.0	1.14	∞	6.9
?	2.9	0.0	2.9	0.0	100.0	100.0	1.14	n.a.	7.4
?	1.0	0.0	1.0	0.0	100.0	100.0	1.14	n.a.	1.9
?	5.5	0.0	5.5	0.0	100.0	100.0	1.50	n.a.	2.2
?	10.1	10.0	6.1	10.0	90.0	100.0	1.14	∞	10.1
?	8.8	8.7	4.9	8.7	91.3	100.0	1.14	∞	1.5
45	3.6	1.6	3.6	1.6	98.4	100.0	1.14	∞	7.2
52	3.3	2.8	3.4	2.8	97.2	100.0	1.14	∞	2.5
82	4.2	0.0	4.2	0.0	100.0	100.0	1.14	∞	2.9
?	0.2	0.0	–0.2	0.0	100.0	100.0	1.14	∞	4.4
87	7.1	7.0	3.2	7.0	93.0	100.0	1.14	∞	7.1
68	10.8	10.8	4.8	10.7	89.3	100.0	1.08	∞	3.7
115	3.8	0.0	3.8	2.4	89.6	92.0	1.09	5.50	5.0
52	4.6	0.0	1.9	4.6	91.4	96.0	1.18	11.00	4.8
66	3.6	0.0	2.8	3.6	88.4	92.0	1.30	5.00	3.1

Lithuania

Elections:	TO	EFRG	PFRG	ENEP	ENPP	P3%S	ED
25/10/92	75.2	0.739	0.671	3.83	3.04	4	MM
20/10–04/11/96	52.9	0.861	0.700	7.19	3.33	5	MM

Luxembourg

Elections:	TO	EFRG	PFRG	ENEP	ENPP	P3%S	ED
21/10/45	?	0.715	0.672	3.50	3.05	4	HP
06/06/48–03/06/51	91.8	0.683	0.674	3.15	3.07	4	HP
30/05/54	92.6	0.677	0.626	3.09	2.68	4	MM
01/02/59	92.3	0.700	0.682	3.33	3.14	4	HP
07/06/64	90.6	0.717	0.684	3.53	3.17	5	HP
15/12/68	88.6	0.719	0.706	3.56	3.41	4	HP
26/05/74	90.1	0.769	0.753	4.32	4.06	5	HP
10/06/79	88.9	0.767	0.711	4.29	3.46	5	HP
17/06/84	88.8	0.719	0.690	3.56	3.77	5	HP
18/06/89	87.3	0.785	0.735	4.66	3.90	5	HP
12/06/94	88.3	0.788	0.744	4.72	3.90	5	HP
13/06/99	85.8	0.784	0.769	4.62	4.34	5	HP

Note: The 1948 and 1951 elections were each partial, the first in the South and East constituencies and the second in the North and Center constituencies. The data thus combine the 1948 and 1951 elections.

Macedonia

Elections:	TO	EFRG	PFRG	ENEP	ENPP	P3%S	ED
16–30/10/94	77.3	?	0.695	?	3.29	5	HP
18/10–01/11/98	72.9	0.806	0.747	5.16	3.95	5	HP

Malta

Elections:	TO	EFRG	PFRG	ENEP	ENPP	P3%S	ED
26–28/03/66	89.7	0.581	0.493	2.39	1.97	2	MM
12–14/06/71	92.9	0.510	0.500	2.04	2.00	2	EM

FP	DISP	WV	SBL	SBT2	2PVC	2PSC	SR1:2	SR2:3	TVOL
46	8.8	9.7	7.8	6.4	65.2	71.6	2.61	1.56	—
24	23.8	11.0	19.8	21.1	41.7	62.8	4.38	1.23	41.5

FP	DISP	WV	SBL	SBT2	2PVC	2PSC	SR1:2	SR2:3	TVOL
29	9.9	1.8	7.6	3.2	67.4	70.6	2.27	1.22	—

FP	DISP	WV	SBL	SBT2	2PVC	2PSC	SR1:2	SR2:3	TVOL
30	4.7	0.0	3.5	1.2	75.7	76.9	1.11	2.38	—
30	8.3	2.8	7.6	5.2	77.5	82.7	1.53	2.84	—
24	6.2	0.7	3.5	1.3	71.8	73.1	1.24	1.55	8.6
41	6.2	0.0	6.0	5.8	71.0	76.8	1.05	3.50	12.2
47	5.3	0.4	2.2	2.0	67.7	69.6	1.17	1.64	11.0
23	4.1	1.1	2.6	2.3	57.0	59.3	1.06	1.21	16.0
36	10.3	1.4	6.2	10.3	55.8	66.1	1.60	1.07	14.3
33	5.0	2.6	2.5	3.5	68.4	71.9	1.19	1.50	14.1
27	9.2	4.4	4.3	8.1	58.6	66.7	1.22	1.64	15.9
25	8.9	6.1	4.7	7.6	55.7	63.3	1.24	1.42	13.2
60	6.5	1.8	1.5	4.5	52.2	56.7	1.27	1.15	8.0

FP	DISP	WV	SBL	SBT2	2PVC	2PSC	SR1:2	SR2:3	TVOL
51	?	?	?	?	?	72.5	2.00	2.90	—
30	9.9	4.0	12.7	10.0	53.3	63.3	1.81	1.80	?

FP	DISP	WV	SBL	SBT2	2PVC	2PSC	SR1:2	SR2:3	TVOL
1	9.1	9.1	8.1	9.0	91.0	100.0	1.27	∞	15.1
7	1.1	1.1	0.1	1.1	98.9	100.0	1.04	∞	8.0

continued

Malta *Continued*

Elections:	TO	EFRG	PFRG	ENEP	ENPP	P3%S	ED
17–18/09/76	95.0	0.500	0.499	2.00	2.00	2	EM
12/12/81	94.6	0.500	0.499	2.00	2.00	2	MM
09/05/87	96.1	0.502	0.500	2.01	2.00	2	EM
22/02/92	96.0	0.515	0.499	2.06	2.00	2	EM
26/10/96	96.2	0.514	0.500	2.06	2.00	2	EM
05/09/98	95.4	0.511	0.497	2.04	1.99	2	EM

Note: Only post-independence elections are analyzed.

Moldova

Elections:	TO	EFRG	PFRG	ENEP	ENPP	P3%S	ED
27/02/94	79.3	0.751	0.619	4.01	2.62	4	MM
22/03/98	72.3	0.825	0.725	5.71	3.63	4	HP

The Netherlands

Elections:	TO	EFRG	PFRG	ENEP	ENPP	P3%S	ED
17/05/46	93.1	0.787	0.776	4.68	4.47	6	HP
07/07/48	93.7	0.800	0.786	4.99	4.68	6	HP
25/06/52	95.0	0.800	0.785	5.00	4.65	6	HP
13/06/56	95.5	0.765	0.754	4.26	4.07	6	HP
12/03/59	95.6	0.790	0.759	4.77	4.14	5	HP
15/05/63	95.1	0.792	0.778	4.80	4.50	5	HP
15/02/67	94.9	0.839	0.820	6.22	5.56	8	HP
28/03/71	79.1	0.859	0.844	7.11	6.40	8	HP
29/11/72	83.5	0.854	0.844	6.85	6.41	9	HP
25/05/77	88.0	0.741	0.730	3.87	3.70	4	HP
26/05/81	87.0	0.781	0.728	4.56	3.67	4	HP
08/09/82	81.0	0.764	0.751	4.24	4.02	4	HP
21/05/86	85.8	0.735	0.713	3.77	3.49	4	HP
06/09/89	80.1	0.744	0.733	3.90	3.75	5	HP
03/05/94	78.3	0.824	0.814	5.68	5.36	6	HP
06/05/98	73.2	0.805	0.793	5.14	4.82	6	HP

Note: Compulsory voting in the Netherlands was abolished in 1970.

FP	DISP	WV	SBL	SBT2	2PVC	2PSC	SR1:2	SR2:3	TVOL
7	0.8	0.0	0.8	0.0	100.0	100.0	1.10	∞	1.1
6	3.2	0.0	3.2	0.0	100.0	100.0	1.10	∞	2.4
3	0.5	0.3	–0.2	0.2	99.8	100.0	1.03	∞	0.3
5	1.7	1.7	0.5	1.7	98.3	100.0	1.10	∞	2.6
2	1.5	1.5	0.0	1.5	98.5	100.0	1.03	∞	4.2
2	2.1	1.3	2.0	1.2	98.8	100.0	1.17	∞	4.0

FP	DISP	WV	SBL	SBT2	2PVC	2PSC	SR1:2	SR2:3	TVOL
37	18.2	18.1	10.6	15.6	65.2	80.8	2.00	2.55	—
60	20.8	23.7	8.4	14.2	49.3	63.5	1.54	1.08	?

FP	DISP	WV	SBL	SBT2	2PVC	2PSC	SR1:2	SR2:3	TVOL
47	2.2	1.0	1.2	1.9	59.1	61.0	1.10	2.23	—
31	2.8	1.6	1.0	2.4	56.6	59.0	1.19	2.08	5.6
69	3.4	2.1	1.0	2.3	57.7	60.0	1.00	2.50	5.6
122	1.9	1.4	0.6	1.6	64.4	66.0	1.02	3.27	4.1
68	3.3	2.0	1.1	2.7	62.0	64.7	1.02	2.53	5.7
70	2.5	1.6	1.4	2.1	59.9	62.0	1.16	2.69	5.0
49	3.5	2.6	1.5	2.6	50.1	52.7	1.14	2.18	10.8
69	4.4	2.5	1.4	2.9	46.4	49.3	1.11	2.19	12.0
163	2.7	1.0	1.4	1.7	45.0	46.7	1.59	1.23	12.2
208	3.3	2.0	1.5	2.3	65.7	68.0	1.08	1.75	12.8
108	2.5	2.0	1.2	2.2	59.1	61.3	1.09	1.69	8.8
57	2.9	1.7	0.9	1.5	59.8	61.3	1.04	1.25	9.4
54	3.6	2.3	1.4	2.8	67.9	70.7	1.04	1.93	10.4
62	1.9	1.2	0.7	1.5	67.2	68.7	1.10	2.23	4.6
111	2.9	1.8	0.7	1.2	46.2	47.4	1.09	1.10	21.7
89	2.9	3.0	1.0	1.6	53.7	55.3	1.18	1.31	14.0

Norway

Elections:	TO	EFRG	PFRG	ENEP	ENPP	P3%S	ED
08/10/45	76.4	0.757	0.685	4.12	3.17	6	MM
10/10/49	82.0	0.734	0.626	3.76	2.67	5	MM
12/10/53	79.3	0.717	0.677	3.53	3.09	5	MM
07/10/57	78.3	0.709	0.666	3.44	2.99	5	MM
11/09/61	79.1	0.724	0.689	3.62	3.22	5	HP
12/09/65	85.4	0.744	0.715	3.90	3.51	5	HP
07/09/69	83.8	0.724	0.686	3.63	3.18	5	HP
09/09/73	80.2	0.810	0.759	5.27	4.14	5	HP
11/09/77	82.9	0.739	0.663	3.82	2.97	4	HP
14/09/81	82.0	0.745	0.687	3.92	3.20	4	HP
08/09/85	84.0	0.724	0.677	3.63	3.09	5	HP
11/09/89	84.7	0.793	0.764	4.84	4.24	6	HP
13/09/93	75.8	0.789	0.752	4.74	4.04	6	HP
16/09/97	78.0	0.803	0.770	5.07	4.36	6	HP

Poland

Elections:	TO	EFRG	PFRG	ENEP	ENPP	P3%S	ED
27/10/91	43.2	0.928	0.908	13.83	10.85	10	HP
19/09/93	52.1	0.898	0.742	9.79	3.87	6	HP
21/09/97	47.9	0.800	0.661	5.00	2.95	4	HP

Portugal

Elections:	TO	EFRG	PFRG	ENEP	ENPP	P3%S	ED
25/04/75*	91.7	0.727	0.661	3.67	2.95	4	HP
25/04/76	83.3	0.750	0.708	4.00	3.43	4	HP
02/12/79	89.9	0.667	0.615	3.01	2.60	4	HP
05/10/80	84.5	0.654	0.598	2.89	2.49	4	HP
25/04/83	78.6	0.732	0.701	3.74	3.35	4	HP
06/10/85	75.4	0.790	0.761	4.77	4.18	5	HP

FP	DISP	WV	SBL	SBT2	2PVC	2PSC	SR1:2	SR2:3	TVOL
26	9.7	0.3	9.7	9.4	58.0	67.4	3.04	1.25	—
1	12.6	6.5	11.0	10.4	61.6	72.0	3.70	1.10	7.0
1	4.9	0.0	4.6	4.2	65.1	69.3	2.85	1.80	4.5
1	6.6	0.2	3.7	6.2	65.1	71.3	2.69	1.93	2.3
20	6.7	3.1	2.5	2.5	66.1	68.6	2.55	1.81	3.6
30	7.0	1.4	2.2	2.6	63.4	66.0	2.19	1.72	6.8
2	7.2	4.6	2.8	3.3	65.3	68.6	2.55	1.45	5.4
33	11.0	0.9	4.7	6.2	52.5	58.7	2.14	1.38	15.9
8	10.9	4.2	6.7	8.7	66.8	75.5	1.85	1.86	14.7
30	9.7	1.7	4.7	7.8	68.9	76.7	1.20	3.60	11.2
18	8.8	4.7	4.4	5.8	71.2	77.0	1.42	3.13	4.9
35	5.1	5.1	3.9	4.1	56.5	60.6	1.70	1.68	15.7
24	6.4	1.5	3.7	6.4	53.6	60.0	2.09	1.14	14.9
32	6.5	3.8	4.4	4.5	50.3	54.6	2.60	1.00	33.2

FP	DISP	WV	SBL	SBT2	2PVC	2PSC	SR1:2	SR2:3	TVOL
57	13.0	7.1	1.2	2.2	24.3	26.5	1.03	1.22	—
37	37.5	34.6	16.8	30.1	35.8	65.9	1.30	1.78	29.4
26	18.7	12.8	9.9	18.5	60.9	79.4	1.23	2.73	63.9

FP	DISP	WV	SBL	SBT2	2PVC	2PSC	SR1:2	SR2:3	TVOL
97	9.8	3.7	5.7	9.8	69.0	78.8	1.43	2.70	—
89	6.5	4.2	4.0	6.6	61.9	68.5	1.47	1.74	10.7
32	6.2	3.6	4.9	6.3	74.5	80.8	1.73	1.68	10.6
96	6.2	4.3	5.3	6.2	77.0	83.2	1.81	1.80	4.0
45	5.3	3.5	3.1	5.3	65.1	70.4	1.35	1.70	10.3
31	6.0	3.5	4.6	6.0	52.0	58.0	1.54	1.27	22.5

continued

Portugal *Continued*

Elections:	TO	EFRG	PFRG	ENEP	ENPP	P3%S	ED
19/07/87	72.6	0.665	0.576	2.98	2.36	3	EM
06/10/91	68.2	0.646	0.552	2.83	2.23	3	EM
01/10/95	66.8	0.676	0.608	3.09	2.55	4	HP
10/10/99	61.8	0.673	0.616	3.06	2.61	4	HP

*Elections for a constituent assembly.

Romania

Elections:	TO	EFRG	PFRG	ENEP	ENPP	P3%S	ED
27/09/92	76.3	0.859	0.774	7.09	4.42	7	HP
03/11/96	76.0	0.836	0.746	6.09	3.94	6	HP

Note: For Romania in 1996, vote and seat calculations are done only for blocks.

Russia

Elections:	TO	EFRG	PFRG	ENEP	ENPP	P3%S	ED
12/12/93	54.8	0.879	0.930	8.27	14.41	8	HP
17/12/95	64.4	0.907	0.838	10.73	6.15	5	HP

Slovakia

Elections:	TO	EFRG	PFRG	ENEP	ENPP	P3%S	ED
08–09/06/90	95.4	0.829	0.799	5.85	4.98	7	HP
5–6/06/92	84.2	0.837	0.702	6.14	3.36	5	HP
30/09–01/10/94	75.7	0.830	0.733	5.90	4.41	7	HP
25–26/09/98	84.2	0.813	0.790	5.33	4.75	6	HP

Note: The 1990 and 1992 elections were to the Slovak National Council within then-Czechoslovakia.

Slovenia

Elections:	TO	EFRG	PFRG	ENEP	ENPP	P3%S	ED
06/12/92	76.0	0.882	0.842	8.46	6.33	8	HP
10/11/96	73.7	0.842	0.765	6.34	4.26	7	HP

FP	DISP	WV	SBL	SBT2	2PVC	2PSC	SR1:2	SR2:3	TVOL
29	9.1	4.0	7.9	9.1	74.1	83.2	2.47	1.94	22.6
24	9.6	4.7	8.3	9.6	80.4	90.0	1.88	4.24	11.2
28	9.1	4.4	4.8	9.1	77.9	87.0	1.27	5.87	18.6
11	7.3	1.9	5.1	7.3	77.9	85.2	1.42	4.76	4.1

FP	DISP	WV	SBL	SBT2	2PVC	2PSC	SR1:2	SR2:3	TVOL
38	19.8	19.8	8.0	13.0	47.7	60.7	1.43	1.91	—
39	19.9	19.9	7.0	13.2	51.7	64.9	1.34	1.72	13.5

FP	DISP	WV	SBL	SBT2	2PVC	2PSC	SR1:2	SR2:3	TVOL
n.a.	14.4	0.8	0.1	–8.6	38.4	29.8	1.09	1.33	—
n.a.	18.4	8.3	12.2	14.1	33.0	47.1	2.85	1.08	53.7

FP	DISP	WV	SBL	SBT2	2PVC	2PSC	SR1:2	SR2:3	TVOL
?	7.7	7.7	2.7	4.2	48.5	52.7	1.55	1.41	—
27	23.8	23.8	13.6	18.8	47.9	66.7	2.40	1.67	52.8
73	13.0	13.0	5.7	7.3	45.4	52.7	3.39	1.06	23.3
34	5.8	5.8	1.7	3.4	53.3	56.7	1.02	1.83	20.2

FP	DISP	WV	SBL	SBT2	2PVC	2PSC	SR1:2	SR2:3	TVOL
50	16.4	17.5	1.3	3.8	38.2	42.0	1.47	1.07	—
109	10.3	11.4	1.4	3.6	46.4	50.0	1.32	1.19	32.4

Spain

Elections:	TO	EFRG	PFRG	ENEP	ENPP	P3%S	ED
15/06/77	76.9	0.768	0.657	4.31	2.92	5	HP
01/03/79	68.1	0.766	0.645	4.28	2.81	3	HP
28/10/82	79.8	0.686	0.570	3.19	2.33	4	MM
22/06/86	70.6	0.722	0.626	3.60	2.67	4	MM
29/10/89	69.7	0.759	0.651	4.15	2.86	5	MM
06/06/93	76.4	0.717	0.626	3.53	2.67	4	HP
03/03/96	78.0	0.694	0.633	3.27	2.72	4	HP

Basque Country

Elections:	TO	EFRG	PFRG	ENEP	ENPP	P3%S	ED
09/03/80	60.0	0.787	0.749	4.70	3.98	6	HP
26/02/84	68.5	0.739	0.717	3.83	3.53	5	HP
30/11/86	69.6	0.826	0.809	5.83	5.23	5	HP
28/10/90	61.0	0.819	0.810	5.53	5.26	7	HP
23/10/94	59.7	0.815	0.823	5.41	5.65	7	HP
25/10/98	70.7	0.808	0.799	5.21	4.96	5	HP

Catalonia

Elections:	TO	EFRG	PFRG	ENEP	ENPP	P3%S	ED
20/03/80	61.0	0.818	0.776	5.51	4.46	5	HP
29/04/84	64.4	0.681	0.614	3.14	2.59	5	MM
29/05/88	59.4	0.694	0.633	3.26	2.73	5	MM
15/03/92	54.8	0.699	0.631	3.33	2.71	5	MM
19/11/95	63.6	0.736	0.708	3.79	3.42	5	HP
17/10/99	59.9	0.691	0.663	3.24	2.97	4	HP

Sweden

Elections:	TO	EFRG	PFRG	ENEP	ENPP	P3%S	ED
19/09/48	82.7	0.701	0.673	3.35	3.06	5	HP
21/09/52	79.1	0.695	0.677	3.28	3.09	4	HP
26/09/56	79.6	0.704	0.686	3.37	3.18	4	HP

FP	DISP	WV	SBL	SBT2	2PVC	2PSC	SR1:2	SR2:3	TVOL
19	16.6	5.5	12.3	15.7	65.1	80.8	1.40	7.38	—
29	17.8	6.2	13.0	17.0	65.5	82.5	1.39	12.10	12.1
36	13.7	3.2	9.3	13.4	74.9	88.3	1.91	8.83	41.8
33	12.8	6.9	8.3	12.4	70.4	82.8	1.75	5.53	12.8
37	15.2	6.3	10.4	14.9	65.4	80.3	1.65	5.89	10.6
37	9.4	0.2	6.7	12.2	73.5	85.7	1.13	7.83	6.3
63	8.9	3.2	5.7	8.5	76.4	84.9	1.11	6.71	5.6

FP	DISP	WV	SBL	SBT2	2PVC	2PSC	SR1:2	SR2:3	TVOL
51	8.0	4.1	3.7	5.4	54.6	60.0	2.27	1.22	—
46	3.9	3.9	1.1	3.6	64.4	68.0	1.68	1.73	16.7
85	6.3	2.8	0.6	3.0	45.0	48.0	1.12	1.31	25.3
85	5.7	4.4	0.8	2.2	48.4	50.6	1.38	1.23	12.7
63	6.1	0.3	–0.5	3.5	41.8	45.3	1.83	1.09	17.9
69	4.7	1.1	0.1	1.3	48.0	49.3	1.31	1.14	8.2

FP	DISP	WV	SBL	SBT2	2PVC	2PSC	SR1:2	SR2:3	TVOL
35	10.6	9.3	4.2	6.3	50.0	56.3	1.30	1.32	—
31	7.6	5.7	6.7	7.1	76.6	83.7	1.76	3.73	32.0
?	7.5	4.0	5.6	7.1	75.1	82.2	1.64	4.67	5.9
?	8.3	6.3	5.9	8.1	73.4	81.5	1.75	3.64	5.6
?	4.2	2.1	3.6	4.0	65.6	69.6	1.76	2.00	12.0
30	3.9	2.8	3.4	3.7	76.3	80.0	1.08	4.33	7.7

FP	DISP	WV	SBL	SBT2	2PVC	2PSC	SR1:2	SR2:3	TVOL
39	5.3	0.1	2.6	4.7	68.8	73.5	1.96	1.90	—
1	3.2	0.1	1.8	2.6	70.4	73.0	1.90	1.87	3.8
1	3.8	0.1	1.3	2.6	68.4	71.0	1.83	1.38	3.3

continued

Sweden *Continued*

Elections:	TO	EFRG	PFRG	ENEP	ENPP	P3%S	ED
01/06/58	77.4	0.698	0.684	3.31	3.16	4	HP
18/09/60	85.9	0.693	0.679	3.26	3.12	4	HP
20/09/64	83.9	0.708	0.692	3.42	3.25	5	HP
15/09/68	89.3	0.686	0.653	3.18	2.88	4	EM
20/09/70	88.3	0.713	0.698	3.49	3.31	5	HP
16/09/73	90.8	0.714	0.701	3.50	3.35	5	HP
19/09/76	91.8	0.720	0.709	3.58	3.44	5	HP
16/09/79	90.7	0.725	0.713	3.63	3.49	5	HP
19/09/82	91.5	0.706	0.680	3.40	3.13	5	HP
15/09/85	89.9	0.712	0.704	3.48	3.38	5	HP
18/09/88	86.0	0.742	0.727	3.87	3.67	6	HP
15/09/91	86.7	0.777	0.765	4.49	4.26	7	HP
18/09/94	86.0	0.725	0.715	3.64	3.51	7	HP
20/09/98	81.4	0.779	0.767	4.53	4.29	7	HP

Switzerland

Elections:	TO	EFRG	PFRG	ENEP	ENPP	P3%S	ED
26/10/47	71.7	0.812	0.799	5.33	4.97	7	HP
28/10/51	69.8	0.804	0.792	5.09	4.80	5	HP
30/10/55	68.7	0.800	0.788	4.99	4.71	5	HP
25/10/59	68.5	0.801	0.790	5.04	4.75	5	HP
27/10/63	64.5	0.800	0.791	5.01	4.78	6	HP
29/10/67	63.8	0.820	0.805	5.55	5.13	6	HP
31/10/71	56.8	0.836	0.818	6.08	5.49	7	HP
26/10/75	52.4	0.828	0.800	5.80	5.00	6	HP
21/10/79	48.3	0.819	0.804	5.52	5.11	6	HP
23/10/83	48.9	0.834	0.810	6.03	5.26	6	HP
18/10/87	46.1	0.854	0.826	6.83	5.76	7	HP
20/10/91	46.0	0.865	0.849	7.38	6.62	7	HP

FP	DISP	WV	SBL	SBT2	2PVC	2PSC	SR1:2	SR2:3	TVOL
1	3.0	0.0	1.9	1.9	65.7	67.6	2.47	1.18	7.3
13	2.7	0.1	1.3	1.0	65.3	66.3	2.85	1.03	3.7
14	3.8	1.8	1.2	2.2	64.3	66.5	2.69	1.27	2.6
14	4.2	1.5	3.5	3.7	65.8	69.5	3.38	1.16	5.7
9	2.4	2.3	1.3	1.7	65.2	66.9	2.30	1.22	7.2
45	2.3	2.3	1.0	1.6	68.7	70.3	1.73	1.76	8.5
15	1.8	1.7	0.9	1.4	66.8	68.2	1.77	1.56	3.0
26	2.2	2.2	0.9	1.5	63.5	65.0	2.11	1.14	6.5
19	3.8	3.8	2.0	3.0	69.2	72.2	1.93	1.54	7.9
19	1.5	1.5	0.5	1.0	66.4	67.4	2.09	1.49	8.4
16	3.0	3.0	1.1	1.6	62.0	63.6	2.36	1.50	10.7
19	4.5	3.7	1.3	2.2	60.2	62.4	1.73	2.58	15.0
19	2.2	2.3	0.8	1.3	67.7	69.0	2.01	2.96	11.3
16	2.6	2.6	0.9	1.7	59.3	61.0	1.60	1.91	15.6

FP	DISP	WV	SBL	SBT2	2PVC	2PSC	SR1:2	SR2:3	TVOL
46	5.8	0.5	3.8	2.3	49.2	51.5	1.08	1.09	—
46	4.1	1.4	2.0	1.0	50.0	51.0	1.04	1.02	4.0
46	3.6	1.0	0.0	2.2	50.3	52.5	1.06	1.06	2.3
53	3.5	1.0	–0.4	1.9	50.1	52.0	1.00	1.09	1.5
46	3.2	1.8	0.1	1.5	50.5	52.0	1.04	1.06	1.6
46	4.5	2.3	2.0	3.3	46.7	50.0	1.04	1.09	6.0
38	5.5	2.0	2.8	2.9	44.6	47.5	1.07	1.05	7.6
45	7.2	3.6	2.6	3.9	47.1	51.0	1.17	1.02	5.2
60	4.3	2.2	1.1	2.5	48.5	51.0	1.00	1.16	6.4
57	7.4	3.4	3.6	4.2	46.3	50.5	1.15	1.15	6.1
52	9.2	2.3	2.6	3.6	42.9	46.5	1.21	1.02	8.6
45	8.3	4.0	1.0	3.5	39.5	43.0	1.05	1.17	7.4

continued

Switzerland *Continued*

Elections:	TO	EFRG	PFRG	ENEP	ENPP	P3%S	ED
22/10/95	42.2	0.854	0.822	6.86	5.60	7	HP
24/10/99	43.3	0.822	0.806	5.62	5.16	6	HP

Note: Women were not granted the right to vote in or stand for national elections in Switzerland until 07/02/1971.

Turkey

Elections:	TO	EFRG	PFRG	ENEP	ENPP	P3%S	ED
14/05/50	87.7	0.556	0.240	2.25	1.32	2	EM
02/05/54	86.6	0.556	0.128	2.25	1.15	2	EM
27/10/57	76.6	0.605	0.432	2.53	1.76	2	MM
15/10/61	81.4	0.706	0.694	3.40	3.27	4	HP
10/10/65	71.3	0.631	0.619	2.71	2.62	5	EM
12/10/69	64.3	0.700	0.573	3.34	2.34	3	MM
14/10/73	66.8	0.768	0.699	4.31	3.32	4	HP
05/06/77	70.4	0.680	0.596	3.13	2.47	4	HP
06/11/83	92.3	0.649	0.602	2.85	2.51	3	MM
29/11/87	93.3	0.757	0.513	4.12	2.05	3	MM
20/10/91	83.9	0.786	0.763	4.67	4.21	5	HP
24/12/95	85.2	0.837	0.773	6.15	4.41	5	HP
18/04/99	86.9	0.853	0.795	6.79	4.87	5	HP

Ukraine

Elections:	TO	EFRG	PFRG	ENEP	ENPP	P3%S	ED
27/03–10/04/94	74.8	0.978	0.926	46.20	13.50	4	HP
29/03/98	70.8	0.901	0.899	10.11	9.85	8	HP

United Kingdom

Elections:	TO	EFRG	PFRG	ENEP	ENPP	P3%S	ED
05/07/45	72.6	0.625	0.526	2.67	2.11	2	MM
23/02/50	83.6	0.591	0.518	2.44	2.08	2	MM
25/10/51	81.9	0.531	0.513	2.13	2.05	2	MM

FP	DISP	WV	SBL	SBT2	2PVC	2PSC	SR1:2	SR2:3	TVOL
52	7.0	4.2	5.2	7.5	42.0	49.5	1.20	1.32	6.3
52	5.9	1.5	2.5	1.4	46.1	47.5	1.16	1.02	9.7

FP	DISP	WV	SBL	SBT2	2PVC	2PSC	SR1:2	SR2:3	TVOL
5	33	0.6	32.9	5.9	93.2	99.1	6.67	63.00	—
12	35.5	1.3	36.6	7.5	91.4	98.9	16.29	6.20	9.2
5	21.6	0.1	22.2	10.8	87.9	98.7	2.38	44.50	11.1
36	2.8	0.8	1.7	2.0	71.5	73.5	1.09	2.43	20.5
17	3.2	3.2	0.4	1.5	81.6	83.1	1.79	4.32	28.6
22	14.9	2.7	10.4	14.8	73.9	88.7	1.79	9.53	11.5
103	11.1	1.9	7.8	11.1	63.1	74.2	1.24	3.10	29.6
16	11.0	2.1	5.9	11.0	78.3	89.3	1.13	7.88	18.2
48	7.8	1.2	7.8	6.7	75.6	82.3	1.81	1.65	98.1
31	28.6	19.8	28.6	25.9	61.0	86.9	2.95	1.58	61.0
41	9.6	0.5	8.5	6.7	51.0	57.7	1.60	1.23	18.1
79	17.0	14.4	7.3	12.6	40.6	53.2	1.17	1.02	21.5
52	18.7	18.3	2.5	8.0	40.2	48.2	1.05	1.16	21.2

FP	DISP	WV	SBL	SBT2	2PVC	2PSC	SR1:2	SR2:3	TVOL
n.a.	10.1	1.9	12.7	13.5	17.9	31.4	4.30	1.11	—
n.a.	4.0	4.6	1.7	2.2	35.1	37.3	2.65	1.35	67.7

FP	DISP	WV	SBL	SBT2	2PVC	2PSC	SR1:2	SR2:3	TVOL
22	14.3	0.0	13.4	7.7	84.8	92.5	1.97	16.58	—
5	8.6	0.7	4.3	8.6	89.5	98.1	1.06	33.11	3.9
9	3.4	0.2	3.4	1.8	96.8	98.6	1.09	49.17	7.3

continued

United Kingdom *Continued*

Elections:	TO	EFRG	PFRG	ENEP	ENPP	P3%S	ED
26/04/55	76.8	0.537	0.506	2.16	2.02	2	MM
08/10/59	78.7	0.561	0.497	2.28	1.99	2	MM
15/10/64	77.2	0.605	0.514	2.53	2.06	2	MM
31/03/66	76.0	0.587	0.504	2.42	2.02	2	MM
18/06/70	72.2	0.593	0.516	2.46	2.07	2	MM
28/02/74	78.9	0.680	0.555	3.13	2.25	2	HP
10/10/74	73.0	0.683	0.557	3.15	2.26	2	MM
03/05/79	76.3	0.652	0.534	2.87	2.15	2	MM
09/06/83	72.8	0.679	0.521	3.12	2.09	3	MM
11/06/87	73.2	0.676	0.542	3.08	2.18	3	MM
09/04/92	77.7	0.674	0.559	3.06	2.27	3	MM
01/05/97	71.6	0.687	0.528	3.20	2.12	3	MM

Note: Turnout figures consist only of valid votes counted until 1959.
Beginning with the 1964 elections, the turnout figure provided included both valid and invalid votes.

Northern Ireland

Elections:	TO	EFRG	PFRG	ENEP	ENi?P	P3%S	ED
30/05/96*	64.5	0.829	0.812	5.84	5.31	5	HP
25/06/98	69.9	0.833	0.815	6.00	5.40	6	HP

*Elections to the peace forum.

**Note: The government formed after the 1998 elections did not actually take office until November 1999, due to difficulties with the peace process.

Scotland

Elections:	TO	EFRG	PFRG	ENEP	ENPP	P3%S	ED
06/05/99	58.7	0.771	0.701	4.37	3.34	4	HP

Wales

Elections:	TO	EFRG	PFRG	ENEP	ENPP	P3%S	ED
06/05/99	46.2	0.737	0.669	3.80	3.03	4	HP

FP	DISP	WV	SBL	SBT2	2PVC	2PSC	SR1:2	SR2:3	TVOL
20	5.0	0.5	5.1	2.7	96.1	98.8	1.25	46.17	2.4
8	8.5	0.7	8.5	5.7	93.2	98.9	1.41	43.00	3.4
1	11.1	1.3	6.2	11.1	87.5	98.6	1.04	33.78	6.0
5	9.8	1.1	9.8	8.1	89.9	98.0	1.44	21.08	4.3
1	8.6	1.0	6.0	8.6	89.5	98.1	1.15	48.00	6.1
5	19.3	0.7	10.2	19.1	75.1	94.2	1.01	21.21	14.9
8	18.9	1.0	11.0	18.7	75.1	93.8	1.15	21.31	3.5
2	15.2	1.4	9.5	15.0	80.8	95.8	1.26	24.45	8.5
2	24.2	0.9	18.7	23.3	70.0	93.3	1.90	9.09	12.1
2	20.9	0.8	15.5	19.9	73.0	92.9	1.64	10.41	3.6
2	16.9	1.6	7.7	14.9	78.3	93.2	1.24	13.55	5.2
6	21.5	6.6	20.4	14.7	73.9	88.6	2.54	3.59	12.7

FP	DISP	WV	SBL	SBT2	2PVC	2PSC	SR1:2	SR2:3	TVOL
n.a.	7.9	2.4	3.1	6.1	43.0	49.1	1.25	1.14	—
**	7.1	4.5	4.6	4.8	43.3	48.1	1.17	1.20	6.2

FP	DISP	WV	SBL	SBT2	2PVC	2PSC	SR1:2	SR2:3	TVOL
13	10.6	4.5	9.8	9.6	60.9	70.5	1.6	1.94	—

FP	DISP	WV	SBL	SBT2	2PVC	2PSC	SR1:2	SR2:3	TVOL
6	11.2	4.9	11.2	8.9	66.1	75.0	1.65	1.89	—

CHAPTER 3

Classifying European Party Systems

In a simplified manner, we can use the number of parties with at least 3 percent of the seats to distinguish between three overall categories: two-party systems (P3%S of two), moderate multiparty systems (P3%S of three to five), and extreme multiparty systems (P3%S of more than five). The breakpoints here thus follow Sartori's (1976) analysis of fragmentation. However, with additional factors we are able to thus expand the categories into more precise situations. In this analysis a party system is thus considered one of eight different types, depending on various mathematical results in an election or series of elections. A polity may thus go through, or shift among, various party systems over time, or its party system may remain constant throughout the period under study. Certainly a party system that is the output of only one election cannot be considered durable, unless we are looking at the most recent elections in which case it *might* have some durability. Thus, earlier single-election party systems should either be seen as deviant (if the polity then goes back to the old party system) or transitional (if the polity then goes on to a new party system for at least a couple of elections). In the data following, such single-election party systems are indicated with square brackets.

Party-system classification is determined by a combination of the following factors, all taken from the data in Chapter 2: (1) the mean number of parties with at least 3 percent of the seats—P3%S; (2) the mean two-party seat concentration—2PSC; (3) the medium seat ratio between the first and second party—SR1:2; and (4) the medium seat ratio between the second and third party—SR2:3. The breakpoints for factors

(3) and (4) remain constant. In a few select cases the criteria are indicative rather than truly deterministic.

(1) *Two-party systems* are those with a mean 2PSC of at least 95 percent. Usually the P3%S value will be exactly 2, and can never be more than 3. Given the very high 2PSC, it is normally the case that one of the parties will have a majority of seats.

(2) *Moderate multiparty systems,* which are in fact *two-and-a-half party systems,* are those with a mean P3%S of 3 to 5 (although normally 3 to 4), a mean 2PSC of between 80 and 95 percent, a median SR1:2 below 1.6, and a median SR2:3 of 1.8 or more. In other words, the gap between the second and third parties is clearly greater than the gap between the first and second parties. Given these parameters, it is certainly possible that one of the two main parties will have a majority of the seats.

(3) *Moderate multiparty systems with one dominant party* are those with a mean P3%S of 3 to 5, and a median SR1:2 of 1.6 or more. Given these parameters, it is certainly possible that the dominant party will have a majority of the seats. In any case, it will be clearly above the other parties. Finally, for such a system to continue across time we must be dealing with the same party; otherwise the polity has a *sequence* of moderate multiparty systems with one dominant party.

(4) *Moderate multiparty systems with two main parties* are those with a mean P3%S of 3 to 5 (although normally 4 to 5), a median SR1:2 below 1.6, and a median SR2:3 of 1.8 or more. Just as in two-and-a-half-party systems, here the gap between the second and third parties is clearly greater than the gap between the first and second parties. However, it is unlikely that either of the two main parties will have a majority of the seats.

(5) *Moderate multiparty systems with a balance among the parties* are those with a mean P3%S of 3 to 5 (although normally 4 to 5), a median SR1:2 below 1.6, and a median SR2:3 below 1.8. There is thus not a huge gap between the first and second parties, nor between the first and third parties. Indeed, there may also not be a huge difference between the first and third parties.

(6) *Extreme multiparty systems with one dominant party* are those with a mean P3%S of more than 5, and a median SR1:2 of 1.6 or more. Given these parameters, it is unlikely that the dominant party will have a majority of the seats. As such, it could be kept out of office; in fact, however, it tends to be in a strong position for government formation, even if this

requires an executive or at least a legislative coalition. Finally, as in system (3), for party system (6) to continue across time we must be dealing with the same party; otherwise it is a *sequence* of moderate multiparty systems with one dominant party.

(7) *Extreme multiparty systems with two main parties* are those with a mean P3%S of more than 5, a median SR1:2 below 1.6, and a median SR2:3 of 1.8 or more. Although not definitional, these systems also tend to have a median 2PSC of from 55 to 75 percent. Consequently, neither of the two main parties will have a majority of the seats.

(8 Finally, *extreme multiparty systems with a balance among the parties* are those with a mean P3%S of more than 5, a median SR1:2 below 1.6, and a median SR2:3 below 1.8. There is, thus, not a huge gap between the top parties. However, since the tendency here is to have a mean 2PSC of below 60 percent, unless the top two parties combine, then at least three parties would be necessary to achieve a majority of the seats.

Based on the above criteria, and using the data given in Chapter 2, European party systems are classified in the following Table 3.1. Data on ENPP are also given. End years in round brackets indicate the most recent elections; if a given pattern holds, then said year can obviously be extended down the road. France since 1978 is an intriguing case: it seems to alternate between two types of party systems, that is, systems (3) and (5). Consequently, although these are technically six unique systems, they will be treated only as two. (See also the individual case analysis of France.)

Two further qualifications are to be noted. First, as discussed, where a particular situation existed for only one election in the past, the data are given in square brackets to indicate that this was a transitional or perhaps a deviant situation rather than an ongoing party system. Second, party systems of more than one election that have experienced moderate or high levels of volatility within the period—that is, not counting the first elections—are indicated by an asterisk or two. (Volatility, to repeat, is a comparison with the previous elections.) Such systems, though staying within their given classifications, are obviously less stable in their elections-to-elections realities.

Most countries, thus, have experienced multiple-party systems; this information is also given chronologically in the country analyses. The "record" seems to be that of Belgium, which has gone through six party systems since the Second World War. On the other hand, Finland, Luxembourg, and Switzerland have each had the same party system in a classificatory sense throughout the postwar era.

Finally, in addition to the four factors used to classify systems, data are also given on mean ENPP. This does indicate how these systems are ever more fragmented in terms of their mean of means (excluding the single-event cases in square brackets, and then weighting the remaining cases within each category equally), as follows:

two-party systems—1.92;

two-and-a-half-party systems—2.56;

moderate multiparty systems with one dominant party—2.95;

moderate multiparty systems with two main parties—3.17;

moderate multiparty systems with a balance among the parties—3.69;

extreme multiparty systems with one dominant party*—3.96;

extreme multiparty systems with two main parties—4.41;

extreme multiparty systems with a balance among the parties—5.56.

*excludes Ukraine 1998 due to very high number of independents

On the other hand, an ENPP of, say, 4.00, just by itself, could be one of perhaps three different categories; this is why this measure is not used directly for classification!

Table 3.1 Party System Classifications

Two-Party Systems	**mean P3%S**	**mean 2PSC**	**median SR1:2**	**median SR2:3**	**mean ENPP**
[Austria 1945	2.0	97.6	1.12	19.00	2.09]
Greece 1981–85	3.0	95.7	1.39	9.68	2.12
Liechtenstein 1945–89	2.0	100.0	1.14	∞	1.99
Malta 1966–(98)	2.0	100.0	1.10	∞	1.99
[TRNC 1990	2.0	100.0	2.13	∞	1.77]
Turkey 1950–57 *	2.0	98.9	6.67	44.50	1.41
United Kingdom 1945–79	2.0	96.9	1.15	33.11	2.10

Note: Turkey 1950–57 and the TRNC 1990 would appear to be *one-party predominant systems*, period, but given that we are only dealing with four elections in total it seems unnecessary to create a new category for these.

Moderate Multiparty, but in Fact Two-and-a-Half-Party Systems

	mean P3%S	mean 2PSC	median SR1:2	median SR2:3	mean ENPP
Austria 1949-1986	3.2	92.6	1.11	8.00	2.30
Belgium 1946–61	3.5	84.4	1.28	3.64	2.65
Bulgaria 1990–91 **	3.5	89.4	1.26	5.34	2.42
Germany 1961–(98)	3.5	87.3	1.20	5.21	2.60
Greece 1989–(96)	3.6	91.3	1.22	6.47	2.32
Ireland 1954–82	3.1	84.1	1.39	2.89	2.64
Liechtenstein 1993–(97)	3.0	93.3	1.18	5.50	2.25
Portugal 1995–(99)	4.0	86.1	1.35	5.32	2.58
Spain 1977–79 *	4.0	81.6	1.39	9.74	2.86
Spain 1993–(96)	4.0	84.2	1.12	7.27	2.70
Turkey 1961–77 **	4.0	81.8	1.24	4.32	2.80
[United Kingdom 1992	3.0	93.2	1.24	13.55	2.27]

Moderate Multiparty Systems with One Dominant Party

	mean P3%S	mean 2PSC	median SR1:2	median SR2:3	mean ENPP
[Bulgaria 1994	5.0	80.9	1.81	3.83	2.73]
Bulgaria (1997–)	5.0	81.3	2.36	3.22	2.52
Catalonia 1984–95	5.0	79.3	1.75	3.68	2.86
Croatia 1992–(95)	3.5	72.5	5.12	1.39	2.55
[Cyprus 1976	3.0	85.7	2.33	2.25	2.28]
[Czech Republic 1990	4.0	79.5	3.97	1.45	2.22]
France 1981, 1988, 1997	4.7	70.5	2.00	1.24	3.12
Germany 1953–57	4.5	84.6	1.61	3.63	2.59
Georgia 1995–(99) **	3.0	64.4	3.15	1.10	3.52
Greece 1974–77 **	3.5	90.9	2.78	6.68	2.03
Ireland 1948–51	5.0	70.8	1.96	2.36	3.43
[Lithuania 1992	4.0	71.6	2.61	1.56	3.04]
Lithuania (1996–)	5.0	62.8	4.38	1.23	3.33

continued

Table 3.1 *Continued*

Moderate Multiparty Systems with One Dominant Party *Continued*	**mean P3%S**	**mean 2PSC**	**median SR1:2**	**median SR2:3**	**mean ENPP**
[Macedonia 1994	5.0	72.5	2.00	2.90	3.28]
[Moldova 1994	4.0	80.8	2.00	2.55	2.62]
Norway 1949–77	4.9	68.8	2.55	1.76	3.22
Portugal 1987–91 *	3.0	86.6	2.18	3.09	2.29
Russia (1995–)	5.0	47.1	2.85	1.08	6.17
Scotland (1999–)	4.0	70.5	1.60	1.94	3.34
Spain 1982–89	4.3	83.8	1.75	5.89	2.62
Sweden 1948–85	4.6	69.0	2.09	1.38	3.22
Turkey 1983–87 **	3.0	84.6	2.36	1.62	2.28
TRNC 1976–85 **	4.0	79.8	2.00	2.17	2.56
TRNC (1998–)	4.0	74.0	1.85	1.86	3.01
[Ukraine 1994	4.0	31.4	4.30	1.11	13.51]
United Kingdom 1983–87	3.0	93.1	1.77	9.75	2.14
United Kingdom (1997–)	3.0	88.6	2.54	3.59	2.12
Wales (1999–)	4.0	75.0	1.65	1.89	3.03

Moderate Multiparty Systems with Two Main Parties	**mean P3%S**	**mean 2PSC**	**median SR1:2**	**median SR2:3**	**mean ENPP**
[Austria 1990	4.0	76.5	1.33	1.82	2.99]
Catalonia (1999–)	4.0	80.0	1.08	4.33	2.97
Czech Republic (1998–)	5.0	68.5	1.17	2.63	3.71
[France 1958	5.0	71.2	1.49	2.33	3.44]
Ireland 1987–(97) *	4.0	76.5	1.47	3.41	3.08
Norway 1981–85	4.5	76.8	1.36	3.37	3.14
Poland (1997–)	4.0	79.4	1.23	2.73	2.95

Moderate Multiparty Systems with a Balance among the Parties

	mean P3%S	mean 2PSC	median SR1:2	median SR2:3	mean ENPP
Austria 1994–(99)	4.7	65.2	1.25	1.24	3.54
[Belgium 1965	4.0	66.5	1.20	1.33	3.59]
[Catalonia 1980	5.0	56.3	1.30	1.32	4.46]
Cyprus 1981–(96) *?	4.3	67.1	1.08	1.57	3.50
France 1978, 1986, 1993	4.7	65.9	1.16	1.14	3.65
Iceland 1946–79	4.3	67.5	1.28	1.79	3.53
Iceland (1999–)	5.0	68.3	1.53	1.42	3.45
Luxembourg 1945–(99) *	4.6	69.5	1.23	1.53	3.50
Macedonia (1998–)	4.0	60.8	1.52	1.16	4.01
Moldova (1998–)	4.0	63.5	1.54	1.08	3.63
Netherlands 1977–(98) *	4.7	61.8	1.09	1.72	4.12
Portugal 1975–85	4.2	63.6	1.51	1.72	3.17
Turkey 1991–(99) **	5.0	53.0	1.17	1.16	4.50
[TRNC (1993)	4.0	64.0	1.00	1.23	3.54]

Extreme Multiparty Systems with One Dominant Party

	mean P3%S	mean 2PSC	median SR1:2	median SR2:3	mean ENPP
Basque Country 1980–84 *	5.5	64.0	1.97	1.47	3.76
[Belgium 1978	8.0	39.2	2.19	1.04	6.80]
[Czech Republic 1992	8.0	55.5	2.17	2.19	4.80]
Denmark 1950–(98) *	6.7	57.2	1.80	1.26	4.58
[Estonia 1992	6.0	55.4	2.29	1.13	4.39]
[Estonia 1995	7.0	59.0	2.16	1.19	4.22]
France 1962–73	6.0	66.3	2.38	1.51	3.57
[Georgia 1992	6.0	31.3	1.61	1.29	~10.00]
[Hungary 1990	6.0	66.3	1.78	2.09	3.80]
[Hungary 1994	6.0	72.2	2.99	1.89	2.90]

continued

Table 3.1 *Continued*

Extreme Multiparty Systems with One Dominant Party *Continued*	**mean P3%S**	**mean 2PSC**	**median SR1:2**	**median SR2:3**	**mean ENPP**
Iceland 1983–(95) *	5.8	59.1	1.66	1.35	4.28
Italy 1946–58 *	5.5	70.2	1.82	1.79	3.49
[Norway 1945	6.0	67.4	3.04	1.25	3.17
Norway 1989–(97) **	6.0	58.4	2.09	1.14	4.21
Slovakia 1992–94 **	6.0	59.7	2.89	1.37	3.88
Sweden 1988–(98) *	6.75	64.0	1.87	2.24	3.93
Ukraine (1998–)	8.0	37.3	2.65	1.35	9.85

Extreme Multiparty Systems with Two Main Parties	**mean P3%S**	**mean 2PSC**	**median SR1:2**	**median SR2:3**	**mean ENPP**
Belgium 1971–77	7.0	52.6	1.18	2.00	5.58
[Czech Republic 1996	6.0	64.5	1.11	2.77	4.15]
[Germany 1949	7.0	67.2	1.06	2.52	4.01]
Hungary (1998–)	6.0	73.0	1.10	2.79	3.45
Italy 1963–87	5.4	70.3	1.32	2.71	3.65
Netherlands 1946–71	6.25	59.3	1.10	2.36	4.81
[Poland 1993	6.0	65.9	1.30	1.78	3.87]
Romania 1992–(96) *	6.5	62.8	1.38	1.82	4.24
Slovakia (1998–)	6.0	56.7	1.02	1.83	4.75

Extreme Multiparty Systems with a Balance among the Parties

	mean P3%S	mean 2PSC	median SR1:2	median SR2:3	mean ENPP
Basque Country 1986–(98) *	6.0	48.3	1.34	1.19	5.28
[Belgium 1968	6.0	51.4	1.18	1.07	4.93]
Belgium 1981–(99)	8.7	35.6	1.17	1.21	8.09
Denmark 1945–47	5.5	65.9	1.21	2.17	4.02
Estonia (1999–)	7.0	45.5	1.56	1.00	5.50
Finland 1945–(99)	6.4	50.4	1.12	1.17	5.05
France 1945–56 *	5.6	51.1	1.10	1.08	4.86
Italy 1992–(96) **	7.3	44.1	1.39	1.16	6.39
Latvia 1993–(98) **	7.7	43.7	1.14	1.15	6.04
[Netherlands 1972	9.0	46.7	1.59	1.23	6.41]
Northern Ireland 1996–(98)	5.5	48.6	1.21	1.17	5.36
[Poland 1991	10.0	26.5	1.03	1.22	10.85]
[Russia 1993	9.0	37.1	1.53	1.06	8.63]
[Slovakia 1990	7.0	52.7	1.55	1.41	4.98]
Slovenia 1992–(96) **	7.5	46.0	1.40	1.13	5.30
Switzerland 1947–(99)	6.1	49.7	1.06	1.08	5.22

*Mean within-period volatility above 10 percent.

**Mean within-period volatility above 20 percent.

We have thus classified 110 systems mathematically. What do these categories mean in a more practical sense? For two-party systems, there may literally be only two parties, such as the CHP and the DP in 1950s Turkey, or Labour and the Nationalists until recently in Malta. There may however be only two parties that matter in any sense of the term, even if some other party (or parties) wins a few seats. For example, in Greece from 1981 to 1985 the communists did get (just) above 3 percent of the seats, but the elections were clearly head-to-head competition between the conservatives (New Democracy) and the socialists (Pasok), with the latter the decisive winners. Indeed, in a two-party system "someone always wins."

In two-and-a-half-party systems there is a relevant "half" consisting of one or more smaller (or third) parties. This party (or these parties) is clearly much smaller than the main two, but its strength is often (although not always) enough to produce a hung parliament. Except for 1957, hung parliaments have always occurred in Germany (where the public seems to prefer them federally to single-party majorities). However, they have not always occurred in postwar Ireland, where Fianna Fáil has been able to win outright majorities from time to time. In any case, if there is a hung parliament, and unless the two main parties choose to form a grand coalition as in Austria and Liechtenstein, the smaller party or a smaller party may well get into the cabinet as a junior partner. This has been the situation, for example, of the Free Democrats and now the Greens in Germany, or the Labour Party in Ireland. Even if they do not get into the cabinet, their support for a minority government of one of the main parties will come at a price. In Spain, the regional parties, especially the CiU in Catalonia, have been very adept at trading support for concessions from each of the main parties (socialists and conservatives) in turn.

In a moderate multiparty system with one dominant party, said dominant party is in a very strong position. First of all, it often wins a majority of seats outright, as has occurred, for example, with the nationalist CiU in Catalonia 1984–92, New Democracy in Greece 1974–77, Labour in Norway 1949–57, the conservative Social Democrats in Portugal 1987–91, the socialists in Spain 1982–89, the Conservatives in the United Kingdom 1983–87, Labour in the United Kingdom 1997, and the Citizens' Union of Georgia in 1999. Even where the dominant party does not win an outright majority, it is the central force in government formation (in other words, the system is effectively unipolar). In such cases where there is a hung parliament, one main outcome is for the dominant party to lead a coalition government, as has occurred, for example, with the socialists in France 1981/1988/1997, the conservatives in Lithuania 1996, and the National Unity Party in the Turkish Republic of Northern Cyprus earlier on and again in 1998. The other main outcome is for the dominant party to form a minority government, as occurred with the Labour Party in Norway in the 1960s and 1970s, and the Social Democrats in Sweden for most of 1948 to 1985. A third, but much rarer scenario, is for all of the other parties (and normally all are required) to "gang up" together in government so as to exclude the dominant party. This occurred in Ireland in 1948 (to keep Fianna Fáil out) and in Sweden from 1976 to 1982 (to keep the Social Democrats out).

The category of moderate multiparty systems with two main parties is the rarest in postwar Europe, with six cases, only one of which—Ireland 1987–97—has lasted more than two elections. Here we are dealing with, by definition, two main parties but also two or more smaller parties. Thus, there are multiple coalition possibilities, but given the bipolar rivalry between the two main parties, it is likely that only one of them will be in the government. (Austria 1990 is an exception given its historical tendency to grand coalitions.)

In the category of moderate multiparty systems with a balance among the parties, there is rarely such a sense of bipolarity, although France in 1986/1993 is an exception—but France is shaped in this regard by the key role of the president. Normally, in this category, there are three or four reasonably large parties. Coalition government is always the norm here. Such coalitions tend to include at least two of the top three or four parties. This could even involve the two largest of the larger parties (unlike in the previous category), for example, the Christian Socials and the Socialists in Luxembourg. If the largest of the various larger parties is relatively flexible, it can normally get itself into government, as has been true for the Independence Party in Iceland 1946–79 and the Christian Socials in Luxembourg. This was also the case for the Dutch Christian Democrats after 1977 until their electoral disaster of 1994. However, if the largest party is relatively extreme, then it will find it difficult to get into (or stay in) government, since there are various alternatives that would exclude it. This has been the recent reality of the Welfare Party in Turkey, and it now appears also to be true of the post-communists in Moldova.

The category of extreme multiparty systems with one dominant party seems to be close in practice to the category of moderate multiparty systems with one dominant party. That is, the dominance of the one party provides a clear pole of competition. Indeed, with some help from the electoral system the dominant party may very occasionally win an outright majority of seats, such as the French Gaullists in 1968 or the Norwegian Labour Party in 1945. Nevertheless, the dominant party is not the only pole, and it is rather rare for the dominant party to be continually in power in such a category. However, this was true for, again, the Gaullists in France 1962–73, as well as the Christian Democrats in Italy 1946–58. What is more common in this category is that dominant party-led coalitions (or single party minorities) are interspersed with coalitions of some or all of the other parties. Within the longer-term examples of this category, this has been the situation in Denmark since 1950 and Sweden since 1988 (whose dominant parties are the Social Democrats), Iceland since 1985 (whose dominant party is the Independence Party), and Norway since 1989 (whose dominant party is the Labour Party).

The category of extreme multiparty systems with two main parties combines the bipolarity of all systems with two main parties with the reality that a majority coalition is likely to need at least three parties (one large and two small), unless of course the two main parties choose to get together. Such coalitions involving the two main parties certainly occurred in the Netherlands 1946–58 (with the two main parties being the Catholic Peoples Party and the Labour Party), but in fact these coalitions tended to involve at least four parties as an expression of Dutch consociationalism. The Dutch case notwithstanding, since in this category one main party tends to govern with more than one smaller party, the main parties need to have a particularly broad appeal. Thus if one of the main parties is more broadly appealing than the other, it will govern while the other main party is excluded from office. This was the case with the Christian Democrats in Germany 1949 and Italy 1963–87, with the German Social Democrats and the Italian Communists, respectively, being excluded from government. This also is the case in Slovakia 1998 with the Slovak Democratic coalition entering government and excluding the Movement for a Democratic Slovakia, although the former alliance was formed for this election and may not prove durable.

Finally, the category of extreme multiparty systems with a balance among the parties contains, as noted earlier, clearly the most fragmented systems in Europe. As such, there is rarely a sense of bipolarity, although Italy since 1992 is an exception here. Indeed, in many of these systems no less than three parties compete credibly to be the largest. In the French Fourth Republic, this was the case with the Communists, the Socialists, and the Christian democratic MRP. In Finland, through the 1970s, anyway, this was the case with the Communists, the Socialists, and the Agrarian Union/Center Party. In Switzerland, this pattern remains to this day, with the Christian Democrats, the Radicals, and the Socialists all usually quite close to each other. It is also common in these systems for all of the larger parties to be in government together, at least from time to time.

REFERENCE

Sartori, Giovanni (1976). *Parties and Party Systems: A Framework for Analysis.* New York: Cambridge University Press.

CHAPTER 4

Electoral Systems and Their Effects

To what extent are the different party systems in Europe "produced," at least in part, by their electoral systems? For those who view the world of electoral systems through the dichotomy of single member plurality (SMP) versus proportional representation (PR), Europe hardly provides a balanced sample. SMP now exists only in the United Kingdom, with everywhere else (save France) using either all proportional representation (including the single transferable vote variant) or a mixture including PR. In this analysis we shall not get into all the minutia of electoral systems (for this, Lijphart 1990 is recommended), although the formula used for PR is given in the country analyses, and data on districts for the current systems are given in the appendix table for this chapter. One point worth stressing, however, is the presence of thresholds, which, if they exist, are given in Table 4.1.

Table 4.1 National Electoral Systems

Austria 1945–99	party-list, proportional representation
Belgium 1946–99	party-list, proportional representation
Bulgaria 1990	party-list, proportional representation
Bulgaria 1991–97	party-list, proportional representation, with 4 percent national threshold
Croatia 1992–95	mixture of single-member plurality and party-list, proportional representation (5 percent threshold for PR)

continued

Table 4.1 *Continued*

Cyprus 1976	single member plurality *
Cyprus 1981–96	party-list, proportional representation
TRNC 1981	party-list, proportional representation
TRNC 1976 and 1990	party-list, proportional representation, with bonus for larger parties
TRNC 1985 and 1993	party-list, proportional representation, with an 8 percent national threshold
Czech Republic 1990–98	party-list, proportional representation, with a 5 percent national threshold
Denmark 1945–98	party-list, proportional representation (very low 2 percent threshold since 1970)
Estonia 1992–99	party-list, proportional representation, with a 5 percent national threshold
Finland 1945–99	party-list, proportional representation
France 1945–46	party-list, proportional representation
France 1951–56	party-list, proportional representation, with bonuses for majority cartels
France 1958–81/1988–97	single-member majority-plurality
France 1986	party-list, proportional representation
Georgia 1992–95	mixture of single-member plurality and party-list, proportional representation, with a 5 percent national threshold
Georgia 1999	mixture of single-member plurality and party list, proportional representation, with a 7 percent national threshold
Germany 1949	mixture of single-member plurality and fully compensatory party list PR, with a 5 percent regional threshold
Germany 1953–98	mixture of single-member plurality and fully compensatory party list PR, with a 5 percent national threshold
Greece 1974–81	three-tiered party-list, proportional representation, with a 17 percent threshold for upper level seats
Greece 1985–96	three-tiered party-list, proportional representation
Hungary 1990–98	mixture of single-member plurality and two-tiered party list PR, with a 5 percent national threshold

Iceland 1946–06/1959	mixture of single-member plurality and party-list, proportional representation
Iceland 08/1959–99	party-list, proportional representation
Ireland 1948–97	single transferable vote
Italy 1946–92	party-list, proportional representation
Italy 1994–96	mixture of single-member plurality and somewhat compensatory party list PR, with a 4 percent national threshold
Latvia 1992–98	party-list, proportional representation, with a 5 percent national threshold
Liechtenstein 1945–97	party-list, proportional representation, with an 8 percent national threshold
Lithuania 1992–96	mixture of single-member plurality and party-list, proportional representation, with a 4 percent national threshold
Luxembourg 1945–99	party-list, proportional representation
Macedonia 1994	single-member plurality
Macedonia 1998	mixture of single-member plurality and party-list, proportional representation, with a 4 percent national threshold
Malta 1966–81	single transferable vote
Malta 1987–98	single transferable vote, with extra seats added if needed to change a manufactured minority (or, from 1995, a plurality) into an earned majority
Moldova 1994–98	party-list, proportional representation, with a 4 percent national threshold
Netherlands 1946–98	party-list, proportional representation
Norway 1945–85	party-list, proportional representation
Norway 1989–97	two-tiered party-list, proportional representation, with a 4 percent national threshold for the upper tier
Poland 1991	party-list, proportional representation
Poland 1993–97	two-tiered party-list, proportional representation, with 5 percent or more national thresholds for the upper tier
Portugal 1975–99	party-list, proportional representation

continued

Table 4.1 National Electoral Systems

Country	System
Romania 1992–96	party-list, proportional representation, with a 3 percent national threshold
Russia 1993–95	mixture of single-member plurality and party-list, proportional representation, with a 5 percent national threshold
Slovakia 1990–98	party-list, proportional representation, with 5 percent or more national thresholds
Slovenia 1992–96	party-list, proportional representation, with a 3 percent national threshold
Spain 1977–96	party-list, proportional representation
Basque Country	party-list, proportional representation
Catalonia	party-list, proportional representation
Sweden 1948–68	party-list, proportional representation
Sweden 1970–98	two-tiered party-list, proportional representation, with a 4 percent national threshold for the upper tier
Switzerland 1947–99	party-list, proportional representation
Turkey 1950–77	party-list, proportional representation
Turkey 1983–99	party-list, proportional representation, with a 10 percent national threshold
Ukraine 1994–98	mixture of single-member plurality and party-list, proportional representation, with a 4 percent national threshold
United Kingdom 1945–97	single-member plurality
Northern Ireland	single transferable vote
Scotland	mixture of single-member plurality and somewhat compensatory party list PR
Wales	mixture of single-member plurality and somewhat compensatory party list PR

*Note that because of insufficient information, the 1976 system in Cyprus cannot be analyzed.

Germany, as the table notes, is fully compensatory PR, and also one-half of the seats are PR—and this can be expanded by (a few) seats if, say, one party sweeps the SMP seats in a state with under half the vote. In Scotland and Wales, the PR seats are compensatory, however since (1) these are less than half of the total, (2) they are based on multiple districts, and (3) there is no ability to expand the size of the legislature, the system is not fully compensatory. Finally, Italy does take into effect results in single-member districts in a complicated way (using the results of second-place candidates) that does allow some compensation at the expense of parties that did not win their single-member seats by much, but only a quarter of Italian seats are PR—not enough to compensate fully, in any case.

In all remaining mixture systems, the PR results are calculated separately from the single-member ones, thus—all other things being equal—greater proportionality is expected the greater the ratio of PR seats to others. In Croatia two-thirds of the seats are proportional; in Georgia, some 60 percent; in Hungary, Lithuania, Russia, and Ukraine one-half or close to one-half of the total seats are PR; but in Macedonia (1998) less than one-third of the seats are proportional.

Overall disproportionality, that is, the overall differences between vote shares and seat shares, divided by two, ranges from over 20 percent in the systems used in Georgia, Poland, France, and Croatia down to less than 3 percent in Malta, Sweden, and the Netherlands. Table 4.2 ranks electoral systems in descending order of disproportionality and gives for each system the party system(s) to which the electoral system has been related. One can hypothesize that the more disproportional an electoral system, the more likely that the party system is concentrated and, thus, is one of the ones with a lower category number.

Table 4.2 Electoral Systems, Disproportionality, and Party Systems

1. Two-party system
2. Two-and-a-half-party system
3. Moderate multiparty system with one dominant party
4. Moderate multiparty system with two main parties
5. Moderate multiparty system with a balance among the parties
6. Extreme multiparty system with one dominant party
7. Extreme multiparty system with two main parties
8. Extreme multiparty system with a balance among the parties

	Mean	Related Party Systems*							
Electoral System	**Disproportionality**	**1.**	**2.**	**3.**	**4.**	**5.**	**6.**	**7.**	**8.**
Georgia 1995	33.5			(X)					
Poland 1993–97	28.1							(X)	X
France 1958–81/1988–97	23.6				(X)	X	X		
Croatia 1992–95	22.0			X					

continued

Table 4.2 *Continued*

Electoral System	Mean Disproportionality	Related Party Systems* 1.	2.	3.	4.	5.	6.	7.	8.
Romania 1992–96	19.9							X	
Moldova 1994–98	19.5			(X)		X			
Hungary 1990–98	19.0						X	X	
Greece 1974–81	17.3	(X)		X					
TRNC 1976 and 1990	17.3	(X)		(X)					
Russia 1993–95	16.9						X		X
Turkey 1950–77	16.7	X	X						
Lithuania 1992–96	16.3			X					
Turkey 1983–99	16.3			X		X			
Bulgaria 1991–97	16.1		X						
Italy 1994–96	15.8								X
Georgia 1999	14.6			(X)					
Czech Republic 1990–98	13.7			(X)	(X)		(X)	(X)	
United Kingdom 1945–97	13.7	X	(X)	X					
Spain 1977–96	13.5		X	X					
Slovenia 1992–96	13.4								X
Estonia 1992–99	13.3						X		X
Poland 1991	13.0								
France 1986	12.6					(X)			
Slovakia 1990–98	12.6						X	X	
TRNC 1985 and 1993–98	12.4			X					
Latvia 1992–98	12.0								X
Wales 1999	11.2				X				
Scotland 1999	10.6				X				
Ukraine 1994	10.1			X					
Macedonia 1998	9.9					X			
Iceland 1946–06/1959	9.7					X			
France 1951–56	8.9								X

Electoral System	**Mean Disproportionality**	**Related Party Systems*** 1.	**2.**	**3.**	**4.**	**5.**	**6.**	**7.**	**8.**
Norway 1945–85	8.6			X	X		(X)		
Greece 1985–96	8.1	(X)	X						
Portugal 1975–99	7.7		X	X		X			
Northern Ireland 1996–98	7.5								X
Bulgaria 1990	7.1		X						
Catalonia 1980–99	7.0			X	(X)	(X)			
Luxembourg 1945–99	7.0					X			
TRNC 1981	6.3								
Belgium 1946–99	6.2		X			X		(X)	X
Germany 1949	6.2							(X)	
Norway 1989–97	6.0						X		
Basque Country 1980–98	5.8						X		X
Switzerland 1947–99	5.7								X
Finland 1945–99	5.6								X
Ireland 1948–97	5.6		X	X	X				
France 1945–46	5.4								X
Italy 1946–92	4.9						X	X	
Liechtenstein 1945–97	4.6	X	X						
Cyprus 1981–96	4.2					X			
Germany 1953–98	4.1	X		X					
Ukraine 1998	4.0						X		
Iceland 10/1959–99	3.8					X	X		
Austria 1945–99	3.7	(X)	X		(X)	X			
Sweden 1948–68	3.7			X					
Malta 1966–81	3.5	X							
Denmark 1945–98	3.1					X	X		
Netherlands 1946–98	2.9					X		X	(X)
Sweden 1970–98	2.6			X			X		
Malta 1987–98	1.4	X							

*Brackets indicate only a single example.

Disproportionality can arise from having single-member seats, or from partial use of SMP, or from high thresholds, but also from not very high thresholds if there are many small parties that fail to clear the threshold. Georgia in 1995 is the extreme example of this situation but there are also various other Central and Eastern European cases. The related party systems are given in decreasing order of concentration (mean effective number of parliamentary parties). One would have hypothesized a downward sloping relationship; that is, countries at the top of the list would have few parties and possibly one dominant party, as these parties would benefit from the disproportionality. In contrast, systems at the bottom of the list would tend to have extreme multiparty systems. As the figure shows, this relationship is in no sense so clear-cut. In part, this is because low disproportionality simply means that parties are, in fact, treated proportionately. However, if the system has few cleavages or reinforcing cleavages, there will not be a "need" for more than a couple of main parties. This is the case in Austria until recently, Germany since the 1950s, and especially Liechtenstein and Malta.

The other way in which the overall relationship is not so clear-cut is that there are many systems with very high disproportionality, which does not however prevent the occurrence of an extreme multiparty system. The issue here is which parties are most disadvantaged by the system. If, for example, smaller parties had somewhat fewer seats and in turn larger parties got a seat bonus, then the party system would be relatively concentrated and probably moderate multiparty. This in fact has been the "Mediterranean" scenario, in that it has occurred in Greece, Spain, Turkey (until recently), the Turkish Republic of Northern Cyprus, and now in Italy. There is also some element of this in Bulgaria. However, as noted above, in much of Central and Eastern Europe a different pattern has emerged in which those parties that do clear the national threshold are treated proportionally vis-à-vis each other, but there are many parties that fail to clear the threshold. The cumulative wasted votes of these parties' supporters is substantial, hence producing high overall disproportionality, but not disproportionality specifically in favor of the larger/largest parties. We see this pattern in the Czech Republic, Estonia, Latvia, Poland, Romania, Slovakia, Slovenia, and most sharply in Georgia. Rational choice theory would predict that these smaller parties would dissolve or merge, thus ending this pattern. However, this may not occur, especially given a bit of hope combined with the fact that the national thresholds in these systems are certainly not extremely high!

* * *

This discussion has made it clear that we need a more refined way of measuring electoral-system effects than simple disproportionality. Dieter Nohlen (1989: 113) has suggested various ways in which electoral systems can penalize smaller parties and benefit larger ones. In Table 4.3 we shall build on this to examine six of these. For simplicity's sake, each factor will be transferred from the raw data into a low/medium/high measure. Occasionally, judgment calls are made at the margins. The first three factors relate to parliamentary concentration.

The first factor is the mechanical (as opposed to the psychological) concentration of the party system. This will be measured by mean electoral fragmentation less parliamentary fragmentation (EFRG minus PFRG), for which a reduction of 0.100 or more is considered high mechanical concentration; EFRG minus PFRG of between 0.050 and 0.100 is considered medium; and EFRG minus PFRG of less than 0.050 is considered low concentration. Second, there is the extent to which small parties are completely excluded from gaining seats. This is the measurement of wasted votes (WV), for which WV of 2.0 or less is considered low exclusion, WV from 2.0 to 4.0 is considered medium, and WV of 4.0 or more is considered high. Third, there is the extent to which the main (two) parties are jointly advantaged by the electoral system. SBT2—the "seat bias of the top two parties"—is designed to measure this. Mean SBT2 of 5.0 or less is considered low bias, SBT2 from 5.0 to 10.0 is considered medium, and SBT2 of 10.0 or more is considered high.

The remaining three factors speak to advantages for the largest or leading party. The fourth factor is, thus, simply the mean SBL, or seat bias of the leading party. Mean SBL of 4.0 or less is considered low bias, SBL from 4.0 to 8.0 is considered medium, and SBL of 8.0 or more is considered high. The fifth factor is the extent to which the leading party wins an overall majority of seats, whether this is earned through a concentration of the votes or manufactured by the electoral system (Rae 1967: 74). For a given election, this is of course a dichotomous result (either it happens or it does not). Here, we thus measure the frequency of its occurrence over the period. Parliamentary majorities occurring less than 20 percent of the time are considered low, those occurring from 20 to 80 percent of the time are considered medium, and those occurring more than 80 percent of the time are considered high. Of course, in most cases here "low" actually means "never." Eighty percent is obviously a high cutoff (and 20 percent a low one), but it is felt that only when a majority occurs at least four times out of five can the polity and the parties take it to be the "normal" outcome. Finally, the sixth factor measures the frequency of manufactured majorities alone and uses the same scale as for parliamentary majorities. It is worth noting that in the overall data set of elections, there are twice as many manufactured majorities as earned majorities (63 to 30). Europe thus confirms Rae's (1967: 74–77) general point that most parliamentary majorities are manufactured majorities.

Table 4.3 Electoral System Effects

1. Mechanical concentration of party system (EFRG—PFRG)
2. Exclusion of smaller parties (WV)
3. Advantages for principal parties (SBT2)
4. Advantages for largest party (SBL)
5. Frequency of parliamentary majorities (EM + MM)
6. Frequency of manufactured majorities (MM)

*Measures from Nohlen 1989, with addition

Bias in the System

	1.	**2.**	**3.**	**4.**	**5.**	**6.**	
High							
Bulgaria 1991–97	H	H	H	H	M	M	16
Croatia 1992–95	H	H	M	H	H	H	17
France 1958–81, 1988–97	H	H	H	H	M	M	16
Georgia 1999	H	H	H	H	H	H	18
Greece 1974–81	H	M	H	H	H	M	16
Hungary 1990–98	H	H	H	H	M	M	16
Lithuania 1992–96	H	H	H	H	H	H	18
Moldova 1994–98	H	H	H	H	M	M	16
Spain 1977–96	H	H	H	H	M	M	16
Turkey 1983–99	M	H	H	H	M	M	15
United Kingdom 1945–97	(H)	L	H	H	H	H	16
Medium-High							
Catalonia 1980–99	L	H	M	M	M	M	12
Czech Republic 1990–98	M	H	M	M	M	M	13

	1.	2.	3.	4.	5.	6.	
Georgia 1995	H	H	H	H	L	L	14
Macedonia 1998	M	H?	M	H	L	L	12
Poland 1993–97	H	H	H	H	L	L	14
Romania 1992–96	M	H	H	M	L	L	12
Scotland 1999	M	H	M	H	L	L	12
Turkey 1950–77	H	L	M	H	M	M	13
TRNC 1976 and 1990	H	L	M	H	H	L	13
Wales 1999	M	H	M	H	L	L	12
Medium							
Bulgaria 1990	L	L	L	M	H	H	11
Estonia 1992–99	M	H	M	M	L	L	11
Greece 1985–96	M	M	M	M	M	M	12
Liechtenstein 1945–97	L	M	L	L	H	M	10
Malta 1966–81	L	M	L	L	H	M	10
Malta 1987–98	L	L	L	L	H	L	8
Norway 1945–85	M	M	M	M	M	M	12
Portugal 1975–99	M	M	M	M	M	L	11
Russia 1993–95	L	H	M	H	L	L	11
Slovakia 1990–98	M	H	M	M	L	L	11
TRNC 1985 and 1993–98	M	H	M	M	L	L	11
Ukraine 1994	M	L	H	H	L	L	11
Medium-Low							
Austria 1945–99	L	M	L	L	M	L	8
France 1986	L	M	L	M	L	L	8
Germany 1949	L	H	M	L	L	L	9
Germany 1953–98	L	H	L	L	L	L	8
Iceland 1946–06/1959	L	M	M	L	L	L	8
Italy 1994–96	L	M?	M	L	L	L	8
Latvia 1993–98	L	H	L	L	L	L	8

continued

Table 4.3 *Continued*

	1.	2.	3.	4.	5.	6.	
Medium-Low *Continued*							
Northern Ireland 1996–98	L	H	L	L	L	L	8
Norway 1989–97	L	M	L	M	L	L	8
Poland 1991	L	H	L	L	L	L	8
Slovenia 1992–96	M	H	L	L	L	L	9
TRNC 1981	M	L	M	L	L	L	8
Ukraine 1998	L	H	L	L	L	L	8
Low							
Basque Country 1980–98	L	M	L	L	L	L	7
Belgium 1946–99	L	M	L	L	L	L	7
Cyprus 1981–96	L	M	L	L	L	L	7
Denmark 1945–98	L	M	L	L	L	L	7
Finland 1945–99	L	L	L	L	L	L	6
France 1945–46	L	L	L	L	L	L	6
France 1951–56	L	L	L	L	L	L	6
Iceland 10/1959–99	L	M	L	L	L	L	7
Ireland 1948–97	L	L	L	L	L	L	6
Italy 1946–92	L	L	L	L	L	L	6
Luxembourg 1945–99	L	L	L	M	L	L	7
Netherlands 1946–98	L	L	L	L	L	L	6
Sweden 1948–68	L	L	L	L	L	L	6
Sweden 1970–98	L	M	L	L	L	L	7
Switzerland 1947–99	L	M	L	L	L	L	7

One can use this data to rearrange the linkage between electoral systems and party systems. That is, instead of ranking systems by descending disproportionality, one can rank them as in Table 4.4 by total overall bias (the figure on the right of Table 4.3, which counts a low as "1," a medium as "2," and a high as "3").

Table 4.4 Electoral Systems, Overall Bias, and Party Systems

1. Two-party system
2. Two-and-a-half-party system
3. Moderate multiparty system with one dominant party
4. Moderate multiparty system with two main parties
5. Moderate multiparty system with a balance among the parties
6. Extreme multiparty system with one dominant party
7. Extreme multiparty system with two main parties
8. Extreme multiparty system with a balance among the parties

	Total	Related Party Systems							
Electoral System	**Bias**	**1.**	**2.**	**3.**	**4.**	**5.**	**6.**	**7.**	**8.**
Georgia 1999	18			(X)					
Lithuania 1992–96	18			X					
Croatia 1992–95	17			X					
Bulgaria 1991–97	16		X						
France 1958–81/1988–97	16				(X)	X	X		
Greece 1974–81	16	(X)		X					
Hungary 1990-98	16						X	X	
Moldova 1994–98	16			(X)		X			
Spain 1977–96	16		X	X					
United Kingdom 1945–97	16	X	(X)	X					
Turkey 1983–99	15			X		X			
Georgia 1995	14			(X)					
Poland 1993–97	14				X			(X)	
Czech Republic 1990–98	13			(X)	(X)		(X)	(X)	
Turkey 1950–77	13	X	X						
TRNC 1976 and 1990	13	(X)		(X)					
Catalonia 1980–99	12			X	(X)	(X)			
Greece 1985–96	12	(X)	X						
Macedonia 1998	12					X			
Norway 1945–85	12			X	X		(X)		
Romania 1992–96	12							X	

continued

Table 4.4 *Continued*

Electoral System	Total Bias	Related Party Systems							
		1.	2.	3.	4.	5.	6.	7.	8.
Scotland 1999	12				X				
Wales 1999	12				X				
Bulgaria 1990	11		X						
Estonia 1992–99	11						X		X
Portugal 1975–99	11		X	X		X			
Russia 1993–95	11						X		X
Slovakia 1990–98	11						X	X	
TRNC 1985 and 1993–98	11			X					
Liechtenstein 1945–97	10	X	X						
Malta 1966–81	10	X							
Germany 1949	9							(X)	
Slovenia 1992–96	9								X
Austria 1945–99	8	(X)	X		(X)	X			
France 1986	8					(X)			
Germany 1953–98	8	X		X					
Iceland 1946–06/1959	8					X			
Italy 1994–96	8								X
Latvia 1992–98	8								X
Malta 1987–98	8	X							
Northern Ireland 1996–98	8								X
Norway 1989–97	8						X		
Poland 1991	8								(X)
TRNC 1981	8								
Ukraine 1998	8						X		
Basque Country 1980–98	7						X		X
Belgium 1946–99	7		X			X		(X)	X
Cyprus 1981–96	7					X			
Denmark 1945–98	7					X	X		
Iceland 10/1959–99	7					X	X		
Luxembourg 1945–99	7					X			

Electoral System	Total Bias	Related Party Systems 1.	2.	3.	4.	5.	6.	7.	8.
Sweden 1970–98	7			X			X		
Switzerland 1947–99	7								X
Ukraine 1994	7			X					
Finland 1945–99	6								X
France 1945–46	6								X
France 1951–56	6								X
Ireland 1948–97	6		X	X	X				
Italy 1946–92	6						X	X	
Netherlands 1946–98	6					X		X	(X)
Sweden 1948–68	6			X					

*Measures from Nohlen 1989, with addition

One can also extrapolate for the electoral systems with clear bias what the party system effects would be if this bias were less or minimal. That is, if these electoral systems were not so biased, would the resulting party systems still be the same? The following are estimates of this process for the electoral systems with high or medium-high bias, focusing again just on the mechanical effects and not the psychological ones:

high bias

old system(s)
new system(s)

Bulgaria 1991–97

two-and-a-half-party system in 1991
moderate multiparty system with one dominant party in 1994
moderate multiparty system with one dominant party since 1997
extreme multiparty system with two main parties in 1991–94
extreme multiparty system with one dominant party since 1997

Croatia 1992–95

moderate multiparty system with one dominant party since 1992
no change

France 1958–81, 1988–97

moderate multiparty system with two main parties in 1958
extreme multiparty system with one dominant party from 1962 to 1973

moderate multiparty system with a balance among the parties in 1978 and 1993

moderate multiparty system with one dominant party in 1981, 1988, and 1997

no change in 1978, otherwise extreme multiparty system with a balance among the parties

Georgia 1999–

moderate multiparty system with one dominant party in 1999

extreme multiparty system with one dominant party in 1999

Greece 1974–81

moderate multiparty system with one dominant party in 1974–77

two-party system in 1981

two-and-a-half-party system in 1974–81

Hungary 1990–98

extreme multiparty systems with one dominant party in 1990 and 1994

extreme multiparty system with two main parties since 1998

extreme multiparty system with a balance among the parties in 1990–94 and possibly 1998

Lithuania 1992–96

moderate multiparty systems with one dominant party in 1992 and 1996

moderate multiparty system with two main parties in 1992

extreme multiparty system with a balance among the parties in 1996

Moldova 1994–98

moderate multiparty system with one dominant party in 1994

moderate multiparty system with a balance among the parties since 1998

extreme multiparty system with one dominant party in 1994

extreme multiparty system with a balance among the parties since 1998

Spain 1977–96

two-and-a-half-party system in 1977–79

moderate multiparty system with one dominant party from 1982 to 1989

two-and-a-half-party system since 1993

moderate multiparty system with one dominant party in 1982, otherwise moderate multiparty system with two main parties since 1977

Turkey 1983–99

moderate multiparty system with one dominant party in 1983–87
moderate multiparty system with a balance among the parties in 1991–99
moderate multiparty system with a balance among the parties in 1983–91
extreme multiparty system with a balance among the parties since 1995

United Kingdom 1945–97

two party system from 1945 to 1979
moderate multiparty system with one dominant party in 1983–87
two-and-a-half-party system in 1992
moderate multiparty system with one dominant party since 1997
two-party system from 1945 to 1959
two-and-a-half-party system from 1964 to 1979
moderate multiparty system with a balance among the parties in 1983–87
moderate multiparty system with two main parties since 1992

medium-high bias

old system(s)
new system(s)

Catalonia 1980–99

moderate multiparty system with a balance among the parties in 1980
moderate multiparty system with one dominant party from 1984 to 1995
moderate multiparty system with two main parties in 1999
extreme multiparty system with a balance among the parties in 1980
moderate multiparty system with two main parties since 1984

Czech Republic 1990–98

moderate multiparty system with one dominant party in 1990
extreme multiparty system with one dominant party in 1992
extreme multiparty system with two main parties in 1996

moderate multiparty system with two main parties since 1998
extreme multiparty system with one dominant party in 1990–92
extreme multiparty system with two main parties since 1996

Georgia 1995

moderate multiparty system with one dominant party in 1995
extreme multiparty system with a balance among the parties in 1995

Macedonia 1998

moderate multiparty system with one dominant party since 1998
moderate multiparty system with a balance among the parties since 1998

Poland 1993–97

extreme multiparty system with two main parties in 1993
moderate multiparty system with two main parties since 1997
extreme multiparty system with a balance among the parties in 1993
extreme multiparty system with two main parties since 1997

Romania 1992–96

extreme multiparty system with two main parties since 1992
extreme multiparty system with a balance among the parties since 1992

Turkey 1950–77

two-party system from 1950 to 1957
two-and-a-half-party system from 1961 to 1977
two-and-a-half-party system from 1950 to 1957
moderate multiparty system with two main parties from 1961 to 1977

TRNC 1976 and 1990

moderate multiparty system with one dominant party in 1976
two-party system in 1990
moderate multiparty system with two main parties in 1976
two-party system in 1990

Scotland 1999–

moderate multiparty system with one dominant party since 1999
moderate multiparty system with two main parties since 1999

Wales 1999–

moderate multiparty system with one dominant party since 1999
moderate multiparty system with two main parties since 1999

In the French Fifth Republic, Hungary, Romania, and now Turkey, the electoral system has clearly prevented the most extreme fragmentation, such as occurred in the French Fourth Republic. Perhaps even more striking, in Bulgaria, Spain, Turkey 1961–77, and the United Kingdom, the electoral system does seem to have compressed party politics into two- or two-and-a-half-party systems, with even occasional periods of one-party dominance.

Furthermore, at the other end, almost all of our extreme multiparty systems with a balance among the parties (the most fragmented category) are found in electoral systems with medium bias or less. The one exception here is Poland in 1993, but by the 1997 elections the Polish party system had become a moderate multiparty one. Ironically, the attempt in the French Fourth Republic to give more seats to centrist alliances did not change the overall picture of minimal overall bias and highly fragmented party politics.

REFERENCES

Lijphart, Arend, et al. (1990). *Electoral Systems and Party Systems.* Oxford: Oxford University Press.

Nohlen, Dieter (1989). *Wahlrecht und Parteiensystem: Über die politischen Auswirkungen von Wahlsystem.* Opladen: Leske and Budrich.

Rae, Douglas (1967). *The Political Consequences of Electoral Laws.* New Haven: Yale University Press.

Appendix Table Current Electoral System Data (December 1999)

System	Total Seats	Single-Member Seats	Multimember Seats Total	#D	Seat Range	Seats from a National List
Austria	**183**	**none**	**170**	9	6–39	**13**
Belgium	**150**	**none**	**all**	20	2–22	**none**
Bulgaria	**240**	**none**	**all**	31	*	**none**
			* varies by turnout			
Croatia	**127**	**35**	**12**	1 *	12	**80**
			* for the Croatian diaspora			
Cyprus (Greek)	**56**	**none**	**all**	6	3–21	**none**

continued

Appendix Table *Continued*

System	Total Seats	Single-Member Seats	Multimember Seats Total	#D	Seat Range	Seats from a National List
TRNC	**50**	**none**	**all**	5	6–15	**none**
Czech Republic	**200**	**none**	**all**	8	8–32	**none**
Denmark	**179**	**none**	**all**	19	2–21	**none**
Estonia	**101**	**none**	**all**	11	8–11	**none**
Finland	**200**	**1**	**199**	20	7–30	**none**
France	**577**	**all**	**none**			**none**
Georgia	**235**	**85**	**none**			**150**
Germany	**656 ***	**328**	**328 ***	16	3–77	**none**
	* may be more if a party or parties win "overhang seats"					
Greece	**300**	**5**	**283**	51	2–32	**12**
Hungary	**386**	**176**	**152**	20	4–28	**58**
Iceland	**63**	**none**	**50**	8	5–19	**13**
Ireland	**166**	**none**	**all**	41	3–5	**none**
Italy	**630**	**475**	**155**	26	1–11	**none**
Latvia	**100**	**none**	**all**	5	14–27	**none**
Liechtenstein	**25**	**none**	**all**	2	10—15	**none**
Lithuania	**141**	**71**	**none**			**70**
Luxembourg	**60**	**none**	**all**	4	7–23	**none**
Macedonia	**120**	**85**	**none**			**35**
Malta	**65**	**none**	**all**	13	5	**none**
Moldova	**104**	**none**	**none**			**all**
Netherlands	**150**	**none**	**none**			**all**
Norway	**165**	**none**	**157**	19	4–15	**8**
Poland	**460**	**none**	**391**	37	3–17	**69**
Portugal	**230**	**none**	**all**	20	3–50	**none**
Romania	**341 ***	**none**	**all**	42	4–29	**none**

* plus additional reserved seats for minorities

Appendix Table *Continued*

System	Total Seats	Single-Member Seats	Multimember Seats Total	#D	Seat Range	Seats from a National List
Russia	**450**	**225**	**none**			**225**
Slovakia	**150**	**none**	**all**	4	12–50	**none**
Slovenia	**90**	**2 ***	**88**	8	11	**none**
* one each for Hungarian and Italian minorities						
Spain	**350**	**2**	**348**	50	3–33	**none**
Basque Country	**75**	**none**	**all**	3	25	**none**
Catalonia	**135**	**none**	**all**	4	15–85	**none**
Sweden	**349**	**none**	**310**	28	2–22	**39**
Switzerland	**200**	**5**	**195**	21	2–35	**none**
Turkey	**550**	**none**	**all**	104	3–6	**none**
Ukraine	**450**	**225**	**none**			**225**
United Kingdom	**659**	**all**	**none**			**none**
Northern Ireland	**108**	**none**	**all**	18	6	**none**
Scotland	**129**	**73**	**56**	8	7	**none**
Wales	**60**	**40**	**20**	5	4	**none**

#D = number of districts

CHAPTER 5

Types of Party Systems and Governments

To what extent do the different types of party systems have different outcomes in terms of governments? Do two-party systems (almost) always yield single-party majorities? Are dominant parties in multiparty systems also dominant around the cabinet table? This chapter will provide relevant data and answers for these questions. First of all, though, for a party system to have any causal effect on a system's government there must be a linkage between the composition of parliament and the resulting government. Such a linkage occurs by definition in a parliamentary system. However, in a presidential system wherein the government is not accountable to the legislature, the composition of the cabinet reflects presidential wishes, not legislative outcomes. Thus the governments in the two presidential systems of this analysis—Cyprus (Greek) and now Georgia—cannot be analyzed as reflections of their party systems. A similar exclusion should also be done for Croatia, Russia, and Ukraine—all three are semipresidential systems, but ones with extremely strong presidencies where the parliament and parliamentary elections matter little for the composition of government. In all the remaining polities, and thus in the vast majority of European party systems, we can analyze their subsequent governmental patterns.

However, we must first be clear on what we mean by a government, or more precisely a government change, before we can count and analyze governments. This study takes what may be called a "maximalist" approach, in that it considers a new government to occur when any of the following happens: (a) a change in the party membership of a cabinet, that is, a party or parties either entering or leaving the government (but not merely changing their relative weights); (b) the formation of a government after a governmental resignation, even if (a) does not occur; (c) the change of a prime minister; or (d) the (re)formation of a government after an election, even if nothing else occurs. Each criterion but the first is controversial, and various scholars do use varying definitions (Laver and Schofield 1990: 145–47).

This analysis will be in two parts (see Table 5.1). The first part deals with the formation of a government and what the median, that is, "typical," government is in each case. The second part deals with the different types of governments formed and links this to cabinet duration. The raw data for this analysis are provided in the appendix table to this chapter. For each polity, it lists all postwar or postdemocratization governments and gives for each, first, the month and year it took office, the month and year it broke up, resigned, or faced the voters, and then the consequent number of months in office [#MON]. It then gives the number of parties in the government [#P] and the combined parliamentary base of these parties [PARL BASE]. Of course, for a single-party government the parliamentary base is just the number of seats held by that party. Next is given the type of government in terms of five key categories, although these are seven in number with qualifications. These five key categories are as follows: a single-party majority government [SP MAJ]; a single-party minority government [SP MIN]; a multiparty, minority-coalition government [MP MIN]; a multiparty, minimal-winning coalition [MP MWC], that is, one in which removing any one party would cost it its parliamentary majority; or a multiparty oversized coalition [MP OVC], that is, one that contains "extra parties" beyond those needed to have a (bare) majority in parliament. In addition, if a multiparty coalition of two parties contains the two largest parties, this is what is known in Germany as a "grand coalition" [GC]. Such systems have been quite common in Austria and Liechtenstein, but also have occurred elsewhere. They are thus indicated as such in the appendix table, although these are ultimately subtypes of either multiparty, minimal-winning coalitions or multiparty oversized coalitions, as the case may be. Finally, the appendix table gives a measure of cabinet dominance [CAB DOM], that is, the percentage of cabinet seats held by the party with the largest number and, thus, percentage of seats. If one party holds all the seats, then this value is 100. Independents—which are indicated in the case studies with an "(I)"—are certainly considered part of the cabinet and thus part of the denominator for this calculation.

In terms of government formation, it is important to note the difference between negative and positive parliamentarianism. Under negative parliamentarianism, a government once sworn in is assumed to have the support, or at least the tolerance, of the parliament. If this assumed or implicit support is not truly the case, then it is up to the opposition party or parties to move a motion of nonconfidence. Under positive parliamentarianism, a new government must show that it has the explicit support of parliament. This is done by holding a *vote of investiture,* which a government must pass before it can assume the powers of office. Even if a government has already been sworn in by the head of state, it does not properly take over until it has passed a vote of investiture. Should a government fail a vote of investiture, then it is "stillborn" and does not count as ever having been a government.

The vast majority of European governments use the system of positive parliamentarianism. Indeed, apparently every new democracy in Central and Eastern Europe has adopted it. Negative parliamentarianism is thus used only in the Nordic countries (but in all five of them), in the United Kingdom, the French Fifth Republic (where a government can call a vote of investiture if it wishes but need not do so), Austria, Malta, and Portugal. The French Fourth Republic used positive parliamentarianism. Two other countries have changed their systems: Sweden adopted the requirement of a vote of investiture in its 1975 constitution, however this is framed so as to count abstentions and absences on the government side; thus, as Bergman (1993: 287) stresses, it still functions as negative parliamentarianism in terms of government formation. Finally, the Turkish Republic of Northern Cyprus adopted positive parliamentarianism in its 1983 constitution.

As Bergman notes, negative parliamentarianism tends to lead to minority governments after a hung parliament, since a minority party may be able to get support from different parties on different issues and thus separate its agenda, unlike under positive parliamentarianism. Indeed, sometimes—especially, as Bergman (1993) stresses, in the Nordic countries—these minority governments are not even close to a majority, in that they hold 40 percent or less of the seats. Finally, governments take longer to form under positive parliamentarianism. Part of this is just the procedure of calling back parliament, debating the proposed government's program, and holding the actual vote of investiture. These additional steps seem to add at least a week to government formation. Under negative parliamentarianism, a government can be simply appointed or reappointed, and it takes office right there and then. Of course, what usually takes much longer than the formalities under positive parliamentarianism are the negotiations needed to form a coalition and/or ensure that the investiture vote is a success.

Since the type of parliamentarianism is quite separate from the type of party system, in taking the mean of all the cases in a category, systems with negative parliamentarianism will be adjusted by a conservative additional value of ten days, so as to approximate the procedural time "saved." If we do this, then the adjusted mean number of formation days for each type of system (with the cases weighted equally) is as follows:

- two party systems—32 days;
- two-and-a-half-party systems—39 days;
- moderate multiparty systems with one dominant party—28 days;
- moderate multiparty systems with two main parties—43 days;
- moderate multiparty systems with a balance among the parties—54 days;
- extreme multiparty systems with one dominant party—41 days;
- extreme multiparty systems with two main parties—42 days; and
- extreme multiparty systems with a balance among the parties—59 days

Thus, what seems to matter for quick government formation is not fewer parties per se, but rather the absence of a multiparty system (extreme or moderate) with a balance among the parties. In such a case, there is a much greater number of probable outcomes, compared with having one dominant party or two main parties.

In terms of classifying the "normal" governmental outcome, first we note the median number of parties of all the governments in a specific national party system. The median is used to provide a clear integer value if possible. Then, of all the governments with said number of parties, we note the median cabinet dominance for these governments. This has the advantage of inevitably excluding extreme values in terms of the number of parties, which, of course, are likely also extreme in their cabinet dominance scores.

What, then, are the typical governments for each of the eight categories of party systems? For a two-party system, not surprisingly, the typical government is a single-party one in which said party holds all of the seats. Austria 1945 and Liechtenstein 1945–89 are exceptions here, though, in that instead of presumably the larger of the two main parties governing alone, the two main parties chose to form grand coalitions. In a two-and-a-half-party system, one of two things tends to occur. In some cases one of the main parties will govern alone, either because it has a majority (as is usually the case in Greece since 1989) or because it is close to a majority (as in Spain 1977–79 and 1993 onward, and in Portugal 1995 and 1999). In other cases, one of the two main parties will govern with one of the smaller parties, and this larger party will keep most of the cabinet portfolios. This has been the case in Germany since 1961, and was the case in Belgium 1946–61 and Turkey 1961–77.

In a moderate multiparty system with one dominant party, that party does indeed dominate the cabinet. In most cases this is because it forms a single-party government. Even where it forms a multiparty coalition, the dominant party is clearly in the majority in the cabinet. A good example of this latter scenario is France 1981, 1988, 1997, in which the French Socialists invariably govern with a couple of other parties (or, since 1997, four other parties), but where the socialists as the pole of the French left dominate in the cabinet. In the few cases of moderate multiparty systems with two main parties, the most common pattern is for there to be two parties in government, but this does not necessarily involve one big and one small party (in terms of cabinet seats). Again, most of these cases are short-lived, so generalizations are risky.

The category of moderate multiparty systems with a balance among the parties has more coherence. To repeat, in this system there are perhaps three or four reasonable-sized parties. The typical government pattern is, thus, for two of these parties to get together in government, with the cabinet portfolios divided up more or less equally. Iceland 1945–79 is an interesting example of this pattern—even though the Independence Party (the conservatives) was always somewhat larger than the other three main parties, it was not always in government, and when it was, it tended to claim only half or perhaps 50 percent plus one of the cabinet seats.

In the case of extreme multiparty systems with one dominant party, the dominant party in question is normally not so dominant as to govern alone. The two main exceptions here are Norway since 1989 and Sweden since 1988, where the social democrats tend to form single-party minority governments. Both countries, it should be stressed, use negative parliamentarianism. In most such systems, however, coalition governments are formed, and the dominance comes in the fact that the dominant party gets most of the cabinet seats. Perhaps the key exception here is Iceland 1983–95, where the newly dominant Independence Party rarely pressed such claims, perhaps because its dominance was due to greater fragmentation rather than an increase in its absolute size.

For the extreme multiparty systems with two main parties, the standard cabinet seems to be a coalition of three to four parties. This tends to mean one (but not both) of the two main parties and two or three smaller ones. Cabinet dominance values range greatly here, but in five of the nine cases with the system, the value is 50 percent or less. In other words, the more likely pattern is no true cabinet dominance. Among the other cases, it should be stressed that Italy 1963–87 seemed to behave more like a system of dominance, in that the Christian Democrats were always in the government and almost always had the majority of cabinet seats. This resulted from the fact that the other main party in Italy 1963–87, the Italian Communist Party, was not seen as an acceptable party of government by the other relevant parties. Of the group of parties that did tend to be in government, the Christian Democrats were mathematically always necessary to achieve a majority, and among just these parties, the Christian Democrats were clearly dominant in the sense of their seat ratios vis-à-vis the Socialist Party.

Finally, the category of extreme multiparty systems with a balance among the parties has a typical government that contains four or even five parties, none of which are dominant. The Swiss case is illustrative: there, the four main parties have controlled the government and distributed the seven cabinet portfolios in the same 2:2:2:1 ratio since 1959.

Table 5.1 Government Formation and Median Types

	Type of Parliamentarianism	Mean Formation Period in Days	Median Number of Parties in Government	Of These Governments Median Cabinet Dominance
Two-Party Systems				
Austria 1945	NEG	54	2	46
Greece 1981–85	POS	3	1	100
Liechtenstein 1945–89	POS	67	2	50
Malta 1966–(98)	NEG	4	1	100
TRNC 1990	POS	55	1	100

	Type of Parliamentarianism	Mean Formation Period in Days	Median Number of Parties in Government	Of These Governments Median Cabinet Dominance
Turkey 1950–57	POS	7	1	100
United Kingdom 1945–79	NEG	7	1	100

Moderate Multiparty, but in fact Two-and-a-Half-Party Systems

Austria 1949–86	NEG	49	2	54
Belgium 1946–61	POS	34	2	55
Bulgaria 1990–91	POS	66	3	56
Germany 1961–(98)	POS	36	2	76
Greece 1989–(96)	POS	8	1	100
Ireland 1954–82	POS	19	1	100
Liechtenstein 1993–(97)	POS	78	2	60
Portugal 1995–(99)	NEG	28	1	78
Spain 1977–79	POS	24	1	95
Spain 1993–(96)	POS	50	1	74
Turkey 1961–77	POS	39	2	61
United Kingdom 1992	NEG	2	1	100

Moderate Multiparty Systems with One Dominant Party

Bulgaria 1994	POS	39	3	56
Bulgaria (1997–)	POS	32	1	100
Catalonia 1984–95	POS	~31	1	100
Czech Republic 1990	POS	?	3	43
France 1981, 1988, 1997	NEG	12	3	83
Germany 1953–57	POS	44	3	73
Greece 1974–77	POS	6	1	100
Ireland 1948–51	POS	14	2.5	72
Lithuania 1992	POS	46	1	100

continued

Table 5.1 *Continued*

	Type of Parliamentarianism	Mean Formation Period in Days	Median Number of Parties in Government	Of These Governments Median Cabinet Dominance
Moderate Multiparty Systems with One Dominant Party *Continued*				
Lithuania (1996–)	POS	24	3	69
Macedonia 1994	POS	51	3.5	50
Macedonia (1998–)	POS	30	3	?
Moldova 1994	POS	37	1	100
Norway 1949–77	NEG	12	1	100
Portugal 1987–91	NEG	27	1	86
Scotland (1999–)	POS	13	2	82
Spain 1982–89	POS	35	1	100
Sweden 1948–85	NEG	17	1	100
Turkey 1983–87	POS	29	1	100
TRNC 1976–85	both	30	1	100
TRNC (1998–)	POS	36	2	73
United Kingdom 1983–87	NEG	2	1	100
United Kingdom (1997–)	NEG	6	1	100
Wales (1999–)	POS	6	1	100
Moderate Multiparty Systems with Two Main Parties				
Austria 1990	NEG	71	2	47
Catalonia (1999–)	POS	30	1	100
Czech Republic 1998	POS	32	1	100
France 1958	NEG	46	3	36
Ireland 1987–(97)	POS	29	2	87
Norway 1981–85	NEG	24	2	80
Poland (1997–)	POS	26	2	50

	Type of Parliamentarianism	Mean Formation Period in Days	Median Number of Parties in Government	Of These Governments Median Cabinet Dominance
Moderate Multiparty Systems with a Balance among the Parties				
Austria 1994–(99)	NEG	66	2	50
Belgium 1965	POS	69	2	64
Catalonia 1980	POS	35	2	38
France 1978, 1986, 1993	NEG	6	2	52
Iceland 1946–79	NEG	52	2	50
Iceland (1999–)	NEG	20	2	50
Luxembourg 1945–(99)	NEG	34	2	50
Moldova (1998–)	POS	60	2	64
Portugal 1975–85	NEG	65	3	?
Netherlands 1977–(98)	POS	98	3	56
Turkey 1991–(99)	POS	58	2	59
TRNC (1993)	POS	31	2	55
Extreme Multiparty Systems with One Dominant Party				
Basque Country 1980–84	POS	49	1	100
Belgium 1978	POS	115	4	30
Czech Republic 1992	POS	27	4	43
Denmark 1950–(98)	NEG	11	2	64
Estonia 1992	POS	31	2	60
Estonia 1995	POS	43	3	73
France 1962–73	NEG	6	3	61
Hungary 1990	POS	45	3	53
Hungary 1994	POS	27	2	79
Iceland 1983–95	NEG	35	2	50
Italy 1946–58	POS	39	2	81

continued

Table 5.1 *Continued*

	Type of Parliamentarianism	Mean Formation Period in Days	Median Number of Parties in Government	Of These Governments Median Cabinet Dominance
Extreme Multiparty Systems with One Dominant Party *Continued*				
Norway 1945	NEG	26	1	100
Norway 1989–(97)	NEG	30	1	100
Slovakia 1992–94	POS	50	3	48
Sweden 1988–(98)	NEG	18	1	100
Extreme Multiparty Systems with Two Main Parties				
Belgium 1971–77	POS	63	5	39
Czech Republic 1996	POS	4	3	50
Germany 1949	POS	37	3	64
Hungary (1998–)	POS	45	2	65
Italy 1963–87	POS	57	3.5	62
Netherlands 1946–71	POS	66	4	41
Poland 1993	POS	37	2	40
Romania 1992–(96)	POS	38	2.5	76
Slovakia (1998–)	POS	34	4	45
Extreme Multiparty Systems with a Balance among the Parties				
Basque Country 1986–(98)	POS	76	2.5	61
Belgium 1968	POS	89	2	59
Belgium 1981–(99)	POS	68	4	31
Denmark 1945–47	NEG	22	1	93
Estonia (1999–)	POS	18	3	33
Finland 1945–(99)	NEG	51	4	40

	Type of Parliamentarianism	Mean Formation Period in Days	Median Number of Parties in Government	Of These Governments Median Cabinet Dominance
France 1945–56	POS	34	4	35
Italy 1992–(96)	POS	61	5	53
Latvia 1993–(98)	POS	34	5	33
Netherlands 1972	POS	163	5	44
Northern Ireland 1996–(98)	POS	n.a.	4	33
Poland 1991	POS	57	5	25
Slovakia 1990	POS	?	3	57
Slovenia 1992–(96)	POS	79	3	47
Switzerland 1947–(99)	POS	49	4	29

Regarding the duration of a government, this seems to relate strongly to the specific type of government in question. As Laver and Schofield (1990: 151) note, there is general agreement that minority governments are less stable than majority ones, given that they are more likely to be defeated in parliament. Laver and Schofield (ibid.) then note that, "[a]rguing along the same lines, minimal winning majority [coalition] governments should be less susceptible to change than surplus majority [coalition] governments," since the latter can shed one or perhaps more members and the rest of the parties can still have a majority. (Of course, this would still be a new government.) Laver and Schofield's (1990: 151–52) evidence from twelve West European countries bears out these assumptions, although it shows that single-party majorities are even longer lasting than multiparty minimal-winning coalitions.

Consequently, the data in Table 5.2 are arranged with these assumptions in mind. The two most stable government types—single-party majorities and multiparty, minimal-winning coalitions—are listed first, followed by the theoretically less stable types. The number of each type of government is given for each system, as is the number of the first types as a percentage of all types. Finally, the mean duration of governments, in months, is given for each type. The summary totals for each category are given at the bottom, as are the overall category values for percentage of the most stable types and mean duration. Note that for the latter two values, the calculations are based on all governments within the category type, which obviously weights more toward the longer lasting systems wherein, we would argue, "typical" government patterns are more stabilized.

What do we find? First of all, two-party systems, with the notable exception of Liechtenstein 1945–89, do tend to have single-party majority governments. Their mean cabinet duration is also the longest of any category, at just over three years. Two-and-a-half-party systems also have a reasonable number of single-party governments, but their most frequent government type is the minimal winning coalition. Moderate multiparty systems with a dominant party reflect this party dominance, in that they normally have single-party governments and of these, more majorities than minorities. Moderate multiparty systems with two main parties, in contrast, tend toward multiparty, minimal-winning coalitions. Such multiparty, minimal-winning coalitions are very much the pattern in moderate multiparty systems with a balance among the parties. All four of these moderate multiparty systems (that is, including two-and-a-half-party systems) have moderate government duration, each averaging around two years.

The extreme multiparty system with one dominant party is the one category with no clear pattern. Single-party minorities, multiparty minority coalitions, and multiparty minimal-winning coalitions are all frequent occurrences. The frequency of minority governments is apparently driven by the three Scandinavian countries, which, again, use negative parliamentarianism. In this category, government duration is also around two years. Finally, extreme multiparty systems with two main parties and extreme multiparty systems with a balance among the parties both tend to multiparty oversized coalitions. Not surprisingly, these two categories have the shortest mean cabinet durations, at clearly less than two years. Indeed, if one takes Switzerland (which has no possibility of nonconfidence motions) out of the last category, the mean for the remaining cases is only fourteen months—the lowest value overall.

Table 5.2 Range of Government Types and Cabinet Durability

	SP MAJ [A]	MP MWC [B]	MP OVC [C]	SP MIN [D]	MP MIN [E]	Others [F]	% A+B	Mean Cabinet Duration (Months)
Two-Party Systems								
Austria 1945		1	1				50	24
Greece 1981–85	2						100	46
Liechtenstein 1945–89			14				0	36
Malta 1966–(98)	9						100	49
TRNC 1990	1						100	30
Turkey 1950–57	3						100	40
United Kingdom 1945–79	14			1			93	30
Category totals	*29*	*1*	*15*	*1*	*0*	*0*		
Weighted category means							*65*	*37*
Moderate Multiparty, but in Fact Two-and-a-Half Party Systems								
Austria 1949–86	4	10		1			93	32
Belgium 1946–61	3	9		1			92	17
Bulgaria 1990–91	1		1	1		2	20	10
Germany 1961–(98)		17		3			85	23
Greece 1989–(96)	4	1	1				83	17
Ireland 1954–82	7	3		2	1		77	30
Liechtenstein 1993–(97)	1	2					100	22
Portugal 1995–(99)				2			0	48
Spain 1977–79				3			0	18
Spain 1993–(96)				2			0	33
Turkey 1961–977	3	4		3	2	1	54	14
United Kingdom 1992	1						100	60
Category totals	*24*	*46*	*2*	*18*	*3*	*3*		
Weighted category means							*74*	*23*

continued

Table 5.2 *Continued*

	SP MAJ [A]	MP MWC [B]	MP OVC [C]	SP MIN [D]	MP MIN [E]	Others [F]	% A+B	Mean Cabinet Duration (Months)
Moderate Multiparty Systems with One Dominant Party								
Bulgaria 1994		1				1	50	56
Bulgaria (1997–)	1						100	..
Catalonia 1984–(95)	3			1			75	45
Czech Republic 1990			1				0	24
France 1981, 1988, 1997			4		1		0	19
Germany 1953–57	1		4				20	19
Greece 1974–77	3						100	28
Ireland 1948–51				1	1		0	37
Lithuania 1992	2						100	24
Lithuania (1996–)		1	1				50	27
Macedonia 1994			2				0	24
Moldova 1994	1					1	50	24
Norway 1949–77	5	2		7	2		44	24
Portugal 1987–91	2						100	49
Scotland (1999–)		1					100	..
Spain 1982–89	3						100	42
Sweden 1948–85	2	5		11	1		37	25
Turkey 1983–87	4						100	23
TRNC 1976–85	4	4		1			89	18
TRNC (1998–)		1					100	..
United Kingdom 1983–87	3						100	35
United Kingdom (1997–)	1						100	..
Wales (1999–)				1			0	..
Category totals	*35*	*15*	*12*	*22*	*5*	*2*		
Weighted category means							*55*	*25*

	SP MAJ [A]	MP MWC [B]	MP OVC [C]	SP MIN [D]	MP MIN [E]	Others [F]	% A+B	Mean Cabinet Duration (Months)
Moderate Multiparty Systems with Two Main Parties								
Austria 1990		1					100	47
Catalonia (1999–)				1			0	..
Czech Republic (1998–)				1			0	..
France 1958		1	2				33	15
Ireland 1987–(97)		4		2	1		57	20
Norway 1981–85		1		2	1		25	24
Poland (1997–)		1					100	..
Category totals	*0*	*8*	*2*	*6*	*2*	*0*		
Weighted category means							*44*	*22*
Moderate Multiparty Systems with a Balance among the Parties								
Austria 1994–(99)		3					100	19
Belgium 1965		2					100	16
Catalonia 1980					1		0	47
France 1978, 1986, 1993		2			2		50	19
Iceland 1946–79		10	3	4			59	25
Iceland (1999–)		1					100	..
Luxembourg 1945–(97)		16	1		1		89	37
Macedonia (1998–)			1				0	..
Moldova (1998–)		2					100	9
Netherlands 1977–(98)		5	4		1		50	27
Portugal 1975–85		5		2		3	50	12
Turkey 1991–(99)		4		1	2		57	14
TRNC (1993)		4					100	13
Category totals	*0*	*54*	*9*	*7*	*7*	*3*		
Weighted category means							*67*	*23*

continued

Table 5.2 *Continued*

	SP MAJ [A]	MP MWC [B]	MP OVC [C]	SP MIN [D]	MP MIN [E]	Others [F]	% A + B	Mean Cabinet Duration (Months)
Extreme Multiparty Systems with One Dominant Party								
Basque Country 1980–84				1			0	46
Belgium 1978			5				0	6
Czech Republic 1992		1					100	48
Denmark 1950–(98)		4		12	14		13	19
Estonia 1992					1	1	0	15
Estonia 1995		3	1				75	12
France 1962–73		4	5		1		40	18
Hungary 1990			2				0	24
Hungary 1994			1				0	47
Iceland 1983–(95)		4	1		1		67	31
Italy 1946–58		3	6	7	2		17	11
Norway 1945	1						100	47
Norway 1989–(97)				3	2		0	24
Slovakia 1992–94		2			1		67	25
Sweden 1988–(98)				5	1		0	24
Category totals	*1*	*21*	*21*	*28*	*23*	*1*		
Weighted category means							*23*	*19*
Extreme Multiparty Systems with Two Main Parties								
Belgium 1971–77		2	5				29	11
Czech Republic 1996					1	1	0	11
Germany 1949		1					100	47
Hungary (1998–)		1					100	..
Italy 1963–87		3	18	8	3		17	11
Netherlands 1946–71		4	7		2		31	25

	SP MAJ [A]	MP MWC [B]	MP OVC [C]	SP MIN [D]	MP MIN [E]	Others [F]	% A + B	Mean Cabinet Duration (Months)
Poland 1993		3					100	15
Romania 1992–(96)			2	1	1		0	21
Slovakia (1998–)			1				0	..
Category totals	*0*	*14*	*33*	*9*	*7*	*1*		
Weighted category means							*22*	*15*
Extreme Multiparty Systems with a Balance among the Parties								
Basque Country 1986–(98)		1	1		4		17	25
Belgium 1968		1					100	41
Belgium 1981–(99)		4	3		1		50	28
Denmark 1945–47				2			0	28
Estonia (1999–)		1					100	..
Finland 1945–(99)		5	22	4	7	7	11	14
France 1945–56		1	23	1	2		4	6
Italy 1992–(96)		3	2		2	1	38	10
Latvia 1993–(98)			3		2		0	11
Netherlands 1972			1				0	48
Northern Ireland 1996–(98)			1				0	..
Poland 1991					2		0	10
Slovakia 1990		1			1		50	12
Slovenia 1992–(96)		1	2				33	23
Switzerland 1947–(99)		2	13				14	43
Category totals	*0*	*20*	*71*	*7*	*21*	*8*		
Weighted category means							*16*	*17*

REFERENCES

Bergman, Torbjörn. (1993). "Constitutional Design and Government Formation: The Expected Consequences of Negative Parliamentarianism." *Scandinavian Political Studies,* Vol. 16, pp. 285–304.

Laver, Michael, and Norman Schofield. (1990). *Multiparty Government: The Politics of Coalition in Europe.* Oxford: Oxford University Press.

Appendix: Governments in Office from First Postwar Free Elections through December 1999

pe = postelections
SP MAJ = single-party majority
SP MIN = single-party minority
MP MIN = multiparty minority (coalition)
MP MWC = multiparty minimal-winning coalition
MP MWGC = multiparty minimal-winning grand coalition *
MP OVC = multiparty oversized coalition
MP OVGC = multiparty oversized grand coalition *
*A "grand coalition" involves the top two parties and only these.

Country/Region

Prime Minister or Equivalent	Government In (M / Y)	Out/ Elections
Austria		
Figl	12/45pe	11/47
Figl	11/47	11/49
Figl	11/49pe	02/53
Raab	04/53pe	05/56
Raab	06/56pe	05/59
Raab	07/59pe	04/61
Gorbach	04/61	03/63
Gorbach	03/63pe	04/64
Klaus	04/64	03/66
Klaus	04/66pe	03/70

Number of Months in Office	Number of Parties	Parliamentary Base	Cabinet Type	Cabinet Dominance
23	3	100	MP OVC	38
24	2	98	MP MWGC	54
39	2	87	MP MWGC	54
37	2	89	MP MWGC	54
35	2	95	MP MWGC	62
21	2	95	MP MWGC	54
23	2	95	MP MWGC	50
13	2	90	MP MWGC	50
23	2	90	MP MWGC	54
47	1	52	SP MAJ	100

Country/Region

Prime Minister or Equivalent	Government In (M / Y)	Out/ Elections
Austria *Continued*		
Kreisky	04/70[pe]	10/71
Kreisky	11/71[pe]	10/75
Kreisky	10/75[pe]	05/79
Kreisky	06/79[pe]	04/83
Sinowatz	05/83[pe]	06/86
Vranitzky	06/86	11/86
Vranitzky	01/87[pe]	10/90
Vranitzky	12/90[pe]	10/94
Vranitzky	11/94[pe]	12/95
Vranitzky	03/96[pe]	01/97
Klima	01/97	10/99
Belgium		
van Acker	04/46[pe]	07/46
Huysmans	08/46	03/47
Spaak	03/47	11/48
Spaak	11/48	06/49
Eyskens	08/49[pe]	06/50
Duvieusart	06/50[pe]	08/50
Pholien	08/50	01/52
van Houtte	01/52	04/54
van Acker	04/54[pe]	06/58
Eyskens	06/58[pe]	11/58
Eyskens	11/58	09/60
Eyskens	09/60	03/61

continued

Number of Months in Office	Number of Parties	Parliamentary Base	Cabinet Type	Cabinet Dominance
18	1	49	SP MIN	100
47	1	51	SP MAJ	100
43	1	51	SP MAJ	100
46	1	52	SP MAJ	100
37	2	56	MP MWC	72
5	2	56	MP MWC	71
45	2	86	MP MWGC	50
47	2	77	MP MWGC	47
13	2	64	MP MWGC	50
10	2	68	MP MWGC	50
33	2	68	MP MWGC	50
3	3	54	MP MWC	39
7	3	54	MP MWC	35
20	2	80	MP MWGC	45
7	2	80	MP MWGC	48
10	2	63	MP MWC	55
2	1	51	SP MAJ	94
17	1	51	SP MAJ	94
27	1	51	SP MAJ	94
50	2	52	MP MWC	53
5	1	49	SP MIN	100
22	2	59	MP MWC	67
6	2	59	MP MWC	65

Country/Region		
Prime Minister or Equivalent	**Government In (M / Y)**	**Out/ Elections**
Belgium *Continued*		
Lefevre	04/61[pe]	05/65
Harmel	07/65[pe]	03/66
Vandenboeynants	03/66	03/68
Eyskens	06/68[pe]	11/71
Eyskens	01/72[pe]	11/72
Leburton	01/73	03/74
Tindemans	04/74[pe]	06/74
Tindemans	06/74	12/76
Tindemans	12/76	04/77
Tindemans	06/77[pe]	10/78
Vandenboeynants	10/78	12/78
Martens	04/79[pe]	01/80
Martens	01/80	04/80
Martens	05/80	10/80
Martens	10/80	04/81
Eyskens	04/81	11/81
Martens	12/81[pe]	10/85
Martens	11/85[pe]	10/87
Martens	10/87	12/87
Martens	05/88[pe]	09/91
Martens	09/91	11/91
Dehaene	02/92[pe]	05/95
Dehaene	06/95[pe]	06/99
Verhofstadt	07/99[pe]	.....

continued

Number of Months in Office	Number of Parties	Parliamentary Base	Cabinet Type	Cabinet Dominance
49	2	85	MP MWGC	57
8	2	67	MP MWGC	60
24	2	59	MP MWC	68
41	2	60	MP MWGC	59
11	3	60	MP MWC	48
14	4	70	MP OVC	36
2	4	54	MP MWC	40
30	5	56	MP OVC	38
4	5	56	MP OVC	39
16	5	81	MP OVC	40
2	6	81	MP OVC	31
9	5	71	MP OVC	31
3	4	66	MP OVC	29
5	6	76	MP OVC	24
6	4	66	MP OVC	31
7	4	66	MP OVC	30
46	4	49	MP MIN	33
23	4	53	MP MWC	28
2	4	53	MP MWC	28
39	6	71	MP OVC	30
2	4	63	MP OVC	31
39	4	57	MP MWC	31
48	4	55	MP MWC	37
..	6	63	MP OVC	28

Country/Region

Prime Minister or Equivalent	Government In (M / Y)	Out/ Elections
Bulgaria		
Lukanov	09/90pe	12/90
Popov	12/90	10/91
Dimitrov	11/91pe	12/92
Berov	12/92	09/94
Indzhova	10/94	12/94
Videnov	01/95pe	02/97
Sofiyanski	02/97	04/97
Kostov	04/97pe	.....
Turkish Republic of Northern Cyprus		
Konuk	07/76pe	03/78
Örek	04/78	11/78
Çağatay	12/78	07/81
Çağatay	08/81pe	12/81
Çağatay	03/82	12/83
Konuk	12/83	06/85
Eroğlu	07/85pe	08/86
Eroğlu	09/86	05/88
Eroğlu	05/88	05/90
Eroğlu	06/90pe	12/93
Atun	01/94pe	02/95
Atun	06/95	11/95
Atun	12/95	07/96
Eroğlu	08/96	12/98
Eroğlu	01/99pe	.....

Number of Months in Office	Number of Parties	Parliamentary Base	Cabinet Type	Cabinet Dominance
3	1	53	SP MAJ	89
10	3	93	MP OVC	56
13	1	46	SP MIN	100
22			government of "experts"	
2			caretaker government	
25	3	52	MP MWC	56
2			caretaker government	
..	1	..	SP MAJ	100
20	1	75	SP MAJ	100
7	1	75	SP MAJ	100
31	1	?	SP MAJ	100
4	1	45	SP MIN	100
21	3	53	MP MWC	73
18	2	53	MP MWC	45
13	2	68	MP MWC	73
20	2	56	MP MWC	91
24	1	50	SP MAJ	91
30	1	68	SP MAJ	100
13	2	56	MP MWC	55
5	2	56	MP MWC	55
7	2	56	MP MWC	55
28	2	?	MP MWC	?
..	2	62	MP MWC	73

Country/Region

Prime Minister or Equivalent	Government In (M / Y)	Out/ Elections

Czech Republic

Prime Minister or Equivalent	Government In (M / Y)	Out/ Elections
Pithart	06/90[pe]	06/92
Klaus	07/92[pe]	01/93
Klaus *	01/93	07/96
Klaus	07/96[pe]	11/97
Tosovsky	12/97	06/98
Zeman	07/98[pe]	.....

*No actual government change, but the Czech Republic now a sovereign country.

Denmark

Prime Minister or Equivalent	Government In (M / Y)	Out/ Elections
Kristensen	11/45[pe]	10/47
Hedtoft	11/47[pe]	09/50
Hedtoft	09/50[pe]	10/50
Eriksen	10/50	04/53
Eriksen	05/53[pe]	09/53
Hedtoft	09/53[pe]	01/55
Hansen	02/55	05/57
Hansen	05/57[pe]	02/60
Kampmann	02/60	11/60
Kampmann	11/60[pe]	09/62
Krag	09/62	09/64
Krag	09/64[pe]	11/66
Krag	11/66[pe]	01/68
Baunsgaard	02/68[pe]	09/71
Krag	10/71[pe]	10/72
Jørgensen	10/72	12/73
Hartling	12/73[pe]	01/75
Jørgensen	02/75[pe]	02/77

Number of Months in Office	Number of Parties	Parliamentary Base	Cabinet Type	Cabinet Dominance
24	3	75	MP OVC	43
(6)	4	56	MP MWC	53
(42)	4	56	MP MWC	53
16	3	49	MP MIN	50
6			caretaker government	
..	1	37	SP MIN	100
23	1	26	SP MIN	93
34	1	39	SP MIN	94
1	1	40	SP MIN	93
30	2	40	MP MIN	53
4	2	40	MP MIN	53
16	1	42	SP MIN	100
27	1	42	SP MIN	100
33	3	53	MP MWC	60
9	3	53	MP MWC	60
22	2	49	MP MIN	65
24	2	49	MP MIN	67
26	1	43	SP MIN	100
14	1	39	SP MIN	100
43	3	56	MP MWC	40
12	1	40	SP MIN	95
14	1	40	SP MIN	95
13	1	13	SP MIN	100
24	1	30	SP MIN	100

continued

Country/Region

Prime Minister or Equivalent	Government In (M / Y)	Out/ Elections
Denmark *Continued*		
Jørgensen	02/77[pe]	08/78
Jørgensen	08/78	10/79
Jørgensen	10/79[pe]	12/81
Jørgensen	12/81[pe]	09/82
Schlüter	09/82	01/84
Schlüter	01/84[pe]	09/87
Schlüter	09/87[pe]	05/88
Schlüter	06/88[pe]	12/89
Schlüter	12/89	12/90
Schlüter	12/90[pe]	01/93
Rasmussen	01/93	09/94
Rasmussen	09/94[pe]	01/97
Rasmussen	01/97	03/98
Rasmussen	03/98[pe]	.....
Estonia		
Laar	10/92[pe]	10/94
Tarand	10/94	03/95
Vähi	04/95[pe]	11/95
Vähi	11/95	11/96
Vähi	12/96	02/97
Siimann	03/97	03/99
Laar	03/99[pe]	.....

Note: In listing the number of parties in government, Estonian party groupings are treated as single parties.

Number of Months in Office	Number of Parties	Parliamentary Base	Cabinet Type	Cabinet Dominance
18	1	37	SP MIN	100
14	2	49	MP MIN	64
26	1	39	SP MIN	100
9	1	34	SP MIN	100
16	3	35	MP MIN	39
44	3	42	MP MIN	39
8	3	38	MP MIN	48
18	3	38	MP MIN	50
12	2	33	MP MIN	52
25	2	34	MP MIN	53
20	4	51	MP MWC	63
28	3	43	MP MIN	75
14	2	40	MP MIN	78
..	2	39	MP MIN	81
24	2	41	MP MIN	60
6			caretaker government	
7	2	56	MP MWC	64
12	2	59	MP MWC	60
2	1	41	SP MIN	80
24	1	41	SP MIN	86
..	3	52	MP MWC	33

Finland

Country/Region

Prime Minister or Equivalent	Government In (M / Y)	Out/ Elections
Paasikivi	04/45[pe]	07/45
Paasikivi	07/45	03/46
Pekkala	03/46	07/48
Fagerholm	07/48[pe]	03/50
Kekkonen	03/50	01/51
Kekkonen	01/51	07/51
Kekkonen	09/51[pe]	07/53
Kekkonen	07/53	11/53
Tuomija	11/53	03/54
Törngren	05/54[pe]	10/54
Kekkonen	10/54	03/56
Fagerholm	03/56	05/57
Sukselainen	05/57	07/57
Sukselainen	07/57	09/57
Sukselainen	09/57	11/57
von Fieandt	11/57	04/58
Kuuskoski	04/58	07/58
Fagerholm	08/58[pe]	01/59
Sukselainen	01/59	07/61
Miettunen	07/61	02/62
Karjalainen	04/62[pe]	12/63
Lehto	12/63	09/64
Virolainen	09/64	03/66
Paasio	05/66[pe]	03/68
Koivisto	03/68	03/70
Aura	05/70[pe]	07/70
Karjalainen	07/70	03/71

Number of Months in Office	Number of Parties	Parliamentary Base	Cabinet Type	Cabinet Dominance
3	5	86	MP OVC	28
8	4	82	MP OVC	28
28	4	82	MP OVC	33
20	1	27	SP MIN	94
10	3	38	MP MIN	67
6	4	65	MP OVC	41
22	3	60	MP OVC	41
4	2	33	MP MIN	57
4			caretaker government	
5	3	60	MP OVC	43
17	2	54	MP MWC	50
14	4	67	MP OVC	40
1	3	40	MP MIN	50
2	2	33	MP MIN	62
3	3	36	MP MIN	44
5			caretaker government	
3			caretaker government	
5	5	74	MP OVC	33
30	1	24	SP MIN	93
7	1	24	SP MIN	93
20	4	56	MP MWC	33
9			nonparty government	
18	4	56	MP MWC	47
22	4	76	MP OVC	40
24	5	82	MP OVC	38
2			caretaker government	
8	5	72	MP OVC	29

continued

Country/Region

Prime Minister or Equivalent	Government In (M / Y)	Out/ Elections
Finland *Continued*		
Karjalainen	03/71	10/71
Aura	10/71	01/72
Paasio	02/72[pe]	09/72
Sorsa	09/72	06/75
Liinamaa	06/75	09/75
Miettunen	11/75[pe]	09/76
Miettunen	09/76	05/77
Sorsa	05/77	03/78
Sorsa	03/78	03/79
Koivisto	05/79[pe]	02/82
Sorsa	02/82	12/82
Sorsa	12/82	03/83
Sorsa	05/83[pe]	03/87
Holkeri	04/87[pe]	08/90
Holkeri	09/90	03/91
Aho	04/91[pe]	03/95
Lipponen	04/95[pe]	03/99
Lipponen	04/99[pe]	.....
France—Fourth Republic		
Gouin	01/46	06/46
Bidault	06/46[pe]	11/46
Blum	12/46[pe]	01/47
Ramadier	01/47	05/47
Ramadier	05/47	10/47
Ramadier	10/47	11/47
Schuman	11/47	07/48

Number of Months in Office	Number of Parties	Parliamentary Base	Cabinet Type	Cabinet Dominance
7	4	56	MP OVC	47
3			caretaker government	
7	1	28	SP MIN	100
33	4	54	MP MWC	44
3			caretaker government	
10	5	76	MP OVC	28
8	3	29	MP MIN	56
10	5	76	MP OVC	33
12	4	71	MP OVC	33
33	4	67	MP OVC	35
10	4	67	MP OVC	35
3	3	51	MP MWC	47
46	4	62	MP OVC	47
40	4	66	MP OVC	44
4	3	61	MP OVC	47
47	4	58	MP OVC	47
47	5	72	MP OVC	31
..	5	70	MP OVC	35
5	3	81	MP OVC	35
5	4	81	MP OVC	35
1	1	21	SP MIN	100
4	5	86	MP OVC	35
5	4	69	MP OVC	46
1	4	69	MP OVC	50
8	5	70	MP OVC	40

continued

Country/Region

Prime Minister or Equivalent	Government In (M / Y)	Out/ Elections
France—Fourth Republic *Continued*		
Marie	07/48	09/48
Schuman	09/48	09/48
Queuille	09/48	10/49
Bidault	10/49	02/50
Bidault	02/50	07/50
Queuille	07/50	07/50
Pleven	07/50	03/51
Queuille	03/51	06/51
Pleven	08/51[pe]	01/52
Faure	01/52	03/52
Pinay	03/52	01/53
Mayer	01/53	06/53
Laniel	06/53	06/54
Mendès-France	06/54	02/55
Faure	02/55	01/56
Mollet	01/56[pe]	06/57
Bourgès-Maunoury	06/57	11/57
Gaillard	11/57	05/58
Pflimlin	05/58	05/58
deGaulle	06/58	01/59

Note: Given the divisions and the lack of discipline within parties, effective parliamentary support was normally less than the above nominal figures.

Prime Minister or Equivalent	Government In (M / Y)	Out/ Elections
France—Fifth Republic		
Debré	01/59[pe]	04/62
Pompidou	04/62	05/62
Pompidou	05/62	11/62
Pompidou	12/62[pe]	01/66
Pompidou	01/66	03/67

Number of Months in Office	Number of Parties	Parliamentary Base	Cabinet Type	Cabinet Dominance
2	4	69	MP OVC	32
(0)	4	69	MP OVC	40
13	5	70	MP OVC	33
4	5	70	MP OVC	33
5	4	53	MP OVC	47
(0)	4	53	MP OVC	43
8	5	70	MP OVC	27
3	5	70	MP OVC	32
5	4	65	MP OVC	33
2	4	65	MP OVC	31
10	4	65	MP OVC	35
5	4	65	MP OVC	35
12	5	65	MP OVC	36
8	4	50	MP MWC	31
11	4	65	MP OVC	32
17	3	33	MP MIN	50
6	3	33	MP MIN	50
6	6	87	MP OVC	29
1	5	76	MP OVC	36
7	5	84	MP OVC	13
39	4	88	MP OVC	29
1	3	61	MP OVC	36
6	2	53	MP MWC	50
37	2	53	MP MWC	59
14	2	53	MP MWC	56

continued

Country/Region

Prime Minister or Equivalent	Government In (M / Y)	Out/ Elections
France—Fifth Republic *Continued*		
Pompidou	04/67[pe]	06/68
Couve de Murville	07/68[pe]	06/69
Chaban-Delmas	06/69	07/72
Messmer	07/72	03/73
Messmer	04/73[pe]	02/74
Messmer	03/74	05/74
Chirac	05/74	08/76
Barre	08/76	03/78
Barre	04/78[pe]	05/81
Mauroy	05/81	06/81
Mauroy	06/81[pe]	03/83
Mauroy	03/83	07/84
Fabius	07/84	03/86
Chirac	03/86[pe]	05/88
Rocard	05/88	06/88
Rocard	06/88[pe]	05/91
Cresson	05/91	04/92
Bérégovoy	04/92	03/93
Balladur	03/93[pe]	05/95
Juppé	05/95	06/97
Jospin	06/97[pe]	.....
Germany		
Adenauer	09/49[pe]	09/53
Adenauer	10/53[pe]	07/55
Adenauer	07/55	03/56
Adenauer	03/56	09/57

Number of Months in Office	Number of Parties	Parliamentary Base	Cabinet Type	Cabinet Dominance
14	2	49	MP MIN	45
11	2	74	MP OVC	63
37	3	79	MP OVC	58
8	3	79	MP OVC	70
10	3	53	MP MWC	59
3	3	53	MP MWC	62
27	4	60	MP OVC	31
19	4	56	MP OVC	28
37	2	56	MP MWC	45
1	2	22	MP MIN	90
21	3	66	MP OVC	83
16	3	66	MP OVC	83
20	2	57	MP OVC	96
26	2	49	MP MIN	52
1	2	36	MP MIN	73
35	2	48	MP MIN	64
11	3	48	MP MIN	73
11	2	48	MP MIN	76
26	2	80	MP MWC	50
25	2	80	MP MWC	52
..	5	55	MP OVC	64
47	3	52	MP MWC	64
21	4	68	MP OVC	62
8	3	63	MP OVC	73
18	3	54	MP OVC	72

continued

Country/Region

Prime Minister or Equivalent	Government In (M / Y)	Out/ Elections
Germany *Continued*		
Adenauer	10/57[pe]	06/60
Adenauer	07/60	09/61
Adenauer	11/61[pe]	11/62
Adenauer	11/62	12/62
Adenauer	12/62	10/63
Erhard	10/63	09/65
Erhard	10/65[pe]	10/66
Erhard	10/66	11/66
Kiesinger	12/66	09/69
Brandt	10/69[pe]	05/72
Brandt	05/72	11/72
Brandt	12/72[pe]	05/74
Schmidt	05/74	10/76
Schmidt	12/76[pe]	10/80
Schmidt	11/80[pe]	09/82
Schmidt	09/82	10/82
Kohl	10/82	03/83
Kohl	03/83[pe]	01/87
Kohl	03/87[pe]	10/90
Kohl	01/91[pe]	10/94
Kohl	11/94[pe]	09/98
Schröder	10/98[pe]	.....

Number of Months in Office	Number of Parties	Parliamentary Base	Cabinet Type	Cabinet Dominance
32	2	58	MP OVC	89
14	1	54	SP MAJ	100
12	2	62	MP MWC	76
1	1	48	SP MIN	100
10	2	62	MP MWC	76
23	2	62	MP MWC	76
12	2	59	MP MWC	77
1	1	49	SP MIN	100
33	2	90	MP MWGC	55
31	2	51	MP MWC	80
6	2	50	MP MWC	81
17	2	55	MP MWC	72
29	2	55	MP MWC	75
46	2	51	MP MWC	75
22	2	55	MP MWC	76
1	1	44	SP MIN	100
5	2	56	MP MWC	71
46	2	56	MP MWC	76
43	2	54	MP MWC	74
45	2	60	MP MWC	75
46	2	54	MP MWC	83
..	2	52	MP MWC	75

Country/Region

Prime Minister or Equivalent	Government In (M / Y)	Out/ Elections
Greece		
Karamanlis	11/74[pe]	11/77
Karamanlis	11/77[pe]	05/80
Rallis	05/80	10/81
Papandreou	10/81[pe]	06/85
Papandreou	06/85[pe]	06/89
Tzannetakis	07/89[pe]	11/89
Zolotos	11/89[pe]	04/90
Mitsotakis	04/90[pe]	10/93
Papandreou	10/93[pe]	01/96
Simitis	01/96	09/96
Simitis	09/96[pe]	.....
Hungary		
Antall	05/90[pe]	12/93
Boross	12/93	05/94
Horn	06/94[pe]	05/98
Orbán	07/98[pe]	.....
Iceland		
Thors	07/46[pe]	10/46
Stefansson	02/47	10/49
Thors	12/49[pe]	03/50
Steinthorsson	03/50	06/53
Thors	09/53[pe]	06/56
Jonasson	07/56[pe]	12/58
Jonsson	12/58	06/59
Jonsson	07/59[pe]	10/59

Number of Months in Office	Number of Parties	Parliamentary Base	Cabinet Type	Cabinet Dominance
36	1	73	SP MAJ	100
30	1	58	SP MAJ	100
17	1	58	SP MAJ	100
44	1	57	SP MAJ	100
48	1	54	SP MAJ	100
4	2	58	MP MWC	91
5	3	99	MP OVC	29
42	1	51	SP MAJ	100
27	1	57	SP MAJ	100
8	1	57	SP MAJ	100
..	1	..	SP MAJ	100
43	3	60	MP OVC	53
5	3	60	MP OVC	53
47	2	72	MP OVC	79
..	3	55	MP OVC	65
3	3	75	MP OVC	33
32	3	67	MP OVC	33
3	1	37	SP MIN	100
39	2	69	MP MWGC	50
33	2	54	MP MWC	50
29	3	63	MP MWC	33
6	1	15	SP MIN	100
3	1	12	SP MIN	100

continued

Country/Region

Prime Minister or Equivalent	Government In (M / Y)	Out/ Elections
Iceland *Continued*		
Thors	11/59[pe]	06/63
Benediktsson	11/63[pe]	06/67
Benediktsson	06/67[pe]	07/70
Hafstein	07/70	06/71
Johannesson	07/71[pe]	06/74
Hallgrimsson	08/74[pe]	06/78
Johannesson	08/78[pe]	10/79
Gröndal	10/79	12/79
Thoroddsen	02/80[pe]	04/83
Hermannsson	05/83[pe]	04/87
Palsson	07/87[pe]	09/88
Hermannsson	09/88	09/89
Hermannsson	09/89	04/91
Oddsson	04/91[pe]	04/95
Oddsson	04/95[pe]	04/99
Oddsson	05/99[pe]	.....
Ireland		
Costello	02/48[pe]	05/51
de Valera	06/51[pe]	04/54
Costello	06/54[pe]	03/57
de Valera	03/57[pe]	06/59
Lemass	06/59	10/61
Lemass	10/61[pe]	04/65
Lemass	04/65[pe]	11/66
Lynch	11/66	06/69

Number of Months in Office	Number of Parties	Parliamentary Base	Cabinet Type	Cabinet Dominance
43	2	53	MP MWC	50
43	2	53	MP MWC	57
37	2	53	MP MWC	57
11	2	53	MP MWC	57
35	3	53	MP MWC	43
46	2	70	MP MWGC	50
14	3	67	MP MWC	44
2	1	23	SP MIN	100
38	3	82	MP OVC	40
47	2	62	MP MWGC	60
14	3	65	MP MWC	36
12	3	49	MP MIN	33
19	4	65	MP OVC	27
48	2	57	MP MWC	50
48	2	63	MP MWC	50
..	2	60	MP MWC	50
39	4	46	MP MIN	43
34	1	47	SP MIN	92
33	3	50	MP MWC	64
27	1	53	SP MAJ	100
28	1	53	SP MAJ	100
42	1	49	SP MIN	100
19	1	50	SP MAJ	100
31	1	50	SP MAJ	100

continued

Country/Region

Prime Minister or Equivalent	Government In (M / Y)	Out/ Elections
Ireland *Continued*		
Lynch	07/69[pe]	02/73
Cosgrave	03/73[pe]	06/77
Lynch	07/77[pe]	12/79
Haughey	12/79	06/81
Fitzgerald	06/81[pe]	02/82
Haughey	03/82[pe]	11/82
Fitzgerald	12/82[pe]	02/87
Haughey	03/87[pe]	06/89
Haughey	07/89[pe]	02/92
Reynolds	02/92	10/92
Reynolds	10/92	11/92
Reynolds	01/93[pe]	12/94
Bruton	12/94	06/97
Ahern	06/97[pe]	.....
Italy		
de Gasperi	07/46[pe]	02/47
de Gasperi	02/47	05/47
de Gasperi	05/47	12/47
de Gasperi	12/47	04/48
de Gasperi	05/48[pe]	01/50
de Gasperi	01/50	07/51
de Gasperi	07/51	06/53
de Gasperi	07/53[pe]	08/53
Pella	08/53	01/54
Fanfani	01/54	02/54

Number of Months in Office	Number of Parties	Parliamentary Base	Cabinet Type	Cabinet Dominance
43	1	52	SP MAJ	100
51	2	51	MP MWC	67
29	1	57	SP MAJ	100
18	1	57	SP MAJ	100
8	2	48	MP MIN	67
8	1	49	SP MIN	100
50	2	52	MP MWC	71
27	1	49	SP MIN	100
31	2	50	MP MWC	88
8	2	50	MP MWC	87
1	1	46	SP MIN	100
23	2	61	MP MWC	60
30	3	47	MP MIN	53
..	2	50	MP MWC	93
7	5	88	MP OVC	41
3	3	77	MP OVC	47
7	2	45	MP MIN	65
4	4	70	MP OVC	40
20	4	64	MP OVC	55
18	3	60	MP OVC	68
23	2	55	MP OVC	81
1	1	45	SP MIN	100
5	1	45	SP MIN	100
1	1	45	SP MIN	95

continued

Country/Region

Prime Minister or Equivalent	Government In (M / Y)	Out/ Elections
Italy *Continued*		
Scelba	02/54	07/55
Segni	07/55	05/57
Zoli	05/57	05/58
Fanfani	07/58[pe]	02/59
Segni	02/59	03/60
Tambroni	03/60	07/60
Fanfani	07/60	02/62
Fanfani	02/62	04/63
Leone	06/63[pe]	12/63
Moro	12/63	07/64
Moro	07/64	02/66
Moro	02/66	05/68
Leone	07/68[pe]	12/68
Rumor	12/68	08/69
Rumor	08/69	03/70
Rumor	03/70	08/70
Colombo	08/70	02/71
Colombo	02/71	02/72
Andreotti	02/72	05/72
Andreotti	06/72[pe]	09/73
Rumor	09/73	03/74
Rumor	03/74	11/74
Moro	11/74	02/76
Moro	02/76	06/76
Andreotti	07/76[pe]	03/78
Andreotti	03/78	03/79
Andreotti	03/79	06/79

Number of Months in Office	Number of Parties	Parliamentary Base	Cabinet Type	Cabinet Dominance
17	3	50	MP MWC	57
22	3	50	MP MWC	62
12	1	45	SP MIN	95
7	2	49	MP MIN	85
13	1	46	SP MIN	100
4	1	46	SP MIN	100
19	1	46	SP MIN	100
14	3	51	MP MWC	75
6	1	41	SP MIN	100
7	4	61	MP OVC	62
19	4	61	MP OVC	62
27	4	61	MP OVC	65
5	1	42	SP MIN	100
8	3	58	MP OVC	59
7	1	42	SP MIN	100
5	4	58	MP OVC	59
6	4	58	MP OVC	64
12	3	57	MP MWC	67
3	1	42	SP MIN	100
15	3	50	MP MWC	65
6	4	59	MP OVC	55
8	3	57	MP OVC	58
15	2	45	MP MIN	80
4	1	42	SP MIN	100
20	1	42	SP MIN	95
12	1	42	SP MIN	95
3	3	46	MP MIN	71

continued

Country/Region

Prime Minister or Equivalent	Government In (M / Y)	Out/ Elections
Italy *Continued*		
Cossiga	08/79[pe]	04/80
Cossiga	04/80	10/80
Forlani	10/80	06/81
Spadolini	06/81	08/82
Spadolini	08/82	12/82
Fanfani	12/82	06/83
Craxi	08/83[pe]	08/86
Craxi	08/86	04/87
Fanfani	04/87	06/87
Goria	07/87[pe]	04/88
De Mita	04/88	07/89
Andreotti	06/89	03/91
Andreotti	04/91	04/92
Amato	06/92[pe]	04/93
Ciampi	04/93	04/93
Ciampi	05/93	03/94
Berlusconi	05/94[pe]	12/94
Dini	01/95	02/96
Prodi	04/96[pe]	10/97
Prodi	10/97	10/98
D'Alema	10/98	.....
Latvia		
Birkavs	07/93[pe]	09/94
Gailis	09/94	09/95
Skele	12/95[pe]	02/97
Skele	02/97	07/97
Krasts	08/97	10/98
Kristopans	09/98[pe]	07/99
Skele	07/99	.....

Number of Months in Office	Number of Parties	Parliamentary Base	Cabinet Type	Cabinet Dominance
8	3	46	MP MIN	61
6	3	54	MP OVC	54
8	4	57	MP OVC	48
14	5	58	MP OVC	54
4	5	58	MP OVC	54
6	4	56	MP OVC	46
36	5	58	MP OVC	53
8	5	58	MP OVC	53
2	1	36	SP MIN	59
9	5	60	MP OVC	52
15	5	60	MP OVC	53
21	5	60	MP OVC	48
12	4	56	MP MWC	53
10	4	53	MP MWC	40
(0)	7	76	MP OVC	31
10	5	57	MP OVC	31
7	3	58	MP MWC	35
13			caretaker government	
18	5	45	MP MIN	43
12	5	45	MP MIN	43
..	7	53	MP MWC	31
14	2	48	MP MIN	?
12	2	49	MP MIN	64
14	7	84	MP OVC	25
5	5	65	MP OVC	29
12	5	73?	MP OVC	36
10	3	..	MP MIN	44
..	3	62	MP MWC	38

Country/Region		
Prime Minister or Equivalent	**Government In (M / Y)**	**Out/ Elections**
Liechtenstein		
Frick	09/45[pe?]	02/49
Frick	03/49[pe]	02/53
Frick	03/53[pe]	06/53
Frick	07/53[pe]	09/57
Frick	10/57[pe]	03/58
Frick	04/58[pe]	03/62
Frick	04/62[pe]	06/62
Batliner	07/62	02/66
Batliner	03/66[pe]	02/70
Hilbe	03/70[pe]	02/74
Kieber	03/74[pe]	02/78
Brunhart	04/78[pe]	02/82
Brunhart	03/82[pe]	02/86
Brunhart	04/86[pe]	03/89
Brunhart	05/89[pe]	02/93
Büchel	05/93[pe]	10/93
Frick	12/93[pe]	02/97
Frick	04/97[pe]	.....
Lithuania		
Slezevicius	12/92[pe]	08/96
Stankevicius	08/96	11/96
Vagnorius	12/96[pe]	05/99
Paksas	06/99	10/99
Kubilius	11/99	.....

Number of Months in Office	Number of Parties	Parliamentary Base	Cabinet Type	Cabinet Dominance
44	2	100	MP OVGC	50
47	2	100	MP OVGC	50
3	2	100	MP OVGC	50
50	2	100	MP OVGC	50
5	2	100	MP OVGC	50
47	2	100	MP OVGC	50
2	2	100	MP OVGC	50
43	2	100	MP OVGC	50
47	2	100	MP OVGC	60
47	2	100	MP OVGC	60
47	2	100	MP OVGC	60
46	2	100	MP OVGC	60
47	2	100	MP OVGC	60
35	2	100	MP OVGC	60
45	2	100	MP OVGC	60
5	2	92	MP MWGC	60
38	2	96	MP MWGC	60
..	1	52	SP MAJ	100
44	1	52	SP MAJ	100
3	1	52	SP MAJ	100
27	3	70	MP OVC	69
4	2		MP MWC	40
..	2		MP MWC	

Country/Region

Prime Minister or Equivalent	Government In (M / Y)	Out/ Elections
Luxembourg		
Dupong	11/45[pe]	02/47
Dupong	03/47	06/48
Dupong	07/48[pe]	06/51
Dupong	07/51[pe]	12/53
Bech	12/53	05/54
Bech	06/54[pe]	03/58
Frieden	03/58	02/59
Werner	02/59[pe]	06/64
Werner	07/64[pe]	01/67
Werner	01/67	12/68
Werner	01/69[pe]	05/74
Thorn	06/74[pe]	06/79
Werner	07/79[pe]	06/84
Santer	07/84[pe]	06/89
Santer	07/89[pe]	06/94
Santer	07/94[pe]	12/94
Juncker	01/95	06/99
Juncker	08/99[pe]	.....
Macedonia		
Crvenovski	12/94[pe]	05/97
Crvenovski	05/97	11/98
Georgievski	12/98[pe]	.....

Number of Months in Office	Number of Parties	Parliamentary Base	Cabinet Type	Cabinet Dominance
15	4	98	MP OVC	37
15	2	65	MP MWC	57
35	2	60	MP MWC	57
29	2	75	MP MWGC	50
5	2	75	MP MWGC	50
45	2	83	MP MWGC	50
11	2	83	MP MWGC	50
64	2	62	MP MWC	57
30	2	77	MP MWGC	50
23	2	77	MP MWGC	50
64	2	57	MP MWC	57
60	2	49	MP MIN	50
59	2	66	MP MWC	63
59	2	72	MP MWGC	56
59	2	67	MP MWGC	50
5	2	63	MP MWGC	50
53	2	63	MP MWGC	55
..	2	57	MP MWGC	50
29	4	88	MP OVC	42
18	3	88	MP OVC	58
..	3	60	MP OVC	..

Country/Region

Prime Minister or Equivalent	Government In (M / Y)	Out/ Elections
Malta		
Olivier	03/66[pe]	06/71
Mintoff	06/71[pe]	09/76
Mintoff	09/76[pe]	12/81
Mintoff	12/81[pe]	12/84
Bonnici	12/84	05/87
Fenech-Adami	05/87[pe]	02/92
Fenech-Adami	02/92[pe]	10/96
Sant	10/96[pe]	09/98
Fenech-Adami	09/98[pe]	.....
Moldova		
Sangheli	03/94[pe]	01/97
Ciubuc	01/97	03/98
Ciubuc	05/98[pe]	02/99
Sturza	03/99	11/99
Netherlands		
Beel	07/46[pe]	07/48
Drees	08/48[pe]	03/51
Drees	03/51	06/52
Drees	09/52[pe]	06/56
Drees	10/56[pe]	12/58
Beel	12/58	03/59
de Quay	05/59[pe]	05/63
Marijin	07/63[pe]	04/65

Number of Months in Office	Number of Parties	Parliamentary Base	Cabinet Type	Cabinet Dominance
63	1	56	SP MAJ	100
63	1	51	SP MAJ	100
63	1	52	SP MAJ	100
36	1	52	SP MAJ	100
29	1	52	SP MAJ	100
57	1	51	SP MAJ	100
56	1	52	SP MAJ	100
23	1	51	SP MAJ	100
..	1	54	SP MAJ	100
34	1	?	SP MAJ	100
14			nonparty government	
9	3	59	MP MWC	?
8	51		MP MWC	?
24	2	61	MP MWGC	38
31	4	76	MP OVC	40
15	4	76	MP OVC	40
45	4	81	MP OVC	37
26	4	85	MP OVC	36
15	3	51	MP MWC	53
48	4	63	MP OVC	46
21	4	61	MP OVC	46

continued

Country/Region

Prime Minister or Equivalent	Government In (M / Y)	Out/ Elections
Netherlands *Continued*		
Cals	04/65	11/66
Zijlstra	11/66	02/67
de Jong	04/67[pe]	03/71
Biesheuvel	06/71[pe]	08/72
Biesheuvel	08/72	11/72
den Uyl	05/73[pe]	05/77
van Agt	12/77[pe]	05/81
van Agt	09/81[pe]	11/81
van Agt	11/81	05/82
van Agt	05/82	09/82
Lubbers	11/82[pe]	05/86
Lubbers	07/86[pe]	09/89
Lubbers	11/89[pe]	05/94
Kok	08/94[pe]	05/98
Kok	08/98[pe]	05/99
Kok	06/99	.....
Norway		
Gerhardsen	11/45[pe]	10/49
Gerhardsen	10/49[pe]	11/51
Torp	11/51	10/53
Torp	10/53[pe]	01/55
Gerhardsen	01/55	10/57
Gerhardsen	10/57[pe]	09/61
Gerhardsen	10/61[pe]	08/63

Number of Months in Office	Number of Parties	Parliamentary Base	Cabinet Type	Cabinet Dominance
19	3	71	MP OVC	43
15	2	42	MP MIN	62
47	4	57	MP MWC	43
14	5	55	MP MWC	37
3	4	49	MP MIN	43
48	5	66	MP OVC	44
41	2	51	MP MWC	67
2	3	73	MP OVC	40
6	3	73	MP OVC	40
4	2	41	MP MIN	64
42	2	54	MP MWC	57
38	2	54	MP MWC	64
54	2	69	MP MWGC	57
45	3	61	MP MWC	36
9	3	65	MP OVC	36
..	3	65	MP OVC	36
47	1	50	SP MAJ	100
25	1	57	SP MAJ	100
23	1	57	SP MAJ	100
15	1	51	SP MAJ	100
33	1	51	SP MAJ	100
47	1	52	SP MAJ	100
23	1	49	SP MIN	100

continued

Country/Region

Prime Minister or Equivalent	Government In (M / Y)	Out/ Elections
Norway *Continued*		
Lyng	08/63	09/63
Gerhardsen	09/63	09/65
Borten	10/65[pe]	09/69
Borten	09/69[pe]	03/71
Brattelli	03/71	10/72
Korvald	10/72	09/73
Brattelli	10/73[pe]	01/76
Nordli	01/76	09/77
Nordli	09/77[pe]	02/81
Brundtland	02/81	09/81
Willoch	10/81[pe]	06/83
Willoch	06/83	09/85
Willoch	09/85[pe]	05/86
Brundtland	05/86	09/89
Syse	10/89[pe]	11/90
Brundtland	11/90	09/93
Brundtland	10/93[pe]	10/96
Jagland	10/96	09/97
Bondevik	10/97[pe]	.....
Poland		
Olszewski	12/91[pe]	06/92
Suchocka	07/92	09/93
Pawlak	10/93[pe]	03/95
Oleksy	03/95	01/96
Cimoszewicz	02/96	09/97
Buzek	10/97[pe]	.....

Note: In listing the number of parties in government, the Solidarity Electoral Alliance (AWS) is counted as a single party.

Number of Months in Office	Number of Parties	Parliamentary Base	Cabinet Type	Cabinet Dominance
1	4	49	MP MIN	33
24	1	49	SP MIN	100
47	4	53	MP MWC	40
18	4	50	MP MWC	40
19	1	49	SP MIN	100
11	3	31	MP MIN	40
27	1	40	SP MIN	100
20	1	40	SP MIN	100
41	1	49	SP MIN	100
7	1	49	SP MIN	100
20	1	35	SP MIN	100
27	3	52	MP MWC	61
8	3	49	MP MIN	44
40	1	45	SP MIN	100
13	3	39	MP MIN	39
34	1	40	SP MIN	100
36	1	41	SP MIN	100
11	1	41	SP MIN	100
..	3	25	MP MIN	47
6	3	26	MP MIN	24
14	7	42	MP MIN	25
17	2	66	MP MWC	40
10	2	66	MP MWC	38
19	2	66	MP MWC	43
..	2	57	MP MWC	50

Country/Region

Prime Minister or Equivalent	Government In (M / Y)	Out/ Elections
Portugal		
Soares	07/76[pe]	12/77
Soares	01/78	07/78
Nobre da Costa	08/78	09/78
Mota Pinto	11/78	06/79
Pintassilgo	07/79	12/79
Sá Carneiro	01/80[pe]	10/80
Pinto Balsemão	01/81[pe]	09/81
Pinto Balsemão	09/81	12/82
Soares	06/83[pe]	10/85
Cavaco Silva	11/85[pe]	04/87
Cavaco Silva	08/87[pe]	10/91
Cavaco Silva	10/91[pe]	10/95
Guterres	10/95[pe]	10/99
Guterres	10/99[pe]	.....
Romania		
Vacaroiu	11/92[pe]	08/94
Vacaroiu	08/94	11/96
Ciorbea	12/96[pe]	04/98
Vasile	04/98	12/99
Slovakia		
Mečiar	06/90[pe]	03/91
Carnogursky	04/91	06/92
Mečiar	06/92[pe]	03/94
Moravčik	03/94	12/94
Mečiar	12/94[pe]	09/98
Dzurinda	10/98[pe]	.....

Number of Months in Office	Number of Parties	Parliamentary Base	Cabinet Type	Cabinet Dominance
17	1	41	SP MIN	70
7	2	57	MP MWC	69
1			presidential government	
7			presidential government	
5			presidential government	
10	3	53	MP MWC	60
9	3	53	MP MWC	56
15	3	53	MP MWC	53
28	2	70	MP MWGC	53
17	1	35	SP MIN	81
50	1	59	SP MAJ	83
48	1	59	SP MAJ	89
48	1	49	SP MIN	78
..	1	49	SP MIN	
21	1	34	SP MIN	73
27	2	43	MP MIN	64
16	3	58	MP OVC	79
20	3	58	MP OVC	79
9	3	57	MP MWC	57
14	3	43	MP MIN	?
21	2	59	MP MWC	93
9	3	44	MP MIN	29
45	3	55	MP MWC	67
..	4	62	MP OVC	45

Country/Region		
Prime Minister or Equivalent	**Government In (M / Y)**	**Out/ Elections**
Slovenia		
Drnovsek	01/93[pe]	03/94
Drnovsek	03/94	11/96
Drnovsek	02/97[pe]	.....
Spain		
Suárez	07/77[pe]	03/79
Suárez	03/79[pe]	02/81
Calvo Sotelo	02/81	10/82
González	12/82[pe]	06/86
González	07/86[pe]	12/89
González	12/89[pe]	06/93
González	06/93[pe]	03/96
Aznar	05/96[pe]	.....
Basque Country		
Garaicoetxea	04/80[pe]	02/84
Garaicoetxea	04/84[pe]	12/84
Ardanza	01/85	11/86
Ardanza	02/87[pe]	10/90
Ardanza	01/91[pe]	09/91
Ardanza	09/91	10/94
Ardanza	12/94[pe]	06/98
Ardanza	06/98	10/98
Ibarretxe	01/99[pe]	.....

Number of Months in Office	Number of Parties	Parliamentary Base	Cabinet Type	Cabinet Dominance
14	5	68	MP OVC	37
31	3	68	MP OVC	47
..	3	54	MP MWC	47
20	1	47	SP MIN	95
23	1	48	SP MIN	92
10	1	48	SP MIN	100
42	1	58	SP MAJ	100
41	1	53	SP MAJ	100
42	1	50	SP MAJ	84
33	1	45	SP MIN	67
..	1	45	SP MIN	80
46	1	42	SP MIN	?
8	1	43	SP MIN	100
22	1	43	SP MIN	100
32	2	48	MP MIN	50
8	3	49	MP MIN	62
37	3	59	MP OVC	60
42	3	56	MP MWC	55
4	2	40	MP MIN	?
..	2	36	MP MIN	77

Country/Region

Prime Minister or Equivalent	Government In (M / Y)	Out/ Elections
Catalonia		
Pujol	05/80[pe]	04/84
Pujol	05/84[pe]	05/88
Pujol	06/88[pe]	03/92
Pujol	04/92[pe]	11/95
Pujol	12/95[pe]	10/99
Pujol	11/99[pe]	.....
Sweden		
Erlander	10/48[pe]	09/51
Erlander	09/51	09/52
Erlander	09/52[pe]	09/56
Erlander	09/56[pe]	10/57
Erlander	10/57	06/58
Erlander	06/58[pe]	09/60
Erlander	10/60[pe]	10/64
Erlander	10/64[pe]	09/68
Erlander	09/68[pe]	10/69
Palme	10/69	09/70
Palme	09/70[pe]	09/73
Palme	10/73[pe]	09/76
Fälldin	10/76[pe]	10/78
Ullsten	10/78	09/79
Fälldin	10/79[pe]	05/81
Fälldin	05/81	09/82

Note: Until 1970 Sweden was bicameral, and in the combined upper and lower houses—which met jointly to pass financial bills—the governing Social Democrats had a continuous majority.

Number of Months in Office	Number of Parties	Parliamentary Base	Cabinet Type	Cabinet Dominance
47	2	42	MP MIN	38
48	1	53	SP MAJ	100
45	1	51	SP MAJ	100
43	1	52	SP MAJ	100
46	1	44	SP MIN	100
..	1	41	SP MIN	100
35	1	49 *	SP MIN *	84
12	2	62	MP MWC	56
48	2	59	MP MWC	56
13	2	54	MP MWC	53
8	1	46 *	SP MIN *	87
27	1	48 *	SP MIN *	93
48	1	49 *	SP MIN *	93
47	1	48 *	SP MIN *	100
13	1	54	SP MAJ	100
11	1	54	SP MAJ	100
36	1	47	SP MIN	100
35	1	45	SP MIN	100
24	3	52	MP MWC	45
11	1	11	SP MIN	95
19	3	50	MP MWC	38
16	2	29	MP MIN	56

continued

Country/Region

Prime Minister or Equivalent	Government In (M / Y)	Out/ Elections
Sweden *Continued*		
Palme	10/82[pe]	09/85
Palme	10/85[pe]	02/86
Carlsson	03/86	09/88
Carlsson	09/88[pe]	02/90
Carlsson	02/90	09/91
Bildt	10/91[pe]	09/94
Carlsson	10/94[pe]	03/96
Persson	03/96	09/98
Persson	10/98[pe]	.....
Switzerland		
	12/47[pe]	10/51
	12/51[pe]	12/53
	12/53	10/55
	12/55[pe]	10/59
	12/59[pe]	10/63
	12/63[pe]	10/67
	12/67[pe]	10/71
	12/71[pe]	10/75
	12/75[pe]	10/79
	12/79[pe]	10/83
	12/83[pe]	10/87
	12/87[pe]	10/91
	12/91[pe]	10/95
	12/95[pe]	10/99
	12/99[pe]	.....

Note: Switzerland has no prime minister.

Number of Months in Office	Number of Parties	Parliamentary Base	Cabinet Type	Cabinet Dominance
35	1	48	SP MIN	100
4	1	46	SP MIN	100
30	1	46	SP MIN	100
17	1	45	SP MIN	100
19	1	45	SP MIN	100
35	4	49	MP MIN	38
17	1	46	SP MIN	100
30	1	46	SP MIN	100
..	1	38	SP MIN	100
46	4	83	MP OVC	43
24	4	86	MP OVC	43
22	3	61	MP MWC	43
46	3	59	MP MWC	43
46	4	86	MP OVC	29
46	4	87	MP OVC	29
46	4	83	MP OVC	29
46	4	80	MP OVC	29
46	4	85	MP OVC	29
46	4	85	MP OVC	29
46	4	83	MP OVC	29
46	4	79	MP OVC	29
46	4	73	MP OVC	29
46	4	81	MP OVC	29
..	4	86	MP OVC	29

Country/Region

Prime Minister or Equivalent	Government In (M / Y)	Out/ Elections
Turkey—First Republic		
Menderes	05/50[pe]	05/54
Menderes	05/54[pe]	10/57
Menderes	10/57[pe]	05/60
[military coup in 1960]		
Turkey—Second Republic		
Inönü	11/61[pe]	05/62
Inönü	06/62	12/63
Inönü	12/63	10/65
Demirel	10/65[pe]	10/69
Demirel	11/69[pe]	02/70
Demirel	03/70	03/71
[military coup in 1971]		
Ecevit	01/74[pe]	09/74
Irmak	11/74	03/75
Demirel	03/75	06/77
Ecevit	06/77[pe]	08/77
Demirel	08/77	12/77
Ecevit	01/78	10/79
Demirel	11/79	09/80
[military coup in 1980]		
Turkey—Third Republic		
Ozal	12/83[pe]	11/87
Ozal	12/87[pe]	11/89
Akbulut	11/89	06/91

Number of Months in Office	Number of Parties	Parliamentary Base	Cabinet Type	Cabinet Dominance
48	1	84	SP MAJ	100
41	1	93	SP MAJ	100
31	1	70	SP MAJ	95
6	2	74	MP MWGC	50
18	3	65	MP MWC	48
22	1	38	SP MIN	87
48	1	53	SP MAJ	100
3	1	57	SP MAJ	100
12	1	57	SP MAJ	100
8	2	52	MP MWC	72
4			caretaker government	
27	4	47	MP MIN	53
2	1	47	SP MIN	94
4	3	51	MP MWC	55
21	3	48	MP MIN	88
10	1	42	SP MIN	100
47	1	53	SP MAJ	91
23	1	65	SP MAJ	100
19	1	65	SP MAJ	100

continued

Country/Region

Prime Minister or Equivalent	Government In (M / Y)	Out/ Elections
Turkey—Third Republic *Continued*		
Yilmaz	06/91	10/91
Demirel	10/91[pe]	05/93
Çiller	06/93	12/95
Yilmaz	03/96[pe]	05/96
Erbakan	06/96	06/97
Yilmaz	06/97	11/98
Ecevit	01/99	04/99
Ecevit	06/99[pe]	.....
United Kingdom		
Attlee	07/45[pe]	02/50
Attlee	02/50[pe]	10/51
Churchill	11/51[pe]	04/55
Eden	04/55	05/55
Eden	05/55[pe]	01/57
Macmillan	01/57	10/59
Macmillan	10/59[pe]	10/63
Douglas-Home	10/63	10/64
Wilson	10/64[pe]	03/66
Wilson	04/66[pe]	06/70
Heath	06/70[pe]	02/74
Wilson	03/74[pe]	10/74
Wilson	10/74[pe]	04/76
Callaghan	04/76	05/79
Thatcher	05/79[pe]	06/83

Number of Months in Office	Number of Parties	Parliamentary Base	Cabinet Type	Cabinet Dominance
4	1	65	SP MAJ	100
19	2	59	MP MWC	62
30	2	59	MP MWC	62
2	2	49	MP MIN	55
12	2	53	MP MWGC	50
17	3	39	MP MIN	53
3	1	14	SP MIN	?
..	3	64	MP MWC	37
55	1	61	SP MAJ	100
20	1	50	SP MAJ	100
41	1	51	SP MAJ	100
1	1	51	SP MAJ	100
20	1	55	SP MAJ	100
33	1	55	SP MAJ	100
48	1	58	SP MAJ	100
12	1	57	SP MAJ	100
17	1	50	SP MAJ	100
50	1	58	SP MAJ	100
44	1	52	SP MAJ	100
7	1	47	SP MIN	100
18	1	50	SP MAJ	100
37	1	50	SP MAJ	100
49	1	53	SP MAJ	100

continued

Country/Region

Prime Minister or Equivalent	Government In (M / Y)	Out/ Elections
United Kingdom *Continued*		
Thatcher	06/83^{pe}	06/87
Thatcher	06/87^{pe}	11/90
Major	11/90	04/92
Major	04/92^{pe}	04/97
Blair	04/97^{pe}	.....
Northern Ireland		
Trimble	07/98^{pe}	.....
Scotland		
Dewar	05/99^{pe}	.....
Wales		
Michael	05/99^{pe}	.....

Number of Months in Office	Number of Parties	Parliamentary Base	Cabinet Type	Cabinet Dominance
48	1	63	SP MAJ	100
41	1	58	SP MAJ	100
17	1	57	SP MAJ	100
60	1	52	SP MAJ	100
..	1	63	SP MAJ	100
..	4	83	MP OVC	30
..	2	57	MP MWC	82
..	1	47	SP MIN	100

PART II

Individual Case Analyses

In this part of the book descriptions are given of the party systems of each of the forty-four cases analyzed. The sections follow a set format, in that first we note the national party system or systems, using the classifications from Chapter 2 of Part I. Then a brief historical overview of the polity is given. Then the electoral system(s) is (are) explained. This is followed by a discussion of the main parties and political divisions, and then specific analysis of certain elections (or in some cases all elections), and finally some comments on the nature of governments. For each case, at least two tables are provided: the first (or first ones) gives the results of selected elections, or in some cases all elections, in terms of both percentage of the total valid votes [%V] and the number of seats won [#S]. The last table lists all governments, giving for each the month the government passed its investiture vote and/or took office; the prime minister (or equivalent); the number of ministers in the government [#M]; of these, the number of independents [(I)], if any; the parties in the government; and in some cases the parties providing external support. Finally, all of the party acronyms of the parties discussed are listed alphabetically, and in most cases references or suggested further readings are given.

Austria

SUMMARY OF PARTY SYSTEMS

1945	two-party system (ÖVP and SPÖ)
1949–86	two-and-a-half-party system
1990	moderate multiparty system with two main parties (SPÖ and ÖVP)
1994–(99)	moderate multiparty system with a balance among the parties

HISTORY

Centuries of imperial rule gave way at the end of World War I to the first Austrian Republic, which was characterized by extreme polarization between Socialists and Christian Socials. The country often seemed on the brink of civil war, and a brief civil war did actually occur in 1934. This conflict was followed by an authoritarian Catholic regime, and then annexation into Nazi Germany in 1938. After World War II Austria, like Germany, was divided between the western powers and the Soviet Union. Full sovereignty was not restored until the Austrian State Treaty of 1955. The second Austrian Republic had, however, been set up in 1945. Within the country, a conscious effort was made after the war to avoid the mistakes of the interwar period. As such, the political system became consociational, with the two main parties governing together. Austria also became known for its strong corporatism and labor peace, institutionalized in various commissions and bodies.

ELECTORAL SYSTEM

Since 1970 Austria has used a two-tier system of party-list proportional representation with the d'Hondt formula. The cutoff to receive seats is 4 percent of the national vote.

CLEAVAGES, PARTIES, AND ELECTORAL CHANGE

The postwar Austrian party system was one of the most stable in Europe, based as it was on deeply rooted subcultures, two of which were central. The first of these *Lager* (camps) was the Catholic, conservative Lager, represented by the **Austrian People's Party (ÖVP)**, founded in 1945. The ÖVP has been the party of Catholics, but also of farmers and business people. Indeed, these economic interests have had specific representation within the ÖVP organization. The other main Lager is the socialist one, represented primarily by the **Socialist Party of Austria (SPÖ)**, founded in 1889, but also for a time after the war by the **Communist Party of Austria (KPÖ)**, founded in 1918. In contrast to the ÖVP, the SPÖ has been the party of industrial workers as well as secular white-collar employees. There was also a third, much smaller Lager of secular pan-German nationalists who were not allowed by the Allies to form such a party in the first elections of 1945, but who would be represented ultimately by the **Freedom Party of Austria (FPÖ)**, formed in 1955 and now known as the **Freedom Movement**. From 1945 to 1947, the ÖVP, SPÖ, and the tiny KPÖ formed an all-party coalition that gave way to a long-lasting ÖVP-SPÖ "Grand Coalition."

In the 1945 elections, the communists were the third force, but a very distant third, and third only because the nationalist camp was not allowed to compete. With the onset of the Cold War, the KPÖ lost its relevance. In contrast, the **League of Independents (VdU)** and, from 1956, the FPÖ would become the third force in Austria's two-and-a-half-party politics. Through through 1962, the ÖVP was normally slightly stronger than the SPÖ, but the spread between these two parties was never very big during this period. In the 1966 elections, however, the ÖVP won an absolute majority and formed a single-party government. After the 1970 elections there was a brief SPÖ minority—the only minority government in postwar Austria—followed by three straight SPÖ majorities in 1971, 1975, and 1979. These majorities were in part due to the personal popularity of Socialist Chancellor Bruno Kreisky. From 1966 until the 1983 elections, then, there were, thus, single-party governments and a very concentrated party system.

In the 1980s, realignment became evident in the emergence of various Green parties, first the **United Greens of Austria (VGÖ)**, founded in 1982, and then the **Green Alternative (GA)**, founded in 1986. These two parties have a working electoral alliance. Although the Greens did not win any seats in 1983 (as they have since 1986), they took enough votes away from the SPÖ in that year to cost the socialists their majority.

The SPÖ thus formed a coalition with the FPÖ. This coalition collapsed in 1986 after the national FPÖ was taken over by Jörg Haider, who would take the party in a far-right populist direction. Thus, in 1987 a "Grand Coalition" was reformed—but now under an SPÖ chancellor—that continues to this day. Initially, Haider's strategy largely hurt the ÖVP, so that after 1990 the ÖVP was no longer clearly one of two main parties. Yet by the 1990s the FPÖ was also able to make inroads into the SPÖ's blue-collar base, especially among younger workers. More liberal-minded members of the FPÖ finally broke away in 1993 to form the **Liberal Forum (LF)**, and thus there were five parties in the Austrian Nationalrat.

Over the postwar period, then, there has thus been a clear shift in the plurality/majority party from the ÖVP to the SPÖ. There seem to have been three main reasons for this (see Müller and Steininger [1994]). First, the ÖVP has been affected more than the SPÖ by social-structural changes. Its core group of farmers and other self-employed has shrunk greatly, and like most religious parties, the ÖVP has been hurt by secularization. In contrast, Austria remained a highly industrialized country, and trade union density as a share of the total labor force has remained around 50 percent. This preserved the SPÖ until Haider began to target blue-collar workers. Second, although aware of its problems, attempts to modernize the organization and image of the ÖVP have essentially failed. Third, the ÖVP has had weaker and certainly less popular leaders and "chancellor-candidates" than the SPÖ. It is thus not surprising that whereas the ÖVP monopolized the chancellorship until 1970, the SPÖ has provided the chancellor since then.

Selected Elections in Austria

	1945		**1949**		**1962**		**1971**	
	%V	**#S**	**%V**	**#S**	**%V**	**#S**	**%V**	**#S**
SPÖ	44.6	76	38.7	67	44.0	76	50.0	93
ÖVP	49.8	85	44.0	77	45.4	81	43.1	80
KPÖ	5.4	4	5.1	5	3.0	0	1.4	0
VdU/FPÖ	—	—	11.7	16	7.0	8	5.5	10
others	0.2	0	0.5	0	0.5	0	0.0	0
TOTAL SEATS		165		165		165		183

continued

Selected Elections in Austria *Continued*

	1986		1990		1994		1995		1999	
	%V	#S	%V	#S	%V	#S	%V	#S	%V	#S
SPÖ	43.1	80	42.8	80	35.2	65	38.1	71	33.2	65
ÖVP	41.3	77	32.1	60	27.7	52	28.3	53	26.9	52
FPÖ	9.7	18	16.6	33	22.6	42	21.9	40	26.9	52
Greens	4.8	8	4.8	10	6.5	13	4.8	9	7.4	14
LF	—	—	—	—	5.5	11	5.5	10	3.7	0
others	1.1	0	3.7	0	1.6	0	1.4	0	1.9	0
TOTAL SEATS		183		183		183		183		183

RECENT ELECTIONS

During the 1994 campaign, as in 1990, the dominant parties were criticized by the upstart FPÖ, which blamed both for the culture of corruption that it felt was rampant in the governmental bureaucracy. The FPÖ's hostile campaign also focused on calls for stricter immigration laws, because the party claimed that immigrants were a major reason for the rising crime rate. The 1994 elections in Austria marked the first time that the two main parties failed to win a two-thirds majority, crucial if they wanted to make changes easily to the constitution. The SPÖ dropped fifteen seats while the ÖVP was down eight seats from the previous elections. This represented the worst results for these two parties since 1945. These elections also marked the first time that five parties won representation in parliament. The newest party to enter parliament was the Liberal Forum, which had split from the FPÖ in 1993.

In September 1995 the ongoing SPÖ-ÖVP coalition reached an impasse over how to reduce the budget deficit to the level needed to meet the Maastricht criterion for Economic and Monetary Union. The ÖVP was particularly opposed to the SPÖ's willingness to raise taxes, preferring instead to cut social spending. The ÖVP thus withdrew from the coalition in October, leading to December elections. In these, economic issues were front and center, which aided the SPÖ—it having more experience and inspiring trust in these matters. In contrast, the lack of focus on immigration and foreigners hurt the FPÖ, which saw its vote drop back slightly, thus ending its trend of sharp increases. After three months of negotiations, the SPÖ and ÖVP reformed their coalition.

In the 1999 elections, the FPÖ achieved its best ever result and in fact narrowly jumped into second place ahead of the ÖVP (albeit by a mere 415 votes out of the 4.62 million cast). With its traditional themes of nationalism and xenophobia, in this case focussed on opposition to the expansion of the EU into Eastern Europe, the FPÖ made further inroads into blue-collar voters. The Freedom party's gains were thus largely at the expense of the SPÖ, which in turn dropped back to the 65 seats it had won in 1994 (thus negating its 1995 rise). Although commentaries focussed on the three main (and now quite close) parties, one should also note that the falure of the Liberal Forum to clear the 4 percent threshold further tilted the parliamentary balance away from the liberal left.

GOVERNMENTS

Austria has mainly been governed by "Grand Coalitions" of the ÖVP and SPÖ. These do not, however, form all that quickly, and in 1995 the collapse of such a coalition occurred. However, given that the third largest party, the FPÖ, is not seen as an acceptable coalition partner, the two larger parties are in some sense stuck with each other. In the 1970s the SPÖ set a European record of sorts by winning three straight-earned majorities.

Austrian Governments since 1945

In Office Date (M/Y)	Chancellor (party)	#M (I)	Parties in Cabinet
12/45	Figl, L. (ÖVP)	13(2)	ÖVP SPÖ KPÖ
11/47	Figl, L. (ÖVP)	13	ÖVP SPÖ
11/49	Figl, L. (ÖVP)	13	ÖVP SPÖ
04/53	Raab, J. (ÖVP)	13(1)	ÖVP SPÖ
06/56	Raab, J. (ÖVP)	13	ÖVP SPÖ
07/59	Raab, J. (ÖVP)	13	SPÖ ÖVP
04/61	Gorbach, A. (ÖVP)	14	ÖVP SPÖ
03/63	Gorbach, A. (ÖVP)	14	ÖVP SPÖ

continued

Austrian Governments since 1945 *Continued*

In Office Date (M/Y)	Chancellor (Party)	#M (I)	Parties in Cabinet
04/64	Klaus, J. (ÖVP)	13	ÖVP SPÖ
04/66	Klaus, J. (ÖVP)	14	ÖVP
04/70	Kreisky, B. (SPÖ)	14	SPÖ
11/71	Kreisky, B. (SPÖ)	15	SPÖ
10/75	Kreisky, B. (SPÖ)	14	SPÖ
06/79	Kreisky, B. (SPÖ)	14	SPÖ
05/83	Sinowatz, F. (SPÖ)	18	SPÖ FPÖ
06/86	Vranitzky, F. (SPÖ)	17	SPÖ FPÖ
01/87	Vranitzky, F. (SPÖ)	18(1)	SPÖ ÖVP
12/90	Vranitzky, F. (SPÖ)	19(1)	SPÖ ÖVP
11/94	Vranitzky, F. (SPÖ)	16(1)	SPÖ ÖVP
03/96	Vranitzky, F. (SPÖ)	16(1)	SPÖ ÖVP
01/97	Klima, V. (SPÖ)	16(1)	SPÖ ÖVP

ACRONYMS

FPÖ	Freedom Party of Austria
GA	Green Alternative
KPÖ	Communist Party of Austria
LF	Liberal Forum
ÖVP	Austrian People's Party
SPÖ	Socialist Party of Austria (since 1991, Social Democratic Party of Austria)
VdU	League of Independents
VGÖ	United Greens of Austria

REFERENCES

Luther, Kurt Richard (1999). "Austria: From Moderate to Polarized Pluralism?." in David Broughton and Mark Donovan, eds., *Changing Party Systems in Western Europe* (London: Pinter), pp. 118–142.

Luther, Kurt Richard, and Wolfgang C. Müller, eds. (1992). *Politics in Austria: Still a Case of Consociationalism?* London: Frank Cass.

Müller, Wolfgang C., and Barbara Steininger (1994). "Christian Democracy in Austria: The Austrian People's Party," in David Hanley, ed. *Christian Democracy in Europe: A Comparative Perspective.* London: Pinter, pp. 87–100.

Belgium

SUMMARY OF PARTY SYSTEMS

1946–1961	two-and-a-half-party system
1965	moderate multiparty system with a balance among the parties
1968	extreme multiparty system with a balance among the parties
1971–77	extreme multiparty system with two main parties (Socialists and CVP)
1978	extreme multiparty system with one dominant party (CVP)
1981–(99)	extreme multiparty system with a balance among the parties

HISTORY

Belgium became independent from the Netherlands in 1830. It was established as a religiously homogeneous Catholic polity. With universal male suffrage in 1919, the two main political forces became the Christian Socials and the Socialists, each of which was backed up by a social "pillar," that is, an institutionalized subculture of schools, trade unions, media, sports associations, and so forth. In part because Belgium was a "pillarized" society, the language conflict between the Dutch-speaking Flemish and the dominant French was rather latent. With the decline of the pillars and the rise of nationalist parties, the language issue has been at the center stage of Belgian politics since the 1960s. On no less than four occasions—1970, 1980, 1988, and 1993—the constitution was amended, so that since 1993 Belgium has been a federal state.

ELECTORAL SYSTEM

Belgium uses party list proportional representation based on the d'Hondt system in multimember districts. With the 1993 constitutional reforms, the number of seats in the House of Representatives was cut from 212 to 150. Voting is compulsory.

POLITICAL PARTIES AND CLEAVAGES

The Belgian party system was relatively straightforward right after the war. Religiosity and social class were what determined one's vote. The largest party—to the point of winning an outright majority in 1950—was the **Catholic Party**, dating back to 1888, with constituent parties going back earlier. Its views were typical of European Christian-democratic parties, stressing Christian personalism, cross-class solidarity, and social conservatism.

In the nineteenth century Belgium was one of the most industrialized countries in Europe, and in 1885 the **Belgian Labour Party (POB)** was formed. In 1946, after the Second World War, the POB was relaunched as the **Belgian Socialist Party (PSB)**. The PSB was strongest in the heavy industry areas of Wallonia. Right after the war, it faced a strong rival on the left in the form of the **Communist Party of Belgium (PCB in French, KPB in Flemish)**, formed in 1921. However, the Communist vote would drop steadily through the late 1940s and 1950s.

The Catholics and Socialists were the two main parties in what was a two-and-a-half-party system. The "half" was that of the **Liberal Party (PL)**. Dating back to 1846, it was the oldest of the Belgian parties. It was supported by the largely Francophone middle class, and was particularly strong in Brussels. At various times the Liberals formed a secular alliance with the Socialists. For example, the 1954–58 Socialist-Liberal government reduced subsidies to Catholic schools and increased the number of state schools—despite massive Catholic opposition. However, after increasing class conflicts and the formation of a Catholic-Socialist government in 1961, the Liberals decided to reformulate themselves, becoming less militant in their secularism and stressing more free-market economics. This was done under the name of the **Party of Liberty and Progress (PLP in French, PVV in Flemish)** and they almost doubled their vote.

Flemish nationalists were first elected to parliament in 1919 and were particularly successful in the late 1930s. However, collaboration with the Nazi occupiers destroyed their credibility, and it would be a few years after the war before a new Flemish party would be again in parliament. This party, the *Volksunie,* or **People's Union (VU)**, was formed in 1954. Clearly right of center, the party was for a time the sole proponent of Flemish autonomy in a decentralized Belgium. Its participation in government in the 1970s, and the resulting compromises on constitutional matters, led hard-liners to break away and form in 1977 the

Vlaams Blok, or **Flemish Bloc (VB)**. Over time the Flemish Bloc would become a radical right party as well as a nationalistic one.

The rise of nationalist parties in Flanders led to the formation of similar parties in the French-speaking parts of Belgium. Of these, the most important have been the **Francophone Democratic Front (FDF)**, formed in 1965 largely to protect the Francophone majority in Brussels, and the **Wallon Gathering (RW)**, which formed in 1968 and fragmented in 1981. In contrast to the rightism of the Flemish nationalist parties, the FDF has been centrist, and the RW on the center left.

The rise of the nationalist parties was largely "checked," especially in Wallonia, by the linguistic fragmentation of the traditional national parties. The first of these was the Catholics, who in 1968 split into the **Christian People's Party (CVP)** in Flanders and the **Christian Social Party (PSC)** in the French-speaking areas. In 1972 the liberals followed suit: in Flanders they were still the **Party of Liberty and Progress (PVV)**, whereas in Brussels and Wallonia they were split into many evolving forces, some of which were allied with regional parties, until in 1979 a unified **Liberal Reform Party (PRL)** was formed. Seeking an image which was less tied to the traditional system, PVV leader Guy Verhofstadt wound up the party in November 1992 and replaced it with the **Flemish Liberal Democrats (VLD)**. Finally, in 1978 the Socialists split into a French **Socialist Party (PS)** and a Flemish **Socialist Party (SP)**. Thus, by the late 1970s nobody was pretending that Belgium could have a national party anymore. Indeed, right from their creation, two linguistically distinct Green parties were set up: the Flemish **Agalev** ("Live Differently") in 1977 and the French **Ecolo** in 1978.

It is important to stress that the formerly national parties are not merely organizationally distinct from each other, but that they have become somewhat ideologically different from each other as well. For example, on economic affairs the Flemish SP is more moderate than the French PS, yet in the 1980s the SP stood out for its strong opposition to the deployment of new nuclear missiles. Also, the French PSC is seen as more flexible than the Flemish CVP. Perhaps the key difference is relative size: in Flanders, which has always been more religious, the CVP is the largest party and has achieved a largely "catchall" nature. In contrast, in Wallonia with its traditional heavy industry (as opposed to the high tech of Flanders), the PS is the main party. Moreover, the PS has become such a clear exponent of Wallonia's interests that Wallon-named parties have been marginalized.

Given that regional parties are stronger in Flanders, one may wish to view the Flemish party system as follows:

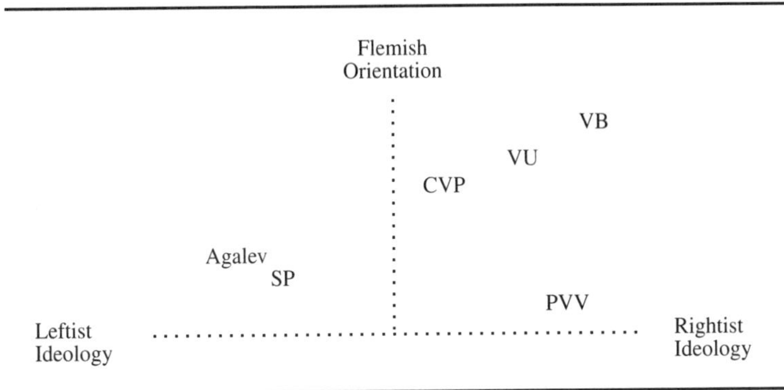

SELECTED ELECTIONS

The 1978 elections were the first in which all the main parties had been divided. Nevertheless, the Flemish CVP still polled over a quarter of the total *Belgian* vote and thus was in a position of relative dominance. However, dissatisfaction with its handling of national economic issues caused the CVP to lose a fifth of its vote in the 1981 elections, with these votes going mainly to the PVV and the VU. The 1991 elections were notable for the national breakthrough of the Vlaams Blok—with a quarter of the vote, it became the leading party in Antwerp. This result built on the 20 percent of the vote it had won in the 1988 municipal elections. The 1995 national elections were conducted against a background of voter cynicism, but showed little change overall.

The 1999 elections were held in the context of a series of scandals, most notably one involving dioxin which contaminated animal feed and led to the paralysis of domestic food production. Governmental mishandling of the food crisis outweighed its successes in reducing unemployment and public debt, and getting Belgium accepted as a member of the EU's single currency. All of the governing Christian democratic and socialist parties lost seats. The biggest gains were registered by the green parties and by the Vlaams Blok. However, even though they only gained slightly, the Liberal "family" was seen as the big winner because for the first time in a century they were the largest force.

Selected Elections in Belgium

	1946		1950		1961		1965	
	%V	#S	%V	#S	%V	#S	%V	#S
Liberals	9.3	17	11.8	20	12.3	20	21.6	48
Catholics	42.5	92	47.7	108	41.5	96	34.4	77
Socialists	32.8	69	35.8	77	36.7	84	28.8	64
Communists	12.7	23	4.7	7	3.1	5	4.6	6
VU	—	—	—	—	3.5	5	6.7	12
FDF	—	—	—	—	—	—	2.3	5
others	2.7	1	0.0	0	2.9	2	2.1	0
TOTAL SEATS		202		212		212		212

	1978		1981		1991		1995		1999	
	%V	#S	%V	#S	%V	#S	%V	#S	%V	#S
CVP	26.1	57	19.3	43	16.8	39	17.2	29	14.1	22
PSC	10.1	25	7.1	18	7.7	18	7.7	12	5.9	10
PS	13.0	32	12.7	35	13.5	35	11.9	21	10.1	19
SP	12.4	26	12.4	26	12.0	28	12.6	20	9.6	14
PRL	(5.3	14)	8.6	24	8.1	20	10.3	18	10.1	18
PVV/VLD	10.3	22	12.9	28	12.0	26	13.1	21	14.3	23
VU	7.0	14	9.7	20	5.9	10	4.7	5	5.6	8
FDF+RW	7.1	15	4.2	8	1.5	3	(allied with PRL)			
VB	1.4	1	1.4	1	6.6	12	7.8	11	9.9	15
Agalev	0.9	1	2.7	3	4.9	7	4.4	5	7.0	9
Ecolo	0.8	0	4.8	4	5.1	10	4.0	6	7.3	11
others	5.6	5	4.2	2	5.9	4	6.3	2	6.1	1
TOTAL SEATS		212		212		212		150		150

GOVERNMENTS

Belgian governments have almost always been coalitions, and presence in government over time has related to relative size. That is, the Catholics and their successor parties have almost always been in government, the Socialists and their successor parties have often been in government, and the Liberals and their successor parties have sometimes been in government. However, Verhofstadt is the first liberal prime minister since 1884. The main regional parties—VU, FDF, and RW—have been in government as well. The Green parties finally entered government in 1999, leaving only the extreme VB off of the list of "acceptable" parties.

Belgian Governments since 1946

In Office Date (M/Y)	Prime Minister (Party)	#M (I)	Parties in Cabinet
04/46	van Acker, A. (BSP)	23(3)	BSP PL PCB/KPB
08/46	Huysmans, C. (BSP)	20(3)	BSP PL PCB/KPB
03/47	Spaak, P. H. (BSP)	20(2)	BSP CVP/PSC
11/48	Spaak, P. H. (BSP)	21(2)	BSP CVP/PSC
08/49	Eyskens, G. (CVP)	20	CVP/PSC PL
06/50	Duvieusart, J. (CVP)	17(1)	CVP/PSC
08/50	Pholien, J. (CVP)	17(1)	CVP/PSC
01/52	van Houtte, J. (CVP)	17(1)	CVP/PSC
04/54	van Acker, A. (BSP)	17(2)	BSP PL
06/58	Eyskens, G. (CVP)	16	CVP/PSC
11/58	Eyskens, G. (CVP)	21	CVP/PSC PL
09/60	Eyskens, G. (CVP)	20	CVP/PSC PL
04/61	Lefevre, T. (CVP)	21	CVP/PSC BSP
07/65	Harmel, P. (CVP)	25	CVP/PSC BSP
03/66	Vandenboeynants, P. (CVP)	22	CVP/PSC PLP/PVV
06/68	Eyskens, G. (CVP)	29	CVP/PSC BSP
01/72	Eyskens, G. (CVP)	21	BSP CVP PSC

continued

Belgian Governments since 1946 *Continued*

In Office Date (M/Y)	Prime Minister (Party)	#M (I)	Parties in Cabinet
01/73	Leburton, E. (BSP)	28	BSP CVP PLP/PVV PSC
04/74	Tindemans, L. (CVP)	25	CVP PSC PLP PVV
06/74	Tindemans, L. (CVP)	26	CVP PSC PLP PVV RW
12/76	Tindemans, L. (CVP)	31	CVP PSC PLP PVV FDF
06/77	Tindemans, L. (CVP)	30	BSP CVP PSC FDF VU
10/78	Vandenboeynants, P. (CVP)	29	CVP SP PSC PS FDF VU
04/79	Martens, W. (CVP)	32	CVP PS SP PSC FDF
01/80	Martens, W. (CVP)	31	CVP PS PSC SP
05/80	Martens, W. (CVP)	33	CVP PS PVV PSC SP PRL
10/80	Martens, W. (CVP)	36	PS CVP PSC SP
04/81	Eyskens, G. (CVP)	33	CVP PS PSC SP
12/81	Martens, W. (CVP)	24	PRL CVP PSC PVV
11/85	Martens, W. (CVP)	25	PRL CVP PSC PVV
10/87	Martens, W. (CVP)	25	PRL CVP PSC PVV
05/88	Martens, W. (CVP)	27	PS CVP SP PSC VU PW
09/91	Martens, W. (CVP)	16	CVP PS SP PSC
02/92	Dehaene, J.-L. (CVP)	16	CVP PS SP PSC
06/95	Dehaene, J.-L. (CVP)	16	CVP PS SP PSC
07/99	Verhofstadt, G. (VLD)	18	VLD PRL PS SP Ecolo Agalev

ACRONYMS

Agalev	"Live Differently" (Flemish ecologists)
CVP	Christian People's Party (Flemish)
Ecolo	Ecologists (French)
FDF	Francophone Democratic Front (French)
KPB	Communist Party of Belgium
PCB	Communist Party of Belgium
PL	Liberal Party

POB	Belgian Labour Party
PRL	Liberal Reform Party (French)
PS	Socialist Party (French)
PSB	Belgian Socialist Party
PSC	Christian Social Party (French)
PVV	Party of Liberty and Progress (Flemish)
RW	Wallon Gathering (French)
SP	Socialist Party (Flemish)
VB	Flemish Bloc
VLD	Flemish Liberal Democrats
VU	People's Union (Flemish)

REFERENCES

Deschouwer, Kris. (1994). "The Decline of Consociationalism and the Reluctant Modernization of Belgian Mass Parties," in Richard S. Katz and Peter Mair, eds. *How Parties Organize: Change and Adaption in Party Organization in Western Democracies.* London: SAGE. pp. 80–108.

de Winter, Lieven, and Patrick Dumont (1999). "Belgium: Party System(s) on the Eve of Disintegration?," in David Broughton and Mark Donovan, eds., *Changing Party Systems in Western Europe* (London: Pinter), pp. 183–206.

Fitzmaurice, John. (1996). *The Politics of Belgium: A Unique Federalism.* Boulder: Westview Press.

Bulgaria

SUMMARY OF PARTY SYSTEMS

1990–91	two-and-a-half party system
1994	moderate multiparty system with one dominant party (BSP)
(1998–)	moderate multiparty system with one dominant party (ODS)

HISTORY

Bulgaria achieved independence from the Ottoman Empire following the Russo-Turkish war of 1877–78, but the country did not gain full independence until 22 September 1908. In the period following 1878 there was initially a party system comprised of two main parties—"liberals" and "conservatives"—however, by the early 1880s a multiparty system began to develop. By 1906 there were ten parties, and by the start of the First World War the number of parties and factions increased rapidly to the point where there were fifteen parties represented in the National Assembly. In 1934 a royal dictatorship ushered in a period of nonparty administration, after which only six parties were revived: the Bulgarian Communist Party (BKP), the Radical Democratic Party, the Bulgarian Social Democratic Party (BSDP), the Bulgarian Agrarian National Union (BZNS), the "Zveno" Circle, and the Democratic Party (DP). All of these parties, save the Democratic Party, formed the Fatherland Front, which took over government and established a communist-dominated "People's Republic" on 4 December 1947. During this period all other parties were banned. Communist rule lasted until 1989, after which multiparty democracy returned.

ELECTORAL SYSTEM

The National Assembly, a unicameral body of now 240 members, is elected to a four-year term by a system of proportional representation using thirty-one multiseat constituencies, closed party-list, proportional representation, and the d'Hondt method. Only parties obtaining at least 4 percent of the nationwide popular vote are entitled to parliamentary representation. Deputies are deemed to represent the entire nation as well as their constituencies. Members of the Council of Ministers may not concurrently hold their seats in the National Assembly.

PARTIES AND CLEAVAGES

Bulgarian parties are often grouped into coalitions and electoral alliances that form, break up, and are revived on a fairly frequent basis. The **Union of Democratic Forces (SDS)** is emblematic of the entire Bulgarian party system. Like the system as a whole, the SDS has had a membership that has changed from year to year and from election to election. Originally formed in December 1989, the SDS was a political union of around ten independent organizations, including intellectual, environmental, trade union, and other groups. Throughout its history, membership in the SDS has been unstable at the best of times. As a result, there has existed much internal strife and conflict within the SDS. This resulted in three distinct SDS lists being represented in the October 1991 elections: the main SDS-Movement, the SDS-Center, and the SDS-Liberals. The SDS-Movement was, however, the only one to gain seats. The SDS is headed by a National Coordination Council (NCC) in which all member parties are represented. In 1996, at the behest of its smaller members and at the chagrin of its larger ones, the SDS took steps to transform the coalition into a single party. In the 1997 elections it, therefore, ran as a member of the larger **United Democratic Forces (ODS)** along with the BSDP, BZNS, and the DP. All of these, with the exception of the BZNS, were one-time members of the SDS. In terms of its policies, the SDS has been prodemocratic, anti-Communist, committed to fast market reform, and pro-Western in orientation.

The other main political force in Bulgaria has been the **Bulgarian Socialist Party (BSP)**. The BSP is descended from the Bulgarian Workers' Social Democratic Party—the former ruling Communist Party. After its name change in 1990 the BSP was the first party to form a government following the end of Communist rule. Since then it has alternated holding power with SDS. The BSP describes itself as a modern left-socialist party, and its views and policies do espouse the ideas of democratic socialism and the social market economy, but at the same time it panders to its traditional communist membership. Like most of

Bulgaria's political parties, it as had elements split off from it and form separate entities, and like most other parties it has taken up membership in electoral alliances. For the October 1991 election the BSP teamed up with the **Fatherland Party of Labor (OPT),** which had competed independently in the 1990 elections. For the 1997 elections the BSP, along with **Ecoglasnost Political Club (EPC),** which has supported the BSP since 1990, formed the **Democratic Left (DL)**.

The Turkish **Movement for Rights and Freedoms (DPS)** has never formed governments but has played a crucial role in supporting and ousting them. The heir to the Bulgarian Turks Organization, the DPS represents the interests of Bulgaria's Turkish minority—a status that instigated legal attempts to ban it as a political party, attempts that were eventually thwarted by Bulgaria's Supreme Court. The DPS served as the "swing party" in the outcome of the October 1991 elections, giving their support to the SDS government that formed shortly thereafter. One year later the DPS was responsible for bringing down the government by withdrawing that support. Weakened from 1993 on by defections, splits, and mass immigration of Bulgaria's Turkish population to Turkey, the DPS, along with other smaller monarchist and centrist groups, formed the **Union of National Salvation (ONS)** for the 1997 elections.

Other parties that have received representation in the National Assembly include the **Bulgarian Business Bloc (BBB)**. The BBB is a right-wing, populist, pro-market party. It advocates the transformation of Bulgaria into a tariff- and tax-free zone. On the center left there is the **Bulgarian Social Democratic (BSDP)**, which traces its existence back to the historic Social Democratic Party that formed in 1891, and more specifically its nonrevolutionary wing, which separated in 1903. Becoming independent in 1989 from a period of forced integration with the ruling communist party, the BSDP original was named the Socialist Party but than switched to BSDP when the BSP formed. The BSDP, as mentioned, was a member of the SDS and led the SDS-Center list during the 1991 elections. In 1994 the BSDP established the **Democratic Alternative of the Republic (DAR)** as an election alliance with the **Alternative Social-Liberal Party (ASP),** the **Alternative Socialist Association (ASO),** the **Bulgarian Labor Social Democratic Party (BRSP)**, and the **Green Party (ZP)**. In the 1994 elections the DAR alliance narrowly missed the 4 percent threshold by less than 0.3 percent.

The **Bulgarian Agrarian People's Union (BZNS)**, not to be confused with the **Bulgarian Agrarian People's Union–Aleksandur Stamboliyski (BZNS-AP)**, which is allied closely with the BSP, nor the **Bulgarian Agrarian People's Union–Nikola Petkov (BZNS-NP)**, which is in the SDS, is the only one of the Agrarian parties to gain individual representation in the National Assembly. Like the BSDP it is descended from a historic party that was founded in 1899. After 1945 the party underwent a gradual suppression and forced integration into the communist-dominated Fatherland Front. It, too, was in the SDS for a time but then left in 1992 to later form the **People's Union (NZ)**, which was successful in gaining seats in the 1994 election.

The other member of the NZ was the **Democratic Party (DP)**, which was the 1990 continuation of the historic conservative Christian party of the same name founded in 1896. It, too, was a member of the SDS for a time, until leaving in 1994 to join with the BZNS. Both the BZNS and the DP joined into the ODS with the SDS and BSDP.

The **Fatherland Union**, which won two seats in the 1990 elections is the remnant of the communist-dominated Fatherland Front that ruled Bulgaria from 1945 to 1989.

A new party, the **Euro-Left Coalition (EL)**, was formed for the 1997 elections and won fourteen seats.

ELECTIONS

The first elections were those held on 10 and 17 June 1990. These elections were conducted using a mix of PR and single-member-majority voting whereby a second round was used to determine winners who had not obtained a first-round majority. Due to this method many parties were able to gain representation, including parties that either received a very small proportion of the vote, like the BSDP, or did not even contest the proportional vote, such as the Fatherland Party of Labor and the Fatherland Union.

The purpose of these initial elections was primarily to elect a body that would draft a new constitution. For this reason, turnout was high—90.6 percent for the PR seats and 90.8 percent for the constituency seats in the first round (84.14 percent for the second round).

Elections in Bulgaria

	1990		1991		1994		1997	
	%V	#S	%V	#S	%V	#S	%V	#S
BSP	47.2	211	33.1	106	43.5	125	—	—
DL	—	—	—	—	—	—	22.1	58
ODS	—	—	—	—	—	—	52.3	137
SDS	37.8	144	34.4	110	24.2	69	—	—
BZNS	8.0	16	3.9	0	—	—	—	—
NZ	—	—	—	—	6.5	18	—	—
BSDP	0.1	1	?	0	—	—	—	—
DAR	—	—	—	—	3.8	0	—	—
DPS	6.0	23	7.6	24	5.4	15	—	—
ONS	—	—	—	—	—	—	7.6	19
BBB	—	—	1.3	0	4.7	13	4.9	12
EL	—	—	—	—	—	—	5.5	14
OPT	—	1	—	—	—	—	—	—
Fatherland Union	—	2	—	—	—	—	—	—
independents	—	2	—	—	0.2	0	—	—
others	0.9	0	19.7	0	11.6	0	7.6	0
TOTAL SEATS		400		240		240		240

The BSP and the SDS were by far the biggest winners, getting 211 and 144 seats, respectively, of the 400 seats up for grabs. This difference was largely due to the difference produced by the constituency voting, wherein the BSP candidates benefited from being much more well known than the SDS candidates. The seat share was also a result of the fact that the SDS campaigned too far on a virulent and intimidating anti-Communist platform. This coupled with poor organization on the part of the SDS and the fact that the former communists, now the BSP, campaigned for social change, introduction of the market economy, political pluralism, and justice made the SDS not as attractive an option as the BSP.

The October 1991 elections, conducted with a new constitution and new electoral law, featuring thirty-one medium-sized voting districts and a 4 percent threshold, saw the number of parties gaining representation drop significantly. The total number of seats in the newly named National Assembly decreased, as well, to 240. As in 1990 the short period of preparation for the elections led to the late registration of candidates and party lists. This time, however, the SDS came out on top winning a plurality of seats but not a majority. The vote shares for both the SDS and the BSP dropped, although not as severely for the SDS. The BSP was hurt by its experience forming the first government, and the SDS lost votes to the two other SDS lists that were presented. The BZNS vote dropped below the new 4 percent threshold and therefore it lost all of the sixteen seats it had received in 1990. The DSP was the big winner in the election, increasing its vote share by 1.5 percent but, more significantly, doubling its percentage share of seats, thus enabling it to play the role of king maker to the SDS.

The 18 December 1994 elections saw turnout drop once again. However, the number of parties competing increased from forty in 1992 to fifty, and the number of parties represented in the National Assembly also increased, from three in 1991 to five in 1994. For the first time, the BBB got seats and the BZNS returned to the National Assembly as part of the newly formed People's Union with the Democratic Party. Power shifted once again, this time away from the SDS and to the BSP, which had formed an alliance with both the Ecoglasnost Political Club and the BZNS-AP that enabled the party to gain an outright majority of the seats.

The April 1997 elections came early because the BSP relinquished its efforts to form a new government and bowed to the massive public pressure following collapse of the old one in December 1996. These elections saw competition between three newly formed coalitions and one new party that called itself a coalition. The BBB was the only entity that competed in 1997 as they had in 1994. The big winner was the United Democratic Forces coalition, which comprised the similarly named SDS and the component elements of the People's Union and the DAR alliance, which had competed in the 1994 election. The ODS received 137 seats as compared with the BSP-led Democratic Left, which finished a distant second with 58 seats.

GOVERNMENTS

Governments in Bulgaria have alternated between SDS and BSP leadership with caretaker or independently led governments filling in between. The Lukanov Government of 1990 was replaced after only three months due to two weeks of mass protests and a four-day general strike to protest Lukanov's role in the former communist regime. He was replaced by Prime Minister–designate Popov whose cabinet included Socialists, the SDS, and the BZNS. Following the 1991 elections the SDS was able to form a government thanks to the support of the DPS. A year later the DPS withdrew its support leading to the government's defeat in a confidence vote. The new government was formally independent, but it did rely on the support of the BSP and SDS dissidents. This government was replaced by a clear caretaker government two months prior to the December 1994 elections that saw the return of the BSP to government. This BSP government did not last its full mandate and was replaced by another caretaker government in the months leading to the 1997 elections. Following these, the SDS was again returned to government, this time thanks to the performance of the ODS, the broad coalition to which it belongs.

Bulgarian Governments since 1990

In Office Date (M/Y)	Prime Minister (Party)	#M (I)	Parties in Cabinet	Supporting Parties
09/90	Lukanov, A. (BSP)	18(2)	BSP	
12/90	Popov, D. (Ind)	18(5)	BSP SDS	
11/91	Dimitrov, F. (SDS)	14	SDS	DPS
12/92	Berov, L. (Ind)	(14)		BSP SDS
10/94	Indzhova, R. (Ind)		(caretaker government)	
01/95	Videnov, Z. (BSP)	18(8)	BSP	
02/97	Sofiyanski, S. (UDF)		(caretaker government)	
04/97	Kostov, I. (SDS)	17	SDS	

ACRONYMS

ASP	Alternative Social-Liberal Party
ASO	Alternative Socialist Association
BBB	Bulgarian Business Bloc
BKP	Bulgarian Communist Party
BRSP	Bulgarian Labor Social Democratic Party
BSP	Bulgarian Socialist Party
BSDP	Bulgarian Social Democratic Party
BZNS	Bulgarian Agrarian People's Union
BZNS-AZ	Bulgarian Agrarian People's Union–Aleksandur Stamboliyski
BZNS-NP	Bulgarian Agrarian People's Union–Nikola Petkov
DAR	Democratic Alternative for the Republic
DL	Democratic Left
DP	Democratic Party
DPS	Movement for Rights and Freedoms
EL	Coalition Euro-Left
EPS	Ecoglasnost Political Club
NZ	People's Union
OPT	Fatherland Party of Labor
ODS	United Democratic Forces
ONS	Union for National Salvation
SDS	Union of Democratic Forces
ZP	Green Party

REFERENCES

Karasimeonov, Georgi. (1995). "Parliamentary Elections of 1994 and the Development of the Bulgarian Party System," *Party Politics,* Vol. 1, pp. 579–87.

Zloch-Christy, Iliana, ed. (1996). *Bulgaria in a Time of Change: Economic and Political Dimensions.* Avebury; Aldershot, England.

Croatia

SUMMARY OF PARTY SYSTEM

1992–(95) moderate multiparty system with one dominant party (HDZ)

HISTORY

In the twelfth century Croatia came under the personal rule of the Hungarian monarch. From 1526 to the early eighteenth century it was under Turkish rule. In 1918 Croatia became part of the Kingdom of Serbs, Croats, and Slovenes, which was renamed Yugoslavia in 1929. An independent Croatian state under Nazi tutelage was established in 1941. In 1945 Croatia was again part of the (People's Republic of) Yugoslavia. In 1991 Croatia (and Slovenia) became independent from Yugoslavia. Croatia fought a war with the Serb-dominated Yugoslav People's Army, which occupied a third of the country until finally driven out by Croat forces in 1995.

ELECTORAL SYSTEM

The Croatian parliament currently has 127 seats; these are elected mainly through a combination of thirty-five single-member plurality constituencies and one national constituency of eighty members, which uses proportional representation and the d'Hondt method. Any list winning less than 5 percent of the votes is excluded from the distribution of these seats. A further twelve deputies are chosen by proportional representation and the d'Hondt method to represent Croatians residing abroad. Members of ethnic and national communities, or minorities whose share of the country's population exceeds 8 percent, are also entitled to be represented in proportion to their number; their representatives are chosen by simple plurality from party lists and currently number seven (including three Serbs). Vacancies arising between general elections are filled by substitutes elected at the same time as titular members.

POLITICAL PARTIES AND CLEAVAGES

The main party in Croatia is the ruling **Croatian Democratic Union (HDZ)** of Franjo Tudjman. The party is right wing but is a member of the Christian Democrat International. The party has created an electoral system that works to its benefit and maintains it in power.

The opposition in Croatia is made up of a group of parties that formed the **Joint List (ZL)** bloc for the 1995 elections. The ZL includes: the **Croatian Peasant Party (HSS)**, a party committed to pacifism, localism, and economic privatization; the **Croatian Party of Slavonia and Baranja (SBHS)**, which represented ethnic Croats in Serb-occupied territory from 1991 to 1995; the **Istrian Democratic Assembly (IDS)**, which represents ethnic Italians and other minorities in Istria and advocates the creation of a transborder region encompassing Croatian, Slovenia, and Italian areas; the **Croatian National Party (HNS)**, an antitraditionalist party committed to political pluralism and a free market economy; and the **Croatian Christian Democratic Union (HKDU)**, which was formally the **Croatian Christian Democratic Party (HKDS)** until its name change in 1992. Of these parties the HNS and the HSS contested and won seats in the 1992 elections as individual parties.

The single largest party after the HDZ is the **Croatian Social Liberal Party (HSLS)**, which is a traditional European liberal grouping committed to a free-market economy and speedy reforms. The ex-Communists are represented by the **Social Democratic Party of Croatia–Party of Democratic Change (SPH-SDP)** and the nationalists have the **Croatian Party of Rights (HSP)**, whose military wing was heavily involved in ethnic conflict during the war.

LACK OF COMPLETELY FAIR ELECTIONS

The HDZ has in part engineered the results of the only two elections held (as of this writing) in the country since it gained independence from Yugoslavia. While this is not outright rigging as in some countries, the HDZ—which in any case would clearly still be the largest party—has nevertheless manipulated the electoral laws and falsified some results to ensure itself a majority of seats in parliament.

ELECTIONS

One of the main ways in which the HDZ has ensured victory is through the votes of the so-called Croatian Diaspora. In the Croatian electoral law, 12 of the parliament's current 127 seats are allocated to election by members of the Croatian Diaspora—those Croatians living abroad for one reason or another. To qualify as a member of this Diaspora a person must have Croatian citizenship or claim to have a Croatian parent or just claim to have the intention of seeking Croatian citizenship at some time in the future. Votes are cast abroad by various polling stations established by Croatian embassies—often in churches, consular missions, clubs, and in one case a bowling alley. To say the least, these votes were hardly cast in a manner conforming to any strict procedural regulations concerning privacy and legitimacy. The results are then telephoned to the government in Croatia. No more precise measures are taken to calculate exactly how many votes were cast or which parties actually received votes. Not surprisingly all twelve of these seats were won by the HDZ in both 1992 and 1995.

The number of votes cast abroad was estimated in 1995 at around 97,000. If these votes had been added to the total number of votes received nationally and then used to determine seats as part of the state party lists, the HDZ would only have received one extra seat, thereby reducing the number of seats it received in total to sixty-four from seventy-five and giving it only a 50 percent share of the total seats instead of the 60 percent it in fact has.

The HDZ has also used more mundane methods for ensuring victory—through intimidation and multiple ballot casting. In many ballot stations in both elections, privacy to cast votes was lacking, which therefore made it much easier for intimidation to be successful.

In 1992—using a mixed system of voting that included 60 seats by PR, 60 by single-member majority, and 18 allocated to Croats abroad, Serbs, and other ethnic minorities—the HDZ captured 42.6 percent of the vote and 64 percent of the elected seats.

In 1996 the number of seats elected by PR was increased to eighty, with twenty-eight now elected by single-member majority, and a total of nineteen seats going to represent Croats abroad, Serbs, and other ethnic minorities. In these elections the HZD polled a slightly higher share of the vote and received 75 of the total 127 seats.

Croatian Elections

	1992		1995	
	%V	#S	%V	#S
HDZ	42.6	85	45.2	75
HSLS	17.7	14	11.6	12
ZL	—	—	18.3	18
SHP-SDP	5.8	11	8.9	10
HNS	6.9	5	—	—
HSP	6.4	5	5.0	4
HSS	—	3	—	—
independents	—	6	—	—
Serbs	1.1	3	—	3
other minorities	—	6	—	4
others	19.5	0	11.0	1
TOTAL SEATS		138		127

GOVERNMENTS

Governments in Croatia, although in theory accountable to the parliament, have in fact been determined by the HDZ's leader, President Franjo Tudjman, until his death.

ACRONYMS

HDZ	Croatian Democratic Union
HKDS	Croatian Christian Democratic Party
HKDU	Croatian Christian Democratic Union
HNS	Croatian National Party
HSLS	Croatian Social Liberal Party
HSP	Croatian Party of Rights
HSS	Croatian Peasant Party

continued

ACRONYMS *Continued*

IDS	Istrian Democratic Assembly
SBHS	Croatian Party of Slavonia and Baranja
SPH-SDP	Social Democratic Party–Party of Democratic Change
ZL	Joint List

REFERENCE

Tanner, Marcus. (1998). *Croatia: A Nation Forged in War.* New Haven: Yale University Press.

Cyprus (Greek)

SUMMARY OF PARTY SYSTEMS

1976	moderate multiparty system with one predominant party (DIKO)
1981–(96)	moderate multiparty system with a balance among the parties

HISTORY

Cyprus was a British colony until 1960. Upon independence, a consociational institutional structure was planned to recognize the division between the Greek majority and the Turkish minority on the island. The president was to be Greek, the vice president Turkish, and other positions distributed in a 7:3 ratio. However, tensions and sporadic violence persisted between the communities, leading to the arrival of United Nations peacekeepers. A 1974 attempt to unite the island with Greece led to the invasion of the northern, Turkish part of the island by the armed forces of Turkey. The two communities have been de facto separate political entities ever since. As a consequence of this de facto division, some 200,000 Greek Cypriots fled south.

For our purposes, Cyprus (Greek) is thus analyzed from the mid-1970s onward.

ELECTORAL SYSTEM

In 1976 Cyprus used a single-member system and in part because of this never seemed to release the vote totals! Since then, Cyprus has used a proportional-representation system in multimember districts. Voting is compulsory. Although the assembly has fifty-six members, technically there are eighty; the remainder are unfilled Turkish Cypriot seats.

POLITICAL PARTIES AND CLEAVAGES

The **Democratic Rally (DISY)** was formed in 1976. The party has a strongly pro-Western orientation, supports free enterprise, and espouses traditional liberal economic policies. The party is generally regarded as the furthest to the right of the country's political parties. In terms of the issue of the TRNC the party has at times adopted a more conciliatory position then the hard-line positions taken by other parties. The party has enjoyed a fairly broad base of support.

The **Progressive Party of the Working People (AKEL)** is Cyprus's main left-of-center party. AKEL originated as the Communist Party of Cyprus in 1941 and is therefore the only party to have a history that predates independence. While this history has meant that the party's rhetoric has been rather orthodox, in practice the party has supported more pragmatic and revisionist policies. The party is strongly tied to Cyprus's labor movement and this is therefore a large base of support for the party. Like the DISY, the AKEL has avoided hard-line rhetoric on the issue of the TRNC, and has supported talks on reunification through the efforts supervised by the UN.

The **Democratic Party (DIKO)** is the last of Cyprus's three main parties. The DIKO was founded in 1976 as a center-right grouping originally known as the Democratic Front. The party has never been strong on ideology and has instead relied on the popularity of personalities within the party. The DIKO did, until very recently, consistently support the idea of a "long-term struggle" against the Turkish occupation of northern Cyprus.

Consistently the fourth party in Cyprus politics, the **Unified Democratic Union of Cyprus (EDEK)** (commonly known as the **Socialist Party**), is a moderate left-of-center party that has supported a unified and independent Cyprus. Because of the AKEL's domination of the left, the EDEK has been largely unable to secure electoral success.

The **Free Democrats Movement (KED)**, which was formed in 1993 as a party on the center left that is pro-EU, managed to win two seats in the most recent elections. This has further weakened the EDEK.

ELECTIONS

The 1976 elections were dominated by the three-party alliance of the DIKO, AKEL, and EDEK, which contested the elections as one entity in many of the country's constituencies. Despite the fact that the DISY secured a large portion of the popular vote, the party did not win any seats due to the majority electoral system. During the campaign the DISY had argued that a solution to Turkey's occupation of the north could be had if the European Community and the United States intervened on Cyprus's behalf and put pressure on the Turkish government. The other parties all argued that the country needed to remain nonaligned and that long-term struggle would solve the problem.

With a change in the electoral system and the breakup of the three-party alliance, the 1981 elections featured large gains by both the DISY and AKEL at the expense of the DIKO.

The 1985 elections were called early, after the dissolution of the AKEL-DIKO government, because of the DIKO's position vis-à-vis the north and primarily the position of the DIKO president. The campaign therefore centered around the issue of the TRNC, with both the DISY and AKEL being highly critical of the president's failure to reach agreement with the north in UN-sponsored talks. The two parties hoped to secure the necessary two-thirds majority in parliament to amend the constitution and force out the president. The EDEK supported the hard-line stance of DIKO. The position taken by the DISY and AKEL was not strongly supported by the voters, and the AKEL saw their share of the popular vote drop while both the EDEK and DIKO doubled their number of seats in parliament.

Elections in Cyprus since 1976

	1976	1981		1985	
	#S	%V	#S	%V	#S
DISY	0	31.9	12	33.6	19
DIKO	21	19.5	8	27.7	16
AKEL	9	32.8	12	27.4	15
EDEK	4	8.2	3	11.1	6
others	1	7.6	0	0.2	0
TOTAL SEATS	35		35		56

continued

Elections in Cyprus since 1976 *Continued*

	1991		1996	
	%V	#S	%V	#S
DISY	35.8	20	34.5	20
DIKO	19.5	11	16.4	10
AKEL	30.6	18	33.0	19
EDEK	10.9	7	8.1	5
KED	—	—	3.7	2
others	3.2	0	4.3	0
TOTAL SEATS		56		56

In 1991 the DISY and AKEL once again campaigned on reunification, and this time the results were seen as support for the continuation of UN-sponsored talks with the north. All parties made gains at the expense of the DIKO, which lost five seats.

The issue of the north was not the primary issue of the 1996 campaign. This was largely due to the fact that there was widespread agreement among all parties with respect to the United Nations resolutions that called for the establishment of a federal and bicommunal republic, and the withdrawal of all foreign military troops from the island. There was, however, some disagreement over how this should be attained.

The main issue in the campaign turned out to be the prospect of the country's entry into the EU, which Cyprus had been seeking since 1990. Most parties were in support of this even to the extent that most argued that EU membership should come before union with the north.

The results were largely similar to those of 1991. The biggest change occurred at the bottom end of the results, with the EDEK losing two of their seats to the newly formed KED. This may have been in part due to the fact that the KED was more openly supportive of the EU than the EDEK, which had traditionally argued for a nonaligned position for Cyprus in international affairs.

GOVERNMENTS

Cyprus is a presidential system. As such, even though members of political parties sit in the cabinet, parliamentary elections as such do not determine the composition of the government.

ACRONYMS

AKEL	Progressive Party of the Working People
DIKO	Democratic Party
DISY	Democratic Rally
EDEK	Unified Democratic Union of Cyprus (Socialist Party)
KED	Free Democrats Movement

Turkish Republic of Northern Cyprus (TRNC)

SUMMARY OF PARTY SYSTEMS

1976–85	moderate multiparty system with one dominant party (UBP)
1990	two party system
1993	moderate multiparty system with a balance among the parties
(1998–)	moderate multiparty system with one dominant party (UBP)

HISTORY

In June 1964 Turkish Cypriots withdrew from participation in the government of the Republic of Cyprus. That same year United Nations peacekeepers began their mission on Cyprus. In 1967 a provisional government was established to provide services in Turkish areas in the north. In 1975 an autonomous state was established on 13 February following the Greek army coup and the subsequent Turkish military occupation of the north. An independent republic was declared on 15 November 1983, but this regime has been recognized only by Turkey. Nevertheless, a new TRNC constitution was approved on 6 May 1985 in a referendum, and the Republic clearly functions as a de facto state.

ELECTORAL SYSTEM

There are now five electoral districts in the TRNC; previously there had been three. The details of the electoral system have been different in each of the elections up to and including 1990. In 1976, proportional representation using a split ticket and the d'Hondt method of distribution was used with seats also automatically going to any candidate winning 50 percent of the votes in a given constituency. In 1981 all seats were allocated using the d'Hondt method. In 1985 an 8 percent threshold for representation was introduced. The number of seats in the assembly were also increased from forty to fifty. Finally, in 1990 the option of splitting one's vote (for either party or candidate) was eliminated. Also, any party receiving more than 33 percent of the vote in a given district received extra seats at the rate of one per extra percentage point up to a maximum of one-third (rounded down) of the total seats available in the district. This bonus existed only for that election.

POLITICAL PARTIES AND CLEAVAGES

The **National Unity Party (UBP)** has consistently won the plurality of votes in each election held in the TRNC. The party was formed in 1975 as an outgrowth of the National Solidarity Movement, which strived for an independent northern Turkish state in Cyprus. Despite its history, the party was initially committed to the establishment of a bicommunal federal state but gradually moved away from this position to encompass a less conciliatory position regarding the Greek Cypriot population. This increasingly extreme position adopted by the party caused internal division and led to the secession of party members to newly formed breakaway parties. These parties in turn drained much of the support for the UBP and explain the latter's failure in the 1993 elections to win the plurality of seats. The party is considered on the right wing of the political spectrum.

The **Democratic Party (DP)** was formed in 1992 by dissidents of the much larger UBP. The founding members of the DP advocated a more conciliatory posture in regard to the intercommunal talks with the Greek population compared to the more extreme position taken by the party mainstream of the UBP. In the first elections it contested, the party won the same number of seats as the UBP and subsequently entered into a governing coalition with the CTP. This proved to be an unstable coalition, collapsing three times in two years.

The **Republican Turkish Party (CTP)** was originally formed in 1970 as a Marxist formation. The party campaigned against the 1985 constitution because of its alleged repressive and militaristic content. For the 1990 elections the party organized an electoral coalition with the TKP and YDP in order to compete with the UBP under the new changes in the electoral law, this coalition being named the **Democratic Struggle Party (DMP)**.

Joining the CTP to form the DMP for the 1990 elections was the **Communal Liberation Party (TKP)**, which is also known as the Socialist Salvation Party. The TKP is a left-of-center party that was founded in 1976 and originally supported a federal solution the Cyprus problem. The party was briefly in government from July 1985 to August

1986. In 1989 the party absorbed the smaller **Progressive People's Party (AHP)**, which itself was formed in 1986 by the merger of the smaller **Democratic People's Party (DHP)** and the centrist **Communal Endeavor Party (TAP)**. These two smaller parties were founded in 1979 and 1984, respectively. The DHP, which itself was founded by dissidents of the UBP, advocated an independent nonaligned biregional Cypriot state.

The third member of the 1990 DMP coalition was the **New Dawn Party (YDP)**, which can be translated into English as New Birth, Revival, or Renaissance Party. The party occupies a center-right position on the political spectrum and is primarily concerned with the representation of Turkish immigrants to the TRNC. The party is generally supportive of the DP, and in 1993 the party contested the general elections with the DP, however, the two remain separate political entities.

ELECTIONS

The 1976 elections were the first since the TRNC had been established as a federated state. The TKP proved be the strongest opposition party to the UBP, which had been formed in 1975 by a majority of the members of the governing assembly. The TKP, which had only been formed a short time before the election, campaigned on a platform calling for no dictatorial rule, more planning, a minimum standard of living, and public employee salaries that were in tune with the increase in the cost of living. The resulting proportion of the vote won by the TKP was an encouraging sign for the left-wing opposition, however, the party was frustrated with the small number of seats allotted to them by the electoral system. Despite winning only a slim majority of the votes, the UBP ended up with an overwhelming majority of 75 percent of the seats.

The 1981 elections came at a time when the UBP was suffering heavily from infighting. Various crises had also weakened the party's popularity among the population. The desire for change was evident in the fact that voter turnout rose by more than 14 percent to 88.6 percent. The Cyprus problem was not a major issue in the election campaign because all parties were in agreement in their support for a federal solution. The left-wing opposition parties campaigned on platforms criticizing the UBP's previous government and calling for more support for the TRNC's working population. The increase in turnout, the crises of the previous UBP government, and the change in the electoral system—

using a more pure d'Hondt method of distribution—all contributed to the outcome of the elections. The UBP share of votes dropped by 10 percent from 1976 but more crucially the party's share of seats dropped from 75 percent to 45 percent.

The 1985 elections were the first held since the TRNC declared its independence and a new constitution was approved in a referendum held one month before the election. The UBP's share of votes dropped further compared with previous elections, however it did manage to increase its share of seats to 48 percent. The elections also saw the CTP usurp the TKP's status as the main opposition party. Turnout remained high at 85.7 percent.

In 1990 the change in the electoral system, which granted bonus seats to parties receiving more than 33 percent of the vote in a given district, prompted the left-wing opposition parties to contest the elections as the Democratic Struggle Party. The parties making up the coalition struggled to come up with a coherent platform, and this benefited the UBP, which was once again able to win a majority of both seats and votes. The three parties that made up the DMP had won, on their own, a combined 46 percent in the 1985 elections (essentially the same total); however, the main difference in 1990 was that there were not any other strong parties to win votes away from the UBP. In 1985 a third force, represented by the DHP, had managed 7.4 percent of votes but no seats due to the 8 percent threshold, however in 1990 the only other party competing other than the UBP and the DMP won a mere 0.8 percent of the votes. Turnout for the 1990 elections reached an all-time high of 91.5 percent.

Both the TKP and CTP, the largest of the opposition parties, protested the results of the elections and the bias they felt existed in the electoral system by taking their seats in the assembly. By-elections were then held in November 1991 for twelve of the sixteen seats won by the DMP that CTP and the TKP refused to occupy. The smaller member of the DMP coalition, the YDP, had decided to occupy its seats, as had two members of the TKP who formed a new party. The CTP and TKP boycotted the by-elections, which saw turnout drop to a low 67.0 percent and the UBP win eleven seats while the newly formed and short-lived **Free Democratic Party (HDP)** won one.

After continued popular protest, the all-opposition boycott of parliamentary committees and the threat of a boycott of parliament itself, as well as pressure from both the president of the TRNC and the government of Turkey, the TRNC prime minister was forced into calling early elections for December 1993. As a result of the elections, the UBP received a record-low 30 percent of the vote, and the first non-UBP government was formed by the DP and CTP. However, this government degenerated into a pattern of collapse and reformation. The UBP would be back in power in 1996 and would argue successfully in the 1998 elections that only it could lead the TRNC.

Elections in the TRNC

	1976		1981		1985	
	%V	#S	%V	#S	%V	#S
UBP	53.7	30	42.5	18	36.7	24
CTP	12.9	2	15.1	6	21.4	12
AHP	11.8	2	—	—	—	—
DHP	—	—	8.1	2	7.4	0
TKP	20.2	6	28.5	13	15.8	10
YDP	—	—	—	—	8.8	4
DMP	—	—	—	—	—	—
others	1.4	0	5.8	1	9.9	0
TOTAL SEATS		40		40		50

	1990		1993		1998	
	%V	#S	%V	#S	%V	#S
UBP	54.7	34	29.9	16	40.3	24
CTP	—	—	24.2	13	13.4	6
TKP	—	—	13.3	5	15.4	7
DP	—	—	29.2	16	22.6	13
DMP	44.5	16	—	—	—	—
others	0.8	0	3.5	0	8.4	0
TOTAL SEATS		50		50		50

GOVERNMENTS

Until 1993 the UBP (National Unity Party) enjoyed effective one-party dominance, inasmuch as it either formed single-party governments or was the dominant player in a coalition. After the 1993 elections, a series of three shaky coalitions were formed between the DP and the CTP. After the last of these collapsed in 1996, the UBP returned to power, supported by the president.

TRNC Governments since 1976

In Office Date (M/Y)	Prime Minister (Party)	#M (I)	Parties in Cabinet
07/76	Konuk, N. (UBP)	11	UBP
04/78	Örek, O. (UBP)	10	UBP
12/78	Cağatay, M. (UBP)	10	UBP
08/81	Cağatay, M. (UBP)	9	UBP
03/82	Cağatay, M. (UBP)	11	UBP DHP TBP
12/83	Konuk, N. (ind)	11(5)	UBP DHP
07/85	Eroğlu, D. (UBP)	11	UBP TKP
09/86	Eroğlu, D. (UBP)	11	UBP YDP
05/88	Eroğlu, D. (UBP)	11(1)	UBP
06/90	Eroğlu, D. (UBP)	11	UBP
01/94	Atun, H. (DP)	11	DP CTP
06/95	Atun, H. (DP)	11	DP CTP
12/95	Atun, H. (DP)	11	DP CTP
08/96	Eroğlu, D. (UBP)	11	UBP DP
01/99	Eroğlu, D. (UBP)	11	UBP TKP

ACRONYMS

AHP	Progressive People's Party
CTP	Republican Turkish Party
DHP	Democratic People's Party
DMP	Democratic Struggle Party
DP	Democratic Party
HDP	Free Democratic Party
TAP	Communal Endeavor Party
TKP	Communal Liberation Party
UBP	National Unity Party
YDP	New Dawn Party

REFERENCE

Dodd, C. H. ed. (1993). *The Political, Social, and Economic Development of Northern Cyprus.* Huntington, England: The Eothen Press.

Czech Republic

SUMMARY OF PARTY SYSTEMS

1990	moderate multiparty system with one dominant party (OF)
1992	extreme multiparty system with one dominant party (ODS)
1996	extreme multiparty system with two main parties (ODS and CSSD)
(1998–)	moderate multiparty system with two main parties (CSSD and ODS)

HISTORY

The first Czechoslovak republic lasted from 1918 to 1938. It was the only Eastern European nation to experience a continuous democracy between the wars, until it was dismantled by the Munich agreement of 1938. This democracy was a multiparty system using PR to elect members of parliament. The "Petka"—a five party coalition—was the dominant form of cabinet. After the Second World War, by February 1948, the communists finally achieved full control of the government. Massive prodemocratic protests beginning in November 1989 led to the first non-communist-dominated government in forty-one years being sworn in on 10 December 1989. Czechoslovakia itself was peacefully dissolved by the leaders of the Czech Republic and Slovakia at the end of 1992—what was called the "velvet divorce." What follows pertains only to the Czech lands from 1990, and the Czech Republic from 1992.

ELECTORAL SYSTEM

The Czech Chamber of Deputies contains two hundred members elected by PR in eight districts with thirteen to forty-one seats each. Elections use a proportional representation system with the Hagenbach-Bischoff method and greatest-remainders calculation for leftover seats. There is an electoral threshold of 5 percent for single parties, 7 percent for coalitions of two parties, 9 percent for coalitions of three parties, and 11 percent for a coalition of more than three parties.

POLITICAL PARTIES AND CLEAVAGES

The **Civic Forum (OF)**, launched in November 1989 with Václav Havel as its leader, precipitated the downfall of the communist regime and was the first party with which the communist entered talks to turn over power. It was a broad social movement and won 49.5 percent of the vote and 63.5 percent of seats in the 1990 National Council elections. The OF split off into various parties prior to the 1992 elections. The **Civic Movement (OH)** attempted to carry on the mandate of the OF as a broad movement but failed to win representation in the 1992 elections.

The **Civic Democratic Party (ODS)** was one of two conservative parties to form from the breakup of the OF. A conservative center-right party and intensely anti-Communist, the ODS led every government in the Czech Republic until the caretaker government of December 1997. The ODS was the driving force behind the period of economic and political transition from 1992 to 1996. In 1996 the ODS formally absorbed its long-time electoral ally, the **Christian Democratic Party (KDS)**, into the ODS rubric; the ODS did likewise in 1997 with the ODA. However, the domineering leadership of Václav Klaus eventually proved too much for some ODS members, who broke away at the start of 1998 to form the Czech **Freedom Union (US)**.

The second of the two conservative parties to form from the OF was the **Civic Democratic Alliance (ODA)**, which was slightly to the right of the ODS. It supported the creation of the Czech state and like the ODS was pro-market. One thing that did distinguish the ODA from the ODS was the fact that the ODA put greater emphasis on regional self-government. The ODA had been a minor partner in the three ODS governments. In November 1997 it merged into the ODS.

The **Christian Democratic Union–Czech People's Party (KDU-CSL)** is the descendant of the historic Czechoslovak People's Party, which was founded in 1918 and banned in 1938. The party was then revived in 1945 as a component of the communist-dominated National Front. The party participated in the 1990 elections as the Christian and Democratic Union and then in April of 1992 formally adopted the KDU-CSL rubric. Until 1993 the KDU-CSL advocated for the autonomy of Moravia, a region from which it got a lot of support. The KDU-CSL is a pro-reform centrist party of Christian-Democratic orientation that supports a social market economy. The KDU-CSL has proved to be a valuable coalition partner and has had ministers in all Czech governments.

On the left of the Czech political spectrum, one finds the **Communist Party of Bohemia and Moravia (KSCM)**. An orthodox Communist party that works within the existing parliamentary structure, it is descended from the **Communist Party of Czechoslovakia (KSC)**, which was founded in 1921 by the pro-Bolshevik wing of the CSSD. The KSC was the only Eastern European Communist party to retain its legal status in the 1930s—until it was banned in 1938. The KSCM was relaunched in 1990 one year before the KSC officially dissolved. The KSCM resisted the breakup of the Czechoslovak federation and has remained Czechoslovak in orientation along with its Slovak counterpart since the "velvet divorce." Both the **Left Block Party (SLB)** and the **Party of Democratic Left (SDL)** split from the KSCM. The SLB split because it opposed the conservative leadership of the KSCM, and the SDL because it styled itself an advocate of a more contemporary form of socialism than that offered by the KSCM. In the 1992 elections the KSCM and the SLB seats are listed as part of the **Left Bloc (LB)**.

The other traditional left-of-center party is the **Czech Social Democratic Party (CSSD)**. The CSSD was the plurality party of Czechoslovakia's first parliamentary election in 1920 but went underground in 1939. The CSSD was forced to merge into the KSC in 1948. In 1989 it reemerged as a separate party occupying a left-centrist position in favor of reform toward a social and ecological market economy. It initially argued against the "velvet divorce," instead wanting a confederal system, but it soon came to accept the separation. In February 1993 the party officially replaced the "Czechoslovak" in its party name with "Czech."

The **Association for the Republic–Republican Party of Czechoslovakia (SPR-RSC)** is on the far, far right of the Czech political spectrum. The party was founded in 1990 but did not get any seats in parliament until 1992. The party advocates the return of capital punishment, economic protectionism, drastic cuts in the state bureaucracy, military neutrality, and nonparticipation in international organizations. It also argues that "measures" should be taken against groups such as Gypsies. The party is also anti-German. The main area of support for the party is in northern Bohemia. The party has been weakened by a series of defections and was eliminated from parliament after the 1998 elections.

Another party that has won seats in the past but currently does not have representation in parliament is the **Czech-Moravian Center Union (CMUS)**, which is the successor to **Movement for Autonomous**

Democracy–Society for Moravia and Silesia (HSD-SMS). The HSD-SMS, formed in 1990, won representation in both the 1990 and 1992 National Council elections. In 1994 the HSD-SMS changed its name but won no seats in 1996. The party, under both names, has argued for Moravia-Silesia to have the same status as Bohemia and Slovakia. The party supports the market economy but advocates the retention of Communist-era social achievements.

Finally, the **Liberal Social Union (LSU)** was created in 1991 by the merger of four small Czech parties, and it won seats in the 1992 elections. The LSU dissolved the following year, however, when its largest component, the **Liberal National Socialist Party (LSNS)**, left to join forces with the **Free Democrats (SD)**, which was the renamed remnant of the OH. The new party, the **Free Democrats–Liberal National Socialist Party (SD-LSNS)** failed to retain any of its seats in the 1996 election.

ELECTIONS

The 1990 elections to the National Council of the Czech Republic were the first since the Civic Forum movement had rested power away from the communists, and the election results reflected the popular support for the role that the OF had played. It won 63.5 percent of the seats; the communists were a distant second capturing only 16 percent of the seats. Only four parties out of thirteen that put forward party lists managed to surpass the 5 percent threshold.

Czech Elections

	1990		1992		1996		1998	
	%V	#S	%V	#S	%V	#S	%V	#S
OF	49.5	127	—	—	—	—	—	—
ODS	—	—	29.7	76	29.6	68 }	27.7	63
ODA	—	—	5.9	14	6.4	13 }		
KSC	13.2	32	—	—	—	—	—	—
LB	—	—	14.1	35	—	—	—	—
KCMS	—	—	—	—	10.3	22	11.0	24
KDU-CSL	8.4	19	6.3	15	8.1	18	9.0	20

	1990		1992		1996		1998	
	%V	#S	%V	#S	%V	#S	%V	#S
HDS-SMS	10.0	22	5.9	14	?	—	—	—
CSSD	—	—	6.5	16	26.4	61	32.3	74
SPR-RSC	—	—	6.0	14	8.0	18	3.9	0
LSU	—	—	6.5	16	—	—	—	—
US	—	—	—	—	—	—	8.6	19
others	18.8	0	19.1	0	11.2	0	7.4	0
TOTAL SEATS		200		200		200		200

Note: The 1990 and 1992 elections were to the Czech National Council within then-Czechoslovakia. From 1996 onwards elections are to the Czech Chamber of Deputies.

The 1992 elections were the first elections with more fully developed political parties, rather than the movements and organizations that had successfully contested the 1990 elections. The main successor party to the OF, the OOS, was only able to capture 30 percent of the vote, some 20 percent less than the united OF had received two years earlier. In this election the number of parties gaining representation doubled.

The 1996 elections were the first to the chamber of deputies of the independent Czech Republic. The ODS/ODA share of seats dropped slightly to 40 percent. Thc big winner was the CSSD, which received the second largest number of votes and seats. The KSCM and the SPR-RSC both increased their number of seats. The big loser was the HSD-SMS, which lost all fourteen seats it had had following the 1992 elections.

The 1998 elections reflected more of an emphasis on personalities than on policy differences, but it did result in an overall shift to the left in two ways. First, the CSSD gained enough votes to become the largest party. Second, the far right SPR-SRC fell below the threshold for representation. However, the gains for the CSSD were not as high as expected.

GOVERNMENTS

The governments of the Czech Republic remained relatively static from 1992 to 1996, with the only change being the absorption of the KDS into the ODS. The 1996 ODS government was, however, a minority one, having control over only ninety-nine of the two hundred seats in the chamber of deputies. It could not survive more than two years, and from the end of 1997 a caretaker government ran the country until the elections of 1998. After these elections the Social Democrats came into office—the first time the left had governed the Czech Republic, and a much later date for this event than most elsewhere in postcommunist Europe. Although pundits were expecting the CSSD to form a coalition, at least with the KDU-CSL, instead they formed a minority government, which the ODS agreed to "tolerate."

Czech Governments since 1990

In Office Date (M/Y)	Prime Minister (Party)	#M (I)	Parties in Cabinet
06/90	Pithart, P. (OF)	21(9)	OF KDU-CSL HSD-SMS
07/92	Klaus, V. (ODS)	17	ODS KDU-CSL ODA KDS
01/93 *	Klaus, V. (ODS)	19	ODS KDU-CSL ODA KDS
07/96	Klaus, V. (ODS)	16	ODS KDU-CSL ODA
12/97	Tosovsky, J. (Ind)		(caretaker government)
07/98	Zeman, M. (CSSD)	19	CSSD

* Czech Republic becomes fully sovereign, but not a new government per se.

ACRONYMS

CSSD	Czech Social Democratic Party
CMUS	Czech-Moravian Center Union
HSD-SMS	Movement for Autonomous Democracy–Society for Moravia and Silesia
KDS	Christian Democratic Party
KDU-CSL	Christian Democratic Union–Czech People's Party
KSC	Communist Party of Czechoslovakia
KSCM	Communist Party of Bohemia and Moravia
LB	Left Bloc
LSNS	Liberal National Socialist Party
LSU	Liberal Social Union
ODA	Civic Democratic Party
ODS	Civic Democratic Alternative

OF	Civic Forum
OH	Civic Movement
SD	Free Democrats
SDL	Party of the Democratic Left
SD-LNSS	Free Democrats–Liberal National Socialist Party
SLB	Left Block Party
SPR-RSC	Association for the Republic–Republican Party of Czechoslovakia
US	Freedom Union

REFERENCES

Klíma, Michal. (1998). "Consolidation and Stability of the Party System in the Czech Republic." *Political Studies,* Vol. 46, pp. 492–510.

Olson, David M. (1997). "Democratization and Political Participation: The Experience of the Czech Republic," pp. 150–96, in Karen Dawisha and Bruce Parrott, eds. *The Consolidation of Democracy in East-Central Europe.* Cambridge: Cambridge University Press.

Turnovec, Frantisek. (1997). "Votes, Seats, and Power: The 1996 Parliamentary Election in the Czech Republic." *Communist and Postcommunist Studies,* Vol. 30, pp. 289–305.

Denmark

SUMMARY OF PARTY SYSTEMS

1945–47	extreme multiparty system with a balance among the parties
1950–(98)	extreme multiparty system with one dominant party (SD)

HISTORY

Denmark has been an independent monarchy for centuries. It was a great power from the fourteenth century onward, with control over southern Sweden (for a time), Norway, and Iceland. Royal absolutism was installed in 1660, but in 1949 elections and semidemocracy were introduced. Fully responsible government came in 1901.

ELECTORAL SYSTEM

There are 179 seats in the Danish Folketing. Of these, 175 are elected from "mainland" Denmark, and these seats only are the focus of our analysis. There are, however, two additional seats each for the Faroe Islands and for Greenland.

Of the 175 seats elected in Denmark proper, 135 are elected in 17 multimember constituencies, and the remaining 40 are national "top-up" seats. To quality for these additional seats, a party must either have won a constituency seat or received 2 percent of the national vote. This 2 percent threshold is the lowest legal threshold in Europe and, not surprisingly, hardly limits the number of parties.

POLITICAL PARTIES AND CLEAVAGES

Traditionally the largest political party in Denmark, the **Social Democratic Party (SD)** was formed in 1871. The party is a pragmatic social-democratic party and, like many of its Scandinavian and west European counterparts, emphasizes the importance of social welfare, economic planning, and environmental policies. From the mid-1940s to the mid-1960s the party polled near or more than 40 percent of the popular vote. Since this period, however, the party has not managed to hurdle the 40 percent barrier, largely due to the sheer number of parties that now contest Danish elections. Nevertheless no other party has managed to win the plurality of votes or seats in Denmark's post–World War II electoral history.

The **Center Democrats (CD)** were formed in 1973 by members of the SD who opposed that party's more progressive stance on moral and social issues. While supportive of the economic policies associated with the social democrats, the Center Democrats have taken a more conservative stance on such issues as education and the teaching of traditional values. As well, the CD has called for a more independent and objective media.

The **Socialist People's Party (SF)** was formed in 1958 when members of the **Communist Party of Denmark (DKP)** split in protest over that party's support of the Soviet intervention in Hungary in 1956. From its inception the SF presented itself as a party that supported far-left positions but wanted these to be independent of the Moscow line. The party is opposed to both NATO and the EU and gets support mainly from disenchanted social democrats and left-wing intellectuals. In 1967 the SF suffered its own split when members left to form the **Left Socialist Party (VS)**.

In 1989 the aforementioned Communist and Left-Socialist Parties, along with the Socialist Workers' Party, formed the far-left **Red-Green Unity List**. The party's main goals have been to work for socialist democracy in Denmark and to solve environmental problems facing Denmark and Europe. The party is against the European Union as it argues that the EU is simply out to exploit the countries of Eastern Europe.

Until the late 1960s, and once again in the 1990s, the main opposition party to the SD has been the **Liberal Party (V)**, which was founded in 1876. The party was originally formed to serve the interests of the country's rural and agrarian population. The party supports a traditional liberal position on economic policies and has called for further liberalization of the national economy. The Liberals have also argued for more personal freedoms. The party is still supported most strongly by those who live in small towns and in rural areas of the country.

The **Radical Liberal Party (RV)** (also known as the Social Liberal Party) was founded in 1905 by less conservative members of the Liberal Party. The RV supports traditional liberal economic policies and has been gradually more supportive of the EU in recent years. The party's main source of support comes from intellectuals and small landholders. Despite being unable to match the electoral success of the Liberal Party, the Radical Liberals have been members of Social Democrat–led governments. Indeed, in much of the postwar period the RV has been the "hinge" party containing the median MP in a left-right sense.

During the 1980s the position of dominance on the center-right was claimed by the **Conservative People's Party (KF)**, which was founded in 1916. Despite maintaining traditional center-right positions on various policies both social and economic, such as lower taxes, the Conservatives have given their support to the concept of the welfare state. The KF receives its strongest electoral support from business and financial groups. During the mid-1970s levels of popular support for the party dropped below 10 percent and hit a historic low of 5.5 percent in 1975. This slump was in large part due to the emergence of the newly formed Progress Party.

The **Progress Party (FP)** was founded in 1972 as a protest party with a strong anti-tax platform. The party argued for the gradual but complete dissolution of personal income tax in Denmark. It is no coincidence that the leader of the party was convicted for tax evasion in the early 1980s. The party also argues for a smaller governmental bureaucracy and tougher laws regulating immigration. On two separate occasions, in 1973 and 1977, the party managed to win the second highest number of votes after the Social Democrats, but since then the FP has seen its levels of popular support fall behind many of the other right-of-center parties. In 1995 more conservative members of the FP split from the party and formed the **Danish People's Party (DFp)**. The Danish People's Party adopted a platform staunchly opposing immigration, increases in taxes, and what the party sees as European rapprochement. This split took further votes away from the FP.

The **Christian People's Party (KrF)** was formed in 1970 in response to what some conservatives saw as a decline in the morals of Danish society, the specific proof of which, they argued, was the liberalization of abortion and pornography laws. The party received support mainly from members of religious groups but lost strength as the issues on which it was founded became less relevant.

Other smaller parties in Denmark include the anti-EU **Justice Party (JP)**, which was founded as the **Single-Tax Party** in 1919. The party was at its strongest during the late 1940s and 1950s but since only has managed to win representation in three elections.

RECENT ELECTIONS

The 1981 election campaign centered on the economy and in particular the high unemployment rate and the increasing budget deficit. In response, the Liberals and Conservatives came up with a joint plan to reduce state budget expenditures by cutting social spending. This was met with resistance by the left-of-center parties. The turnout, which was 82.7 percent, was the lowest reached since 1953. The most impressive gains were made by the smaller Center Democrats, who more than doubled their representation in parliament from six to fifteen seats, and the Socialist People's Party, which saw an increase from eleven to twenty seats. In large part, these increases came at the expense of the Social Democrats, who lost nine seats after recording three consecutive election increases following their worst post–World War II showing in 1973. Of the center and center-right parties, only the Conservatives were able to increase their share of seats while all others suffered moderate losses. The Progress Party's drop was in part due to the failure of the appeal launched by the party's leader against the jail sentence imposed on him for tax invasion.

In the 1994 election campaign the high unemployment rate and future of the welfare state were the major issues. The Liberal Party campaigned on a platform promising greater restrictions on public spending and lower taxes. The results were a major success for the Liberals who increased their share of seats from twenty-nine to forty-two. The Radical Liberals increased their share of seats by one, and the Red Green Unity List won six seats after a disappointing showing in their first election in 1990 in which they failed to win a single seat. Every other party, including the four that had participated in the previous government, lost support both in terms of votes and seats.

During the 1998 election campaign issues such as immigration, tax cuts, welfare spending, and the economy as a whole were the main source of debate. The Social Democrats and their allies the Radical Party, campaigned in defense of the record of their government, highlighting the fact that the rate of unemployment had dropped and the economy was generally much improved. The center-right parties spent much of the campaign fighting among themselves as tensions arose between the more moderate and extreme parties. For the two main parties, the Social Democrats and Liberals, the results were virtually the same as in the previous election. The big changes occurred among the center-right parties. The more moderate Conservatives and Progress Party suffered significant drops in support largely due to the emergence of the far-right Danish People's Party and the resurgence of the Christian People's Party, which recovered from its poor showing in 1994.

Selected Elections in Denmark

	1947		**1960**		**1966**		**1968**	
	%V	**#S**	**%V**	**#S**	**%V**	**#S**	**%V**	**#S**
SD	40.6	57	42.1	76	38.2	69	34.2	62
V	28.0	49	21.1	38	19.3	35	18.5	34
KF	12.6	17	17.9	32	18.7	34	20.4	37
RV	7.0	10	5.8	11	7.3	13	15.0	27
VS	—	—	—	—	—	—	2.0	4
DKP	6.8	9	1.1	0	0.7	0	1.1	0
Single-Tax	4.6	6	2.2	0	0.7	0	0.7	0
SF	—	—	6.1	11	10.9	20	6.1	11
others	0.4	0	3.7	7	4.2	4	2.0	0
TOTAL SEATS		148		175		175		175

	1973		1981		1994		1998	
	%V	#S	%V	#S	%V	#S	%V	#S
SD	25.6	46	32.9	59	34.6	62	35.9	63
V	12.3	22	11.3	21	23.3	42	24.0	42
KF	9.2	16	14.5	26	15.0	27	8.9	16
FP	15.9	28	8.9	16	6.4	11	2.4	4
DFp	—	—	—	—	—	—	7.4	13
RV	11.2	20	5.1	9	4.6	8	3.8	7
KrF	4.0	7	2.3	4	1.8	0	2.5	4
Red-Greens	—	—	—	—	3.1	6	2.7	5
VS	1.5	0	2.7	5	—	—	—	—
DKP	3.6	6	1.1	0	—	—	—	—
Single-Tax	2.9	5	1.4	0	—	—	—	—
SF	6.0	11	11.3	20	7.3	13	7.6	13
CD	7.8	13	8.3	15	2.8	5	4.3	8
others	0.0	1	0.2	0	1.0	1	0.5	0
TOTAL SEATS		175		175		175		175

GOVERNMENTS

Danish governments have tended to be led by the Social Democrats, either as a minority or in coalition with smaller centrist parties. Only from 1966 to 1968 was there a clearly leftist government, in the sense of relying for support on the SF. However, Social Democratic control has not been as complete as in Norway and Sweden, and from 1982 to the start of 1993 the Social Democrats were excluded from office.

Danish Governments since 1945

In Office Date(M/Y)	Prime Minister (Party)	#M(I)	Parties in Cabinet	Supporting Parties
11/45	Kristensen, K. (V)	15(1)	V	RV
11/47	Hedtoft, H. (SD)	16(1)	SD	RV
09/50	Hedtoft, H. (SD)	15(1)	SD	
10/50	Eriksen, E. (V)	15	KF	V
05/53	Eriksen, E. (V)	15	KF	V
09/53	Hedtoft, H. (SD)	16	SD	
02/55	Hansen, H. C. (SD)	16	SD	RV
05/57	Hansen, H. C. (SD)	20	SD	RV JP
02/60	Kampmann, V. (SD)	20	SD	RV JP
11/60	Kampmann, V. (SD)	17	SD	RV
09/62	Krag, J. 0. (SD)	17	SD	RV
09/64	Krag, J. O. (SD)	17	SD	RV SF
11/66	Krag, J. O. (SD)	21	SD	SF
02/68	Baunsgaard, H. (RV)	20	KF RV V	
10/71	Krag, J. O. (SD)	21(1)	SD	
10/72	Jørgensen, A. (SD)	21(1)	SD	
12/73	Hartling, P. (V)	18	V	
02/75	Jørgensen, A. (SD)	20	SD	RV SF DKP
02/77	Jørgensen, A. (SD)	20	SD	
08/78	Jørgensen, A. (SD)	22	SD V	
10/79	Jørgensen, A. (SD)	20	SD	
12/81	Jørgensen, A. (SD)	20	SD	
09/82	Schlüter, P. (KF)	23	V KF CD KrF	
01/84	Schlüter, P. (KF)	23	V KF CD KrF	
09/87	Schlüter, P. (KF)	23	KF V CD KrF	
06/88	Schlüter, P. (KF)	22	KF V RV	
12/89	Schlüter, P. (KF)	21	KF V	

In Office Date(M/Y)	Prime Minister (Party)	#M(I)	Parties in Cabinet	Supporting Parties
12/90	Schlüter, P. (KF)	19	KF V	
01/93	Rasmussen, P. N. (SD)	24	SD CD RV KrF	
09/94	Rasmussen, P. N. (SD)	20	SD RV CD	
12/96	Rasmussen, P. N. (SD)	20	SD RV	
03/98	Rasmussen, P. N. (SD)	21	SD RV	

ACRONYMS

CD	Center Democrats
DFp	Danish People's Party
DKP	Communist Party of Denmark
FP	Progress Party
JP	Justice Party
KF	Conservative People's Party
KrF	Christian People's Party
RV	Radical Liberal Party
SD	Social Democrats
SF	Socialist People's Party
V	Liberal Party
VS	Left Socialist Party

REFERENCE

Miller, Kenneth E. (1991). *Denmark: A Troubled Welfare State.* Boulder, Colo.: Westview Press.

Estonia

SUMMARY OF PARTY SYSTEMS

1992	extreme multiparty system with one dominant party (RKI)
1995	extreme multiparty system with one dominant party (KMÜ/EK)
(1999–)	extreme multiparty system with a balance among the parties

HISTORY

In late medieval period Estonia was ruled by Livonian Knights. From the fifteenth century to 1700 the country was ruled by Sweden until the Swedes were defeated by Peter the Great. Estonia was under Russian rule until 1917 when Estonia was granted local autonomy, but it was then occupied by Germany in 1918. The country was granted sovereign status in the Treaty of Versailles in 1919. From 1921 to 1934 the country was democratic. In 1940 Estonia came under Soviet rule. From 1941 to 1945 it was temporarily under German occupation once again. In 1989 the Estonian Supreme Soviet unilaterally annulled the 1940 annexation by the Soviet Union, and in 1990 it abolished provisions in the constitution that gave a "leading role" to the Communist Party. In August 1991 Estonia made a declaration of independence that was accepted by the USSR in September of that same year.

ELECTORAL SYSTEM

Estonia uses direct party-list voting with proportional distribution of seats in three rounds of counting according to a simple electoral quotient, the distribution of leftover "compensation mandates" taking place on the basis of a modified d'Hondt method. Mandates not assigned at the district level are distributed as national "compensation mandates" on the basis of a modified d'Hondt method among those parties and electoral coalitions whose candidates obtained at least 5 percent of the national vote. Vacancies that occur between general elections are filled by candidates who are "next in line" on the list of the party or electoral coalition that formerly held the seat. They are also known as "substitute members."

POLITICAL PARTIES AND CLEAVAGES

The political parties of Estonia can be divided along rural/urban lines as well as according to how anti-Communist they are. There are also some parties that support national minorities—most particularly the Russian minority. Overall, then, the standard left-right ideological divide has not always been that applicable in Estonian party politics. Electoral coalitions were the norm in the first two elections, but these have largely transformed themselves into cohesive parties.

One of Estonia's oldest parties is the **Estonian National Independence Party (ERSP)**, which was officially (but still illegally) formed in 1988. At the time it was the only non-Communist party in the entire USSR. The party declined to participate in the 1990 elections to the Estonian Supreme Soviet but was nevertheless given a position in the body that drafted Estonia's new constitution. In the 1992 elections the party campaigned on its own and won enough seats to enable it to become a partner in the first postindependence government. Following the elections the party was given the opportunity to join forces more officially with the **Pro Patria** group, but declined. The party then suffered from infighting and the formation of splinter parties. For the 1995 elections, the ERSP did join with Pro Patria in an electoral alliance. Then in December of that same year the ERSP and Pro Patria officially merged to form the Fatherland Union (Isamaalitt), which has however come to be known as the **Pro Patria Union**.

Pro Patria itself is also know by its Estonian name of ***Isamaa***. In 1992 the party was known as the **Pro-Fatherland Nation Coalition (RKI)**, which was an electoral alliance of five smaller parties, including two Christian parties formed in 1989, a small conservative party, a liberal-democratic party, and a republican party, which had all formed in 1990. The alliance was a right-center grouping that advocated a complete break with the communist era. This grouping was formed into a unified party following the 1992 elections. Like the ERSP, Pro Patria suffered from defections and the formation of splinter parties—including the departure of some of its original constituent elements.

The second of the three major Estonian political groupings is the **Moderates**, which was formed in 1990 as an electoral coalition of three smaller parties. The first of these was the **Estonian Social Democratic Party (ESDP)**, which was itself formed in 1990 as a fusion of several smaller social-democratic parties and groupings. The second component was the **Estonian Rural Center Party (EMKE)**, which was founded in 1990 originally to bring about the restoration of private ownership and private farms. It differs from Estonian's other rural parties in that it gives full backing to pro-market reform policies. The last member of the Moderates is the **Farmer's Assembly (PK)**. The PK, another rural party, had contested the 1995 elections in alliance with the EME (a member of the KMÜ coalition) but then withdrew from the government in 1996 to join up again with the Moderates.

The third key bloc in Estonia has been the **Estonian Coalition Party (EK)**, which was set up as a single party prior to the 1999 elections to unite most of the **Coalition and Rural People's Union (KMÜ)** alliance. The KMÜ itself was created for the 1995 elections and campaigned on a platform of agricultural subsidies and increased social expenditure. Included in the KMÜ was an antecedent **Coalition Party**, the **Estonian Rural Union (EM)**, the **Estonian Pensioners' and Families' League (EPPL)**, and the **Estonian Rural People's Party (EME)**. The Coalition Party was founded in 1991 by former managers of small- and medium-size state enterprises and therefore contained many former members of the Communist Party. The EM, also founded in 1991, dates back to a 1989 grouping that was closely allied with the rural wing of the Communist Party. The EPPL represented the pensioners and invalids of Estonia. The Coalition Party, EM, and EPPL—that is, the bulk of the KMÜ—contested the 1992 elections under the **Safe Home** rubric. The one component part of the KMÜ that did not join the EK is the EME; this was founded in 1994 and, for a time, helped rally agrarian support to the KMÜ. The KMÜ/EK is broadly conservative in orientation and still contains many former members of the Communist Party.

Apart from these main blocs there exist some important individual parties. The **Reform Party (ER)** was founded in 1994 as a self-described "liberal-rightist" party. The party includes a breakaway faction of the RKI, which withdrew from the Pro Patria–led coalition government to protest the leadership style of the prime minister.

The **Estonian Center Party (EKe)** (also known as the **People's Center Party [RKe]**) was formed as an offshoot of the Popular Front movement. The **Popular Front** was formed in 1988 and called for all

Soviet republics to receive recognition as sovereign states. The movement advocated cooperation with the Estonian Communist Party in order to accomplish its objectives, which included improved health care, restrictions on further immigration of non-Estonians into Estonia, and a nuclear-free Baltic region. The movement fragmented following independence and what was left had a disappointing result in the 1992 elections. A year later the Popular Front was formally dissolved. The EKe absorbed the smaller **Estonian Entrepreneurs' Party (EEE)** prior to the 1995 elections.

The Russian minority in Estonia is represented by thc **United People's Party (EUR)**. The EUR was formed as a single party from the **Our-Home-Is-Estonia** bloc of smaller ethnic Russian parties that had been founded for the 1995 elections. The United People's Party, not surprisingly, strongly opposes Estonia's citizenship laws, which have made it very difficult for nonethnic Estonians to vote.

Two parties that won several seats in the 1992 elections but then withered were the **Independent Royalist Party** and the **Estonian Citizens Party (ETE)**. So, too, did the Green Party, which won one seat in 1992. The Greens would merge into the EKe in 1998.

The **Republican and Conservative People's Party (VKR)** (or "Right-Wingers" as they liked to be called in English) was formed in 1994 by the merger of smaller rightist and conservative parties that had earlier split from the RKI. It did not contest the 1999 elections.

ELECTIONS

The 1992 elections were the first after independence in 1991. The key election issue was how to continue with the democratization and reconstruction of a postindependence Estonia. The anti-Communist parties did well given the popular desire to break with the past. The RKI, ERSP, and Moderates all campaigned on a similar platform of rapid political and economic reform.

As is true most everywhere, noncitizens of Estonia were unable to vote; however, this included almost all of the large ethnic Russian population, which makes up more than 30 percent of the Estonian population. At the time, citizens were defined as the people, or the direct descendants of people, who held Estonian citizenship in the Estonian Republic prior to 1940.

The elections of 5 March 1995, in fact, saw turnout go up slightly to 69.6 percent of the registered voters. In competition were 1,256 candidates (including twelve independents). Of the thirty parties that competed in the elections, only nine competed on their own while the rest were grouped into seven coalitions. The main campaign issue was the state of the national economy and the concern over the pace of privatization. Other issues included the agrarian policy of the previous government, the powers of the president, and aspects of Estonia's foreign policy. The KMÜ, relying on rural support, won the plurality of seats, campaigning on the ambiguous message of continued pro-market reform and increased protectionism and social benefits. The ER benefited from urban support and the largest amount of campaign funds to spend, while the EKe stressed the plight of pensioners and renters in the face of privatization. With the size of the Russian electorate increasing from 50,000 in 1992 to 150,000 in 1995 the Our-Home-Is-Estonia bloc of ethnic Russian parties was able to win six seats. The ERSP–Pro Patria bloc dropped nearly 23 percent in support due to their experience in the first postindependence government.

Going into the 1999 elections, the KMÜ/EK minority government was plagued by infighting, and support for it collapsed. The EKe (the Center Party) gained in strength to become the largest party. Nevertheless, what was new in these elections was that a bloc of (other) opposition parties chose to unite *before* the elections. Specifically, the ER (Reform Party), the Pro Patria Union, and the Moderates were united in promising faster reforms. Even though the ER vote stagnated, both the Pro Patria Union and the Moderates gained sharply (although Pro Patria still remained well below its 1992 level). These three parties thus were able to get a narrow but absolute majority of seats between them, and quickly formed a coalition.

Estonian Elections

	1992			1995		1999	
	%V	#S		%V	#S	%V	#S
RKI	22.0	29	}				
ERSP	8.8	10	}				
Pro Patria Union	—	—	}	7.9	8	16.1	18
Safe Home	13.6	17					
→ KMÜ/EK	—	—		32.2	41	7.6	7
ER	—	—		16.2	19	15.9	18
Popular Front	12.3	15	}				
EEE	2.4	1	}				

	1992		1995		1999	
	%V	#S	%V	#S	%V	#S
→ EKe			14.2	16	23.4	28
Moderates	9.7	12	6.0	6	15.2	17
Royalists	7.1	8	—	—	—	—
ETE	6.9	8	—	—	—	—
Greens	2.6	1	?	0	(into EKe)	
EUR	—	—	5.9	6	6.1	6
VKR	—	—	5.0	5	—	—
EME			(part of KMÜ)		7.3	7
others	6.4	0	12.6	0	10.5	0
TOTAL SEATS		101		101		101

GOVERNMENTS

The first postcommunist government, that of Pro Patria and ERSP, did not complete its term due to internal splits. From 1995 to 1999, the new dominant party, the KMÜ/EK, did better, remaining in office continuously; however from the end of 1996 onward it could not find any more formal coalition partners. After 1999 Pro Patria returned to government and likewise its leader Mart Laar returned to the Prime Minister's Office.

Estonian Governments since 1992

In Office Date(M/Y)	Prime Minister (Party)	#M(I)	Parties in Cabinet
10/92	Laar, M. (Pro Patria)	15	Pro Patria ERSP
11/94	Tarand, A. (Moderates)	15	(caretaker government)
04/95	Vähi, T. (KMÜ)	14	KMÜ EKe
11/95	Vähi, T. (KMÜ)	15	KMÜ ER
12/96	Vähi, T. (KMÜ)	15(3)	KMÜ
03/97	Siimann, M. (KMÜ)	14(2)	KMÜ
	government supported by EME from 04/98 to 10/98		
03/99	Laar, M. (Pro Patria)	15	Pro Patria ER Moderates

ACRONYMS

EEE	Estonian Entrepreneurs' Party
EK	Estonian Coalition Party
EKe	Estonian Center
EM	Estonian Rural Union
EME	Estonian Rural People's Party
EMKE	Estonian Rural Center Party
EPPL	Estonian Pensioners' and Families' League
ER	Estonian Reform Party
ERSP	Estonian National Independence Party
ESDP	Estonian Social Democratic Party
ETE	Estonian Citizens Party
EUR	United People's Party
KMÜ	Coalition and Rural Union
RKI	Pro-fatherland National Coalition
VKR	Republican and Conservative People's Party

REFERENCES

Arter, David. (1996). *Parties and Democracy in the Post-Soviet Republics: The Case of Estonia.* Aldershot, England: Dartmouth.

Taagepera, Rein. (1995). "Estonian Parliamentary Elections, March 1995." *Electoral Studies,* Vol. 14, pp. 328–31.

Finland

SUMMARY OF PARTY SYSTEM

1945–(99)	extreme multiparty system with a balance among the parties

HISTORY

Finland was a province of Sweden until 1809, and to this day there are Swedish speakers on its western and southern coasts, and in the Åland Islands. From 1809 to 1917 Finland was a usually autonomous Grand Duchy of Russia. In 1906 universal suffrage (for both sexes) was introduced, and Finland thus became the first European country to enfranchise women. With universal suffrage, the number of parties sharply expanded. Independence from Imperial Russia was followed quickly by a civil war between "Reds" and "Whites," with the latter being victorious. The new constitution of 1919 established a republic, and also a semipresidential system in which the president had a key role in government formation (and, during the Cold War, in foreign policy as well). Political tensions in the interwar period led to right-radical attempts to overthrow the regime; democracy did survive, however the Communists were banned from 1930 to 1945. In the decades after World War II, Finnish foreign policy was constrained by the presence of the Soviet Union.

ELECTORAL SYSTEM

Finland uses a straightforward system of proportional representation in fourteen multimember districts to elect all but one of its two-hundred-member parliament *(Eduskunta),* with calculations using the d'Hondt method. The remaining seat is the constituency of the Swedish-speaking Åland Islands, which uses single member plurality.

POLITICAL PARTIES AND CLEAVAGES

In recent decades the traditional "socialist" and "nonsocialist" ideological division in Finland has lost relevance as parties have more frequently reached across the traditional left-right spectrum to form coalitions. The urban/rural cleavage is still relevant, however.

The **Finnish Social Democratic Party (SSDP)** was originally formed as the Workers' Party in 1899 and adopted its present name in 1903. Early on, the party was divided between more radical and reform-minded members. In 1918 the radical element within the party left to form the Finnish Communist Party. Divisions within the party did not vanish after this schism, however, and in the 1950s further splits resulted in the creation of smaller breakaway parties. Today the SSDP is a predominantly left-of-center party committed to traditional social-democratic ideals such as maintaining the welfare state and increasing employee rights. The party has, however, displayed a measure of pragmatism, arguing for a continued but not all-powerful role for government in the national economy and an economy that should largely develop according to market forces. The party is more heavily supported in southern urban areas as opposed to rural areas. Unlike Scandinavian social-democratic parties, the SSDP is overwhelming pro-EU.

The more hard-line socialists in Finland have formed several parties and electoral coalitions over the years. The most recent creation is the ardently anti-EU **Left-Wing Alliance (Vas or VL)**. The VL was formed in 1990 as a coalition of left-Socialist and Communist groups and political parties, the most prominent of which was the **Finnish Communist Party (SKP)**. The SKP, which was formed by hard-line Social Democrats in 1918 never competed in elections as the Communist Party, and instead, once it became legal in 1944, created the **Finnish People's Democratic League (SKDL)** under whose banner Communist candidates would run. The SKDL, which was supported by the industrial working class in the south and some disadvantaged groups in rural areas, argued for a "Finnish road to democratic socialism," which advocated the nationalization of some industry but not an orthodox communist platform. As a result, the party was not considered radical enough for some socialists and was in turn weakened by hard-line defections and the creation of breakaway parties such as the **Communist Workers' Party (KTP)** and the **Communist Party of Finland–Unity (SKP-Y)**, which together contested the 1987 elections, as the **Democratic Alternative (Deva)**.

The Communists have seen their electoral performance rise and fall. The party even challenged the SSDP for preeminent status on the left in the early postwar elections but lost strength through the 1970s to defections and the creation of smaller parties. The low reached in 1987, when the party polled less than 10 percent, was the worst showing ever for the Communists and was due in large part to the creation of the Democratic Alternative.

The nonsocialist side of Finland's political spectrum is as crowded with parties as the left, but it is slightly less confused. The **National Coalition Party (Kok)** is one of the largest parties on the center right. The party came into being in 1918 when several smaller monarchist forces consolidated into one party. While the party has at times throughout its history been associated with more hard-right attitudes the party today is very much a moderate party. Despite advocating some traditional free enterprise and liberal economic policies such as tax reform in favor of a VAT and smaller bureaucracy, the party maintains a commitment to the concept of a social market economy.

The **Finnish Christian Union (SKL)** was founded in 1958 and is a party committed to advocating Christian ideals and supporting conservative and agrarian interests. The party was against EU membership and this position resulted in its withdrawal from the government coalition in 1994.

The **Finnish Rural Party (SMP)** was founded by ex-members of the Agrarian Union, who split from that party in the late 1950s. It achieved a major breakthrough in the 1970 elections. The party appeals to what it has called "forgotten Finland," or the periphery of society who do not enjoy effective representation in Finnish politics. The party has enjoyed support as a protest party but nevertheless has participated in governments. The party suffered from its own split in 1972 when members left it to form the **Finnish People's Unity Party**. The SMP was against Finland's membership in the EU. After the 1995 elections, they renamed themselves the **True Finns (PS)**.

The **Finnish Center (Kesk)** was originally formed as the **Agrarian Union (AF)** in 1906, was renamed the **Center Party (KP)** in 1965, and adopted its current name in 1988 when it absorbed the smaller **Liberal People's Party (LKP)**. Despite the name changes, which were an attempt to broaden the party's appeal, Kesk still relies most heavily on support from Finland's rural population. The party has attempted to present itself as a party without a strong ideology and has actively criticized both communism and capitalism. This stance has in part been adopted in order to make the party more attractive to potential coalition partners. In early elections the Agrarian Union was the largest party on the center-right but this position was claimed through the 1970s and 1980s by the National Coalition Party. This relative decline was in large part a function of the Rural Party, which during this period won close to 10 percent in three elections, taking support directly from the Agrarians. However, with the absorption of the smaller Liberal People's Party and another name change, Kesk has been able to reestablish itself in the position of preeminence on the center right.

The LKP was created in 1965 when its forerunner, the **Finnish People's Party**, which was founded in 1954, merged with the smaller **Liberal Union**, which was founded in 1951. In an effort to avoid becoming a nonentity in Finnish politics, the party agreed to cooperate with the KP in 1982, while maintaining a separate identity. Six years later the party gave up that identity when it was completely absorbed into Kesk.

The Swedish speakers of Finland also have political representation through the **Swedish People's Party of Finland (SFP)**, which was formed in 1906. The main purpose of the party has been to protect the rights of the Swedish-speaking community in the country. Because of the party's nonideological raison d'être the party has advocated a wide range of economic and social policies.

The main Green Party in Finland is the **Green Union (VL)**, which was formed as an alliance of several environmental organizations. They were first elected to parliament in 1983, the first such electoral success in the Nordic region. Since 1991 they have been the largest of the smaller parties in Finland.

RECENT ELECTIONS

Despite the participation of many parties in Finnish elections in the post–World War II period, four parties have traditionally garnered the overwhelming majority of votes; these are the SSDP, Kok, SKDL (later

Vas), and Kesk (under its many incarnations). Of these, the SSDP has been the strongest, winning the plurality of votes in every election save 1991. Due to the highly fractured nature of the party system, however, this electoral success has not always translated into success in forming the government.

The election held in 1987 was an important one because it could be seen as a sign of the decreasing importance of the nonsocialist/socialist cleavage in Finnish politics. In this election, parties avoided taking strong ideological positions in order to keep coalition options open, and for the first time ever, the SSDP did not rule out potential coalitions with the center-right parties.

The 1991 election was significant not only because it featured the newly created Left-Wing Alliance and the renamed Finnish Center, which for the first time won more seats than the SSDP, but also because it marked the height in success of the nontraditional Finnish parties. In total, twenty-six seats went to parties such as the Greens, Rural Party, and Christian Union. The campaign was described by some as low key due largely to events elsewhere in the world, namely in the Baltic States and Persian Gulf, and also because parties did not want to attack others in fear of alienating potential coalition partners.

The elections held in 1995 came at the end of Finland's 1990-93 recession, one of the worst ever experienced by a western industrialized economy since 1945. The SSDP—campaigning on a platform pledging interventionist measures to bring down the unemployment rate, which stood at 20 percent—was able to regain its position of dominance, winning the most amount of seats and votes by any party in the post–World War II period. The elections were a major rebuke for the center right, which had primarily formed the previous government, with both Kesk and Kok dropping below the 20 percent mark. Also, the SMP lost all but one of its seats in parliament.

In contrast, the elections of 1999 were held against the backdrop of rapid economic improvement but also government cutbacks. These cutbacks, along with a favoritism scandal, hurt the SSDP, which barely held on to remain the largest party. The Kok was the big winner, in part due to a modern, pro-European image.

Selected Elections in Finland

	1945		1954		1970		1979	
	%V	#S	%V	#S	%V	#S	%V	#S
SSDP	25.1	50	26.2	54	23.4	51	23.9	52
SFP	8.4	15	7.0	13	5.7	12	4.6	10
AF/Kesk*	21.4	49	24.1	53	17.1	37	17.3	36
Kok	15.0	28	12.8	24	18.0	37	21.7	47
SKDL	23.5	49	21.6	43	16.6	36	17.9	35
LKP	—	—	7.9	13	5.9	8	3.7	4
SKL	—	—	—	—	1.1	1	4.8	9
SMP	—	—	—	—	10.5	18	4.6	7
others	6.7	9	0.4	0	1.6	0	1.7	0
TOTAL SEATS		200		200		200		200

*Kesk competed as the Agrarian Union (AF) through the 1962 elections, then as the Center Party (KP) up to and including the 1987 elections, then as simply the Finnish Center.

	1987		1991		1995		1999	
	%V	#S	%V	#S	%V	#S	%V	#S
SSDP	24.1	56	22.1	48	28.3	63	22.9	51
SFP	5.6	13	5.5	12	5.1	12	5.1	11
Kesk*	17.6	40	24.8	55	19.9	44	22.4	48
Kok	23.1	53	19.3	40	17.9	39	21.0	46
SKDL	9.4	16	—		—	—	—	—
Vas	—	—	10.1	19	11.2	22	10.9	20
LKP	1.0	0	—	—	—	—	—	—
SKL	2.6	5	3.1	8	3.0	7	4.2	10
SMP/PS	6.3	9	4.8	7	1.3	1	1.0	1
VL	4.0	4	6.8	10	6.5	9	7.3	11
Deva	4.2	4	—	—	—	—	—	—
others	1.9	0	3.5	1	7.8	3	5.2	2
TOTAL SEATS		200		200		200		200

GOVERNMENTS

Governments in postwar Finland have normally been broad multiparty affairs, although caretaker governments also occurred fairly frequently through the 1970s. As well, through the 1970s, Finnish governments tended to be short-lived. Since 1983, however, governments have tended to last longer. The government formed in 1995 and reformed in 1999 ranges from post-communists and Greens through to conservatives.

Finnish Governments since 1945

In office Date (M/Y)	Prime Minister (Party)	#M(I)	Parties in Cabinet
04/45	Paasikivi, J. K. (Ind)	18(4)	SSDP SKDL AF PP SFP
07/45	Paasikivi, J. K. (Ind)	18(2)	SSDP SKDL AF SFP
03/46	Pekkala, M. (SKDL)	18(1)	SKDL SSDP AF SFP
07/48	Fagerholm, K. (SSDP)	17(1)	SSDP
03/50	Kekkonen, U. (AF)	15	AF SFP PP
01/51	Kekkonen, U. (AF)	17(1)	AF SSDP PP SFP
09/51	Kekkonen, U. (AF)	17(1)	AF SSDP SFP
07/53	Kekkonen, U. (AF)	14(3)	AF SFP
11/53	Tuomija, S. (Ind)	15(6)	caretaker government
05/54	Törngren, R. (SFP)	14(1)	AF SSDP SFP
10/54	Kekkonen, U. (AF)	14(1)	SSDP AF
03/56	Fagerholm, K. (SSDP)	15(1)	SSDP AF PP SFP
05/57	Sukselainen, V. J. (AF)	14(1)	AF PP SFP
07/57	Sukselainen, V. J. (AF)	13(1)	AF PP
09/57	Sukselainen, V. J. (AF)	16(2)	AF SDL PP
11/57	von Fieandt, R. (Ind)	14(5)	caretaker government
04/58	Kuuskoski, R. (AF)	14(4)	caretaker government
08/58	Fagerholm, K. (SSDP)	15	SSDP AF Kok PP SFP
01/59	Sukselainen, V. J. (AF)	15(1)	AF
07/61	Miettunen, M. (AF)	15(1)	AF
04/62	Karjalainen, A. (AF)	15(3)	AF Kok PP SFP

continued

Finnish Governments since 1945 *Continued*

In office Date (M/Y)	Prime Minister (Party)	#M(I)	Parties in Cabinet
11/63	Karjalainen, A. (AF)	15(1)	AF Kok PP SFP
12/63	Lehto, R.R. (Ind)	(15)	nonparty government
09/64	Virolainen, J. (AF)	15(1)	AF Kok PP SFP
05/66	Paasio, R. (SSDP)	15	SSDP KP SKDL SDL
03/68	Koivisto, M. (SSDP)	16	SSDP KP SKDL SDL SFP
05/70	Aura, T. (LKP)	13(3)	caretaker government
07/70	Karjalainen, A. (KP)	17(1)	SSDP KP SKDL PP SFP
03/71	Karjalainen, A. (KP)	17(1)	SSDP KP PP SFP
10/71	Aura, T. (LKP)	15(5)	caretaker government
02/72	Paasio, R. (SSDP)	17	SSDP
09/72	Sorsa, K. (SSDP)	16(1)	SSDP KP SFP PP
06/75	Liinamaa, K. (SSDP)	17(6)	caretaker government
11/75	Miettunen, M. (KP)	18(2)	SSDP KP SKDL SFP PP
09/76	Miettunen, M. (KP)	16(1)	KP PP SFP
05/77	Sorsa, K. (SSDP)	15(1)	KP SSDP SKDL PP SFP
03/78	Sorsa, K. (SSDP)	15(1)	KP SSDP SKDL PP
05/79	Koivisto, M. (SSDP)	17(1)	KP SSDP SKDL SFP
02/82	Sorsa, K. (SSDP)	17(1)	KP SSDP SKDL SFP
12/82	Sorsa, K. (SSDP)	17(1)	SSDP KP SFP
05/83	Sorsa, K. (SSDP)	17	SSDP KP SFP SMP
04/87	Holkeri, H. (Kok)	18	SSDP Kok SFP SMP
09/90	Holkeri, H. (Kok)	17	SSDP Kok SFP
04/91	Aho, E. (KP)	17	KP Kok SFP SKL
04/95	Lipponen, P. (SSDP)	16(1)	SSDP Kok SFP VL Vas
04/99	Lipponen, P. (SSDP)	17	SSDP Kok SFP VL Vas

ACRONYMS

AF	Agrarian Union
Deva	Democratic Alternative
Kesk	Center
Kok	National Coalition Party
KP	Center Party
LKP	Liberal People's Party
PS	True Finns
SFP	Swedish People's Party of Finland
SKDL	Finnish People's Democratic League
SKL	Finnish Christian Union
SKP	Finnish Communist Party
SMP	Finnish Rural Party
SSDP	Finnish Social Democratic Party
Vas	Left-Wing Alliance
VL	Green Union

Note: all acronyms are from the Finnish except for the SFP, where the Swedish acronym is the standard.

REFERENCES

Arter, David. (1987). *Politics and Policy-Making in Finland.* New York: St. Martin's Press.

Sundberg, Jan. (1994). "Finland: Nationalized Parties, Professional Organizations," pp. 158–84, in Richard S. Katz and Peter Mair, eds. *How Parties Organize: Change and Adaption in Party Organization in Western Democracies.* London: SAGE.

France

GENERAL HISTORY

Long a united polity, France was Europe's major power in the seventeenth and eighteen centuries. The French Revolution of 1789 created a contested legacy, in that various claimants to the throne had definite support even into the twentieth century. Since 1789, France has had no less than twelve political regimes, of which the Third Republic from 1875 to 1940 was the longest lasting. This analysis looks first at the Fourth Republic (1940–58) and then the Fifth Republic (since 1958).

The French Fourth Republic

SUMMARY OF PARTY SYSTEM

1945–56	extreme multiparty system with a balance among the parties

HISTORY

After liberation in 1944, General de Gaulle more or less personally ran the country until the end of the war. In an October 1945 referendum, 96 percent of the population indicated that they did not wish a simple return to the prewar Third Republic. Consequently elections were held for a constituent assembly. Its first proposal, for a unicameral parliamentary system, was narrowly rejected by the voters. A subsequent proposal, with an upper house and thus a constitution not greatly different from the Third Republic, did pass, but only by nine million votes to eight million, with a further eight million abstentions. The Fourth Republic thus hardly had the strong support of the population, or of all political elites.

ELECTORAL SYSTEM

Initially, a fairly straightforward system of proportional representation in small multimember districts was used. However, in 1951 the system was manipulated to favor the proregime parties. This manipulation involved keeping Paris (where the antiregime Gaullists and Communists were strong) proportional, but allowing parties in the rest of the country to form alliances—not necessarily the same ones—in each department. If and when any alliance collectively won over 50 percent of the vote in the department, the alliance won *all* of the seats, to be then distributed proportionally among its components.

POLITICAL PARTIES AND CLEAVAGES

French politics in the Fourth Republic was structured along two main ideological divisions—attitudes to the Fourth Republic itself, and left versus right—as well as the cleavage of religiosity. These divisions yielded six main parties, of which the first three discussed were normally larger than the rest.

The **French Communist Party (PCF)** was founded in 1920. It was opposed to the Fourth Republic (and indeed to the democratic order), extremely leftist, and secular. The PCF benefited greatly from its role in the resistance and had a certain following among intellectuals. Mainly, of course, it was the party of French workers, and thus strongest in the industrial areas of the north, the east, and the suburbs of Paris. It also had support in secular rural areas of the center and south.

The PCF had, in fact, broken away from the Socialist Party, or more precisely the **French Section of the Workers' International (SFIO)**, founded in 1905. The SFIO was also leftist and secular, but definitely pro-regime. Given the strength of the Communists, manual workers were only a minority of the Socialist electorate, and these were primarily from smaller industries. The majority of SFIO support came from secular white collar workers, especially in the public sector.

The third main party of the French Fourth Republic was a new one, the Christian democratic **Popular Republican Movement (MRP)**, founded in 1944. Like the Socialists, the MRP was very pro-regime. It was also left leaning in socioeconomic policy. On the other hand, it was clearly a religious party and was thus limited to the more religious areas of France in the east and west. Indeed, most of its voters supported it on religious grounds and did not share its progressive socioeconomic goals. As an explicitly cross-class party, it drew from a variety of economic groups.

The MRP would to some extent be the key hinge party in the Fourth Republic. In the Third Republic, however, that role had been filled very clearly by the Radicals, or more precisely the **Radical Socialist**

Republican Party (PRSR), which was founded in 1901 but whose roots went back earlier. There was actually nothing socialist about this party. It was on the center right economically, militantly secular, pro-regime, and a classic office-seeking party as opposed to an ideological one. Its support was mainly found in small towns. The Radicals were hurt after the war by their collaboration during the Nazi occupation. Moreover, women—who had received the vote in 1944—avoided the party, which perhaps "served it right" for opposing female suffrage. Consequently the Radicals were a smaller force than they had been. In the Fourth Republic the Radicals also had a junior partner in the form of the **Democratic and Socialist Union of the Resistance (UDSR)**, now known chiefly because one of its leaders (and cabinet ministers) was the future Fifth Republic president François Mitterrand.

The Fourth Republic also featured a disparate group of conservatives, or **Moderates**, who were pro-regime, right of center, and somewhat more religious than not. They thus differed from the MRP primarily on economics. Despite their generally religious nature, however, the conservatives had perhaps more in common with the Radicals, especially as the conservatives were also discredited by their collaboration. Of the Moderates, the biggest single party was the **National Center of Independents and Peasants (CNIP)**, founded in 1948.

All of the above parties or groups contested each election in the Fourth Republic. In addition, there were two ephemeral anti-system parties on the right. Of these two, the more important was the Gaullist **Rally of the French People (RPF)**. General de Gaulle had opposed the creation of the Fourth Republic, preferring instead a presidential regime. Some pro-Gaullist candidates ran, but only in 1947 did de Gaulle agree to the establishment of a national organization, the RPF. (De Gaulle always saw parties as divisive forces, and thus the RPF did not contain the word *party* but instead was more of a national movement.) The RPF did extraordinarily well in the municipal elections of 1947, but as it turned out, the 1951 national elections were the only ones de Gaulle seriously contested. The Gaullist appeal was based on nationalism and institutional change, and was thus catchall in nature. Nevertheless, the RPF electorate was basically religious, and its voters came largely from the MRP.

Finally, in the 1956 elections there was a flash far-right anti-system protest party called the **Poujadists** after its leader Pierre Poujade. The party was anti-establishment and anti-Semitic and appealed to small shopkeepers and others hurt by economic modernization.

Elections in the French Fourth Republic

	1945		June 1946		November 1946		1951		1956	
	%V	#S	%V	#S	%V	#S	#V	#S	%V	#S
Radicals +UDSR	11.1	35	11.5	39	12.4	55	10.0	77	15.2	73
SFIO	23.8	134	21.1	115	17.9	90	14.5	94	15.2	88
Moderates	13.3	92	12.8	62	12.8	70	14.0	87	15.3	95
PCF	26.1	148	26.2	146	28.6	166	26.7	97	25.9	147
MRP	24.9	141	28.1	160	26.3	158	12.5	82	11.1	71
RPF	—	—	—	—	1.6	5	21.7	107	4.0	16
Poujadists	—	—	—	—	—	—	—	—	11.7	51
others	0.9	2	0.4	0	0.3	0	0.7	0	1.7	3
TOTAL SEATS		552		522		544		544		544

Note: The 1945 elections were for a constituent assembly.

GOVERNMENTS

Governments in the Fourth Republic were notoriously unstable. From 1947, when the Communists were expelled from the government, until 1958, when de Gaulle returned to power, the pro-regime parties monopolized the cabinet table, but also used it to play an ongoing game of "musical chairs."

French Fourth Republic Governments, 1946–1958

In Office Date(M/Y)	Prime Minister (Party)	#M(I)	Parties in Cabinet
01/46	Gouin, F. (SFIO)	20(1)	SFIO MRP PCF
06/46	Bidault, G. (MRP)	23(1)	MRP SFIO PCF PRSR
12/46	Blum, L. (SFIO)	17	SFIO
01/47	Ramadier, P. (SFIO)	26	SFIO MRP PCF PRSR Cons

continued

French Fourth Republic Governments, 1946–1958 *Continued*

In Office Date(M/Y)	Prime Minister (Party)	#M(I)	Parties in Cabinet
05/47	Ramadier, P. (SFIO)	24	SFIO MRP PRSR Cons
10/47	Ramadier, P. (SFIO)	12	SFIO MRP PRSR Cons
11/47	Schuman, R. (MRP)	15	MRP SFIO PRSR UDSR Cons
07/48	Marie, A. (MRP)	19	MRP SFIO PRSR Cons
09/48	Schuman, R. (MRP)	15	MRP PRSR SFIO Cons
09/48	Queuille, H. (PRSR)	15	MRP SFIO PRSR UDSR Cons
10/49	Bidault, G. (MRP)	18	MRP SFIO PRSR UDSR Cons
02/50	Bidault, G. (MRP)	17	MRP PRSR Cons UDSR
07/50	Queuille, H. (PRSR)	21	MRP PRSR Cons UDSR
07/50	Pleven, R. (UDSR)	22	MRP PRSR SFIO Cons UDSR
03/51	Queuille, H. (PRSR)	22	MRP SFIO PRSR UDSR Cons
08/51	Pleven, R. (UDSR)	24	PRSR Cons MRP UDSR
01/52	Faure, E. (PRSR)	26	PRSR MRP Cons UDSR
03/52	Pinay, A. (Cons)	17	Cons PRSR MRP UDSR
01/53	Mayer, R. (PRSR)	23	PRSR Cons MRP UDSR
06/53	Laniel, J. (Cons)	22	Cons MRP PRSR UDSR
06/54	Mendès-France, P. (PRSR)	16(1)	PRSR Cons RPF UDSR
02/55	Faure, E. (PRSR)	19	PRSR Cons MRP RPF
02/56	Mollet, G. (SFIO)	14(1)	SFIO PRSR UDSR
06/57	Bourgès-Maunoury, M. (PRSR)	14	PRSR SFIO UDSR
11/57	Gaillard, F. (PRSR)	17	PRSR SFIO MRP Cons RPF UDSR
05/58	Pflimlin, P. (MRP)	22	PRSR MRP SFIO Cons UDSR
06/58	DeGaulle, C. (RPF)	24(9)	RPF Cons MRP PRSR SFIO

The French Fifth Republic

SUMMARY OF PARTY SYSTEMS

1958	moderate multiparty system with two main parties (UNR and Moderates)
1962–73	extreme multiparty system with one dominant party (UNR/UDR)
1978/1986/1993	moderate multiparty system with a balance among the parties
1981/1988/1997	moderate multiparty system with one dominant party (PS)

HISTORY

The Fourth Republic ultimately proved unable to deal with the uprising in Algeria, and Charles de Gaulle used this crisis as a means to return to power. As part of his demands, a new semipresidential constitution was drawn up and overwhelmingly approved by the voters in a September 1958 referendum. Thus, in January 1959 de Gaulle became the first president of the new Fifth Republic. He was in fact chosen by an electoral college; however, a referendum in October 1962 approved the direct election of the president, the first of which occurred in 1965. The Fifth Republic president has broad powers, including the ability to dissolve the National Assembly once a year.

ELECTORAL SYSTEM

With the exception of the 1986 elections, which used proportional representation, all National Assembly elections in the Fifth Republic have used what is called the single-member majority-plurality system. Under this system, all deputies are elected in single-member constituencies. If any candidate wins an absolute majority on the first ballot, he or she is elected right away. If not, there is a second ballot held a week later, in which a candidate need only win a plurality to get elected. However, participation in this second round is limited to candidates whose first-round votes were at least 12.5 percent of the constituency's *electorate*—in practice, about 18 percent of the first-round vote. This thus eliminates all the smaller candidates. Moreover, parties that are allied tend to practice what is known as *désistement* (withdrawal), in which everyone stands down except for the highest-placed candidate on the first ballot. This avoids splitting the votes of one side, given that the second ballot is a plurality one. To some extent, then, the first ballot plays the role of a primary.

POLITICAL PARTIES AND CLEAVAGES

Presidential elections and the popularity of a given president are often crucial factors in the outcome of a given *parliamentary* election. Moreover, the electoral system has encouraged the formation of two broad groupings of the center-right and the left. Nevertheless, the party system remains multiparty, and underlying cleavages such as social class and religiosity remain.

On the center-right of the spectrum, the **Gaullists** quickly (by 1962) became the dominant party. They stressed nationalism and selective economic interventionism. Especially when de Gaulle himself was president in the 1960s, the Gaullists were a true "catchall" party, garnering a proportionate share of the working-class vote. Since the 1970s, though, the Gaullist electorate has been more clearly conservative, white collar or farmer, and/or religious. We often use the phrase "the Gaullists" to describe the party largely because they have changed their name so frequently: they were the RPF in the Fourth Republic; and in the Fifth Republic they were the **Union for the New Republic (UNR)** from 1958 to 1968, the **Union for the Defence of the Republic (UDR)** from 1968 to 1971, the **Union of Democrats for the Republic (also UDR)** from 1971 to 1976, and since 1976 they have been the **Rally for the Republic (RPR)**. These names have been constant in two ways, though: they always refer to the (Fifth) Republic, and they never contain the word *party*, which—as noted earlier—de Gaulle saw as a divisive concept.

Although initially the MRP and the traditional conservatives or Moderates carried over into the Fifth Republic, they were much weaker as the Gaullists took over many of their voters and as they were squeezed by the single-member electoral system. Moreover, most center-right voters wanted a party that supported de Gaulle, even if it was not actually the Gaullists as such. Nevertheless, those Catholic deputies who were suspicious of de Gaulle and wanted a clear centrist expression formed the **Democratic Center (CD)** in 1966, which became the **Democratic and Social Center (CDS)** in 1976, the **Union of the Center (UDC)** in 1988, and finally the **Democratic Force (FD)** in 1995. The MRP itself was dissolved in 1967. A competing pro-Gaullist centrist force, the **Center for Democracy and Progress (CDP)**, was established in 1969.

The Radical Party persisted into the 1960s, but was pulled between its right of center and more progressive tendencies. Despite differences of religiosity, the right-wing Radicals were part of the CD in 1966. Also, independent conservatives have continued to be elected to the National Assembly. The main other party on the center right, though, was the creation of the ambitious and well-groomed politician Valéry Giscard d'Estaing. Giscard had entered parliament as a member of the CNIP in the late 1950s and supported de Gaulle and his new constitution. He did not, however, want to become a Gaullist proper. Sensing the limited prospects of the CNIP, Giscard left the party with his followers in 1962 and set up the **Independent Republicans (RI)**, which became the **Republican Party (PR)** in 1977 and **Liberal Democracy (DL)** in 1997.

In the 1974 presidential elections, Giscard surpassed a weak Gaullist candidate to become the main center-right candidate and ultimately the president. Within the government side in parliament, however, the Gaullists remained strong, as Giscard's Independent Republicans were only a tiny force. In order to provide more balance, in 1978 Giscard created the **Union for French Democracy (UDF)** out of the Republicans, the CDS, and most of the Radicals. The UDF is first and foremost an electoral alliance—its component parts do not run against each other. It also has a certain ideological cohesion, in particular it has always been more pro-European than the Gaullists. However, the separate component parties remain as separate parties, with national leaders. Usually the UDF forms one bloc in the parliament, but at times specific component parties have chosen to sit separately. Finally, in terms of demographics there is very little to distinguish UDF voters from RPR (Gaullist) voters.

The RPR and the UDF work closely together, practicing mutual *désistement* and at times even having one joint candidate on the first ballot of parliamentary elections. Together they comprise the center right or the moderate right. On the far right, however, is the **National Front (FN)**, formed in 1972 by Jean-Marie Le Pen as a gathering of fascists, Poujadists, ultranationalists, xenophobes, and so on. The FN went nowhere in the 1970s, but in the 1980s it took off in the context of growing unemployment and social unrest and the weakening of the Communist Party, which it basically replaced as the party of protest. The electoral system (except for 1986) has kept the FN out of the National

Assembly, however, it increasingly has enough support to stay on for second ballots, even if it only serves the role of a "spoiler."

The left of the French party spectrum has shown much greater continuity than the right. The PCF's (Communist Party's) traditional fifth of the vote held through the 1960s and 1970s, but dropped in the 1980s as the still pro-Moscow party was seen as increasingly out of touch and limited to an aging electorate that still remembered its role in the resistance. Although in the 1990s it has (finally) become more flexible, it still retains the communist name. The SFIO carried on through the 1960s, but in 1969 François Mitterrand founded a new **Socialist Party (PS)**, which was still supported by public-sector workers but which began to make inroads (back) into the working class at the expense of the Communists. The PS soon allied itself with the **Left Radical Movement (MRG)**, founded in 1972 by the more leftist faction of the Radicals. Mitterrand, as president from 1981 to 1995, would transform the PS into the overwhelming dominant force on the left and at times the main party of government. The party was and is quite factionalized, but Mitterrand was able to keep overall discipline. A more nationalist and socialist PS factional leader, Jean-Pierre Chevènement, did quit the party in 1993 to form the left-nationalist **Citizens' Movement (MdC)**, which is skeptical of European integration, unlike the PS.

Finally, France has two Green Parties, **the Greens** who formed in 1984, and **Ecology Generation (GE)**, which formed in 1990. Personal rivalries between their respective leaders are a big part of the difference. By the late 1990s, the Greens were positioning themselves clearly on the center left and willing to work with the Socialists.

RECENT ELECTIONS

Since 1981, National Assembly elections have followed closely the situation of the presidency. Thus Mitterrand's presidential victory in 1981 was followed the next month by a Socialist majority in the Assembly. Dissatisfaction with Mitterrand and the Socialists led to the center right regaining control of the Assembly in 1986. However, Mitterrand's personal popularity rebounded and he was reelected president in 1988. Again, he dissolved parliament, and again, the left won, though this time the PS had only a plurality. In 1993 the center right would win a sweeping majority in parliament. Jacques Chirac, the RPR leader, would finally be elected president in 1995. In 1997 his decision to call parliamentary elections a year early proved unwise, given his unpopularity and that of his prime minister, Alain Juppé. Lionel Jospin, the Socialist candidate in the 1995 presidential elections, was able to build an effective electoral alliance of the PS, the MRG, and the PCF (all traditional electoral allies), but also of the new MdC and the Greens (but not GE). This alliance was able to stage an upset victory.

One general point to stress is that 1978 was the last time a French government was reelected—there is thus a clear tendency to throw the incumbents out. Another point worth stressing is that whereas the RPR and UDF are relatively equal in strength (but not internal cohesion), the Socialists have become the overwhelming dominant party—or "pole"—on the left. It is thus a foregone conclusion that a PS candidate will be the left's main presidential candidate, and that when the left wins parliamentary elections, the PS will be the dominant party of the system.

Selected French Fifth Republic Elections

	1958		1962		1967		1973	
	%V	#S	%V	#S	%V	#S	%V	#S
PCF	19.2	10	21.8	41	22.5	72	21.4	73
SFIO/PS+MRG	15.4	44	12.7	66	18.9	118	20.8	100
PRSR	7.4	23	7.6	41	—	—	—	—
MRP/CD	11.2	57	8.9	36	12.6	38	12.5	30
RI	—	—	4.4	35	6.2	41	10.3	54
Gaullists	20.5	198	31.9	195	31.6	191	23.9	175
conservatives	22.2	133	9.5	48	3.7	7	6.5	36
others	3.9	0	3.3	3	4.5	3	6.1	5
TOTAL SEATS		465		465		470		473

continued

Selected French Fifth Republic Elections *Continued*

	1978		**1981**		**1986**	
	%V	**#S**	**%V**	**#S**	**%V**	**#S**
PCF	20.6	86	16.1	43	9.7	32
PS + MRG	25.0	112	38.1	281	32.4	211
Greens	—	—	—	—	1.2	0
UDF	21.8	125	19.3	63	15.8	128
RPR	22.4	141	20.8	80	26.8	146
conservatives	3.2	9	2.7	6	1.9	4
FN	—	—	—	—	9.8	35
others	8.4	1	3.3	1	2.2	0
TOTAL SEATS		474		474		556

	1988		**1993**		**1997**	
	%V	**#S**	**%V**	**#S**	**%V**	**#S**
PCF	11.2	24	9.1	23	9.9	37
PS + MRG	37.8	269	19.1	57	25.0	265
MdC	—	—	—	—	1.1	10
Greens	0.4	0	2.1	0	3.6	8
GE	—	—	7.8	0	2.7	0
UDF	18.6	130	19.6	215	14.2	109
RPR	19.1	123	20.2	257	15.7	139
conservatives	2.7	8	4.3	19	6.6	8
FN	9.8	1	12.7	0	14.9	1
others	0.6	0	4.1	6	6.3	0
TOTAL SEATS		555		577		577

Note: Sources vary on both vote shares and seat totals.

GOVERNMENTS

French governments have thus gone through three main stages. Initially they were dominated by the Gaullists. Then, during the Giscard presidency of 1974–81 there was more of a center-right balance. Finally, since 1981—as noted—there has been a continuous alteration between Socialist-led leftist governments and those of the center right.

French Fifth Republic Governments since 1959

In Office Date (M/Y)	Prime Minister (Party)	#M(I)	Parties in Cabinet
01/59	Debré, M. (UNR)	21(7)	UNR MRP RI PRSR
04/62	Pompidou, G. (UNR)	22(8)	UNR MRP RI
05/62	Pompidou, G. (UNR)	20(8)	UNR RI
12/62	Pompidou, G. (UNR)	22(7)	UNR RI
01/66	Pompidou, G. (UNR)	18(7)	UNR RI
04/67	Pompidou, G. (UNR)	22(4)	UNR RI
07/68	Couve de Murville, M. (UDR)	19(3)	UDR RI
06/69	Chaban-Delmas, J. (UDR)	19	UDR CDP RI
07/72	Messmer, P. (UDR)	20	UDR CDP RI
04/73	Messmer, P. (UDR)	22(3)	UDR RI CDP
03/74	Messmer, P. (UDR)	16(2)	UDR RI CDP
05/74	Chirac, J. (UDR)	16(4)	UDR RI CDP PRSR
08/76	Barre, R. (Ind)	18(5*)	UDR RI PRSR CDP
04/78	Barre, R. (UDF)	20(5*)	UDF RPR
05/81	Mauroy, P. (PS)	31(1)	PS MRG
06/81	Mauroy, P. (PS)	36(1)	PS PCF MRG
03/83	Mauroy, P. (PS)	23	PS PCF MRG
07/84	Fabius, L. (PS)	23	PS MRG
03/86	Chirac, J. (RPR)	25(3)	RPR UDF
05/88	Rocard, M. (PS)	25(5)	PS MRG

continued

French Fifth Republic Governments since 1959 *Continued*

In Office Date (M/Y)	Prime Minister (Party)	#M(I)	Parties in Cabinet
06/88	Rocard, M. (PS)	33(9)	PS MRG
05/91	Cresson, E. (PS)	30(3)	PS MRG GE
04/92	Bérégovoy, P. (PS)	21(3)	PS MRG
03/93	Balladur, E. (RPR)	24(1)	RPR UDF
05/95	Juppé, A. (RPR)	27(1)	RPR UDF
06/97	Jospin, L. (PS)	14	PS PCF MDC MRG Greens

*Formally independents, but in fact were considered part of Giscard d'Estaing's "presidential majority."

ACRONYMS—FOURTH AND FIFTH REPUBLICS

CD	Democratic Center
CDP	Center for Democracy and Progress
CDS	Democratic and Social Center
CNIP	National Center of Independents and Peasants
DL	Liberal Democracy
FD	Democratic Force
FN	National Front
GE	Ecology Generation
MdC	Citizens' Movement
MRG	Left Radical Movement
MRP	Popular Republican Movement
PCF	French Communist Party
PR	Republican Party
PRSR	Radical Socialist Republican Party
PS	Socialist Party
RI	Independent Republicans
RPF	Rally of the French People
RPR	Rally for the Republic
SFIO	French Section of the Workers' International
UDC	Union of the Center
UDF	Union for French Democracy

UDR	Union for the Defense of the Republic/Union of Democrats for the Republic
UDSR	Democratic and Social Union of the Resistance
UNR	Union for the New Republic

REFERENCES—FOURTH AND FIFTH REPUBLICS

Cole, Alistair, and Peter Campbell. (1989). *French Electoral Systems and Elections since 1789,* 3d ed. Brookfield, Vt.: Gower.

Frears, John. (1991). *Parties and Voters in France.* New York: St. Martin's Press.

Hanley, David (1999). "France: Living with Instability," in David Broughton and Mark Donovan, eds., *Changing Party Systems in Western Europe.* London: Pinter, pp. 48–70.

Lewis-Beck, Michael S., ed. (2000). *How France Votes.* New York: Chatham House.

MacRae, Duncan, Jr. (1967). *Parliament, Parties, and Society in France, 1946–1958. New York: St. Martin's Press.*

Marcus, Jonathan. (1995). The National Front and French Politics: The Resistible Rise of Jean-Marie Le Pen. New York: New York University Press.

Safran, William. (1998). *The French Polity,* 5th ed. New York: Longman.

Williams, Philip M. (1964). *Crisis and Compromise: Politics in the Fourth Republic.* Hamden, Connecticut: Archon Books.

Georgia

SUMMARY OF PARTY SYSTEMS

1992	extreme multiparty system with one dominant party ("Peace" bloc)
1995–(99)	moderate multiparty system with one dominant party (SMK)

HISTORY

Georgia was absorbed by Russia in the early nineteenth century. It proclaimed its independence in May 1918, and this was recognized by the Soviets in 1920. In 1921, however, the country was overrun by the Red Army and declared a Soviet Republic. In the 1990 elections for the Georgian Supreme Soviet, the pro-independence movement won majority of seats. The Georgian Communist Party split from the CPSU in December 1990 and agitated for independence. The former Soviet foreign minister Eduard Shevardnadze returned to Georgia in March 1992 and has led the country ever since. Georgia has experienced violence and civil strife over two autonomous regions—Abkhazia and South Ossetia. Shevardnadze himself has been the victim of an assassination attempt. The 1995 constitution formally made Georgia a presidential system, although, as the chairman of Parliament, Shevardnadze had effectively been exercising presidential powers.

ELECTORAL SYSTEM

The current mixed-member electoral system was adopted in August 1995. There are a total of 235 seats, of which 85 are single-member districts. The remaining 150 seats are elected by a party list proportional representation system. In 1995, there was a 5 percent (of total votes) threshold to gain party list seats. Prior to the 1999 elections, this threshold was increased to 7 percent of the total votes. The emphasis on total votes is important: in 1999, for example, a party received 7.02 percent of the *valid* votes (by this author's calculations), but this was only 6.59 percent of the total votes—and so it got no party list seats.

Under both the single-member and the party list ballots, at least 50 percent of the registered electors must have voted for the poll to be deemed valid; otherwise it is repeated. For the single-member seats, if no candidate obtains at least 33⅓ percent of the votes cast in the constituency, a runoff vote is held between the two top candidates.

In 1992 the electoral system was different in that the chairman of the Parliament was directly elected by a direct, nationwide ballot. Deputies were elected by PR in ten multimember regions. Voters could vote for up to three parties, and a system of point allocation was then used to determine how many seats a party was given.

POLITICAL PARTIES AND CLEAVAGES

The 1992 elections were dominated, relatively speaking, by three blocs of political parties. The **"Peace" (Mshvidoba)** bloc featured parties representing agrarians, conservatives, and monarchists. The **11th October** bloc (named after the date of the elections) comprised republican parties. The **"Unity" (Ertoba)** bloc was a grouping of liberal parties. Of the three blocks that competed in 1992, "Unity" was the only one to contest the 1995 elections, albeit unsuccessfully.

Post-1992, the party system has been more and more concentrated. Most important, the **Citizens' Union of Georgia (SMK)** was launched by Eduard Shevardnadze in 1993 to obtain a parliamentary majority on which he could rely so he would not have to rule by consensus. The party is closely associated with the **Green Party of Georgia (SMP)**, which contested the 1992 elections on its own. The SMK is a top-down centrist party that includes many ex-communists. Most members claim to believe in Western social democracy, the rule of law, a market economy, and maintaining friendly relations with Russia.

The **Socialist Party of Georgia (SSP)** was founded in 1995 for the elections of that year. It campaigned on a democratic left-wing program but only won single-member constituency seats. The SSP was allied with the SMK.

Initially, the main opposition to the SMK was the **National Democratic Party (EDP)**, which claimed to be the heir to the pre–Soviet era party of the same name. A Christian democratic party, it favored restoration of the monarchy as a means of national unification. The EDP was allied with the smaller **Democratic Party (DP)**. The two parties contested the 1992 separately but campaign together in 1996 under the EDP rubric. The nationalistic EDP is opposed to CIS membership and opposed ratification of a friendship treaty with Russia.

The **All-Georgian Union of Revival (SSAK)** is based in the predominantly Muslim autonomous republic of Adzharia. The AGUR was founded in 1992 and participated in the Peace bloc in the 1992 elections, but then went on its own in 1995. For the 1999 elections, SSAK created an anti-Shevardnadze bloc called the **Union for the Democratic Revival of Georgia**. This very heterogeneous bloc grouped nationalists, monarchists, minorities, and leftists, all in a populist opposition to difficult economic conditions.

ELECTIONS

The 11 October 1992 elections saw 36 parties compete. Ossetian and Abkhazian nationalists boycotted the elections, as did the "Zviadists," supporters of Zviad Gamsakhurdia, who was the leader of the movement that ousted the communist party from power. The elections were generally conducted in an honest and quiet atmosphere. The parties boycotting the elections did disrupt voting in certain districts, but these districts represented on 9.1 percent of the total Georgian electorate. Turnout in the election was 74.3 percent. Shevardnadze himself won the chairman position with a personal vote of 95.9 percent, representing 71.3 percent of the electorate.

The 1995 general elections were the second since independence and the first under the new presidential system (they were held simultaneously with the presidential elections). This time, 54 parties or blocs competed, 30 of which were formed after the 1992 elections. Only three parties made it over the 5 percent threshold, meaning that almost all parties failed to get party list representation. Although this was due in part to the large number of parties contesting the elections, it was more a result of the fact that many parties were "arrogant and amateurish" in their response to the threshold. Many parties simply assumed they would be able to surpass the mark and therefore did not put forward a strong strategy for attaining the needed 5 percent.

Elections in Georgia

	1992	1995		1999	
	#S	%V	#S	%V	#S
"Peace" bloc	29	—	—	—	—
11th October bloc	18	—	—	—	—
"Unity" bloc	14	—	—	—	—
EDP	12	8.4	34	4.7	0
SMP	11	?		0.6	0
DP	10	(with EDP)			
SMK	—	25.0	106	44.5	130
SSP	—	4.0	4	?	0
SSAK	—	7.2	29	(into Revival)	
Revival of Georgia	—	—	—	26.8	56
Industry bloc	—	—	—	7.5	16
Other parties		55.4	10	15.9	2
Independents	56	—	45	—	16
Sub-Total	150		228		220
Unfilled seats	—		7		15
TOTAL SEATS	150		235		235

Note: Vote percentages from 1995 onward refer to the party list ballot only (share of valid votes).

In the eastern region of the country, around the capital of Tbilisi, the elections were fairly well run and there was no evidence of fraud or intimidation. In western Georgia, the story was different. International observers noted that voters were pressured to vote for the main political party in the area, the SSAK. There were also allegations of improprieties in the northwest. For their part, Shevardnadze and the CUG advocated continued economic reform and called for reunification of the country as well as suppression of the private armies that had cropped up since independence. The other prominent issues of the campaign related to the conflict with the breakaway regions of Abkhazia and South Ossetia as well as ramifications of the often-tense relations with the Russian Federation. Of the 85 single-member seats, 7 were not filled in the secessionist regions where polling was indefinitely suspended, and runoffs for 36 others were required on 19 November.

The 1999 elections also did not take place in Abkhazia and South Ossetia. This time, the number of parties or blocs competing dropped to 33, and the race was largely polarized between Shevardnadze's SMK and the anti-Shevardnadze Union for the Democratic Revival of Georgia. Shevardnadze himself contrasted the Western orientation of the SMK with what he called the Stalinist past advocated by the Revival leader Aslan Abashidze. Besides the SMK and Revival, the only other force to clear the new, higher electoral threshold was the **Industry Will Save Georgia** bloc.

GOVERNMENTS

Although from 1992 to 1995 Georgia had a prime minister, Shevardnadze as chairman of Parliament was the key figure. Since the constitutional change to a formal presidential system, the government has been hand picked by President Shevardnadze and has consisted largely of members of his SMK.

ACRONYMS

DP	Democratic Party
EDP	National Democratic Party
SMK	Citizens' Union of Georgia
SMP	Green Party of Georgia
SSAK	All-Georgian Union of Revival
SSP	Socialist Party of Georgia

REFERENCES

Allison, Lincoln (1996), "The Georgian Elections of November 1995," *Electoral Studies,* Vol. 15, pp. 275–280.

Allison, Lincoln, et al. (1993), "The Georgian Election of 1992," *Electoral Studies,* Vol. 12, pp. 174–179.

Germany

SUMMARY OF PARTY SYSTEMS

1949	extreme multiparty system with two main parties (CDU/CSU and SPD)
1953–57	moderate multiparty system with one main party (CDU/CSU)
1961–(98)	two-and-a-half-party system

HISTORY

The Federal Republic of Germany dates from 1949. Germany was unified in 1871, and Imperial Germany (1871–1918) saw full party competition, although for a parliament with only limited powers. The Weimar Republic (1919–33) had a very polarized party system, with the National Socialists ultimately becoming the largest party and Hitler being appointed chancellor in January 1933. All other parties were banned during the Nazi era. After the defeat of Germany, political parties reappeared but these had to be approved by the allied occupiers. Nazi-like parties were definitely not permitted, although the Communist Party was. The occupation ended in 1949. To this day, however, the Federal Constitutional Court retains the power to ban antidemocratic parties.

The four-power occupation gave way to the formal division of Germany into West Germany and East Germany. The East German regime collapsed in 1989 and by 1990 the two Germanies were reunited. This involved the eastern parts joining the Federal Republic of Germany and thus was accomplished with very little formal constitutional change. The number of component states/provinces *(Länder)* has increased to sixteen. The powerful upper house (the *Bundesrat,* or council of states) continues to represent the governments of the Länder. Our concerns are the elections to the *Bundestag,* or lower house.

ELECTORAL SYSTEM

Germany has a complicated electoral system. Since 1953 each voter has two votes—the first for a local constituency candidate and the second for a (regional) party list. Essentially one half of the deputies are elected each way. The second vote is the most important one, as the intention of the system is that the total number of seats won by a party should be proportional to its national second vote. (The vote shares listed below thus always refer to the second vote.) To achieve such proportionality the seats (however many) a party wins on the first vote are "topped up" by seats taken from the regional lists so as to reach the proper total. If, however, a party wins "excess mandates" on the first ballot, it gets to keep these, and the Bundestag is expanded somewhat—the record here being sixteen seats in 1994. The total number of seats, thus, often varies slightly from election to election. Of course, the expansion of the country has increased the base number of seats, from 496 in 1957 (after the Saarland joined to "complete" West Germany) to 656 with reunification in 1990.

Crucially, there are (alternative) hurdles to be cleared for a party to win these additional seats. In 1949, this was one direct mandate (from the first vote) or 5 percent in any *Land.* This led to a proliferation of regional parties so in 1953 this requirement was changed to either one direct mandate or 5 percent of the national vote. In 1956 this was then changed to three direct mandates or 5 percent of the national vote. (If a party wins, for example, only two direct mandates and 4 percent of the national vote, it would keep these two seats but not get any more. In practice, almost every single direct mandate is won by one of the two main parties.) Finally, for the 1990 "reunification" elections—but only for these—the calculations were done separately for each of the former West and the former East Germany. This was done so as to not discriminate against the East. As of 1994, however, the 1956 rules apply to the entire country. In summary, then, the "5 percent cutoff" has been an important method of keeping down the number of parties in parliament, as was its intention.

PARTIES AND CLEAVAGES

The Christian Democratic parties have almost always been the leading force in German elections. Various regional Christian parties were formed in 1945 and Konrad Adenauer soon became their effective leader.

As the first postwar chancellor, Adenauer was able to unite from the top down almost all of these regional parties into the **Christian Democratic Union (CDU)**, founded in 1950. One exception was the Bavarian **Christian Social Union (CSU)**, founded in 1946, which has remained separate. These two parties campaign together, back a common chancellor candidate (except in 1980, always from the CDU), and sit together in parliament. The CDU does not run candidates in Bavaria, whereas the CSU *only* runs there (although it tried, unsuccessfully, to break into Eastern Germany in 1990). The CSU is also clearly more conservative than most of the CDU.

The CDU built on the Catholic **Centre Party (Z)** of Weimar Germany, but was established to be a party for all Christians. Nevertheless, it does do better among Catholics, and obviously among religious voters generally. Its core supporters tend to be small-town or rural, female, and/or the "old middle class" of professionals and farmers. That being said, it has a broad range of appeal as what is called a "catch-all" party (in German, *Volkspartei,* or Peoples Party). On socioeconomic issues the CDU (but not the CSU) prefers to see itself as a centrist rather than a conservative force. Finally, following standard practice, the CDU/CSU is considered one party for electoral purposes, and for all calculations in this book.

The **Social Democratic Party (SPD)** was founded in 1863, and is indeed the only German party with a clear prewar continuity. Founded to defend the specific interests of workers, it was also—most crucially during the Weimar Republic—a strong pro-democratic force. After 1945, under the leadership of Kurt Schumacher, it continued to aim essentially at working class voters. This orientation, combined with its neutralist views in foreign affairs, saw its support stagnate in the 1950s. Party reformers, frustrated at the party being stuck in what they saw as a "30 percent ghetto," finally triumphed at the 1959 Bad Godesberg convention. Thereafter, the SPD would also aim for a broad, catch-all appeal. However, its core supporters still remain manual workers, especially nonreligious ones. One relative postwar advantage enjoyed by the SPD was that its historic leftist rival, the **Communist Party of Germany (KPD)**, formed in 1919, was so tainted by its association with the Soviet Union that it quickly withered and was a spent force before it was banned in 1956.

German liberalism had traditionally been divided into nationalistic-liberal and left-liberal parties. In 1948, a single liberal party was formed, this being the **Free Democratic Party (FDP)**. Never intending to be a catchall force, its appeal is centered on educated, secular, urban professionals and white collar workers. Civil servants and dentists are stereotypical FDP voters. Unlike the other smaller parties of the early years, the FDP not only survived but played (at least until 1998) a key "hinge" role. That is, it normally had enough seats to determine which of the two main parties would govern, for which its price was a disproportionate (to its vote) amount of cabinet seats. It also acted as a moderate force in such coalitions and thus appealed to voters as an anti-extremist party. The FDP also usually benefited from supporters of its larger coalition partner, "loaning" it second votes so that it could clear the 5 percent hurdle.

Until the 1980s these three parties overwhelmingly dominated German politics, and indeed from 1961 through 1980, inclusive, they were the only party to win seats in the parliament. Their underlying cleavages and appeals can be conceived of in the following way:

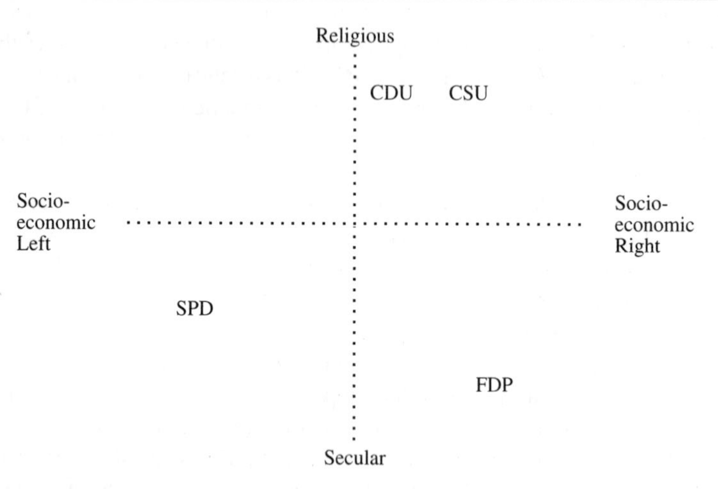

There have, thus, been points of commonality and difference across each pair; for example, the SPD and the CDU each support the welfare state much more than does the FDP.

Although in the early 1970s well-educated younger people were highly supportive of the Brandt government (and Brandt himself), the more conservative style and policies of Helmut Schmidt left a space in the "postmaterialist" part of the electorate that was filled by various regional environmental and alternative parties. At the national level the **Greens** were formed in 1980 and have been in almost all national parliaments since 1983. They finally entered the national government after the 1998 elections. Their supporters are very clearly young, secular, well educated, and based in cities or university towns, with a slightly greater appeal to (young) women. Lack of interest in German reunification caused them to fall just below the separate 5 percent hurdle for Western Germany established for 1990. In 1993 the West German Greens merged with the intellectually based eastern **Alliance 90 (B 90) Party**, and in 1994 the Alliance 90/Greens, as they are now called, easily returned to the Bundestag—making them the first party in postwar Germany to come back after falling below the 5 percent cutoff.

East Germany itself had been governed by the **Socialist Unity Party**, which was created in 1946 as a forced merger of the eastern SPD with the communists. In early 1990, with reunification on the horizon, this party renamed itself the **Party of Democratic Socialism (PDS)**. Although in theory now running everywhere in Germany, its appeal is almost exclusively among those former East Germans who benefited from, or who are nostalgic about, the old regime, or those who simply wish to cast a protest vote against West German dominance. Both the Greens and the PDS are in the same left-secular part of the spectrum as the SPD, although they are both more leftist and the Greens have a post-materialist appeal.

ELECTIONS AND REALIGNMENTS

The first national elections in the Federal Republic of Germany were held in 1949, and various parties were able to win seats. The Christian Democrats and the Social Democrats were far and away the two leading parties, with the former slightly ahead. However, since almost all of the other parties elected were to the right of the SPD (the only exception being obviously the communists), the Christian Democrats were able to form a government. These other parties tended to have either explicit regional appeals **(Bavarian Party (BP)** or implicit regional appeals (the **Centre Party (Z)** to Catholics in the Rhineland, the **German Party (DP)** to northern, Protestant conservatives, and the **Refugee Party (BHE)** to those who had fled from the east to settle in the north). The aforementioned changes to the electoral system thus squeezed out these parties, almost totally to the benefit of the CDU/CSU. The Christian

Democrats had three other strengths in the 1950s: (1) Adenauer was more popular than Schumacher; (2) Adenauer's pro-Western foreign policy was more popular than the SPD's neutralism; and (3) the German economy was booming in its postwar "economic miracle." Thus by 1957 the Christian Democrats had slightly over half the vote, the only time since 1949 that (effectively) one party has won an outright national majority (although the CDU/CSU still kept the German Party in government).

By the 1961 elections Adenauer was eighty-five years old, and, indeed, the FDP campaigned on forming a coalition with the Christian Democrats but under a new chancellor (this was achieved in 1963). Facing them was a more moderate SPD with an attractive young chancellor candidate in Willy Brandt, the mayor (effectively premier) of West Berlin. Thus in the 1960s it was the SPD's turn to grow in support. The party also gained increased legitimacy with middle-class voters by participating successfully in a "Grand Coalition" government with the Christian Democrats from 1966 to 1969, and their policies generally found favor with the new middle class of urban professionals.

The 1960s would also see the rise on the far right of the **National Democratic Party (NPD)**, formed in 1964, which gained the protest votes of dissatisfied conservatives, including CDU/CSU supporters who disliked the Grand Coalition. Although winning seats in most Länder, the NPD failed to clear the 5 percent cutoff in 1969, and withered away thereafter. The far right has yielded other tiny parties since the 1980s, all of which have experienced a similar problem with the national 5 percent hurdle.

For their part, the Free Democrats had quit the government in 1966 (precipitating the Grand Coalition) in large part so as to not appear indistinguishable from the CDU. From 1961 onward a coalition of any two of the three parties in parliament would have provided a mathematical majority, but the FDP was far too conservative in the early 1960s to have anything to do with the SPD. However, by the late 1960s the left-liberal wing of the FDP was ascendant, and the decision was taken to govern with the SPD after the 1969 elections. The numbers were there for this, but just barely, and Brandt became the first SPD chancellor since 1930.

Although often controversial, policies of the SPD-FDP government such as normalizing relations with Eastern Europe were also quite popular. The defection of some FDP MPs to the CDU led Brandt to call early elections in 1972, producing a resounding success for the social-liberal coalition. Indeed, for the first time, the SPD topped the CDU/CSU in votes, 45.9 percent to 44.8 percent. The replacement of Brandt with Helmut Schmidt in 1974 led to more moderate policies, which suited the increasingly conservative FDP. The coalition hung together through the 1980 elections, which featured the only CSU (as opposed to CDU) chancellor candidate in postwar Germany, Franz-Josef Strauss. Strauss's unpopularity with northern CDU voters led to some of these backing the FDP.

After 1980, conflict intensified *within* the SPD between its leftist/postmaterialist wing and the more moderate leadership, especially over the deployment of new nuclear missiles. In 1982 the FDP then played its balancing role, switching sides and putting the Christian Democrats under Helmut Kohl back into power. Early elections in 1983 confirmed the CDU/CSU-FDP government, which has been in office since. The SPD lost many postmaterialist voters to the Greens, and in 1983 also lost working-class support to the CDU. It has regained the latter but not the former. The Kohl government did begin to look tired in the late 1980s, and Kohl himself was seen as weak, but his seizing of the issue of German reunification proved popular, especially given that the Social Democrats were split over how quickly the two Germanies should unify. In both 1990 and 1994 the Christian Democrats were able to win as much support in the former East Germany as in the former West. However one should note that their support level (41 to 44 percent) was still lower than anytime since 1949.

In the 1998 elections, after sixteen years in government, the Christian Democrats appeared tired and bereft of new ideas. They stressed the experience of Chancellor Kohl and his record in foreign affairs, but offered little new. The Social Democrats nominated as chancellor candidate their most "electable" candidate, Gerhard Schröder, the premier of Lower Saxony. Schröder ran a moderate, pragmatic campaign, attacking the government over high unemployment and stressing the need for renewal and innovation. Election polls were predicting a close race, and probably another "Grand Coalition." However, on election night not only did the SPD surpass the CDU/CSU for the first time since 1972, but it did so by over 5 percentage points. Support for the other parties changed little. Consequently, the SPD and the Greens had a clear working majority between them, and the first national "red-green" government was formed.

Selected Elections in the Federal Republic of Germany

	1949		1953		1957		1961	
	%V	#S	%V	#S	%V	#S	%V	#S
SPD	29.2	131	28.8	151	31.8	169	36.2	190
CDU/CSU	31.0	139	45.2	243	50.2	270	45.3	242
FDP	11.9	52	9.5	48	7.7	41	12.8	67
KPD	5.7	15	2.2	0	—	—	—	—
BP	4.2	17	1.7	0	—	—	—	—
Z	3.1	10	0.8	3	—	—	—	—
DP	4.0	17	3.3	15	3.4	17	—	—
BHE	—	—	5.9	27	4.6	0	—	—
others	10.9	21	2.8	0	2.4	0	7.7	0
TOTAL SEATS		402		487		497		499

	1969		1972		1980		1983	
	%V	#S	%V	#S	%V	#S	%V	#S
SPD	42.7	224	45.8	230	42.9	218	38.2	193
CDU/CSU	46.1	242	44.9	225	44.5	226	48.8	244
FDP	5.8	30	8.4	41	10.6	53	7.0	34
NPD	4.3	0	0.6	0	0.2	0	0.2	0
Greens	—	—	—	—	1.5	0	5.6	27
others	1.1	0	0.3	0	1.8	0	0.2	0
TOTAL SEATS		496		496		497		498

	1987		1990		1994		1998	
	%V	#S	%V	#S	%V	#S	%V	#S
SPD	37.0	186	33.5	239	36.4	252	40.9	298
CDU/CSU	44.3	223	43.8	319	41.5	294	35.2	245
FDP	9.1	46	11.0	79	6.9	47	6.2	43
Greens	8.3	42	3.9	0	—	—	—	—
B 90	—	—	1.2	8	—	—	—	—
B 90/Greens	—	—	——		7.3	49	6.7	47
PDS	—	—	2.4	17	4.4	30	5.1	36
others	1.6	0	4.2	0	3.5	0	5.9	0
TOTAL SEATS		497		662		672		669

GOVERNMENTS

German governments have been relatively stable, in that there have only been seven chancellors since 1949. These have always been from either the Christian Democratic Union or the Social Democratic Party. However, as noted, it has been the pivotal Free Democratic Party that has been in government the longest. Moreover, if one views these three parties as forming a triangle, then governments have been formed from each side of this triangle. Most common have been CDU/CSU-FDP governments, but again there were SPD-FDP governments from 1969 to 1982 and a CDU/CSU-SPD government from 1966 to 1969. The post-1998 SPD-Green government is the first clear break with this triangular pattern. These various patterns, along with single-party governments of the larger parties, have also existed at Land level.

German Governments since 1949

In Office Date (M/Y)	Chancellor (Party)	#M(I)	Parties in Cabinet
09/1949	Adenauer, K. (CDU)	14	CDU/CSU FDP DP
10/1953	Adenauer, K. (CDU)	16	CDU/CSU FDP DP BHE
07/1955	Adenauer, K. (CDU)	15	CDU/CSU FDP DP
03/1956	Adenauer, K. (CDU)	18	CDU/CSU FVP DP
10/1957	Adenauer, K. (CDU)	18	CDU/CSU DP
07/1960	Adenauer, K. (CDU)	18	CDU/CSU
11/1961	Adenauer, K. (CDU)	21	CDU/CSU FDP
11/1962	Adenauer, K. (CDU)	16	CDU/CSU
12/1962	Adenauer, K. (CDU)	21	CDU/CSU FDP
10/1963	Erhard, L. (CDU)	21	CDU/CSU FDP
10/1965	Erhard, L. (CDU)	22	CDU/CSU FDP
10/1966	Erhard, L. (CDU)	18	CDU/CSU
12/1966	Kiesinger, K. G. (CDU)	20	CDU/CSU SPD
10/1969	Brandt, W. (SPD)	16 (1)	SPD FDP
05/1972	Brandt, W. (SPD)	16	SPD FDP
12/1972	Brandt, W. (SPD)	18	SPD FDP
05/1974	Schmidt, H. (SPD)	16	SPD FDP
12/1976	Schmidt, H. (SPD)	16	SPD FDP
11/1980	Schmidt, H. (SPD)	17	SPD FDP
09/1982	Schmidt, H. (SPD)	13	SPD
10/1982	Kohl, H. (CDU)	17	CDU/CSU FDP
03/1983	Kohl, H. (CDU)	17	CDU/CSU FDP
03/1987	Kohl, H. (CDU)	19	CDU/CSU FDP
10/1990	Kohl, H. (CDU)	20	CDU/CSU FDP
11/1994	Kohl, H. (CDU)	18	CDU/CSU FDP
10/1998	Schröder, G. (SPD)	16 (1)	SPD Greens

*In 1956 the FVP, an FDP split-off.

**In 1960 the two DP ministers and most of its MPs joined the CDU.

ACRONYMS

B 90	Alliance [19]90
BHE:	"League of those expelled from their homeland and those deprived of their rights"
BP	Bavaria Party
CDU	Christian Democratic Union
CSU	Christian Social Union (Bavaria)
DP	German Party
FDP	Free Democratic Party
KPD	Communist Party of Germany
NPD	National Democratic Party of Germany
PDS	Party of Democratic Socialism
SPD	Social Democratic Party of Germany
Z	Centre Party

REFERENCES

Conradt, David P. (1996). *The German Polity,* 6th ed. New York: Longman.

Jeffery, Charlie (1999). "Germany: From Hyperstability to Change?," in David Broughton and Mark Donovan, eds., *Changing Party Systems in Western Europe.* London: Pinter, pp. 96–117.

Padgett, Stephen, ed. (1993). *Parties and Party Systems in the New Germany.* Aldershot: Dartmouth.

Padgett, Stephen, and Tony Burkett. (1986). *Political Parties and Elections in West Germany: The Search for a New Stability.* New York: St. Martin's Press.

Poguntke, Thomas. (1994). "Parties in a Legalistic Culture: The Case of Germany," pp. 185–215, in Richard S. Katz and Peter Mair, eds. *How Parties Organize: Change and Adaption in Party Organization in Western Democracies.* London: SAGE.

Pulzer, Peter (1999). "The German Federal Election of 1998," *West European Politics,* Vol. 22, No. 3, pp. 241–249.

Smith, Gordon. (1986). *Democracy in Western Germany: Parties and Politics in the Federal Republic,* 3d ed. New York: Holmes and Meier.

Greece

SUMMARY OF PARTY SYSTEMS

1974–77	moderate multiparty with one dominant party (ND)
1981–85	two-party system (PASOK and ND)
1989–(96)	two-and-a-half-party system

HISTORY

Modern Greece became independent in 1827, and a monarchy was established in 1831. Crete and part of Macedonia were added after the 1912 Balkan War. In the interwar period, Greece was bitterly divided between anti- and pro-monarchists, and suffered frequent military interventions. An authoritarian system was eventually established by General Metaxas, who ruled from 1936 until German and Italian conquest in 1941. After the war a civil war occurred between communists and nationalist monarchists. The latter used the army and aid from Britain and the United States to defeat the communists, and from 1950 onward a stable parliamentary system existed, although the Communist Party was banned and the monarch intervened actively in politics. Fears of an electoral swing to the left led the military to stage a coup d'etat in 1967. Failed intervention in Cyprus in 1974 would lead to the collapse of the military regime. Since 1974 Greece has been fully democratic. A December 1974 referendum established a republic. The constitution of 1975 was modified in 1986 to make the president a pure figurehead.

ELECTORAL SYSTEM

Greece has a complicated, multitiered electoral system. In its current version there are 6 single-member constituencies and 50 multimember constituencies for a total of 288 seats. The multimember seats use a single round of voting in accordance with the Hagenbach-Bischoff system of "reinforced" proportional representation, with voting for party lists and preferential voting within each list. Remaining seats after this distribution are allocated in thirteen principal electoral districts according to the same system. The remaining twelve "state deputies" are allocated from one multimember national constituency. The threshold for representation is 3 percent of the national vote. The overall effect is a form of PR biased toward the largest party.

Voting of people under the age of seventy years is compulsory, failure to participate resulting in a term of imprisonment ranging from one month to one year.

POLITICAL PARTIES AND CLEAVAGES

New Democracy (ND) represents Greece's conservative tradition. The party was formed in 1974 as a center-right, antisocialist force. The party is largely a pragmatic one; it has put emphasis on free enterprise and social justice; it has advocated an independent foreign policy and has attempted to distance itself from the extreme right since the period of the dictatorship. The party enjoys a fairly broad base of support. After democratization in 1974, New Democracy's main opponent was initially the liberal-radical **Center Union (EDHK)**. The EDHK had risen in the 1960s to win an absolute majority in the 1964 elections, but its leader was then forced out of office by the king. In the 1970s EDHK was quickly outflanked on the left by the Socialists and barely made it into the 1980s.

The **Panhellenic Socialist Movement (Pasok)** was founded in 1974. The party advocated for the socialization of the Greek economy by way of its theory of the "third road" to socialism. The party regarded this path as less radical than that of the communists but more committed to the ideals of socialism than most other social democratic parties. The party, as a result, was highly critical of many European social democratic parties and admonished them for not being radical enough. At the time, some critics argued that the party was in fact far from the radical group it saw itself as, and instead labeled it a populist, left-centrist party that had long abandoned the Marxist ideology it earlier espoused. In reality the party did in fact officially distance itself from its more radical rhetoric in the early 1990s. In terms of foreign policy the party once argued for the dissolution of European military alliances, for Greek control of U.S. bases and installations in Greece, and for the renegotiating of Greek membership in the EC. But as part of its modernization, the party began to adopted a less hostile position and called for Greece to play a more constructive role in NATO and the EC. Even more recently the party has adopted an even more pro-European position in foreign policy and what may be described as enthusiasm for the EU.

The far left of Greek politics has seen many parties come and go, several different electoral coalitions formed, and as a result it is a somewhat confused collection of political entities. The party furthest to the left, and which has had the most stable existence, relatively speaking, has been the **Communist Party of Greece (KKE)**. The party is Greece's historic orthodox communist party, which was originally founded in 1918 and revived in 1974 after twenty-seven years of nonexistence. The party is opposed both to the EU and NATO and has called for the removal of U.S. military installations in Greece. The KKE was hurt by defections following its support of the Soviet invasion of Afghanistan. A breakaway party was formed in 1968 called the **Communist Party of Greece-Interior (KKEs)**. The KKEs would run jointly with the KKE in the first elections of 1974, but then the KKEs went on to form the **Alliance of Progressive and Left-Wing Forces**, which was later renamed the **Progressive Left Coalition**. This was a coalition of various socialist, communist, and far-left parties in Greece. The KKEs itself was renamed the **Greek Left (EAR)** in 1987. The historic Communist Party became a member of this Progressive Left Coalition for a short period until it left in 1991.

Elections in Greece, 1974–85

	1974		1977		1981		1985	
	%V	#S	%V	#S	%V	#S	%V	#S
KKE	} 9.4	8	9.3	11	10.9	13	9.9	12
KKEs	}		2.7	2	1.3	0	1.8	1
EDHK	20.5	60	11.9	15	0.4	0	—	—
ND	54.3	220	41.8	172	35.9	115	40.8	126
PASOK	13.6	12	25.3	93	48.1	172	45.8	161
others	2.2	0	9.0	7	3.6	0	1.6	0
TOTAL SEATS		300		300		300		300

A new party to enter the left is the **Democratic Social Movement (Dikki)** which was formed in 1995 by a splinter group of Pasok. Dikki claims to be representative of Pasok's true socialist heritage. Another party that recently won representation in the Greek parliament is **Political Spring**. Formed in 1992, the party has called for reform and an end to the rule of the political elites. Although winning ten seats in the 1993 elections, the party did not retain any of these in 1996.

RECENT ELECTIONS

In 1989 Greece had two elections. The first, held on 18 June, resulted in a "hung parliament" with no parties able to form a government. New Democracy and the Progressive Left Coalition finally agreed to form a coalition solely with the intent of overseeing the implementation of a series of investigations into financial and other scandals involving the previous Pasok government, which had been in power from 1981 to 1989. This coalition government resigned in October as prearranged and elections were held on 5 November. This campaign was less passionate than that of the June elections and featured more use of the media and less use of rallies and party events. Campaign issues centered around economic issues such as the public-sector deficit and the high inflation Greece was experiencing. Pasok accused both the ND and the Left Coalition of trying to destroy the party. The results of the November elections were relatively similar to those of June, with New Democracy and Pasok both increasing their number of seats by three at the expense of the Left Coalition. With no party holding a parliamentary majority, once again it was unsure which parties would work to form a government. An all-party coalition was agreed upon and yet another election was scheduled for the following April.

Elections in Greece, 1989–90

	June 1989		**Nov. 1989**		**1990**	
	%V	**#S**	**%V**	**#S**	**%V**	**#S**
ND	44.3	145	46.2	148	46.9	152
Pasok	39.1	125	40.7	128	38.6	124
Left Coalition	13.1	28	11.0	21	10.2	21
others	3.5	2	2.1	3	4.3	3
TOTAL SEATS		300		300		300

The April 1990 elections finally brought the decisive victory for one party that the two elections in the previous eleven months had failed to do. New Democracy received 152 seats and was therefore able to form a government without having to rely on the support of any other party.

The 1993 elections saw a new political party enter into the fold, **Political Spring**. Campaigning for the end of the rule by the political "dinosaurs" of Greece, and as well taking a hard line regarding the name used by the Former Yugoslavian Republic of Macedonia, the party won a surprising ten seats. The KKE competed in this election on its own and not within the Left Coalition rubric. The KKE won ten seats while the Left Coalition did not manage to win the required 3 percent of the national vote in order to gain representation in parliament. Pasok regained its position as the preeminent party in Greek politics largely due to the voters' dissatisfaction with the previous ND government. The party's success was also a result of the modernization Pasok underwent and its new "social democratic" leanings.

Elections in Greece, 1993–96

	1993		1996	
	%V	#S	%V	#S
Pasok	46.9	170	41.5	162
ND	39.3	111	38.1	108
KKE	4.5	9	5.6	11
Left Coalition	2.9	0	5.1	10
Dikki	—	—	4.4	9
Political Spring	4.9	10	2.9	0
others	1.5	0	2.4	0
TOTAL SEATS		300		300

The most recent elections, held in 1996, saw results similar to those of the election before. Pasok held on to its parliamentary majority, which was seen by many as a popular mandate for the party to commence its plans to implement the necessary economic reforms that would give Greece the chance to qualify to participate in the upcoming European single currency. New Democracy remained by far the second-strongest party only losing three of its seats. The biggest changes occurred with the smaller parties. The Left Coalition rebounded from having no representation after the previous election, to winning ten seats, while Political Spring lost all ten seats it had won in 1993. A new party, the Democratic Renewal Movement, did well by securing nine seats, and the KKE increased its representation from nine to eleven. The success of these smaller left-wing parties was in part a result of traditional Pasok voters protesting the party's apparent shift to the right.

GOVERNMENTS

With the exception of the 1989 coalitions discussed above, all Greek governments have been single-party majorities, either of ND or Pasok. Government formation is, thus, normally straightforward and swift.

Greek Governments since 1974

In Office Date (M/Y)	Prime Minister (Party)	#M(I)	Parties in Cabinet
11/74	Karamanlis, C. (ND)	20	ND
11/77	Karamanlis, C. (ND)	22	ND
05/80	Rallis, G. (ND)	24	ND
10/81	Papandreou, A. (Pasok)	21	Pasok
06/85	Papandreou, A. (Pasok)	22	Pasok
07/89	Tzannetakis, T. (ND)	22	ND KKE
11/89	Zolotos, X. (Ind)	21 (8)	ND Pasok KKE
04/90	Mitsotakis, K. (ND)	21	ND
10/93	Papandreou, A. (Pasok)	19	Pasok
01/96	Simitis, K. (Pasok)	20	Pasok
09/96	Simitis, K. (Pasok)	19	Pasok

ACRONYMS

Dikki Democratic Social Movement
EAR Greek Left
EDHK Center Union

continued

ACRONYMS *(Continued)*

KKE	Communist Party of Greece
KKEs	Communist Party of Greece-Interior
ND	New Democracy
Pasok	Panhellenic Socialist Movement

REFERENCES

Dimitras, Panayote Elias. (1994). "The Greek Parliamentary Election of October 1993." *Electoral Studies,* Vol. 13, No. 3, pp. 235–39.

———. (1990). "The Greek Parliamentary Election of November 1989." *Electoral Studies,* Vol. 9, No. 2, pp. 159–63.

Hungary

SUMMARY OF PARTY SYSTEMS

1990	extreme multiparty system with one dominant party (MDF)
1994	extreme multiparty system with one dominant party (MSzP)
(1998–)	extreme multiparty system with two main parties (Fidesz-MPP and MSzP)

HISTORY

Historically, Hungary was part of the Austro-Hungarian Empire, and largely autonomous after 1867. Independent after the First World War, interwar Hungary was initially semidemocratic and then authoritarian in the 1930s. The country was occupied by Soviet forces in late 1944. In free elections held in 1945, the communists got only 17 percent of the vote, whereupon the communists backed by the Soviets seized de facto control of the country. The Hungarian People's Republic was formally established in 1948. The 1956 anticommunist uprising was brutally crushed by Soviet forces. In 1962 the communist government shifted toward a more pragmatic domestic policy. In 1985 around forty-five independents were elected in the last "one-party" general elections. Despite various reforms, the 1988–89 period was one of communist decay and the rise of the opposition, leading to the first multiparty elections in 1990.

ELECTORAL SYSTEM

Hungary has a complicated, three-tiered electoral system. Each elector casts two votes, one for an individual candidate and one for a party list. First, there are 186 single-member constituencies; for these, two rounds of voting are normally held. If within a local constituency, no candidate obtains an absolute majority of the votes in the first ballot, or if less than half of the registered electors have voted, a second ballot is held. In the former case (no absolute majority for any individual), all candidates having gained at least 15 percent of the valid votes may run again; if this number is only one or two, the three having obtained the most first-ballot votes are entitled to continue. In the latter case (fewer than half of the voters), all previous candidates may run again; the one then obtaining the most votes is declared elected. In either event, the candidate with the most votes is then declared elected, provided that at least 25 percent of the constituency's electorate has voted.

Next, there are territorial constituencies; these use proportional representation (simple electoral quotient) in a single ballot, unless voter participation falls below 50 percent. Parties polling less than 5 percent of the vote do not gain a parliamentary seat through this system. Finally, there is a national constituency in which seats are allotted to political parties on a fully proportional basis according to "scrap votes," that is, those cast for previously unsuccessful constituency candidates, or lists, are added together to form a national total. Vacancies arising between general elections are filled through by-elections (in single-member constituencies), while vacancies of territorial or national list seats are filled by the party concerned from among the candidates figuring on its original list.

POLITICAL PARTIES AND CLEAVAGES

Unlike many of its neighbors, Hungary skipped the umbrella-movement stage and went straight to a viable party system. However, a relatively low number of voters actually identify with a particular party, and there are usually a high percentage of undecided voters leading up to elections. Ideological views on both economics and nationalism structure the Hungarian party system, as is shown in the diagram that follows.

The **Hungarian Democratic Forum (MDF)** was founded in 1987 as a nationalist-populist movement occupying a centrist position between the communists and the radical opposition. In 1989 the party dropped its populist nature and built up a Christian-democratic image. The party is pro-market but wants market reform at a slower pace, and it advocates some state control over aspects of public political expression. The party is strongly pro-Hungarian and is very concerned with the status of Hungarians in other countries. Nevertheless, the MDF is in support of western integration. Initially there were also some elements of anti-Jewish and anti-Gypsy sentiments within the party. Divisions within the party on such issues led to expulsion in June 1993 of the leading nationalist István Csurka. That November Csurka formed the right-radical **Hungarian Justice and Life Party (MIEP)**.

On the right of center along with the MDF lies the **Christian Democratic People's Party (KDNP)**. The KDNP claims to be the revival of the Popular Democratic Party, which was the leading opposition party in the immediate post–World War II period. The party is pro-market but like the MDF believes in a more cautious pace of reform. The party is very similar to the MDF in that it also believes in strong Christian values, is strongly pro-Hungarian, supports some restrictions on free speech, and has some policies that are either anti-Jewish or anti-Gypsy.

Like the KDNP, the **Independent Smallholders' Party (FKgP)** is descended from a historic Hungarian party. The FKgP is the 1989 revival of the party that dominated Hungary's first postwar election in 1945. The party is conservative and populist in nature. Strongly pro-Hungarian, the FKgP has been accused, like the two parties mentioned above, of being anti-Jewish and anti-Gypsy. The party is, however, anti-Western, unlike the MDF and the KDNP. The FKgP was a party deeply divided over reparations for property lost during the communist era. Two factions subsequently split from the party. The first, the **National Smallholders and Bourgeois Party (NKPP)**, left for only one year and then rejoined, but the second—the **United Smallholders' Party–Historical Section (EKgP-TT)**—left the party for good following the FKgP's withdrawal from the MDF-led government in 1992.

Another pro-market force that formed in opposition to the communists is the **Federation of Free Democrats (SzDSz)**. The SzDSz was founded in 1988 as the Network of Free Initiatives by a grouping of dissident intellectuals and human rights activists and was regrouped as a formal political party in November of the following year. The party is a member of the Liberal International and is, like the MDF, pro-Western in orientation. The party does not, however, demonstrate the same degree of nationalism as the MDF.

The **Federation of Young Democrats (Fidesz)** is, like the SzDSz, a member of the Liberal International. As well, Fidesz is both pro-market and pro-Western. The difference is that until 1993 the party limited membership to those below the age of thirty-six. In April of that year the party abandoned the age restriction and adopted the Federation of Free Democrats–Hungarian Civic Party (Fidesz-MPP) rubric. Its leader, Viktor Orbán, managed to become prime minister in 1998 at the age of thirty-five.

The **Hungarian Socialist Party (MSzP)** was originally formed in 1948 as the **Hungarian Workers' Party (MMP)** and was a merger of

Hungary's communist and social democratic parties. In 1956, following the Soviet invasion, the party was renamed the **Hungarian Socialist Workers' Party (MSzMP)**. In 1989 the party renounced Marxism and adopted its current name. In 1994 the MSzP became an affiliate of the Socialist International. The party supports state intervention in the market economy. The MSzP is, in part, one of the more anti-Western of all Hungarian parties but it is also one of the least nationalist.

The Hungarian party system can perhaps best be conceived in the following two-dimensional manner:

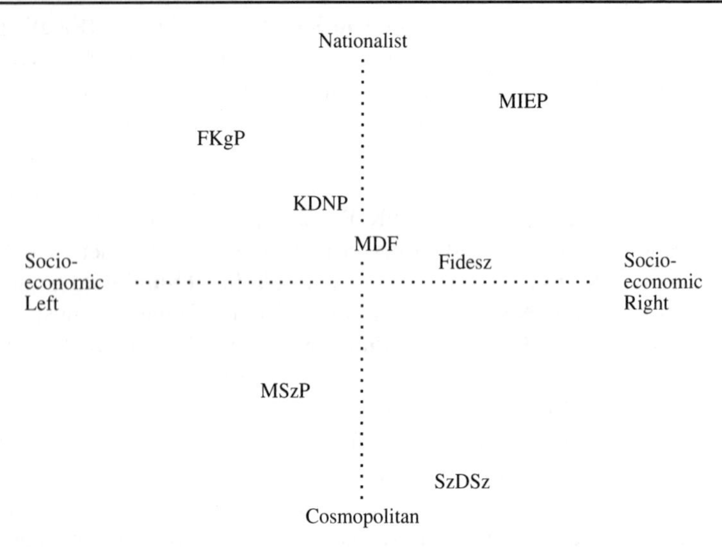

ELECTIONS

The first elections in postindependence Hungary were held in March 1990. Turnout for the elections was only 65 percent in the first round and 45 percent in the second round. This was very low, especially compared with similar founding elections in other postcommunist countries. The main issue of the campaign was what approach the country would take toward reform and at what pace these reforms would be made. The MDF campaigned on a platform of privatization of state property "within the context of a reasonable and socially controlled process." The SzDSz argued for a more radical restructuring and privatization of the economy. As well, the party campaigned for a rapid integration with western Europe and a faster withdrawal of Soviet troops.

The MDF and the SzDSz proved to be the main parties in contention, with the voters largely not interested in maintaining the status quo under the MSzP. The FKgP was able to gain some support with its one-issue campaign—advocating a return of collectivized land to its owners, as listed in the 1947 land register. This strategy proved successful in gaining votes among the rural villagers. The MDF proved strong in rural towns and the SzDSz was especially strong in Budapest.

The elections were conducted in a free and fair manner, with a multiparty committee established to ensure the fairness of the distribution of air-time to candidates and parties.

The 1994 elections represented a swing of support back to left-leaning parties, especially and almost exclusively to the MSzP. The Fidesz, SzDSz, and the MDF all launched vigorous campaigns in the spring—months in advance of the elections, which were held on 8 and 29 May. The MSzP only began to campaign hard in the weeks before the election. This shows to what extent voters had made up their collective mind despite what the government parties said. The main issue of the election was not any specific question over the government's policy, but instead the state of the economy and a sense of nostalgia for what were, in comparative economic terms, the "good old days" of Goulash communism of the late 1980s. Living standards for all but one-fifth of the population had dropped and people were generally unhappy with the pace and direction reforms had taken.

The impending MSzP victory was not responded to with panic or demonstrations in any of the major cities, meaning that voters fully accepted the democratic standing of the former communists. A crude anticommunist campaign was launched by the MDF in the eleventh hour of the elections but this proved to be counterproductive and hurt only the MDF, if anyone.

Turnout for these election increased, compared with 1990, to 68.1 percent. Only 2 of the 176 directly elected members of parliament were elected on the first ballot.

The 1998 elections, held in May, saw the voters' response to four years under the MSzP. Clearly not impressed with what any of the previous parties had been able to offer, the voters turned to the one party that had not yet been in government—the Fidesz, now Fidesz-MPP. The

Fidesz quadrupled its vote share from 1994 and increased its number of seats sevenfold. The MSzP, although seeing a decrease in their votes of only 0.7 percent, lost seventy-five of the seats they had won in 1994.

Elections in Hungary

	1990		1994		1998	
	%V	#S	%V	#S	%V	#S
MSzP	10.9	33	33.0	209	32.3	134
SzDSz	21.4	92	19.7	69	7.9	24
MDF	24.7	164	11.7	38	3.1	17
FKgP	11.8	44	8.8	26	13.8	48
KDNP	6.5	21	7.0	22	2.6	—
Fidesz	8.9	22	7.0	20	28.2	148
MIEP	—	—	1.6	—	5.6	14
others	15.8	10	11.2	2	6.5	1
TOTAL SEATS		386		386		386

GOVERNMENTS

The first two governments in Hungary were led by the MDF and included both the FKgP and the KDNP. These parties formed a natural alliance. All are nationalistic and all harbor somewhat antiminority attitudes. Both the KDNP and MDF are Christian conservatives, both are pro-Western, and both support a more cautious program of reform. The FKgP was included because of the rural base of support it shares with the MDF and to a lesser extent with the KDNP. Problems existed, however, because the FKgP is ardently anti-Western, and, therefore, a government shuffle took place in 1993.

The government formed following the 1994 elections contained somewhat unlikely allies. The MSzP had a majority of seats on its own but no doubt included the SzDSz to lend legitimacy to the party's commitment to democracy and to bolster its pro-Western platform. After the swing back to the right in 1998, the Fidesz-MPP formed a government with the two other center-right parties that had been in opposition.

Hungarian Governments since 1990

In Office Date (M/Y)	Prime Minister (Party)	#M(I)	Parties in Cabinet
05/90	Antall, J. (MDF)	17(3)	MDF FKgP KDNP
12/93	Boross, P. (MDF)	17(3)	MDF FKgP KDNP
06/94	Horn, G. (MSzP)	14	MSzP SzDSz
07/98	Orbán, V. (Fidesz-MPP)	17	Fidesz-MPP MDF FKgP

ACRONYMS

EKgP-TT	United Smallholders' Party–Historical Section
Fidesz	Federation of Young Democrats
Fidesz-MPP	Federation of Young Democrats–Hungarian Civic Party
FKgP	Independents Smallholders' Party
KDNP	Christian Democratic People's Party
MDF	Hungarian Democratic Forum
MIEP	Hungarian Justice and Life Party
MMP	Hungarian Workers' Party
MSzMP	Hungarian Socialist Workers' Party
MSzP	Hungarian Socialist Party
NKPP	National Smallholders and Bourgeois Party
SzDSz	Federation of Free Democrats

REFERENCES

Korosenyi, Andras. (1995). "The Reasons for the Defeat of the Right in Hungary." *East European Politics and Societies,* Vol. 9.

Montgomery, Kathleen. (1999). "Politics in Hungary," pp. 422–65, in Gabriel A. Almond, Russell J. Dalton, and G. Bingham Powell Jr., eds. *European Politics Today.* New York: Longman.

Iceland

SUMMARY OF PARTY SYSTEMS

1946–79	moderate multiparty system with a balance among the parties
1983–95	extreme multiparty system with one dominant party (IP)
(1999–)	moderate multiparty system with a balance among the parties

HISTORY

Iceland was ruled for many centuries by Denmark. In 1918 it acquired autonomous status, and in 1944 it became fully independent. The struggle for independence thus shaped Icelandic politics until relatively recently. Additionally, Icelanders take pride in a parliamentary tradition that goes back to the tenth century. Nowadays, what remains perhaps most distinctive is the ethnic-linguistic homogeneity of the population—Iceland is one the most homogeneous societies in the world, and the most so in Europe.

ELECTORAL SYSTEM

Iceland did not fully adopt proportional representation until 1959, much later than elsewhere in Nordic Europe. Of the now sixty-three seats, fifty are elected in multimember constituencies using the greatest-remainder system. The remaining thirteen are national "top-up" seats for parties winning at least one constituency seat.

POLITICAL PARTIES AND CLEAVAGES

Icelandic party abbreviations are rarely used in a general sense, and more precisely English-language ones are more common. In what follows, the English abbreviation will be given first and used, with the Icelandic acronym then given in square brackets, where one exists.

The role of personalities is a very important one in politics. Politics are also very localized. For these reasons parties do not take up a very firm position on the classic left-right spectrum. The most evident cleavage dividing political parties in Iceland is a rural/urban one or, as some have labeled it, a center/periphery one. Attitudes toward NATO membership and the maintenance of U.S. military forces in Iceland are other issues that produce sharp divisions among the various political parties.

The strongest party in Iceland is the **Independence Party (IP [Sj])**. Founded in 1929 by the union of smaller conservative and liberal groups, the Independence Party has traditionally been the most powerful party in Icelandic politics, having participated in almost all the country's postwar governments. The party has a very broad base of support but is supported most strongly by the nation's fishermen and commercial interests. As well, the party enjoys the highest amount of support from the high-income groups in Iceland as well as professionals, employers, and those with a university education. In terms of the urban/rural cleavage, this party is the most heavily supported party in highly populated urban areas included the capital and surrounding areas. In terms of policy, the party adopts a pro-NATO position, stands for limited state intervention, and espouses a liberal economic policy. However, the party does not strongly adhere to a specific ideology as such. Consequently, the Independence Party has been described as a "highly pragmatic rather than ideological party." The party does have a tradition of strong individualism and has, as a result, been difficult to manage at times and has suffered from splits and defections. Some have left to create new parties, as in 1983 when a popular minister left the Independence Party to form the short-lived **Citizens' Party (CP)**.

Iceland's second-strongest party has traditionally been the **Progressive Party (PP [F])**. The Progressive Party was founded in 1916 and represents largely agrarian interests and therefore does much better in rural as opposed to urban areas. The party began as a relatively conservative party but in the mid-1960s began to move to a slightly left-of-center position on economic policy. The party is against privatization and deregulation largely because these policies would hurt farmers. The party is a qualified supporter of NATO while advocating the withdrawal of U.S. forces from the country.

The **Social Democratic Party (SDP [A])** was founded in 1916 and like both the Progressive Party and Independence Party, it has contested and won seats in all of Iceland's post–World War II elections. While the party was initially in favor of classic social-democratic policies such as state ownership of large enterprises and substantial increases in spending for social welfare, in the latter post–World War II period the party has occupied a more centrist if not slightly right-of-center position with respect to economic policy. This shift occurred most prominently in the 1960s and 1970s when the party abandoned its position that the government play a large role in the national economy and it began to advocate for a freer market, particularly in the agricultural sector. Compared to other political parties in Iceland the Social Democrats have the least firm association with any one particular interest group. It does not enjoy the support of typical social-democratic allies. While it does get some support from workers, it also gets support from the private sector and is particularly weak among public-sector employees. With regard to NATO, the party is second only to the Independence Party in terms of the degree of its support for NATO membership. The Social Democratic Party has suffered from defections as well. One such defection resulted in the creation of the more neutralist **Union of Liberals and Leftists (ULL)** in the 1970s. Another such defection resulted in the creation of the short-lived, populist **Social Democratic Alliance** in 1983, which contested two elections and only managed to win seats in the first. Most recently, in 1995, a splinter group of the Social Democrats formed the **Awakening of the Nation** (or **People's Movement (PM)**).

The only truly left-of-center party in Iceland is the **People's Alliance (PA [Ab])**. This party first appeared in 1956 as an electoral coalition of the former **Socialist Party (SP)**, which contested the first three postwar elections, and more hard-line Social Democrats who had grown disenchanted with their party's shift to the center. The party initially advocated for radical socialist reforms but has gradually softened this rhetoric in recent years. The People's Alliance has, however, remained committed to a neutral foreign policy and maintained its call for Iceland to withdraw from NATO. The party does well in urban areas and is supported most heavily by public-sector employees and intellectuals.

The last of Iceland's opposition parties is the **Women's Alliance (WA [Kv])**. Founded in 1983, the party is the political manifestation of Iceland's modern feminist movement. The party has a very informal structure and prefers to be referred to as a "movement" than a political party. The Women's Alliance strives for more recognition for women in Iceland but also puts emphasis on environmental issues (more emphasis than any other party in Iceland). The Women's Alliance is, however, not explicitly opposed to NATO.

ELECTIONS

Iceland has had seventeen post–World War II elections. In every one of these, the Independence Party has received the plurality of both votes and seats but never has it received the majority of seats.

Some elections of note include the two held in 1959. The first was held on 28 June to elect a parliament to decide on constitutional reforms, and the second, on 25–26 October, was intended to elect a body to ratify the reform proposals adopted. In the first set of elections the Progressive Party saw its share of votes increase by nearly 12 percent at the expense of the Social Democrats and the People's Alliance. The Social Democrats did so badly largely because the Progressive Party ended its electoral cooperation agreement with them. As some have suggested, the People's Alliance lost support due in part to the delayed backlash from the Soviet suppression of the Hungarian uprising three years earlier.

The elections held in October under the new election law greatly benefited parties that relied on urban support. As a result, the electoral law itself was one of the major campaign issues—as was inflation and the possible devaluation of the national currency. The new law reduced the overly large number of constituencies from twenty-seven to eight and changed the method of electing members from a mixed PR system to a pure PR system. The Independence Party, whose share of the vote actually dropped by 3 percent, saw its share of seats go up by four. The changes hurt the Progressive Party by far the most because the party relies most heavily on rural support. The Social Democrats saw their seats and votes increase, not only due to the changes in the electoral law, but also to the party's shift to the right and its good performance in leading the previous government in its successful anti-inflationary measures.

The elections held on 25 April 1987 were also significant because of the poor performance of Iceland's strongest party, the Independence Party. The party polled an all-time low of 27.2 percent and only won eighteen seats. The main reason for this was the personal nature of the campaign and the creation of the new **Citizens' Party (CP)**. The party was founded by the popular ex-minister of energy and industry who was forced to resign by the Independence Party. The new party represented no significant policy change from the Independence Party and was simply a populist party. Another party, the **Social Democratic Alliance**, which was created in very much the same way for the election in 1983, failed to retain any of the seats in 1987 that it had previously won.

Turnout was high at 90 percent, and because of the drop in the voting age from twenty to eighteen, the election saw many first time voters. The election also saw a near doubling in the popular vote gained by the Women's Alliance.

The next elections, held in 1991, saw the Independence Party return to its pre-1987 levels with respect to percentage of votes; and it won more seats than in all previous post–World War II elections. This can be attributed in large part to the complete collapse of the Citizens' Party, which retained none of the seats it won in 1987. The campaign was not centered much on policies, but rather personalities, local issues, and the record of the previous governments were the major areas of debate and conflict. This helped the Independence Party as well, because it did not participate in the coalition governments from September 1988 until the elections.

The next elections, held in 1995, followed a familiar trend in that one of the older parties saw its votes drop because of the creation of a splinter party. In this case it was the Social Democrats who dropped three seats due to the creation of the newly formed **People's Movement**. The campaign was not a very lively one. Potentially divisive issues such as EU membership did not receive the focus some thought they might. Instead the main issues of the campaign included the government's record and potential alternative coalitions.

For the 1999 elections, the three left-of-center parties—the People's Alliance, the Social Democrats, and the Women's Alliance—formed what was called the **Unified Left (UL [IU])**, under Ms. Margrét Frimannssdottir of the People's Alliance. The United Left called for a redistribution of the growing economic wealth and higher welfare spending. However, yet another splinter group arose in 1999, this time from the People's Alliance. Called the **Left-Green Alliance (LGA)**, this group opposed the formation of the Unified Left. For its part, the incumbent right-center government of conservatives and progressives stressed the strong domestic economy, with its high growth, low unemployment, and falling inflation.

The elections themselves produced little change across the left-right divide. Certainly the Unified Left was disappointed with its seventeen seats, but adding in the six won by the Left-Green Alliance yields the same twenty-three leftist deputies as in 1995. The relative victor was clearly the Independence Party, which was back above 40 percent for the first time since 1974.

Selected Elections in Iceland

	June 1959		Oct. 1959		1974		1978	
	%V	#S	#V	#S	%V	#S	#V	#S
IP	42.5	20	39.7	24	42.7	25	32.7	20
PP	27.2	19	25.7	17	24.9	17	16.9	12
SDP	12.5	6	15.2	9	9.1	5	22.0	14
PA	15.3	7	16.0	10	18.3	11	22.9	14
ULL	—	—	—	—	4.6	2	3.3	0
others	2.5	0	3.4	0	0.4	0	2.2	0
TOTAL SEATS		52		60		60		60

	1987		1991		1995		1999	
	%V	#S	#V	#S	%V	#S	#V	#S
IP	27.2	18	38.6	26	37.1	25	40.7	26
PP	18.9	13	18.9	13	23.3	15	18.5	12
SDP	15.2	10	15.5	10	11.4	7	(into UL)	
PA	13.3	8	14.4	9	14.3	9	(into UL)	
WA	10.1	6	8.3	5	4.9	3	(into UL)	
CP	10.9	7	1.2	0	—	—	—	—
PM	—	—	—	—	7.2	4	(into UL)	
UL	—	—	—	—	—	—	26.8	17
LGA	—	—	—	—	—	—	9.1	6
others	4.3	1	3.1	0	1.8	0	4.9	2
TOTAL SEATS		63		63		63		63

GOVERNMENTS

Although it has always been the plurality party in terms of election results, the Independence Party could not be considered a strong party in terms of cabinet formation, in the sense of it always being in government if it so wished. In fact, a wide range of coalitions occurred in Iceland, one of which even included the Independence Party and the People's Alliance together. In the late 1990s, however, a more clear left-right polarization (at least in terms of party strategy) led in 1999 to the first-ever reelection of a right-center government. Also, Prime Minister David Oddsson (IP) is now into a record third-straight term.

Icelandic Governments since 1946

In Office Date (M/Y)	Prime Minister (Party)	#M	Parties in Cabinet
07/46	Thors, O. (IP)	6	IP SP SDP
02/47	Stefansson, S. J. (SDP)	6	SDP IP PP
12/49	Thors, O. (IP)	5	IP
03/50	Steinthorsson, S. (PP)	6	PP IP
09/53	Thors, O. (IP)	6	IP PP
07/56	Jonasson, H. (PP)	6	PP PA SDP
12/58	Jonsson, E. (SDP)	4	SDP
07/59	Jonsson, E. (SDP)	4	SDP
11/59	Thors, O. (IP)	6	IP SDP
11/63	Benediktsson, B. (IP)	7	IP SDP
06/67	Benediktsson, B. (IP)	7	IP SDP
07/70	Hafstein, J. (IP)	7	IP SDP
07/71	Johannesson, O. (PP)	7	PP PA ULL
08/74	Hallgrimsson, G. (IP)	8	IP PP
08/78	Johannesson, O. (PP)	9	PP PA SDP
10/79	Gröndal, B. (SDP)	6	SDP
02/80	Thoroddsen, G. (IP)	10	PP IP PA
05/83	Hermannsson, S. (PP)	10	IP PP
07/87	Palsson, T. (IP)	11	IP PP PA
09/88	Hermannsson, S. (PP)	9	PP PA SDP
09/89	Hermannsson, S. (PP)	11	PP PA SDP CP
04/91	Oddsson, D. (IP)	10	IP SDP
04/95	Oddsson, D. (IP)	10	IP PP
05/99	Oddsson, D. (IP)	12	IP PP

ENGLISH ABBREVIATIONS

CP	Citizens' Party
IP	Independence Party
LGA	Left-Green Alliance
PA	People's Alliance
PM	People's Movement
PP	Progressive Party
SDP	Social Democratic Party
SP	Socialist Party
WA	Women's Alliance
UL	United Left
ULL	Union of Liberals and Leftists

ICELANDIC ACRONYMS

A	Social Democratic Party
Ab	People's Alliance
F	Progressive Party
IU	United Left
Ky	Women's Alliance
Sj	Independence Party

REFERENCES

Kristinsson, Gunnar Helgi. (1995). "The Icelandic Parliamentary Election of 1995." *Electoral Studies,* Vol. 14, pp. 332–35.

———. (1991). "The Icelandic Parliamentary Election of 1991." *Electoral Studies,* Vol. 10, pp. 262–66.

Kristjánsson, Svanur. (1998). "Electoral Politics and Governance: Transformation of the Party System in Iceland, 1970–96", pp. 167–82, in Paul Pennings and Jan-Erik Lane, eds. *Comparing Party System Change.* London and New York: Routledge.

Republic of Ireland

SUMMARY OF PARTY SYSTEMS

1948–51	moderate multiparty system with one dominant party (FF)
1954–82	two-and-a-half-party system
1987–(97)	moderate multiparty system with two main parties (FF and FG)

HISTORY

Centuries of British control of the island of Ireland gave way in 1922 to independence for most of the island as the Irish Free State—but only after a bloody struggle. In 1937 a new constitution proclaimed the Irish Republic, a status finally accepted by Britain in 1949. The terms of the independence settlement and the desire to have Irish sovereignty over the entire island shaped strongly and to some extent continue to shape Irish politics.

ELECTORAL SYSTEM

The Republic of Ireland uses the single-transferable-vote form of proportional representation. STV tends to use smaller multimember districts, and indeed in Ireland these range from three to five members. Since Ireland does not have a large number of electoral parties, STV does not produce much distortion as opposed to party-list proportional representation.

POLITICAL PARTIES AND CLEAVAGES

Political parties in Ireland do not easily fit on a traditional left-right spectrum. Factors such as the largely rural population of Ireland and the influence of the Catholic Church have meant that parties have to be forced to develop in response to a largely rural, morally conservative voting public. And factors such as the divisions over partition with Northern Ireland and the 1921 Treaty with Britain have meant that where divisions do exist they are not necessarily ideological but rather historical. Politics are also very localized.

Throughout the post–World War II period of Irish elections, one party has consistently won the plurality of both seats and votes; that party is **Fianna Fáil (FF)**. The origins of the party stem from the element within Sinn Féin that refused to accept the Treaty with Britain in 1921 and therefore took no part in the parliament that was subsequently formed for the first few years. Because of its origins as a party formed in protest to a historical event, the party has never developed a firm ideology that can be described in left-right terms. If an ideology does exist, some have argued that this would be "Republicanism," as the party has consistently rejected partition. On economic issues the party has at times had a left-leaning approach; they have supported government expenditures to promote economic development and have resisted cuts to welfare. The party has at other times also presented a more liberal policy on economics, calling for reduced government spending and lower taxes. When it comes to social issues, the party occupies a much more consistent and conservative position and has very close ties to the Catholic Church. The party enjoys the widest base of support among all Irish political parties.

Supporters of the Treaty with Britain in 1921 formed their own party and that was **Fine Gael (FG)**. Like Fianna Fáil, Fine Gael has a broad base of support but does best among the upper middle class in urban areas as well as middle and large farm owners. In the late 1970s and early 1980s the party made a concerted effort to increase its support among lower-income groups but this was not entirely successful. The party has never managed to poll more than its main rivals, Fianna Fáil, but it has formed governments in coalition with other parties. Fine Gael advocates a less conservative position on social policy compared with Fianna Fail. The party does, however, share in its rival's support for good relations with Northern Ireland and eventual reunification.

The **Labour Party** was founded in 1912 as the political wing of the Trade Union Congress and became a separate entity in 1930. It has traditionally been the third-place finisher in Ireland's post–World War II elections. The party has been very weak compared with other left-wing parties in the rest of Europe principally because the demographics do not exist in Ireland to provide sufficient support for the left-wing policies traditional labor parties espouse. This hasn't necessarily prevented the party from calling for public ownership of many industries and expanded social welfare but it has meant that it has had to refocus attention in non-traditional areas. The party, for example, has argued for expansion in the agriculture industry in order to appeal to the rural vote. The party has also been forced to tone down rhetoric and make compromises on policy stances in order for it to participate in coalition governments with the other more conservative parties.

Apart from these three parties, Ireland has seen several other short-lived parties that have contested elections. After the war, the two most important were the small farmers-based **Party of the Land (CnT)** and the nationalistic **Party of the Republic (CnP)**. Among those currently active, and that have won significant representation in parliament, is the **Democratic Left Party (DLP)**. This party was founded in 1992 by members of the defunct **Workers' Party (WP)**, which had contested eight elections and won representation in five of these. The DLP is committed to democratic socialism and in 1994 was a member of the so-called rainbow-coalition government along with the Labour Party and Fine Gael.

Another of these smaller parties is the **Progressive Democrats (PD)**. The Progressive Democrats was founded in 1985 by ex-members of Fianna Fáil and did very well in their first election in 1987, when the party won fourteen seats, finishing in third place. The party was formed largely as an option from the more amorphous traditional parties and has firmly positioned itself on the right, advocating tax reform, tax cuts, and support for private enterprise. Despite the drop in support for the party in recent elections, it did form the government with Fianna Fail following the 1997 elections.

The final party to mention is significant less for its electoral performance and more for its history and association with the Irish Republican Army. **Sinn Féin (SF)** won its first seat in parliament in 1997. The party believes in a united socialist republic with the north.

ELECTIONS

Until the 1980s, Irish elections were stable in the sense that the FF would come in first (often with a majority of seats), the FG would come in second, and the Labour Party would come in a distant third. In 1987, however, the Progressive Democrats entered the Irish political stage and did what no new party had done in all previous and subsequent post–World War II elections—it won more seats than any of the three traditional parties. The major reason behind the success of the PD was the fact that it broke with tradition and presented itself as a party with a clear ideology and a clear campaign platform. The party to suffer most from the PD's performance was Fine Gael, whose economic policy most closely matches that of the PD. Fine Gael fought the elections on its record in the previous government and on its budget proposals proposals that had caused the withdrawal of the Labour Party from the government coalition, leading to the government's collapse and the early calling of elections. Fianna Fáil's campaign lacked specifics and Fine Gael attacked them for it. One successful aspect of the Fianna Fáil campaign was, however, the party's argument that a single-party government could offer greater stability, and only it could be that party.

Selected Elections in Ireland

	1948		**1957**		**1973**		**Nov. 1982**	
	%V	**#S**	**#V**	**#S**	**%V**	**#S**	**#V**	**#S**
FF	41.3	68	48.3	78	46.2	69	45.2	75
FG	19.9	31	26.6	40	35.1	54	39.2	70
Labour	9.8	14	9.1	12	13.7	19	9.4	16
CnT	13.0	7	2.4	3	—	—	—	—
CnP	6.0	10	1.7	1	—	—	—	—
WP	—	—	5.3	4	1.1	0	3.3	2
others	10.0	17	6.6	9	3.8	2	2.9	3
TOTAL SEATS		147		147		144		166

	1987		**1989**		**1992**		**1997**	
	%V	**#S**	**#V**	**#S**	**%V**	**#S**	**#V**	**#S**
FF	44.1	81	44.2	77	39.1	68	39.3	77
FG	27.1	51	29.2	55	24.5	45	27.9	54
Labour	6.4	12	9.5	15	19.3	33	10.4	17
WP	3.8	4	5.0	7	0.7	0	—	—
PD	11.8	14	5.5	6	4.7	10	4.7	4
DLP	—	—	—	—	2.8	4	2.5	4
others	6.8	3	6.6	6	8.9	6	15.2	10
TOTAL SEATS		165		166		166		166

The elections held in 1992 saw the participation of yet another new party. This time it was the **Democratic Left Party** that contested elections on a firm ideological platform—for the DLP this was an ardently social-democratic one. The election was called early due to the breakdown of the Fianna Fáil–Progressive Democrat coalition. The main issues of the campaign included unemployment, ethics in government, health service provisions, and rising interest rates. The results showed the people's dissatisfaction with both Fianna Fáil and Fine Gael. Fianna Fáil won the fewest amount of seats since 1954 and Fine Gael won the fewest amount of seats since the 1957 election. Labour had its best results ever, more than doubling its representation from the previous election. This allowed the party to be a major player in the subsequent rainbow-coalition government, which was set up with Fine Gael and the DLP. Both the DLP's and Labour's success came largely at the expense of the Workers' Party which lost all its representation in parliament.

The most recent elections held in Ireland were in 1997. These elections saw virtually the same results from the elections of 1989. The Labour Party lost all the gains it had made in the previous elections and once again Fianna Fáil was able to translate its success into the formation of a new government. These elections also saw a large number of votes and seats go to smaller parties and independents. Among those parties to win a single seat in the parliament was Sinn Féin.

GOVERNMENTS

Until 1989 there were only two types of governments in Ireland. On the one hand there were the single-party governments of Fianna Fáil, and on the other hand there were coalitions of the remaining relevant parties. Initially this "anti-FF" alliance involved Fine Gail, the Labour Party, the CnT, and (briefly) the CnP. By the 1960s only Fine Gail and Labour remained, but they would form a stable alternative government. However, in 1989 Fianna Fáil broke its historic vow of "no coalitions"; since then, it has governed with both the Progressive Democrats and Labour as junior partners.

Irish Governments since 1948

In Office Date (M/Y)	Prime Minister (Party)	#M(I)	Parties in Cabinet
02/48	Costello, J. (FG)	14(2)	FG Labour CnP CnT
06/51	de Valera, E. (FF)	12(1)	FF
06/54	Costello, J. (FG)	14	FG Labour CnT
03/57	de Valera, E. (FF)	12	FF
06/59	Lemass, S. (FF)	14	FF
10/61	Lemass, S. (FF)	15	FF
04/65	Lemass, S. (FF)	15	FF
11/66	Lynch, J. (FF)	15	FF
07/69	Lynch, J. (FF)	14	FF
03/73	Cosgrave, L. (FG)	15	FG Labour
07/77	Lynch, J. (FF)	16	FF
12/79	Haughey, C. (FF)	15	FF
06/81	Fitzgerald, G. (FG)	15(1)	FG Labour
03/82	Haughey, C. (FF)	16	FF
12/82	Fitzgerald, G. (FG)	17(1)	FG Labour
03/87	Haughey, C. (FF)	15	FF
07/89	Haughey, C. (FF)	17	FF PD
02/92	Reynolds, A. (FF)	16	FF PD
10/92	Reynolds, A. (FF)	14	FF
01/93	Reynolds, A. (FF)	15	FF Labour
12/94	Bruton, J. (FG)	15	FG Labour DLP
06/97	Ahern, B. (FF)	15	FF PD

ACRONYMS

CnP Party of the Republic
CnT Party of the Land
DLP Democratic Left Party

continued

ACRONYMS *Continued*

FF	Fianna Fáil
FG	Fine Gael
PD	Progressive Democrats
SF	Sinn Féin
WP	Workers' Party

REFERENCES

Collins, Neil. (1993). "The Irish Election of 1992." *Electoral Studies,* Vol. 12, No. 2, pp. 180–84.

Farrell, David M. (1994). "Ireland: Centralization, Professionalization, and Competitive Pressures," in Richard S. Katz and Peter Mair, eds. *How Parties Organize: Change and Adaption in Party Organization in Western Democracies.* London: SAGE, pp. 216–41.

Farrell, David M. (1999). "Ireland: A Party System Transformed?," in David Broughton and Mark Donovan, eds., *Changing Party Systems in Western Europe.* London: Pinter, pp. 30–47.

Sinnott, Richard. (1995). *Irish Voters Decide: Voting Behaviour in Elections and Referendums Since 1918.* Manchester: Manchester University Press.

Italy

SUMMARY OF PARTY SYSTEMS

1946–58	extreme multiparty system with one dominant party (DC)
1963–87	extreme multiparty system with two main parties (DC and PCI)
1992–(96)	extreme multiparty system with a balance among the parties

HISTORY

Italy was finally unified in 1870 as a secular monarchy. Until World War I, the anti-clerical liberals dominated politics based on a limited franchise. After the war, with universal male suffrage, a fragmented and multiparty system soon developed. This included the Catholic Popular Party, since the pre–World War I papal prohibition of Catholic involvement in the politics of secular Italy was lifted. Growing polarization and instability set the stage for Mussolini's seizure of power in 1922. By 1925 he had consolidated his totalitarian regime.

Defeat in World War II, and Allied occupation, paved the way for another attempt at democratization. A referendum abolished the monarchy in 1946, and another referendum in 1948 approved a new constitution. Under this, voters have the right to repeal legislation through referenda, although the enabling legislation did not pass until 1970. Increasing secularization of Italian society would be evidenced in the 1971 legalization of divorce and the 1978 limited legalization of abortion. A 1974 referendum on repealing the new liberal divorce law was demanded by militant Catholics: despite heavy campaigning by the Christian Democrats and the Vatican in this landmark vote, Italian voters confirmed their support for divorce by 19 million to 13 million.

ELECTORAL SYSTEM

The postwar Italian system used a very proportional PR system; with no national threshold to win seats, many small and smaller parties not only won seats but played a role in national politics. Opposition to political fragmentation and to the entrenched power of the traditional parties—what the Italians called *partitocrazia,* or "partyocracy"—led to a growing movement in the early 1990s for electoral reform so as to allow more decisive elections in which voters could throw out governments. Although certain parties favored a shift to the French single-member, majority-plurality system, the decision was made to move largely to British-style single-member plurality. The term *largely* is used because, in order to preserve some powers of traditional party elites, the electoral system for the lower house adopted in 1993 provided for three-quarters of the seats to be elected by single-member plurality, but one-quarter by proportional representation in twenty-six multimember districts—albeit with a 4 percent national threshold. Voters have two votes under this system.

The allocation of the PR seats in Italy is complicated: this is neither fully compensatory as in Germany or a completely separate calculation as in Russia. Instead, it is somewhat compensatory in that parties winning plurality seats do pay a "price" when it comes to determining PR seats. This price, called the *scorporo* ("unbundling," or "separation"), works as follows in the Chamber of Deputies: for each multimember district, for each plurality seat won, the party will have its total PR votes reduced by the number of votes received by the *second-placed* candidate in the specific single-member plurality constituency, plus one (vote). Only the PR votes remaining after the scorporo for each plurality seat are used to calculate the consistency of PR seats.

A referendum was held in April 1999 on whether to remove these PR seats and thus make the system entirely single-member plurality. Supporters of the remaining proportional seats (mainly the smaller parties), seeing the overall public approval for the change, endeavoured to keep the voter turnout down so as to make the vote invalid. In other words, those people who did want to retain some proportionality deliberately did not vote. Consequently, even though the overwhelming majority of actual voters supported removing these seats, the turnout fell just under the 50 percent threshold for validity.

POLITICAL PARTIES AND CLEAVAGES THROUGH 1992

Without a doubt, the main party of postwar Italy was the **Christian Democrat (DC)** party, founded in September 1943. It dominated government, providing every prime minister until 1981. Intended as a broad catchall party, the DC certainly succeeded in this vein, attracting the support of industrialists and Catholic workers, shopkeepers and housewives, and above all small farmers. This being said, the party was basically on the center right, supporting social programs as well as capitalism, although some of its factors went further left or further right. The appeal of the DC was basically threefold. First, of all the parties in Italy, it was the only explicitly religious one; thus, it gained the votes of practising Catholics. Second, it was seen as a centrist, democratic force in a country with both communists and neofascists. In this sense voting for the DC was more of an "anti-" vote in which one voted against the extremes. Third and finally, the DC was the most important party of clientelism, especially toward farmers and the poorer south. It monopolized key patronage ministries such as agriculture and public works.

The other two key, albeit small, parties on the center right were the **Italian Liberal Party (PLI)** and the **Italian Republican Party (PRI)**, both of which were clearly secular—in contrast to the Christian Democrats. The Liberals dated back to 1848 and, as noted above, dominated Italian politics before the First World War. Their collaboration with Mussolini discredited them after the war. The Republicans, for their part, dated back to 1897. In postwar Italy these parties were backed by key industrialists and business leaders. Of the two, the Liberals were generally more clearly to the right of the DC on economics.

To the right of the DC on most everything was the neofascist **Italian Social Movement (MSI)**, founded in 1946. Strongest in southern Italy, the MSI looked back to the Mussolini era and called for social and economic ultraconservatism and heavy defense spending. With one brief exception in 1960, it was considered an unacceptable pariah by the regime parties.

On the left of the political spectrum, there were initially only two parties in postwar Italy: the **Italian Socialist Party (PSI)**, founded in 1892, and the **Communist Party of Italy (PCI)**, founded in 1921. The Communists benefited from their role in the resistance, and in the 1946 elections would get almost as much support as the Socialists. Both the Socialists and the Communists participated in the basically all-party coalitions that governed Italy from 1945 until early 1947. However, with the Cold War intensifying, the PCI was kicked out of the DC-led government. The majority of the Socialists chose to join the Communists in strongly opposing the DC-led regime. Indeed, in 1948 the two parties ran jointly as the **People's Democratic Front (FDP)**. However, not all Socialists wished to ally with the Communists. Encouraged by the United States, a third of the PSI split off in 1947 to form the **Italian Social Democratic Party (PSDI)**. The PSDI and the PSI would link up once, in 1968, but otherwise remained two parties.

Although the PSI and the PCI remained allies until 1956, they competed separately in the 1953 elections. The Communists, having gained control of the main leftist organs (newspapers, trade unions, and so on), gained almost twice the support of the Socialists. Starting in 1953, then, the PCI would always be the second-largest party and the PSI the third largest. The PCI was strongest in the north-central part of Italy, where it built up a clear subculture. As the main opposition party (except from 1976 to 1979, when it supported a DC government in an attempt to produce a "historic compromise" between the two parties), the PCI benefited from the protest vote in an increasingly stagnant system. It also moderated its ideology and distanced itself from the Soviet Union, so that by the 1970s it was the paradigm of "Eurocommunism." The PCI grew steadily in support from 1958 to 1976, peaking in the latter elections at just over a third of the vote. However, it then went into a slow decline, in part because of the success with younger voters of the libertarian **Radical Party (PR)**, founded in 1976, and later on the **Green Federation (FdV)**, founded in 1987.

Since the Communists were essentially the party of the nonpracticing Catholic working class, the Socialists were left without a clear base. From 1956 onward they moved toward the center left and reentered government as junior partners of the Christian Democrats in 1963. Like the DC, the PSI soon proved adept at colonizing part of the state apparatus and thus acquiring votes through clientelism. With the two larger parties becoming ever closer in support, the PSI's position as number three put it ever more clearly into the king-maker position, and ultimately put Bettino Craxi, its leader since 1976, into the prime minister's office in 1983.

The Italian party system would, however, be completely shaken up by the fall of communism in eastern Europe. The PCI now wished to be seen explicitly as a social-democratic party (in the broader west European sense). In 1991, therefore, it reformed itself as the **Democratic Party of the Left (PDS)**. However, a hard-line minority within the party opposed this evolution and thus broke away to form the **Communist Refoundation (RC)**. The DC was also affected by the evolving situation: without its "anticommunist card," its support fell off in the north to the **Northern League (LN)**, founded in 1991 (but following from the 1987 **Lombard League (LL)**). These regional protest parties targeted Italians angry about corruption and the "waste" of their tax dollars on spending elsewhere in the country. In contrast, in the clientelistic-based south, the DC vote held through the 1992 elections.

Selected Elections in Italy, 1946–92

	1946		1948		1958		1963	
	%V	#S	%V	#S	%V	#S	%V	#S
PLI	6.8	41	3.8	19	3.5	17	7.6	39
PSI	20.7	115	(in FDP)		14.2	84	13.8	87
PRI	4.4	23	2.5	9	1.4	6	1.4	6
PCI	19.0	104	(in FDP)		22.7	140	25.3	166
DC	35.2	207	48.5	305	42.4	273	38.3	260
MSI	—	—	2.0	6	4.8	24	5.1	27
PSDI	—	—	7.1	33	4.5	22	6.1	33
FDP	—	—	31.0	183	—	—	—	—
others	13.9	65	5.1	19	6.5	30	3.0	12
TOTAL SEATS		555		574		596		630

	1976		1979		1987		1992	
	%V	#S	%V	#S	%V	#S	%V	#S
PLI	1.3	5	1.9	9	2.1	11	2.8	17
PSI	9.6	58	9.8	62	14.3	94	13.6	92
PRI	3.1	14	3.0	16	3.7	21	4.4	27
PCI	34.4	228	30.4	201	26.6	177	—	—
DC	38.7	262	38.3	262	34.3	234	29.7	206
MSI	6.1	35	5.3	30	5.9	35	5.4	34
PSDI	3.4	15	3.8	20	3.0	17	2.7	16
PR	1.1	4	3.5	18	2.6	13	1.2	7
FdV	—	—	—	—	2.5	13	2.8	16
LL/LN	—	—	—	—	0.5	0	8.6	55
PDS	—	—	—	—	—	—	16.1	107
RC	—	—	—	—	—	—	5.6	35
others	2.2	9	4.0	12	5.0	15	7.1	18
TOTAL SEATS		630		630		630		630

POLITICAL REALIGNMENT AND RECENT ELECTIONS

Starting just before the 1992 elections, but intensifying after them, an investigation into bribery and kickbacks in Milan soon discredited most of the PSI, which began to disintegrate. The rot then spread into the other governing parties, especially the DC. By early 1993 the leaders of the PSI, the PLI, and the PSDI had all resigned. The DC leadership initially held firm, but a well-known reformer within the party, Mario Segni, broke away. The DC vote dropped in the June 1993 local elections and then almost vanished in other local elections later in the year. The party thus dissolved itself at the beginning of 1994. Two parties would quickly arise out of the ashes of the DC: the **Italian People's Party (PPI)** and the **Christian Democratic Center (CCD)**, which was actually more right of center.

To sum up at this point, by 1993 the traditional governing parties—DC, PSI, PSDI, PRI, and PLI—had all been discredited, whereas those parties that had not been part of postwar Italian governments—PDS, PR, Greens, MSI, and the relatively new LN—survived the corruption scandals as intact forces. In the local elections of 1993 leftist candidates, backed by but not always members of the PDS, thus, did very well, winning many key mayoralty races. Of course, outside of northern Italy where the LN ran, the main opposition candidate was likely from the MSI, so for some voters, certainly, a leftist mayor was the lesser of two evils.

Nevertheless, the left did look like it had the momentum to win the upcoming March 1994 national elections. This prospect was viewed with apprehension by Silvio Berlusconi, the media magnate. Building on his business network, in late 1993 he quickly formed **Forza Italia! (FI)**, a party that was a mixture of media creation, marketing focus, and sporting-club support. (The name itself translates as "Let's Go Italy!" or "Come On Italy!") The FI then struck an electoral and hopefully governmental alliance, the Alliance for Freedom, with the LN in the north, and a similar alliance, the Alliance for Good Government, with the **National Alliance (AN)** in the south. The AN was the new version of the MSI, set up for the 1994 elections. Its leader, Gianfranco Fini, toned down its fascist legacy and tried, fairly successfully, to present the image of a nationalist-conservative party, somewhat akin to the Gaullists in France. As was the case with the PDS and RC, hardline neofascists opposed the change from MSI to AN; however, running separately as **The Flame**, these would get less than 1 percent of the vote in the March elections. Finally, the CCD joined in with Berlusconi's side, as did most of the PR, despite their leftist libertarianism.

Opposing the Alliance for Freedom/Alliance for Good Government were two other electoral alliances. In the center, there was the Pact for Italy, involving the PPI and a list around Mario Segni. The Pact for Italy, thus, was explicitly centrist and implicitly religious, factors that have certainly worked for the DC in the past. On the left, the PDS built a Progressive Alliance that included the Greens, what little was left of the PSI—now the **Italian Socialists (SI)**—some smaller left parties, but also the RC. The presence within the Progressive Alliance of the Refounded Communists certainly hurt its image with moderate voters.

On election day the Alliance for Freedom/Alliance for Good Government easily triumphed over the Progressive Alliance. Berlusconi had, thus, largely filled the political space left by the disappearance of the DC. The Pact for Italy was but a distant third and was squeezed further by the new electoral system. Berlusconi then formed a government in which both domestic and international controversy was aroused by the presence of three AN ministers who had been leaders of the MSI. Moreover, Berlusconi soon ran into problems with personal conflict of interest between his business empire and the prime ministership. Finally, the planned budget, with its welfare cutbacks and amnesty for tax evaders, led to massive public protests in late 1994. Sensing political trouble, and frustrated by the failure to quickly federalize Italy, the LN jumped ship at the end of the year, and the Berlusconi government fell. It was succeeded by a technocratic administration under Lamberto Dini, Berlusconi's finance minister and a former director of the Bank of Italy. Dini's government, although right of center, was flexible and conciliatory; it survived for over a year due to the support of the Progressive Alliance, which wished to show its credentials for moderate fiscal conservatism.

The 1994 Italian Elections

	%V	#S
Progressive Alliance		
PDS	20.4	109
RC	6.0	39
FdV	2.7	11
SI	2.2	14
others	3.1	40
total	*34.4*	*213*

continued

The 1994 Italian Elections *Continued*

	%V	#S
Pact for Italy		
PPI	11.1	33
Segni Pact	4.6	13
total	*15.7*	*46*
Alliance for Freedom/Alliance for Good Government		
LN	8.4	117
FI	21.0	99
AN	13.5	109
CCD		29
ex-PR	3.5	6
others		6
total	*46.4*	*366*
other parties	3.5	5
TOTAL SEATS		630

Note: Vote percentage refers only to PR ballots; seat total combines single-member plurality and proportional districts.

To some extent, the 1996 elections were to be a replay of 1994, in that two broad alliances confronted each other. There would be no centrist alliance, as the PPI split into a center-right group, the **United Christian Democrats (CDU)**, which allied with Berlusconi, and a center-left group. However, there were several more important changes. On the right, Berlusconi's Alliance for Freedom continued to group his FI, the AN, the CCD, and now the CDU. However, the Northern League contested these elections separately. Berlusconi himself was weakened by charges of tax evasion and bribery. On the left, this time the PDS formed the **Olive Tree** alliance, which still included the Greens, the RC, and other leftists but also a list led by outgoing Prime Minister Dini called **Italian Renewal (RI)** and, crucially, many center-left Christian democrats. Indeed, the proposed prime minister of the Olive Tree was Romano Prodi, an economics professor and former member of the DC. Finally, its support for the fiscally responsible Dini administration aided the credibility of the PDS.

On election day the Olive Tree thus won the majority of seats; however, the alliance with the RC was only electoral and this party was not part of the new government, merely a supporter (and the RC would cause the temporary fall of the government in 1997). It is also worth stressing that although the Olive Tree only won slightly more PR votes than the Alliance for Freedom—43.4 percent to 42.1 percent—its vote lead was higher in the single member seats, 44.9 percent to 40.3 percent, thus producing its victory. This outcome arose because the Olive Tree was a more disciplined alliance than the Alliance for Freedom, some of the voters of which opted for an opposition candidate if the particular Alliance for Freedom candidate in their constituency was not to their liking.

Yet another new party would be created in February 1998, when former president Francisco Cossiga attracted Christian democrats away from both the CCD and the CDU to his new **Democratic Union of the Republic (UDR)**. Whereas the CCD and CDU are both right of center in terms of their alliances, the UDR was another attempt to create a truly centrist hinge force. It would, in fact, join in with the PDS-led left-wing government formed in October of that year.

The 1996 Italian Elections

	%V	#S
Olive Tree		
PDS	21.1	171
Prodi Group	6.8	72
Dini List - RI	4.3	26
FdV	2.5	16
sub-total	*34.8*	*285*
RC	8.6	35
total	*43.4*	*320*
Alliance *for* Freedom		
AN	15.7	93
FI	20.6	123
CCD*	5.8	19
CDU*		11
total	*42.1*	*246*
Northern League (LN)	10.1	59
other parties	4.4	5
TOTAL SEATS		630

*CCD and CDU are combined here for a total of 5.8 percent of the vote.

Note: Vote percentage refers only to PR ballots; seat total combines single-member plurality and proportional districts.

GOVERNMENTS

Italy is known for governmental instability. Nevertheless, after the broad coalitions of the immediate postwar period and until the collapse of the old order in 1993, there were two main types of governments. The first, more common earlier on when the DC was clearly dominant, was a single-party minority of the party. The second type was a coalition including some or all of the smaller secular parties (PSDI, PRI, PLI) and/or from 1963 onward the PSI. As the gap between the DC and the PCI narrowed, and thus a left-of-DC government became mathematically possible, the "hinge" parties increased their bargaining power. Thus, ultimately, in the 1980s and early 1990s non–Christian Democrats became prime minister, although the DC was still central in terms of cabinet seats.

Italian Governments since 1946

In Office Date (M/Y)	Prime Minister (Party)	#M(I)	Parties in Cabinet	Supporting Parties
07/46	de Gasperi, A. (DC)	17	DC PSI PCI PRI PLI	
02/47	de Gasperi, A. (DC)	15(2)	DC PCI PSI	
05/47	de Gasperi, A. (DC)	16(5)	DC PLI	
12/47	de Gasperi, A. (DC)	20(5)	DC PSDI PLI PRI	
05/48	de Gasperi, A. (DC)	20(3)	DC PSDI PLI PRI	
01/50	de Gasperi, A. (DC)	20	DC PRI PSDI	
07/51	de Gasperi, A. (DC)	16	DC PRI	
07/53	de Gasperi, A. (DC)	17	DC	PRI
08/53	Pella, G. (DC)	17	DC	PRI PLI PMP
01/54	Fanfani, A. (DC)	19(1)	DC	
02/54	Scelba, M. (DC)	21	DC PSDI PLI	PRI
07/55	Segni, A. (DC)	21	DC PSDI PLI	PRI
05/57	Zoli, A. (DC)	20(1)	DC	MSI PMP
07/58	Fanfani, A. (DC)	20	DC PSDI	PRI
02/59	Segni, A. (DC)	21	DC	PLI PMP
03/60	Tambroni, F. (DC)	22	DC	MSI
07/60	Fanfani, A. (DC)	24	DC	PSDI PRI

In Office Date (M/Y)	Prime Minister (Party)	#M(I)	Parties in Cabinet	Supporting Parties
02/62	Fanfani, A. (DC)	24	DC PSDI PRI	PSI
06/63	Leone, G. (DC)	23	DC	
12/63	Moro, A. (DC)	26	DC PSI PSDI PRI	
07/64	Moro, A. (DC)	26	DC PSI PSDI PRI	
02/66	Moro, A. (DC)	26	DC PSI PSDI PRI	
07/68	Leone, G. (DC)	23	DC	
12/68	Rumor, M. (DC)	27	DC PSI PRI	
08/69	Rumor, M. (DC)	25	DC	PSI PSDI
03/70	Rumor, M. (DC)	27	DC PSI PSDI PRI	
08/70	Colombo, E. (DC)	28	DC PSI PSDI PRI	
02/71	Colombo, E. (DC)	27	DC PSI PSDI	
02/72	Andreotti, G. (DC)	25	DC	
06/72	Andreotti, G. (DC)	26	DC PSDI PLI	PRI
09/73	Rumor, M. (DC)	29	DC PSI PSDI PRI	
03/74	Rumor, M. (DC)	26	DC PSI PSDI	PRI
11/74	Moro, A. (DC)	25	DC PRI	PSI PSDI
02/76	Moro, A. (DC)	22	DC	PSDI
07/76	Andreotti, G. (DC)	22(1)	DC	
03/78	Andreotti. G. (DC)	21(1)	DC	PCI PSI PSDI PRI
03/79	Andreotti, G. (DC)	21	DC PSDI PRI	
08/79	Cossiga, F. (DC)	23(2)	DC PSDI PLI	
04/80	Cossiga, F. (DC)	28	DC PSI PRI	
10/80	Forlani, A. (DC)	27	DC PSI PRI PSDI	
06/81	Spadolini, G. (PRI)	28	DC PSI PSDI PRI PLI	
08/82	Spadolini, G. (PRI)	28	DC PSI PSDI PRI PLI	
12/82	Fanfani, A. (DC)	26	DC PSI PSDI PLI	
08/83	Craxi, B. (PSI)	30	DC PSI PRI PSDI PLI	

continued

Italian Governments since 1946 *Continued*

In Office Date (M/Y)	Prime Minister (Party)	#M(I)	Parties in Cabinet	Supporting Parties
08/86	Craxi, B. (PSI)	30	DC PSI PRI PSDI PLI	
04/87	Fanfani, A. (DC)	27(11)	DC	
07/87	Goria, G. (DC)	31	DC PSI PRI PSDI PLI	
04/88	De Mita, C. (DC)	30	DC PSI PSDI PRI PLI	
07/89	Andreotti, G. (DC)	33	DC PSI PRI PSDI PLI	
04/91	Andreotti, G. (DC)	30	DC PSI PSDI PLI	
06/92	Amato, G. (PSI)	25(4)	DC PSI PLI PSDI	
04/93	Ciampi, C.A. (ind)	26(5)	DC PSI PDS PRI FdV PLI PSDI	
05/93	Ciampi, C.A. (ind)	26(9)	DC PSI PRI PLI PSDI	
05/94	Berlusconi, S. (FI)	26(6)	FI LN AN	
01/95	Dini, L. (ind)	(20)	(caretaker government)	
04/96	Prodi, R. (PPI)	21(3)	PDS PPI RI FdV UD	RC
10/97	Prodi, R. (PPI)	21(3)	PDS PPI RI FdV UD	RC
10/98	D'Alema, M. (PDS)	26(4)	PDS PPI UDR RI FdV PDCI PSDI	

ACRONYMS

AN	National Alliance
CCD	Christian Democratic Center
CDU	United Christian Democrats
DC	Christian Democrats
FDP	People's Democratic Front
FdV	Green Federation
FI	Forza Italia
LL	Lombard League
LN	Northern League
MSI	Italian Social Movement
PCI	Communist Party of Italy
PDS	Democratic Party of the Left
PLI	Italian Liberal Party

PMP	Popular Monarchist Party
PPI	Italian People's Party
PR	Radical Party
PRI	Italian Republican Party
PSDI	Italian Social Democratic Party
PSI	Italian Socialist Party
RC	Communist Refoundation
RI	Italian Renewal
SI	Italian Socialists
UDR	Democratic Union of the Republic

REFERENCES

Bardi, Luciano, and Leonardo Morlino (1994). "Italy: Tracing the Roots of the Great Transformation," pp. 242–77, in Richard S. Katz and Peter Mair, eds. *How Parties Organize: Change and Adaption in Party Organization in Western Democracies.* London: SAGE.

Daniels, Philip (1999). "Italy: Rupture and Regeneration?," in David Broughton and Mark Donovan, eds., *Changing Party Systems in Western Europe.* London: Pinter, pp. 71–95.

Hine, David. (1993). *Governing Italy: The Politics of Bargained Pluralism.* Oxford: Oxford University Press.

Lange, Peter and Sidney Tarrow, eds. (1980). *Italy in Transition: Conflict and Consensus.* London: Frank Cass.

Partridge, Hilary. (1998). *Italian Politics Today.* Manchester and New York: Manchester University Press.

Latvia

SUMMARY OF PARTY SYSTEM

1993–(98)	extreme multiparty system with a balance among the parties

HISTORY

Before being absorbed by Russia in the eighteenth century, Latvia had been ruled in whole or in part by Sweden, Poland, and the Livonian branch of the Teutonic knights. In 1917 Latvia came under Bolshevik rule, and it was occupied by Germany in 1918. The interwar democratic government lasted until the coup of 1934. Latvia was formally incorporated into the USSR in 1940. On 11 January 1990 the Latvian Supreme Soviet voted to abolish the clause in constitution that gave the Communist Party the "leading role" in government. It also condemned the 1940 annexation by the USSR. The pro-independence Popular Front movement won elections in 1990, and its leader was named prime minister. Latvia declared independence in August 1991 after a referendum. The first sovereign democratic elections were in 1993.

ELECTORAL SYSTEM

Latvia uses proportional representation, and the distribution of seats among parties is based on the Saint-Lagüe method. Vacancies that occur between general elections are filled by the "next-in-line" candidates of the same party list.

Only those parties obtaining at least 5 percent of the national vote gain representation in the *Saeima* (parliament). The threshold for representation was 4 percent for the 1993 election but was increased to 5 percent the following year.

POLITICAL PARTIES AND CLEAVAGES

In Latvia, key ideological divisions include the degree to which the parties are nationalist and how they feel about the Russian minority population in Latvia.

The **Democratic Party Saimnieks (DPS)** is descended from the prewar **Democratic Center Party (DCP)** which was relaunched in 1992 and won five seats in the 1993 elections. It became the Democratic Party in 1994 before merging with the Saimnieks parliamentary group to form the DPS in 1995. The DPS holds a liberal position on economic issues and is moderately nationalist. *Saimnieks* means "head of farmstead" and is often translated as "in charge." In 1996 the party absorbed the smaller **Latvian Unity Party (LVP)**. The LVP was formed by orthodox Communists of the Soviet era and resists rapid economic and social reform. The LVP won 0.1 percent of the vote in 1993 but 7.2 percent in 1995, before merging with the DPS.

Latvian Way (LC) (also known as Latvia's Way) contested the 1993 elections as a grouping of "personalities," including ex-communists and many Latvians who had been living abroad and therefore had experience in public service. The LC represented middle-of-the-road views and claimed to be a "non-ideological" coalition. Possessing a liberal-conservative, socioeconomic orientation the party, like the DSP, is non-hostile to the Latvian minority population.

Even more liberal in terms of attitudes toward the Russian minority is the **National Harmony Party (TSP)**, which is the 1994 continuation of what remained of the **Harmony for Latvia and Rebirth of the National Economy (SL)** grouping that contested the 1993 elections. The TSP advocates a policy of coexistence between Latvians and non-Latvians and believes in entrenched rights for minority groups. In terms of foreign policy, the party has advocated a balanced approach between East (Russia) and West (the European Union). In 1996 the party technically lost its parliamentary status because when several of its parliamentarians split to join Saimnieks, the rest of the party members holding seats dropped below the minimum for forming a parliamentary group and therefore were forced to sit as independents.

The **Latvian Socialist Party (LSP)** is the successor to the **Equality** (or Equal Rights) grouping which contested the 1993 elections representing the interests of the non-Latvian population. The party adopted its current name in 1994. The party urges, among other things, the adoption of Russian as Latvia's official second language. The party has lost strength, however, since the creation of other non-Latvian parties representing the interests of the Russian minority.

In the other direction of the political spectrum, vis-à-vis the nationality issue, we find the **Latvian National Conservative Party (LNNK)**. The LNNK was known as the Latvian National Independence Party from 1988 to 1994 but than changed its name. The party is ultranationalist and anti-Russian and has argued for more restrictive citizenship laws. In 1995 it contested the election with the **Latvian Green Party (LZP)**. Unlike traditional European Green parties, the LZP is on the right in terms of its nationalist attitudes, seeing a strong ethnically Latvian Latvia as a necessary step to better environmental conditions. In 1997 the LNNK merged with TUB to form the **For Fatherland and Freedom/Latvian National Conservative Party (FF-LNNK)**.

The second half of the FF-LNNK is the **Fatherland and Freedom Alliance (TUB)**, which was formed in 1993 as an alliance of ultra-right-wing parties. The TUB had a link to the interwar party of the Waffen SS during the period of German occupation. The TUB was officially constituted as a party in 1995, two years before its merger with the LNNK.

Sharing this type of attitude with respect to non-Latvians is the **National Movement for Latvia–Zigerists' Party (TKL-ZP)**, founded in 1995 by Joahims Zigerists. Zigerists is a wealthy German businessman who was born Joachim Siegerist. He claimed Latvian citizenship through his father, an ethnic German who fled Latvia at the end of World War II. Zigerists was originally a deputy from the LNNK but was kicked out of parliament for poor attendance and poor grasp of the Latvian language. The party is ultranationalist and therefore, not surprisingly, both anti-Russian and anti-Communist.

The **Latvian Agrarian Union (LZS)** takes a conservative position on the nationality issue but is not as ultranationalist as the parties mentioned. The LZS is descended from the similarly named party, which was founded in 1917 and disbanded in 1934. The party had dominated Latvian politics during the interwar period. Three of four presidents, and ten of thirteen prime minister came from the LZS during this period. The party was then restarted in 1991. The LZS is now the largest political organization in Latvia with a membership of over 3,800 members. It supports agricultural protectionism.

Taking the middle position on the nationality issue is the **Latvian Christian Democratic Union (LKDS)**. Founded in 1991, the party is descended from a group of prewar parties of similar orientation. The LKDS is supported by the local religious establishment. In 1995 the LKDS contested the election in coalition with the LZS.

ELECTIONS

The 1993 elections were the first elections since Latvia gained independence from Russia. The turnout was 89.4 percent. A large number of parties competed in a short campaign. The main issue that parties debated concerned the appropriate speed of reforms and what parts of the command economy should be kept and what parts dismantled. The campaign showed little in the way of extremist platforms. Eligibility to vote in 1993 was based on the existence of citizenship at the time Latvia was last independent (1940). One was also eligible if one could prove direct descent from such a citizen. Twenty-five percent of the electorate was made up of non-Latvian ethnic groups. Latvians who were living abroad at the time were able to vote in the elections.

In the 1995 elections the threshold for representation increased from 4 to 5 percent. This, however, did not result in fewer parties gaining representation. In fact, one more party won seats in 1995 than in 1993. The main campaign issues revolved around the unrest following the collapse of Latvia's largest bank, as well as the issue of whether or not former members of the ruling communist party should be allowed to run for public office. The DPS promised to soften government reform programs. This campaign had more extremist and overtly anti-Russian platforms, especially the one presented by the Movement for Latvia–Zigerists' Party. In general, parties moved away from the center and expressed more distinctive left and right positions, especially with regard to the nationality issue. Turnout for this election was 71.9 percent—a drop of almost 18 percent from the year before. The electorate of around 1,334,000 did not include 700,000 residents who had not yet gotten Latvian citizenship.

Elections in Latvia

	1993		1995		1998	
	%V	#S	%V	#S	%V	#S
LC	32.3	36	14.6	17	18.2	21
LNNK	13.4	15	—	—	—	—
LNNK/LZP	—	—	6.1	8	—	—
SL	12.0	13	—	—	—	—
TSP	—	—	5.6	6	14.2	16

continued

Elections in Latvia *Continued*

	1993		1995		1998	
	%V	#S	%V	#S	%V	#S
LZS	10.6	12	—	—	—	—
LZS/LKDS	—	—	6.1	7	—	—
Equality	5.8	7	—	—	—	—
LSP	—	—	5.6	6	—	—
LSDA	—	—	—	—	12.9	14
TUB	5.4	6	11.6	14	—	—
FF-LNNK	—	—	—	—	14.2	17
LKDS	5.0	6	—	—	—	—
DCP	4.8	5	—	—	—	—
LVP	0.1	—	7.2	8	—	—
DPS	—	—	15.3	18	—	—
TKL-ZP	—	—	15.0	16	—	—
TP	—	—	—	—	20.9	24
JP	—	—	—	—	7.4	8
others	10.6	0	12.9	0	12.2	0
TOTAL SEATS		100		100		100

GOVERNMENTS

The Latvian governments following the 1993 elections were both led by the LC and featured relatively few parties participating in the government coalition. However, following the 1995 election, with no party winning even 20 percent of the seats, the government coalitions have featured many more parties, and the party heading the government has also changed. The coalitions themselves have featured parties that locate themselves either in the middle or on the right on the nationality issue. The coalitions have not featured "Russia friendly" parties such as the TSP or the LSP, or the far-right TKL-ZP.

Latvian Governments since 1993

In Office Date (M/Y)	Prime Minister (Party)	#M(I)	Parties in Cabinet
07/93	Birkavs, V. (LC)	..	LC LZS
09/94	Gailis, M. (LC)	10(4)	LC Harmony for Latvia
12/95	Skele, A. (DPS)	16	DPS TUB LC LNNK LVP LZS/LKDS LSP
02/97	Skele, A. (DPS)	14	DPS TUB LC LNNK LZS/LKDS
08/97	Krasts, G. (FF-LNNK)	14	FF-LNNK LC DPS LZS LKDS
11/98	Kristopans, V. (LC)	..	LC FF-LNNK JP
07/99	Skele, A. (TP)	13	TP FF-LNNK LC

ACRONYMS

DCP	Democratic Center Party
DPS	Democratic Party–Saimnieks
FF-LNNK	For Fatherland and Freedom/Latvian National Conservative Party
JP	New Party
LC	Latvia's Way
LKDS	Latvian Christian Democratic Party
LNNK	Latvian National Conservative Party
LSP	Latvian Socialist Party
LVP	Latvian Unity Party
LZP	Latvian Green Party
LZS	Latvian Agrarian Union
SL	Harmony for Latvia and Rebirth for the National Economy
TP	People's Party
TKL-ZP	National Movement for Latvia–Zigerists' Party
TSP	National Harmony Party
TUB	Fatherland and Freedom Alliance

REFERENCES

Davies, Philip John, and Andreja Valdis Ozolins. (1994). "The Latvian Parliamentary Elections of 1993." *Electoral Studies,* Vol. 13, pp. 83–86.

Plakans, Andrejs. (1997). "Democratization and Political Participation in Postcommunist Societies: The Case of Latvia," pp. 245–89, in Karen Dawisha and Bruce Parrott, eds. *The Consolidation of Democracy in East-Central Europe.* Cambridge, England: Cambridge University Press.

Liechtenstein

SUMMARY OF PARTY SYSTEMS

1945–89	two-party system (VU and FBP)
1993–(97)	two-and-a-half-party system

HISTORY

Liechtenstein was created in 1719 as a combination of two earldoms, and its sovereignty was recognized in 1809. Until the First World War Liechtenstein had close economic ties with Austria; thereafter, a customs union was reached with Switzerland. Although Liechtenstein is a constitutional monarchy, the prince participates in the government and may veto laws. Popular referenda are also important. Liechtenstein was the last country in Europe to grant women the vote, in 1984 (at the third national referendum on the subject).

ELECTORAL SYSTEM

The Liechtenstein Landtag has only twenty-five members (and through 1986 had only fifteen), making it the smallest parliament under study. The country has only two multimember constituencies, one with fifteen seats and one with ten. The electoral system is one of proportional representation with the remaining seats allocated by greatest remainders. There is an 8 percent national threshold for representation. Voting is compulsory, and the fine for those without a valid excuse is up to Sfr 20 (Liechtenstein uses Swiss currency).

POLITICAL PARTIES AND CLEAVAGES

Prior to the elections of 1993, only two parties had ever won seats in Liechtenstein's parliament. Unlike in other two-party systems, these two parties are very similar and have, as well, worked together to form a coalition government following every election prior to 1997. The major source of opposition to this political arrangement has, therefore, come from the citizens of Liechtenstein, whose frequent use of referenda has blocked or amended many proposals made by the coalition.

The **Fatherland Union (VU)** was founded during World War I as the **People's Party**, which relied heavily on support from the working class. These beginnings were largely forgotten, however, when in 1936 the party adopted the VU rubric when it merged with smaller, conservative political forces. The party today advocates a fairly traditional right-of-center position. It advocates for minimal state interference in the private sector, highlights the importance of the family and individual responsibility, and has worked to limit the amount of foreigners coming into the county. The party has also come out in support of equality of pay and treatment of women, issues of particular relevance in a country where women only received the vote in 1984. Where support is concerned the party shares the same broad base that Liechtenstein's other party does. Early on, there was a geographic tendency for the VU to be more heavily supported in the southern constituency of the country, however this difference disappeared over time. In recent years the party has also been a strong supporter of stricter environmental standards.

The country's other main party is the **Progressive Citizens' Party (FBP)**, which was formed in 1918 as the more conservative alternative to the VU forerunner, the People's Party. The FBP has traditionally been the more successful of the two, leading the coalition government from 1928 to 1970 and again from 1974 to 1978. However, since then, the party has only won one election. The party broke with tradition following the 1997 election and withdrew entirely from the government coalition for the first time. The party, as mentioned, is strikingly similar to the VU. It supports a free-market economy while calling for adequate social-security measures; it puts strong emphasis on family policy, supports equality, and has recently begun to be supportive of environment-friendly policies.

The only other party to win representation is the **Free List (FL)**. This party was formed for the 1986 election and is strongly environmentalist and less conservative in orientation.

ELECTIONS

In the seventeen elections held in Liechtenstein since 1945, only three have seen a margin of victory of more than one seat, and two of these were the most recent elections held in October 1993 and 1997. While these elections have been almost the exclusive battle ground of the FBP and the VU, other parties have had an impact if only a statistical one. Prior to the Free List's electoral successes, beginning in the late 1980s, one other party had managed to win votes but not seats. The **Christian Socialist Party (PSC)** contested the elections held from 1962 through 1978. It managed to win 10.0 percent and 8.7 percent in the 1962 and 1966 elections, respectively, but it was not rewarded with any seats due to the electoral system at the time. Unlike the Christian Socialists, the Free List has not seen its support fade even after the two discouraging elections of 1986 and 1989 when the party won over 7 percent of the national vote but did not receive seats due to the 8 percent cutoff for representation.

Selected Elections in Liechtenstein, 1945–82

	1945		Feb 1953		1966		1982	
	%V	#S	%V	#S	%V	#S	%V	#S
FBP	54.7	8	50.5	8	48.4	8	46.5	7
VU	45.2	7	42.5	7	42.7	7	53.5	8
PSC	—	—	—	—	8.7	0	—	—
others	—	—	6.8	0	—	—	—	—
TOTAL SEATS		15		15		15		15

On two occasions Liechtenstein has had two elections in one calendar year. The first time this occurred was in 1953. In the first elections, held in February, a Workers' Party managed to disrupt the normal course of events by winning nearly 7 percent of the vote, largely at the expense of the VU. An election was held four months later, in June, in which the Workers' Party did not run, and those votes it had won were "returned" to the VU. In 1993 there were once again two elections but this time they occurred because the FBP prime minister lost a vote of confidence shortly after the first elections. The vote of confidence was initiated by his own party because it did not like his style of leadership. The following election, held in October, saw the VU return as the leading party, this time with a rare two-seat majority.

Selected Elections in Liechtenstein, 1986–97

	1986		Feb 1993		Oct 1993		1997	
	%V	#S	%V	#S	%V	#S	%V	#S
FBP	42.7	7	44.2	12	41.3	11	39.2	10
VU	50.1	8	45.4	11	50.1	13	49.2	13
FL	7.0	0	10.4	2	8.5	1	11.6	2
others	—	—	—	—	—	—	—	—
TOTAL SEATS		15		25		25		25

Electoral campaigns in Liechtenstein are often not very heated because, as mentioned, the two main parties present very similar platforms. This was the case prior to the February 1993 elections when both parties gave their support for the treaty creating a European Economic Area, the main issue facing the nation at the time. The parties did, however, differ somewhat on how to alter their bilateral trade agreements with Switzerland in light of that country's decision not to join the EEA.

The most recent elections, held in 1997, saw some of the biggest changes yet to occur in Liechtenstein's electoral history. For the first time one of the two big parties polled less than 40 percent of the popular vote, and a third party almost reached 12 percent. The elections also resulted in the FBP pulling out of the government coalition. In addition, the 1997 elections saw the continuation of the trend of lower voter turnout. In the last three elections, held in the 1990s, turnout has been below 88 percent; prior to this decade the average turnout in the post–World War II period was 94 percent.

GOVERNMENTS

As noted, "grand coalitions" between the two main (or often only) parties had been the norm until 1997, when the first single-party government was formed.

Liechtenstein Governments since 1945

In Office Date (M/Y)	Prime Minister (Party)	#M	Parties in Cabinet
09/45	Frick, A. (FBP)	4	FBP VU
03/49	Frick, A. (FBP)	4	FBP VU
03/53	Frick, A. (FBP)	4	FBP VU
07/53	Frick, A. (FBP)	4	FBP VU
10/57	Frick, A. (FBP)	4	FBP VU
04/58	Frick, A. (FBP)	4	FBP VU
04/62	Frick, A. (FBP)	4	FBP VU
07/62	Batliner, G. (FBP)	4	FBP VU
03/66	Batliner, G. (FBP)	5	FBP VU
03/70	Hilbe, A. (VU)	5	VU FBP
03/74	Kieber, W. (FBP)	5	FBP VU
04/78	Brunhart, H. (VU)	5	VU FBP
03/82	Brunhart, H. (VU)	5	VU FBP
04/86	Brunhart, H. (VU)	5	VU FBP
05/89	Brunhart, H. (VU)	5	VU FBP
05/93	Büchel, M. (FBP)	5	FBP VU
12/93	Frick, M. (VU)	5	VU FBP
04/97	Frick, M. (VU)	5	VU

ACRONYMS

FBP	Progressive Citizens' Party
FL	Free List
PSC	Christian Socialist Party
VU	Fatherland Union

Lithuania

SUMMARY OF PARTY SYSTEMS

1992	moderate multiparty system with one dominant party (LDDP)
(1996–)	moderate multiparty system with one dominant party (TS-LK)

HISTORY

Lithuania was one of the leading states of medieval Europe. It merged with Poland in the sixteenth century and was absorbed by Russia in the eighteenth century, during the period of Polish partitions. Lithuania was independent between the world wars. From 1919 to 1926 it was democratic, but a coup in 1926 established an authoritarian regime. In 1940 it was incorporated into the USSR. In the 1990 Soviet elections the majority of seats went to the Lithuanian Reform Movement. Lithuania was the first Soviet Republic to declare independence, which was recognized in September 1991.

ELECTORAL SYSTEM

The current election law was adopted in June 1996. Lithuania uses a mixed system with 141 seats in total. In seventy-one seats, that is, just over half, there is a direct, absolute-majority vote in single-member constituencies. If no candidate is elected in the first round a runoff election is held between the two leading candidates. Also, such elections are only valid if at least 40 percent of the electorate cast its vote.

The remaining seventy seats are awarded proportionally in one national constituency, on the basis of the simple quotient and greatest remainders rules. In order for these seats to be valid, at least 25 percent of the electorate must have cast its vote. There exists a 5 percent threshold for representation based on proportional-representation votes for parties, which goes up to 7 percent for coalitions. (These thresholds were 4 percent and 5 percent, respectively, for the 1992 elections.)

In 1992 there was a "privileged" 2 percent threshold for ethnic parties, however this was dropped for 1996.

Vacancies arising between general elections are filled through by-elections (in the single-member constituencies) or by the "next-in-line" candidates of the same party (in the multimember constituency).

POLITICAL PARTIES AND CLEAVAGES

Unlike Latvia and Estonia, Lithuania's former ruling Communist Party is well represented in party politics. And unlike Estonia and Latvia, the minority populations in Lithuania are small—ethnic Lithuanians make up over 81 percent of the population; therefore, there are no strong ethnically based parties.

The **Lithuanian Democratic Labor Party (LDDP)** was founded in 1990 by a faction of the former Communist Party that had initially given its support to Gorbachev's reformist program. In 1992 the party campaigned on a program of gradual transition to a market economy. The LDDP went on to form the government following the first election without needing to work in coalition with any other party.

The other main political force in Lithuanian politics had been the **Lithuanian Reform Movement—Sajudis**. This broadly based middle-of-the-road movement was equivalent to the Popular Front in both Estonia and Latvia. Sajudis had performed well in the 1990 elections to the Lithuanian Supreme Soviet, winning a majority of the seats, however, the movement began to disintegrate in 1991 following a failed attempt to transform the movement into a political party. Sajudis competed in the 1992 elections but finished a distant second to the LDDP.

By 1993 Sajudis completely broke down, and the new opposition party to the LDDP, which emerged out of it was the right-of-center **Homeland Union—Lithuanian Conservatives (TS-LK)**. Despite its rightward leanings, the party remained open to former communists. The TS-LK had the reputation and image of a radical right-wing party; however, for the 1996 election it moderated its tone and transformed itself into a pragmatic and competent Western-style party.

The center of Lithuanian politics is taken up by two parties: the **Lithuanian Christian Democratic Party (LKDP)** and the **Lithuanian Center Union (LCS)**, which competed in the 1992 elections under the

Center Movement rubric. The LKDP, a revival pre-Soviet party formed in 1905, presented a joint list in most electoral districts with two smaller parties, one representing Lithuanian's political prisoners and deportees, the other a small democratic party. Both parties competed independently in 1996, however the LKDP still won as many seats in 1996 as the coalition of the three parties had in 1992. The LCS is a pro-market, centrist force that saw a huge increase in both votes and number of seats from the 1992 elections to those in 1996.

The other party to see improvement from 1992 to 1996 is the **Lithuanian Social Democratic Party (LSDP)**. A member of the Socialist International, the LSDP is descended from the historical party of the same name, which was originally founded in 1896 and then reestablished in 1989.

ELECTIONS

The results of the 1992 elections reflected the voters unhappiness with the performance of the Sajudis-led Supreme Soviet and the economic decline that had been the result of the movement's inability to govern. In particular, Lithuanians were fed up with the fuel shortages, the persistent government-sponsored anti-Communist propaganda, and the confrontational style Sajudis had adopted in dealing with Russia. In general the LDDP's victory signaled the people's dissatisfaction with the hardships brought about by the program of marketization and privatization launched by the government. The LDDP, which campaigned on a platform of slowing down economic reform, won 48 percent of the seats, while the Sajudis coalition could only win 17 percent. Only ten of the seventy-one single-member seats were decided by majority vote in the first round.

The very program of slow economic transition that the LDDP had been elected for in 1992 resulted in its loss of the 1996 elections. The LDDP was heavily criticized for the period of economic stagnation that the country had suffered through and now found itself in. The TS-LK attacked the LDDP for alleged corruption and vowed to clean up government. The LKDP argued for the solution of current social problems at the cost of economic efficiency. All the opposition parties agreed on the main issues of foreign policy in the campaign—those being affiliation to NATO and the EU. Most of the votes lost by the LDDP were picked up by the center parties, including the LCS and the LKDP. Only two of the seventy-one majority seats were decided in the first round of voting.

Turnout was only 53 percent in the first found, and fell in the second round to 40 percent.

Elections in Lithuania

	1992		1996	
	%V	#S	%V	#S
LDDP	44.0	73	10.0	12
Sajudis	21.2	28	—	—
TS-LK	—	—	31.3	70
LKDP	12.6	18	10.4	16
LCS	2.5	2	8.7	13
LSDP	6.0	8	6.9	12
others	13.7	11	32.7	10
independents	—	1	—	4
TOTAL SEATS		141		137
Vacant Seats *		—		4

*The vacant seats are a result of less than 40 percent voter turnout in four constituencies. These seats were to be filled in mid-1997.

Note: Vote percentages refer to the national lists.

GOVERNMENTS

There have been only four postindependence governments, two of which have been formed by the LDDP, and two coalitions led by the TS-LK. The TS-LK initially joined forces with both centrist parties, the LCS and the LKDP, to ensure that they had a comfortable majority of support in the parliament. Prime minister Vagnorius resigned in May 1999, after a dispute with the president. He was succeeded by the mayor of Vilnius (the capital), Rolandas Paksas, who formed a minimal winning coalition. However, Paksas himself would resign a few months later, in opposition to an unpopular proposed oil refinery privatization.

Lithuanian Governments since 1992

In Office Date (M/Y)	Prime Minister (Party)	#M	Parties in Cabinet
10/92	Slezevicius, A. (LDDP)	..	LDDP
08/96	Stankevicius, L. (LDDP)	..	LDDP
12/96	Vagnorius, G. (TS-LK)	16	TS-LK LKDP LCS
06/99	Paksas, R. (TS-LK)	15	TS-LK LKDP
11/99	Kubilius, A. (TS-LK)	..	TS-LK LKDP

ACRONYMS

LCS Lithuanian Center Union
LDDP Lithuanian Democratic Labor Party
LKDP Lithuanian Christian Democratic Party
LSDP Lithuanian Social Democratic Party
TS-LK Homeland Union–Lithuanian Conservatives

REFERENCES

Clark, Terry D. (1995). "The Lithuanian Political Party System: A Case Study of Democratic Consolidation." *East European Politics and Societies,* Vol. 9. Winter.

Krupavicius, A. (1997). "The Lithuanian Parliamentary Elections of 1996." *Electoral Studies,* Vol. 16, pp. 541–45.

Luxembourg

SUMMARY OF PARTY SYSTEM

1945–(99)	moderate multiparty system with a balance among the parties

HISTORY

Luxembourg achieved its independence in 1839, although it became part of the German tariff union. The population speaks German, French, and the local Letzeburgesch dialect. Its economic ties have been closest with Belgium: a customs union has existed since 1921, and the Luxembourg franc is set at parity to the Belgian franc (which is also legal tender). Luxembourg joined the Benelux economic union in 1947 and then was a founding member of the European Communities. A grand duke is the ceremonial head of state.

ELECTORAL SYSTEM

Luxembourg uses a party-list, proportional-representation system, with seats allocated by the Hagenbach-Bishoff method. Voters vote for a party list or a specific candidate on the list. The country is divided into four multimember constituencies. Voting is compulsory, under sanction of a fine.

POLITICAL PARTIES AND CLEAVAGES

In Luxembourg, there is a high importance placed on individual candidates. In terms of political parties, the centrist **Christian Social People's Party** (**CSV** in German, **PCS** in French) was formed in 1914. The CSV has traditionally been Luxembourg's strongest party. It has participated in nearly every government since its founding. Since 1945 the party has won the plurality of votes in all but three elections but has nevertheless never failed to win the plurality of seats. The CSV has also provided all but one of the country's post–World War II prime ministers. The party is pro-monarchy, supports the social market economy, is in favor of subsidies for small business and farmers, and is strongly supportive of the EU and NATO. The party's main sources of support are farmers, Catholics, and moderate conservatives.

The second-largest party next to the CSV has been the **Socialist Workers' Party of Luxembourg (LSAP in German, POSL in French)**. The party was founded in 1902 and is a moderately left-of-center party. The party is pro-EU and pro-NATO and supports the concept of a mixed economy so long as the present social-security net is protected and maintained. The party enjoys a fairly broad base of support but is particularly strong among the urban lower-middle classes and trade-union members. In 1971 more conservative members spilt from the party and created the **Social Democratic Party (SDP)**, which was itself dissolved in 1983 after competing in only two elections.

The **Democratic Party (DP in German, PD in French)** is the country's third-largest party and was founded in 1945. The party occupies a liberal-centrist position on most issues. The party supports the concepts of economic liberalism and free enterprise but is nevertheless committed to maintaining social welfare. The DP is pro-EU and pro-NATO and is mildly anti-clerical. The party is mainly supported by the upper middle class and professionals.

The **Communist Party of Luxembourg (KPL in German, PCL in French)** was founded in 1921. The party is an orthodox communist party and calls for the total nationalization of the economy. The KPL was pro-Soviet while the Soviet Union still existed and was the only Western European communist party that gave its approval to the Soviet invasions of Czechoslovakia and Hungary. The party gets support form intellectuals and some of the country's urban and industrial workers. Prior to 1979 the party enjoyed fairly high levels of popular support.

The **Green Alternative (GA)** was formed in 1983 and advocated a mixture of Green and leftist policies. Some of the party's campaigns have centered on calling for a thirty-five-hour work week and developing a more ecologically friendly agricultural sector. In 1986 the **Green List–Ecological Initiative** (**GLEI** in German, **IVE** in French) was formed by a prominent ex-member of the Green Alternative who was forced out of the party. The two parties nevertheless competed together in the 1989 and 1994 elections. In 1995 the two parties united and are now simply known as the **Green Party**.

The **Action Committee for Democracy and Justice (ADR)** was formed in 1989 as the **Five-Sixths Action Committee** but adopted their current name prior to the 1994 elections. The party argues for the introduction of an across-the-board pension plan worth five-sixth of a person's final salary.

RECENT ELECTIONS

The 1994 election campaign centered on the issues of social welfare and the status of foreigners, who constitute a sizable percentage of the work force in the country. The results were very similar to the those of the election before. The CSV and LSAP each lost one seat but the parties together still held a healthy majority in parliament and agreed to renew their governing coalition shortly after the elections.

The 1999 elections were hardly dramatic in terms of vote shifts. However, the vote breakdown across the various constituencies caused the socialists to lose four of their 17 seats. Consequently, the LSAP wound up in third place in terms of seats, even though it was still second in terms of votes. The party thus withdrew from the government, paving the way for the return to a CSV-DP government. For its part, the CSV is now the only Benelux Christian democratic party which as of this writing is still the largest, and indeed pivotal, party in its system. This fact holds despite the continued growth of the ADR in Luxembourg.

Selected Elections in Luxembourg

	1945		**1974**		**1989**		**1994**		**1999**	
	%V	**#S**	**%V**	**#S**	**%V**	**#S**	**%V**	**#S**	**%V**	**#S**
CSV	41.4	25	28.0	18	31.6	22	30.3	21	30.2	19
LSAP	26.0	11	29.0	17	26.2	18	25.4	17	24.2	13
DP	16.7	9	22.1	14	17.2	11	19.3	12	22.0	15
KPL	13.5	5	10.4	5	4.4	1	1.7	0	?	0
SDP	—	—	9.1	5	—	—	—	—	—	—
Greens	—	—	—	—	8.7	4	9.9	5	7.5	5
ADR	—	—	—	—	7.9	4	9.0	5	10.5	7

	1945		1974		1989		1994		1999	
	%V	#S	%V	#S	%V	#S	%V	#S	%V	#S
others	2.4	1	1.4	0	4.4	0	4.4	0	5.6	1
TOTAL SEATS		51		59		60		60		60

GOVERNMENTS

Despite the relative balance of the parties, the larger size of the Christian Socials, combined with their centrist position, has meant, as noted, that the party has provided all but one of the country's post–World War II prime ministers.

Luxembourg Governments since 1945

In Office Date (M/Y)	Prime Minister (Party)	#M	Parties in Cabinet
11/45	Dupong, P. (CSV)	8	CSV LSAP DP KPL
03/47	Dupong, P. (CSV)	7	CSV DP
07/48	Dupong, P. (CSV)	7	CSV DP
07/51	Dupong, P. (CSV)	6	CSV LSAP
12/53	Bech, J. (CSV)	6	CSV LSAP
06/54	Bech, J. (CSV)	8	CSV LSAP
03/58	Frieden, P. (CSV)	8	CSV LSAP
02/59	Werner, P. (CSV)	7	CSV DP
07/64	Werner, P. (CSV)	8	CSV LSAP
01/67	Werner, P. (CSV)	8	CSV LSAP
01/69	Werner, P. (CSV)	7	CSV DP
06/74	Thorn, G. (DP)	8	DP LSAP
07/79	Werner, P. (CSV)	8	DP CSV
07/84	Santer, J. (CSV)	9	CSV LSAP
07/89	Santer, J. (CSV)	10	CSV LSAP
07/94	Santer, J. (CSV)	12	CSV LSAP
01/95	Juncker, J. C. (CSV)	11	CSV LSAP
08/99	Juncker, J. C. (CSV)	10	CSV DP

ACRONYMS (GERMAN LANGUAGE)

ADR	Action Committee for Democracy and Justice
CSV	Christian Social People's Party
DP	Democratic Party
GA	Green Alternative
GLEI	Green List–Ecological Initiative
LSAP	Socialist Workers' Party of Luxembourg
KPL	Communist Party of Luxembourg
SDP	Social Democratic Party

REFERENCE

Smart, Michael. (1995). "Luxembourg: European Parliament and National Elections of 1994." *West European Politics,* Vol. 18: 1, pp. 194–96.

Macedonia

SUMMARY OF PARTY SYSTEMS

1994	moderate multiparty system with one dominant party (SDSM)
(1998–)	moderate multiparty system with one dominant party (VMRO-DPMNE)

HISTORY

Macedonia was ruled by Ottoman Turks for five centuries. In 1913 it was divided between Greece and Serbia—known as Aegean Macedonia and Vardar Macedonia, respectively. A small portion of its territory was given to Bulgaria following World War I. After World War II Macedonia became a constituent republic of the Communist-ruled federal Yugoslavia. The 1990 elections were inconclusive, and renamed Communists held onto to the presidency. On 25 January 1991 the Macedonian Assembly unanimously adopted a declaration of independence; a new constitution was adopted on 17 November 1991. Officially the country is known as the Former Yugoslav Republic of Macedonia (FYROM) because of a dispute with Greece over its name.

ELECTORAL SYSTEM

Initially, in 1994, Macedonia had 120 single-member constituencies, with an absolute majority vote in two rounds. To win a single-member constituency, the number of votes received should not have been smaller than one-third of the registered electors of the constituency concerned. If the number of votes of the leading candidate was insufficient, either absolutely or as a proportion of registered voters, then a second round of voting was held within fourteen days. Candidates who received at least 7 percent of the votes cast in the first round were entitled to be candidates for the second round.

For the 1998 elections this system was modified so that only eighty-five of the seats would come from single-member districts and the remaining thirty-five would come from a national PR calculation with a cutoff of 5 percent. Also, for the second-member districts the second round was changed to a straight runoff between the top two candidates from the first round.

POLITICAL PARTIES AND CLEAVAGES

The main party on the left is **the Social Democratic Alliance of Macedonia (SDSM),** which is the descendant of **the League of Communists (SKM)**. The SKM was first renamed the **League of Communists–Party of Democratic Change (SKM-PDP)** in 1989, and it was under this name that it contested the 1990 elections, when Macedonia was still part of Yugoslavia. In 1991 the Communists adopted their current name.

In 1994 the SDSM created the **Alliance of Macedonia (SM)** with the smaller and far-left-wing **Socialist Party of Macedonia (SPM)**, which was founded in 1990, and the **Liberal Party of Macedonia (LPM)**, which was founded in 1990. The LPM contested the 1990 elections as the **Alliance of Reform Forces of Macedonia (SRSM)**. The LPM adopted the name **Reform Forces of Macedonia–Liberal Party (RSM-LP)** in 1992 but contested the 1994 elections as simply the LPM. The party was, however, ousted from the government and the SM alliance in a cabinet reshuffle in late 1996 and was forced into opposition.

The main opposition party in Macedonia has been the **Internal Macedonian Revolutionary Organization–Democratic Party for Macedonian National Unity (VMRO-DPMNE)**. The VMRO was named after a historic group founded in 1893 that fought for independence from the Turks. The DPMNE was launched by Macedonian migrant workers in Sweden. The two halves merged in June 1990 as an organization of the "democratic center." The party strongly endorses the revival of Macedonian cultural identity. Winning the plurality of seats in 1990, the VMRO-DPMNE got no seats in the 1994 elections due to the boycott it launched in response to alleged ballot fraud. For the 1998 election the party moderated its nationalistic appeals, specifically stating that it no longer aspired to unite parts of Bulgaria and Greece into a "Greater Macedonia." The VMRO-DPMNE also stressed support for greater market reforms and linked up with the new **Democratic Alternative (DA)**, a pro-market party led by Vasil Tupurkovski, a United States–educated international lawyer.

The second party to have largely boycotted the 1994 elections was the **Democratic Party of Macedonia (DPM)**, which was founded in 1993 under the leadership of a former communist-era prime minister.

The Albanian population of Macedonia is represented by the **Party of Democratic Prosperity (PDP)**. The PDP was founded in 1990 and boasts a membership of over 100,000. The party only operates in areas with substantial Albania populations. The PDP was in the first two of Macedonia's governments despite its participation in a boycott of the legislature from February to July of 1995 by Albanian parties. The party has suffered from a series of defections and the creation of splinter parties. The second ethnic Albanian party that has won seats in both elections is the **Democratic Party of Albanians (DPA)**, formerly the **National Democratic Party (NDP)**. The NDP contested the 1990 elections with the PDP but then split off and contested the 1994 elections on their own. The NDP was the largest opposition party in parliament following the 1994 elections, until the LPM got booted out of the government. In 1998 the PDP and the DPA ran together.

ELECTIONS

The elections held on 16 and 30 October, and 13 November 1994, were the first in Macedonia since its independence. Due to irregularities in the balloting, the voting process for the National Assembly was repeated in eleven constituencies, hence the third round on 13 November. The campaign issues focused on the country's ailing economy (due in no small part to the blockade by neighboring Greece, and international trade sanctions on another neighbor, Serbia) and foreign relations. No less than thirty-eight parties and 1,765 candidates (of whom 283 were independents) competed in the first round. The first round results were contested by the two main opposition parties, the DPM and the VMRO-DPMNE, both of which boycotted the second round and sought annulment of the poll, citing numerous irregularities in the conducting of the balloting. The Alliance of Macedonia, therefore, had little standing in its way in achieving a majority with ninety-five seats. Foreign observers, numbering some 150, expressed, however, the view that the elections were generally free and fair, despite certain reservations about the procedures followed by the State Election Commission, especially the compilation of electoral registers.

In the 1998 elections the governing Social Democrats lost heavily, and the opposition electoral alliance of the VMRO-DPMNE and the DA won a narrow majority of seats. These parties had pledged continuity in Macedonia's pro-Western foreign policy, but in domestic affairs promised more foreign investment, growth, and jobs.

Elections in Macedonia since 1994

	1994	1998			
	#S	%V	#S PR	#S SM	total seats
VMRO-DPMNE	boycotted	28.1	11	38	49
DA	—	10.7	4	9	13
SDSM	58	25.2	10	17	27
LPM	29				
DPM	1				
LPM-DPM		7.0	2	2	4
SPM	8	4.7	0	1	1
PDP	10				
NDP	4				
PDP + NDP/DPA		19.3	8	17	25
others	10	5.0	0	1	1
TOTAL SEATS	120		35	85	120

GOVERNMENTS

The first two postindependence governments in Macedonia were headed by the former Communists—the SDSM. The first such government was composed of the parties making up the SM alliance and the Albanian PDP. In all, the government had control of 105 out of 120 seats. The government lost control of 29 of these seats when the LPM was forced out of government. In 1998 the SDSM was removed from power and replaced by the VMRO and its DA allies, along with the smaller of the ethnic Albanian parties.

Macedonia Governments since 1994

In Office Date (M/Y)	Prime Minister (Party)	#M(I)	Parties in Cabinet
12/94	Crvenovski, B. (SDSM)	19(1)	SDSM LPM PDP SPM
05/97	Crvenovski, B. (SDSM)	19	SDSM PDP SPM
12/98	Georgievski, L. (VMRO)	18	VMRO DA NDP

ACRONYMS

DA	Democratic Alternative
DPA	Democratic Party of Albanians
DPM	Democratic Party of Macedonia
LPM	Liberal Party of Macedonia
NDP	National Democratic Party
PDP	Party of Democratic Prosperity
RSM-LP	Reform Forces of Macedonia–Liberal Party
SDSM	Social Democratic Alliance of Macedonia
SKM	League of Communists of Macedonia
SKM-PDP	League of Communists of Macedonia–Party of Democratic Change
SM	Alliance of Macedonia
SPM	Socialist Party of Macedonia
SRSM	Alliance of Reform Forces of Macedonia
VMRO-DPMNE	Internal Revolutionary Organization–Democratic Party for Macedonian National Unity

Malta

SUMMARY OF PARTY SYSTEM

1966–(98) two-party system (MLP and PN)

HISTORY

At the crossroads of the Mediterranean, Malta was subjected to frequent invasions and occupations until it fell under British control. Malta became independent from Britain in 1964, and a republic within the British Commonwealth in 1974. It is a strongly Roman Catholic country, where divorce is still illegal as of this writing.

ELECTORAL SYSTEM

Malta uses a single transferable vote system in which the country is divided into thirteen constituencies, each with five seats. A constitutional amendment in 1987 dictated that the party winning the majority of votes be given the necessary amount of seats to have a parliamentary majority, thus preventing any more "manufactured minorities." A further constitutional amendment in 1995 changed the threshold from a majority of votes to a plurality of votes, thus guaranteeing that the leading party—in terms of votes—will form the government. Such "bonuses" have been awarded twice, in 1987 and 1996.

POLITICAL PARTIES AND CLEAVAGES

Malta has a strictly two-party system that is marked by intense partisanship and extremely high voting turnout. The **Maltese Labour Party (MLP)** has been in power following half of Malta's eight postindependence elections. The MLP adheres to a socialist domestic policy in advocating for universal education and healthcare, in resisting privatization, and in giving government a large role in the economy. It also supports a neutralist foreign policy in which it sees Malta's role as a link between the Arab countries of North Africa and the Middle East and the countries of Europe. While encouraging close participation with EU member countries, the MLP has consistently argued against full membership of Malta in the European Union.

The other main party, and the only other to have won representation in Malta since independence, is the **Nationalist Party (PN)**, which was in power following the 1966, 1987, 1992, and 1998 elections. The PN advocates a more right-of-center policy with regard to the national economy, preferring less government intervention. The party has often run campaigns calling for cleaner government and for guarantees of human rights. The PN has also been active in recent decades in trying to promote Malta as a center for off-shore investment, by lowering taxes and even proposing their elimination. In areas of foreign policy, the party is supportive of EU membership and favors closer cooperation with NATO. Support for the party comes mainly from white-collar professionals and religious adherents.

There are other parties in Malta that, although not represented in parliament, have received a share, albeit a small one, of the popular vote. The strongest of these is the **Democratic Alternative (DA)**. This party was founded prior to the 1992 elections mainly as a form of protest against the two-party system that exists. The party is concerned with policy, primarily regarding ecological and environmental issues.

ELECTIONS

There have been eight postindependence elections in Malta. In all but the first, held in 1966, the percentage of votes going to parties other than the MLP and PN has been less than 1.8 percent. In three cases the vote for other parties has been less than 0.05 percent. It is clear that these elections reflect the extreme polarization of the Maltese political system.

The elections of 17–18 September 1976 stand out because they featured the highest voter turnout in the previous forty years of Maltese electoral history. These elections also saw the voting age reduced from twenty-one to eighteen and therefore many first time voters. The campaign centered largely on issues of foreign policy. The PN criticized the MLP government for its close links to China and argued that closer cooperation with NATO and the then EC should be established. The MLP responded with its "bridge-of-peace" policy, which was designed to ensure Malta's nonaligned position and to give it a role as bridge between Europe and the Arab world. Also at issue was the continued military presence of the British in Malta and the potential loss of revenue resultant from their impending departure in 1979. The PN argued that their departure should be delayed until suitably trained Maltese replacements could be established. The MLP victory in 1976 was a more convincing one than it had secured at the previous election.

The following elections held on 12 December 1981 stand out not so much for the campaign but for the result. The MLP won a majority of seats but at the same time polled a smaller percentage of votes than the PN. The PN accused the MLP of rigging the elections by redrawing electoral districts so it could hold on to its majority. The MLP was also accused of monopolizing state-run TV and radio, forcing the PN to make broadcasts out of Sicily. Again, foreign policy was a key issue, with the PN calling for full membership of Malta in the EC, while the MLP campaign contained an anti-British element.

Maltese Elections since Independence

	1966		**1971**		**1976**		**1981**	
	%V	**#S**	**%V**	**#S**	**%V**	**#S**	**%V**	**#S**
MLP	43.1	22	50.8	28	51.5	34	49.1	34
PN	47.9	28	48.1	27	48.4	31	50.9	31
others	9.0	0	1.1	0	0.1	0	0.0	0
TOTAL SEATS		50		55		65		65

	1987		**1992**		**1996**		**1998**	
	%V	**#S**	**%V**	**#S**	**%V**	**#S**	**%V**	**#S**
MLP	48.9	34	46.5	31	50.7	35*	47.0	30
PN	50.9	35*	51.8	34	47.8	34	51.8	35
others	0.2	0	1.7	0	1.5	0	1.3	0
TOTAL SEATS		69		65		69		65

*Includes 4 bonus seats to create a parliamentary majority.

The problem of the elections of 1981 was addressed by a constitutional amendment made in January 1987 that was agreed upon by both parties. The amendment dictated that the party winning the majority of votes be given the necessary amount of seats to have a parliamentary majority. It is unclear whether the MLP would have agreed to this amendment if the party had known how the elections of 9 May of the same year would have turned out. The results were virtually the same as those of 1981. The MLP received less votes but more initial seats than the PN. However, because of the change in the constitution, the PN was granted four additional seats for having received the majority of votes, thus ensuring the party a parliamentary majority. The campaign issues included the PN's continued push to move Malta's foreign policy toward closer cooperation with Western Europe. The Nationalist Party victory was the party's first since the elections of 1966.

In the 1996 elections it was the MLP that benefited from the constitutional amendment of 1987. The party, like the PN in 1981 and 1987, received the majority of votes but not initially the majority of seats and was therefore given four additional seats to produce a parliamentary majority. In large part these elections were seen as a referendum on the foreign policy of the PN government, which had launched efforts to attain full membership in the EU and maintain current membership in NATO's Partnerships for Peace. The MLP campaigned on reversing both these policies. The MLP also gained support for its campaign promise to abolish the 15 percent value-added tax that the PN had imposed. Turnout was the highest ever at over 96 percent.

The 1996 Labour government soon found itself in a minority position, however, as the former leader and prime minister Dom Mintoff broke ranks in 1997 over the economic austerity measures of the government. Thus, in the summer of 1998, Prime Minister Sant decided to call early elections. These featured the ongoing themes of Maltese politics—membership in the EU or not, and the NP's plans to reintroduce a value-added tax. The two main parties essentially changed vote shares from 1996, and this time the NP won the decisive majority of seats.

GOVERNMENTS

Maltese governments have always been single-party governments, either of Labour or the PN. They form quickly and normally last a full term in office.

Maltese Governments since 1966

In Office Date (M/Y)	Prime Minister (Party)	#M	Parties in Cabinet
03/66	Olivier, G. B. (PN)	8	PN
06/71	Mintoff, D. (MLP)	9	MLP
09/76	Mintoff, D. (MLP)	12	MLP
12/81	Mintoff, D. (MLP)	14	MLP
12/84	Bonnici, M. (MLP)	11	MLP
05/87	Fenech-Adami, E. (PN)	18	PN
02/92	Fenech-Adami, E. (PN)	13	PN
10/96	Sant, A. (MLP)	15	MLP
09/98	Fenech-Adami, E. (PN)	13	PN

ACRONYMS

DA	Democratic Alternative
MLP	Maltese Labour Party
PN	Nationalist Party

REFERENCES

Fenech, Dominic. (1999). "The 1998 Maltese Election," *West European Politics* 22, 2: 193–198.

Hirczy, Wolfgang. (1995). "Explaining Near-Universal Turnout: The Case of Malta." *European Journal of Political Research,* Vol. 27, pp. 255–72.

Howe, Stephen. (1987). "The Maltese General Election of 1987." *Electoral Studies,* Vol. 6, pp. 235–47.

Moldova

SUMMARY OF PARTY SYSTEM

1994	moderate multiparty system with one dominant party (PDAM)
(1998–)	moderate multiparty system with a balance among the parties

HISTORY

Moldovans are not a historic people of Europe but rather a post-Soviet nation of Romanian-speakers. Moldova encompasses the territory of the pre-1940 Moldavian Autonomous Soviet Socialist Republic (located within the Ukraine) which was joined to all but the northern and southern portions of the territory of Bessarabia upon the latter's detachment from Romania in 1940 (part of the Nazi-Soviet pact). In 1989, the communist president endorsed the nationalist demands of the Popular Front of Moldova. The name *Moldova* was adopted in June 1990; it was previously *Moldavia.* In the 1990 elections, Popular Front members running as independents gained election to the previously communist-dominated legislature. The Moldovan government declared the annexation of Bessarabia illegal and vowed to return it to Romania. This statement of purpose prompted the creation in August 1990 of the Republic of Gagauzia by the Gagauz minority in that region. The following month the Dnestr Republic declared itself independent as well. On 21 August 1991 Moldova declared independence. The period 1991–94 was marked by regional strife and economic turmoil. The first postindependence elections were held in 1994.

ELECTORAL SYSTEM

Moldova has one multimember nationwide constituency for 104 deputies. It uses a proportional representation system, with a threshold of 4 percent of the national vote being applicable for parliamentary representation. At least 50 percent of the electorate must cast ballots for the poll to be deemed valid. Vacancies arising between general elections are filled through by-elections.

POLITICAL PARTIES AND CLEAVAGES

In general there existed an overlaying reform/antireform cleavage, a weak communist/anticommunist cleavage, and a strong set of divisions based on nationality. The ethnic Moldovan majority is divided between "Romanian" nationalists and "Moldovan" nationalists. The early party formation in the transition period was the result of positioning by competing party elites.

The **Popular Front of Moldova (PFM)** was the dominant political group following the eclipse of the Communist regime in mid-1991. This party was the first noncommunist party to gain representation in the Moldovan parliament. The party that was founded in 1989 disintegrated in 1992, and one of its largest factions was transformed into the **Christian Democratic Popular Front (FPCD)**. The FPCD was launched as one of Moldova's pro-Romanian parties, which in the lead-up to the 1994 elections, argued for a close integration with Romania. Following its poor showing in 1994, the FPCD joined forces with the **Party of Revival of Accord of Moldova (PRCM)** to form the nationalistic, right-wing **Democratic Convention of Moldova (CDM)**, led by former President Mircea Snegur, for the 1998 elections. The PRCM was launched by Snegur in 1995 and declared a "mass party of the center" but in reality is more to the right of center. The party advocated the transformation of Moldova to a presidential form of government as opposed to a parliamentary system. It also tried to attract the support of the Romanian nationalists by advocating a move to make Romanian and not Moldovan the official language. By 1999 the CDM had decomposed back into Christian Democrats and the PRCM.

The **Agrarian Democratic Party of Moldova (PDAM)**, associated not with farmers but with the republican agro-industrial complex, was made up of village mayors or collective-farm managers, who had a common ideological outlook as reformed communists. A strong political force early on due to clear policy orientation, an institutional power base, and good organization, the PDAM was the core of the government of national unity formed in mid-1992. In 1994 the party advocated Moldovan independence from both Russia and Romania and the cultivation of a "Moldovan" identity while accommodating all ethnic groups in the territory. The party nevertheless supported participation in the Commonwealth of Independent States' economic structures but not its political or military structures. The party moved to a more moderate position on the national issue following the 1994 elections and called for permanent neutrality and the banning of foreign troops from the country.

The **Party of Communists of the Moldovan Republic (PCRM)** was banned in 1991 but regained legal status in 1994 by which time many former communists had either opted for the socialists or given support to the agrarians. The PCRM did not win any seats in 1994 but did poll an incredible 30.1 percent and forty seats in 1998 elections, benefiting largely from a shift in support away from the socialists and agrarians.

The **Socialist Party (PS)** was formed in 1993 as the pro-Russian successor to the former ruling communist party. In the 1994 and 1998 elections it offered a joint list with the **Unity (Edinstvo) Movement**.

Other parties to have won seats in the 1994 elections include the **Peasants' and Intellectuals' Bloc**—a moderate pro-Romanian alliance of smaller parties, some of which had split from the PFM. The parties that made up the bloc went on to form the **United Democratic Forces (CDU)** alliance following the election of 1994, which one year later became the center-right **Party of Democratic Forces (PFD)**. In 1998 the PFD virtually replicated the percentage of votes and number of seats that the Peasants' and Intellectuals' Bloc had received.

The 1998 elections also saw the emergence of a new pro-government centrist alliance, the **Movement for a Democratic and Prosperous Moldova (PMDP)**.

ELECTIONS

The 1994 elections, held on 27 February, focused on the issues of economic reform and the various strategies for the resolution of the separatist conflict but overall were used as a barometer to determine the people's opinion on what Moldova's international orientation should be—either pro-Russian or pro-Romanian. The Socialists and Agrarians, both representing reformed communists, argued for a slower transition to capitalism and for a pro-Russian orientation largely involving closer economic links with the former Soviet republics through membership in the CIS. These parties also argued for the cultivation of a "Moldovan" identity and toleration for the minority ethnic groups in the country.

The ex–Popular Front parties argued for varying degrees of closer Romanian affiliation and "pan-Romanianism." With the extreme position of complete unification taken up by the FPCD while the more moderated bloc of Peasants and Intellectuals argued for a period of independence followed by unification. Members of these pro-Romanian parties complained of harassment at the hands of the Moscow-oriented parties. Voting did take place in the Gagauz region but Transdniestrian authorities did not allow ballots to be cast in their region although they did allow citizens to cross into Moldovan territory to vote.

The results were an overwhelming victory for the pro-Russian and pro-national forces. The main pro-Romanian forces got less than 17 percent and controlled only 19 percent of the seats. The Democratic Agrarian Party emerged with the largest share of votes and seats, ending up with a majority in parliament. Turnout was high—79.3 percent of the electorate participated in the vote.

In the 1998 elections, fifteen parties and some sixty independent candidates vied for the 101 available parliamentary seats (polling being postponed in three constituencies). During the campaign, the Communists pledged a return to a centralized, state-controlled economy and "the rebirth of a socialist society." The PCRM also favored close political and military ties with the Russian Federation. The CDM, on the other hand, backed faster market reforms and a Western-oriented foreign policy. The president of Moldova urged voters to promote stability by supporting moderate forces, a view echoed by the prime minister. Such forces were represented by the newly formed PMDP, which appealed to middle-of-the-road voters with promises of more welfare programs and stronger links with both Russia and the West. The PCM came out on top with forty seats—a clear margin over their two most serious rivals but still short of an absolute majority. Foreign observers considered the elections generally free and fair and calm.

Elections in Moldova

	1994		1998	
	%V	#S	%V	#S
PDAM	43.2	56	3.7	0
PS/Unity	22.0	28	1.8	0
Peasants' and Intellectuals' Bloc	9.2	11	—	—
PFD	—	—	8.8	11

	1994		1998	
	%V	#S	%V	#S
FPCD	7.5	9	—	—
CDM	—	—	19.2	26
PCRM	—	—	30.1	40
PMDP	—	—	18.2	24
others	18.1	0	18.2	3
TOTAL SEATS		104		104

GOVERNMENTS

There have been four postindependence governments in Moldova. The second was headed by the independent Ion Ciubuc but maintained its PDAM support. Following the 1998 elections Cubiuc was kept in as prime minister despite the new parties that composed the cabinet. The parties then in government—the PFD, the PMDP, and the CDM—all represented pro-government, pro-reform, and moderately pro-Romanian forces, a major shift from the PDAM. However, divisions among them led to a government collapse after only a few months, followed by a government of similar forces, but with Ion Sturza of the PMDP as prime minister. Sturza himself resigned a few months later.

Moldovan Governments since 1994

In Office Date (M/Y)	Prime Minister (Party)	#M(I)	Parties in Cabinet
03/94	Sangheli, A.	20(3)	PDAM
01/97	Ciubuc, I.	..	nonpartisan
05/98	Ciubuc, I.	21	CDM PMDP PFD
03/99	Sturza, I. (PMDP)	20	PMDP PRCM PFD

ACRONYMS

CDM Democratic Convention of Moldova
CDU United Democratic Forces

continued

ACRONYMS *Continued*

FPCD	Christian Democratic Popular Front
PCRM	Party of Communists of the Moldovan Republic
PRCM	Party of the Revival and Accord of Moldova
PDAM	Agrarian Democratic Party of Moldova
PFD	Party of Democratic Forces
PFM	Popular Front of Moldova
PMDP	Movement for a Prosperous and Democratic Moldova
PS	Socialist Party

REFERENCE

Dawisha, Karen, and Bruce Parrott. eds. *Democratic Changes and Authoritarian Reactions in Russia, Ukraine, Belarus, and Moldova.* Cambridge, England: Cambridge University Press, 1997.

Netherlands

SUMMARY OF PARTY SYSTEMS

1946–71	extreme multiparty system with two main parties (KVP and PvdA)
1972	extreme multiparty system with a balance among the parties
1977–(98)	moderate multiparty system with a balance among the parties

HISTORY

The modern state of the Netherlands dates from 1815. Before that time the Dutch United Provinces were more of a confederal system, which obviously did not stop them from becoming a center of trade and science in the seventeenth century. The Catholic south revolted and broke away in 1830–31, becoming modern Belgium. However, a Catholic minority remained in the Netherlands. The predominant Dutch Reformed Church would itself suffer a schism in the late 1800s when more fundamentalist Calvinists—the so-called little men of farmers, artisans, and the lower middle class—broke away to form the *Gereformeerde* Church. In short, the country was clearly divided on religious grounds. Responsible government was achieved in 1848, and universal suffrage was achieved by 1919. From around the turn of the century until the 1960s, the Dutch society was clearly segmented into institutional subcultures or "pillars," each with their own schools, media, sporting teams, and political parties. The most institutionalized of these was the pillar of the Catholic minority, but there was also a Dutch Reformed pillar, a Calvinist pillar, and a socialist pillar. The secular middle class was largely outside of a clear pillar. The lack of a majority group and the division of society into top-down pillars facilitated a national "pacification settlement" among the groups in 1913–17, which protected the various minorities and gave each group a favored policy. Secularization and "depillarization" from around 1967 would see these pillars collapse.

ELECTORAL SYSTEM

The Netherlands has perhaps the simplest, and certainly the most proportional, of the proportional representation/party list systems. The entire country serves as one constituency (using the d'Hondt method), and there is no legal threshold for representation. Thus, the only effective threshold is the size of the legislature, which was expanded from 100 to 150 seats in 1956. This meant that a party needed only 1 percent of the vote through 1956 to win a seat, and since then, needs only 0.667 percent of the vote. Voting was compulsory until 1970.

CLEAVAGES, POLITICAL PARTIES, AND DE-ALIGNMENT

The Netherlands has usually had a moderate number of key parties, but because of its extremely proportional electoral system has also had many small parties. In the immediate postwar era, or more precisely from the 1920s to the 1960s, pillarization and the underlying cleavages of religiosity, religion, and social class produced an extremely structured party system, with very little movement of voters. It was the Gereformeerde subculture that had in fact formed the first national party in the Netherlands, when in 1879 it established the **Anti-Revolutionary Party (ARP)**. This party opposed the French Revolution and its secular values. Issues of suffrage expansion, as well as denominational conflicts, caused the more upper-middle-class Dutch Reform members to leave the ARP to the Gereformeerden and set up a separate party in 1908, the **Christian Historical Union (CHU)**. A specific Catholic party, the **Roman Catholic State Party (RKSP)**, was not set up until 1926. After the Second World War, a separate Catholic party was again formed, the **Catholic People's Party (KVP)**, with a new broader-based program. The KVP contained a substantial working-class component and was thus rather progressive in socioeconomic policy.

Besides the major religious parties cited, there are also three smaller, conservative, Protestant parties, each of which in fact splintered off from the ARP and/or the Gereformeerde Church: the **Political Reformed Party (SGP)**, which was formed in 1918; the **Reformed Political Union (GPV)**, which was formed in 1948 and finally won a seat in 1963; and the **Reformed Political Federation (RPF)**, which was formed in 1975. Of these, the SGP is the most orthodox, to the point of opposing both the separation of church and state, and female suffrage.

For nonreligious Dutch, the cleavage of religion was obviously not salient; instead, social class was what mattered. For the secular working class, the main historical party was the **Social-Democratic Workers' Party (SDAP)**, which was organized in 1894. After the Second World War, the Socialists (like the Catholics) thought that a new name and more flexibility would allow them to break through the pillars and pick up new voters. The party thus became the **Labour Party (PvdA)**, or more literally the "Party of Labour." Reference to socialism was thus dropped from the name, as was Marxist terminology from the program. Nevertheless, the Labour Party did not have much appeal beyond the secular working class until the 1960s, when it began to pick up some "new-politics" elements. The increasing influence of this New Left group led some moderates to break away in 1970 and form the **Democratic Socialists '70 (DS'70)**. This was more of a centrist or even center-right force, and, although it was part of a center right government in 1971, it did not have much long-term durability. The DS'70 was disbanded in 1983.

Other smaller leftist parties that existed included the **Communist Party of the Netherlands (CPN)**, dating back to a 1909 split from the SDAP; the anti–Cold War **Pacifist Socialist Party (PSP)**, formed in 1957; and the **Political Party Radicals (PPR)**, which was formed by leftist Catholics in 1970 and quickly became secular.

Finally, various liberal, radical, and (secular) conservative parties had existed before the First World War and between the wars. Finally, in 1948 a unified liberal party, the **People's Party for Freedom and Democracy (VVD)**, was established. The party has been clearly secular and free-market oriented, and after its foundation was the vehicle of the secular middle class.

Starting in the late 1960s, some fundamental changes occurred in Dutch party politics. First and foremost, secularization and "depillarization" led to a drop-off in support for the main religious parties, especially the KVP but also the CHU. Discussions soon arose about merging the main religious parties. The ARP, whose vote was still holding, was hesitant, but the three parties agreed to present a joint list in the 1977 elections as the **Christian Democratic Appeal (CDA)**. In 1980 the parties would formally merge. Left-leaning members of the ARP who opposed this merger broke away and formed the **Evangelical People's Party (EVP)**. The CDA, as a unified entity, was able to stop the collective decline of the main religious parties, but this was in part due to the popularity in the 1980s of CDA Prime Minister Ruud Lubbers, who was able to attract some young secular voters to the party. In the 1990s the CDA has suffered a further loss in support.

Second, the Netherlands has seen the creation of and increased support for, postmaterialist parties. Indeed, it appears that it was the Dutch who created the first of these, in 1966. This party was thus called the **Democrats '66 (D'66)**, and is now known simply as **D66**. The party was not based on a specific social group, but pushed for institutional changes such as a directly elected prime minister (to produce accountability). In its early years the D'66 often spoke of trying to "explode" the structured Dutch party system. In addition to being postmaterialist, it can also been seen as the "left-liberal" alternative to the "right-liberal" VVD; certainly there has been some shifting of voters between these two parties. The other main postmaterialist party is the **Green Left (GL)**, formed in 1989 as a merger of the CPN, PSP, PPR, and EVP. The GL is much more leftist than the D66.

RECENT ELECTIONS

The 1989 election campaign centered around the issue of the environment. All parties, with the exception of the VVD, pledged to support more environment-friendly policies. This focus greatly benefited the new Green Left as well as D66. The CDA focused its campaign on fiscal reform and the importance of implementing a policy of economic austerity. The CDA argued that only once the economy was improved could money be put back into social welfare. The PvdA campaigned for a shorter work week and criticized the CDA plan as something that would hurt the sick, poor, and elderly members of society. The election results showed support for the CDA, as the VVD and PvdA both lost seats. The VVD performance was the party's worst since 1973. The D66, benefiting from its concentration of environmental issues during the campaign, gained three seats.

The key issues of the 1994 campaign centered around the reform of social security, as well as the country's immigration laws. The Christian Democrats wanted to put a freeze on pensions. This proved to be a very unpopular position that—coupled with the resignation of the popular prime minister and leader of the CDA, Ruud Lubbers—resulted in a dramatic drop for the party. The CDA lost twenty seats, which, combined with the twelve seats lost by the PvdA, represented an unprecedented thirty-two-seat drop for the outgoing government coalition. Parties representing the interests of pensioners benefited from the focus the pension issue received during the campaign. The **General Union of the Elderly (AOV)** picked up six seats while **Union 55+** won one. The biggest single gain for a party was made by D66, which increased its number of seats by twelve. As a result of these elections, religious parties were excluded from government for the first time ever.

The 1998 elections were not as dramatic. This time the Labour Party benefited from the popularity of its leader, incumbent Prime Minister Wim Kok. Votes shifted from the D66 to the VVD. The CDA continued to fall, and the pensioners' parties lost all their seats.

Selected Elections in the Netherlands

	1948		1963		1967		1971	
	%V	#S	%V	#S	#V	#S	%V	#S
KVP	31.0	32	31.9	50	26.5	42	21.8	35
ARP	13.2	13	8.7	13	9.9	15	8.6	13
CHU	9.2	9	8.6	13	8.1	12	6.3	10
SGP	2.4	2	2.3	3	2.0	3	2.3	3
PvdA	25.6	27	28.0	43	23.6	37	24.6	39
CPN	7.7	8	2.8	4	3.6	5	3.9	6
VVD	7.9	8	10.3	16	10.7	17	10.3	16
GPV	—	—	0.7	1	0.9	1	1.6	2
PSP	—	—	3.0	4	2.9	4	1.4	2
D'66	—	—	—	—	4.5	7	6.8	11
PPR	—	—	—	—	—	—	1.8	2
DS'70	—	—	—	—	—	—	5.3	8
others	2.9	1	3.7	3	7.4	7	5.1	3
TOTAL SEATS		100		150		150		150

continued

Selected Elections in the Netherlands *Continued*

	1977		1989		1994			1998	
	%V	#S	%V	#S	#V	#S		%V	#S
CDA	31.9	49	35.3	54	22.2	34		18.4	28
SGP	2.1	3	1.9	3	1.7	2		1.8	3
PvdA	33.8	53	31.9	49	24.0	37		29.0	45
CPN	1.7	2	(merged into GL)						
VVD	17.9	28	14.6	22	19.9	31		24.7	39
GPV	1.0	1	1.2	2	1.3	2		1.2	2
PSP	0.9	1	(merged into GL)						
D66	5.4	8	7.9	12	15.5	24		9.0	14
PPR	1.7	3	(merged into GL)						
DS'70	0.7	1	—	—	—	—		—	—
RPF	—	—	1.0	1	1.8	3		2.0	3
GL	—	—	4.1	6	3.5	5		7.3	11
AOV	—	—	—	—	3.6	6	}	0.5	0
Union 55+	—	—	—	—	0.9	1	}		
others	2.7	1	2.1	1	5.6	5		6.1	5
TOTAL SEATS		150		150		150			150

GOVERNMENTS

The relative balance between Dutch parties has meant that coalition negotiations take a long time, and the coalitions are often broad. Governments have tended to be either center left or center right, since from 1951 until 1994 the PvdA and the VVD would not be in government together. This situation gave a strategic advantage to the main religious parties, and later the CDA. Since 1994, however, a "purple" secular coalition has governed. This collapsed for a brief period in May 1999, but was reestablished the following month.

Dutch Governments since 1946

In Office Date (M/Y)	Prime Minister (Party)	#M(I)	Parties in Cabinet
07/46	Beel, L. (KVP)	16(4)	KVP PvdA
08/48	Drees, W. (PvdA)	15(2)	KVP PvdA CHU VVD
03/51	Drees, W. (PvdA)	15(1)	KVP PvdA CHU VVD
09/52	Drees, W. (PvdA)	16(1)	KVP PvdA ARP CHU
10/56	Drees, W. (PvdA)	14	PvdA KVP ARP CHU
12/58	Beel, L. (KVP)	15	KVP CHU ARP
05/59	de Quay, J.E. (KVP)	13	KVP VVD ARP CHU
07/63	Marijin, V. (KVP)	13	KVP VVD ARP CHU
04/65	Cals, J. (KVP)	14	KVP PvdA ARP
11/66	Zijlstra, J. (KVP)	13	KVP ARP
04/67	de Jong, P. (KVP)	14	KVP ARP VVD CHU
06/71	Biesheuvel, B. (ARP)	16	KVP ARP VVD CHU DS70
08/72	Biesheuvel, B. (ARP)	14	KVP ARP VVD CHU
05/73	den Uyl, J. (PvdA)	16	PvdA KVP ARP PPR D66
12/77	van Agt, A. (KVP)	15	KVP VVD ARP CHU
09/81	van Agt, A. (CDA)	15	CDA PvdA D66
11/81	van Agt, A. (CDA)	15	CDA PvdA D66
05/82	van Agt, A. (CDA)	14	CDA D66
11/82	Lubbers, R. (CDA)	14	CDA VVD
07/86	Lubbers, R. (CDA)	14	CDA VVD
11/89	Lubbers, R. (CDA)	14	PvdA CDA
08/94	Kok, W. (PvdA)	14	PvdA VVD D66
08/98	Kok, W. (PvdA)	15	PvdA VVD D66
06/99	Kok, W. (PvdA)	15	PvdA VVD D66

ACRONYMS

AOV	General Union of the Elderly
ARP	Anti-Revolutionary Party
CDA	Christian Democratic Appeal
CHU	Christian-Historical Union
CPN	Communist Party in the Netherlands
D'66	Democrats '66
DS'70	Democratic Socialists '70
EVP	Evangelical People's Party
GL	Green Left
GPV	Reformed Political Union
KVP	Catholic People's Party
PPR	Political Party Radicals
PSP	Pacifist Socialist Party
PvdA	Labour Party
RKSP	Roman Catholic State Party
RPF	Reformed Political Federation
SDAP	Social-Democratic Workers' Party
SGP	Political Reformed Party
VVD	People's Party for Freedom and Democracy

REFERENCES

Andeweg, Rudy B., and Galen A. Irwin. (1993). *Dutch Government and Politics.* Basingstoke, England: Macmillan.

Daalder, Hans, and Galen A. Irwin, eds. (1989). *Politics in the Netherlands: How Much Change?* London: Frank Cass.

Koole, Ruud A. (1994). "The Vulnerability of the Modern Cadre Party in the Netherlands," in Richard S. Katz and Peter Mair, eds. *How Parties Organize: Change and Adaption in Party Organization in Western Democracies.* London: SAGE, pp. 278–303.

ten Napel, Hans-Martien (1999). "The Netherlands: Resilience Amidst Change," in David Broughton and Mark Donovan, eds., *Changing Party Systems in Western Europe.* London: Pinter, pp. 163–182.

Norway

SUMMARY OF PARTY SYSTEMS

1945	extreme multiparty system with one dominant party (DNA)
1949–77	moderate multiparty system with one dominant party (DNA)
1981–85	moderate multiparty system with two main parties (DNA and H)
1989–(97)	extreme multiparty system with one dominant party (DNA)

HISTORY

Norway was under Danish rule for several centuries; in 1814, this was replaced with a union with Sweden under Swedish control. Home rule was achieved in 1884, and full independence came in 1905. The many centuries of foreign domination have made Norwegians wary of control from abroad, evidenced in their rejection in 1972 and again in 1994 of membership in the European Union.

ELECTORAL SYSTEM

Norway uses a party-list, proportional-representation electoral system, with nineteen multimember districts. The modified St. Laguë formula is used. Since 1989, there have been eight "top-up" seats.

POLITICAL PARTIES AND CLEAVAGES

Many of the political parties in Norway tend to be less conservative than in other countries, with there being general agreement on maintaining the welfare state and the role of the government in the economy. The center/periphery cleavage is still an important one, as it has at times led to divisions over foreign policy, such as membership in the European Union.

The **Norwegian Labor Party (DNA)** was founded in 1887 and has been the largest party in Norway since the 1920s. The party has enjoyed a fairly broad base of support among both urban and rural workers and has maintained close relations with the country's trade unions. The DNA has advocated a fairly tradition social democratic platform and has supported NATO, environmental polices, and a nuclear-free Norway. The party was internally very divided over the EU membership issue despite the official pro-EU stance that the party ended up taking.

To the left of the DNA on Norway's political spectrum is the **Socialist Left Party (SV)**, which was founded in 1975. The party's origins lie in an electoral coalition formed by socialists and communists who were opposed to NATO and the DNA's position with respect to NATO. The party was known for a time as the **Socialist People's Party (SF)**. The party is left-socialist in orientation and critical of both social democrats and orthodox communists. The party has campaigned for a more progressive tax system and is against any cuts to the social welfare state.

The **Conservative Party (H)** was formed in the 1880s. The party's name in Norwegian, *Høyre,* literally translates into "the Right." The Conservatives have traditionally been one of the largest of Norway's non-Socialist parties. The party supports a reduction in taxes, less government control of industry, and an emphasis on private investment. Despite these policy stances the party, nevertheless, still believes in a social market economy, only with a smaller bureaucracy. The party takes a rather liberal position on social issues and has also given support to tougher environmental policies. It supported the country's attempts at gaining EU membership, and this stance somewhat divided the party and hurt it in terms of electoral support.

The **Christian People's Party (KrF)** was founded in 1933 to promote Christian values in public life. The party maintains conservative positions on most social issues and has been associated with Norway's temperance movement. In terms of economics, however, the party positions itself between the DNA and the Conservatives. One economic policy that the party has been particularly supportive of is an increase in trade with the developing nations of the world. The party is pro-NATO but campaigned against the EU in 1993. Understandably, the party is most heavily supported by churchgoers and moral conservatives.

The **Center Party (SP)** was founded in 1920 as the Agrarian Party. Like many other Scandinavian agrarian and farmers' parties, the SP adopted its current name (in 1958) in an effort to broaden its appeal outside rural areas. Despite these efforts, the party's main source of support remains farmers and Norway's rural population. The party supports regional aid and subsidies and is more conservative on social and religious issues. Recently, the party has put emphasis on supporting environmental policies.

The **Progress Party (FP)** was founded in 1973 as a populist, libertarian, protest party called the **Anders Lange Party for a Strong Reduction in Taxes and Public Intervention**. The party argued for a reduction of the welfare state, lower taxes, an end to farm subsidies, and tougher immigration and crime laws. The founder of the party, Anders Lange, died in 1974, and as result the party changed its name to the Progress Party in 1977. It has avoided taking a firm stand on EU membership to avoid dividing the party.

The **Liberal Party (V)** was formed in the 1880s as "the left" to the Conservative "right." The party maintains a middle-of-the-road position on social and economic issues. It supports tax reform and a shift to indirect taxation. The party has suffered from splits, especially over EU integration; in 1972 members left to form the **New People's Party**, which, in 1980, was renamed the **Liberal People's Party (DLF)**. The split did not last, however, and the DLF returned to the Liberal Party fold in 1988.

SELECTED ELECTIONS

The 1973 election campaign was completely dominated by the European Community membership issue. Those parties that supported membership, such as the DNA and Conservatives, lost votes. In the case of Labor the loss was sizable. In the previous election, in 1969, the DNA had won 46.5 percent of the vote; in 1973 this total dropped to 35.3 percent. The following election, held in 1977, saw a reversing of the votes won and lost due to the EC issue. Parties, such as the SV and the SP, which had made gains due to their stance against EC membership, returned to their pre-1973 levels. The DNA, which had suffered huge losses, regained almost all the votes lost in 1973.

Selected Elections in Norway, 1949–77

	1949		1961		1973		1977	
	%V	#S	%V	#S	%V	#S	%V	#S
DNA	45.7	85	46.8	74	35.3	62	42.3	76
H	18.3	23	20.0	29	17.4	29	24.8	41
SP	7.9	12	9.4	16	11.0	21	8.6	12
V	13.1	21	8.8	14	3.8	2	3.2	2
SV	—	—	2.4	2	11.2	16	4.2	2

continued

Selected Elections in Norway, 1949–77 *Continued*

	1949		1961		1973		1977	
	%V	#S	%V	#S	%V	#S	%V	#S
KrF	8.4	9	9.6	15	12.3	20	12.4	22
FP	—	—	—	—	5.0	4	1.9	0
DLF	—	—	—	—	3.4	1	1.4	0
others	6.6	0	3.1	0	0.9	0	1.3	0
TOTAL SEATS		150		150		155		155

The 1981 elections featured the best showing for the Conservatives in Norway's post–World War II history. This success was in part due to the lowering of the voting age in Norway from twenty to eighteen years of age, since many of the new younger voters supported the Conservatives as opposed to the DNA. The abortion issue, which had featured prominently in the election campaigns of the 1970s, was not as big an issue in the 1981 campaign. The issue did, however, affect the formation of the next government when talks between the Christian People's Party, Conservatives, and Center Party broke down because the KrF wanted reforms to the abortion law and the others did not.

Selected Elections in Norway, 1981–97

	1981		1989		1993		1997	
	%V	#S	%V	#S	%V	#S	%V	#S
DNA	37.2	65	34.3	63	37.0	67	35.1	65
H	31.7	54	22.2	37	16.9	28	14.3	23
SP	6.7	11	6.5	11	16.8	32	8.0	11
V	3.9	2	3.2	0	3.6	1	4.5	6
SV	4.9	4	10.1	17	7.9	13	5.9	9
KrF	8.9	15	8.5	14	7.9	13	13.7	25
FP	4.5	4	13.0	22	6.3	10	15.3	25
DLF	0.5	0	—	—	—	—	—	—
others	1.2	0	2.2	1	3.6	1	3.3	1
TOTAL SEATS		155		165		165		165

The 1993 elections saw the issue of EU membership return as the primary focus of the campaign. Once again parties that campaigned against it benefited. The Center Party, whose anti-EU position became a centerpiece of its campaign, saw its vote share nearly triple as compared with the previous election. The DNA managed to avoid any drop in votes by concentrating on its efforts to bring down the rate of unemployment and by highlighting the role played in the Oslo peace talks between the government of Israel and the PLO.

The most recent elections, held in 1997, saw the SP lose all the seats it had gained in 1993. The biggest winners of the election were the Progress Party and the Christian People's Party, which managed to tie for the second highest number of seats behind the DNA. This was the first time a party other than the Conservatives or Center Party had finished second. The main issues of the campaign included health care for the elderly, and immigration. Parties also debated over how the government should best spend the profits earned from the country's large petroleum resources.

GOVERNMENTS

The Norwegian Labour Party is the country's "natural party of government"—initially this was through outright dominance of the parliament. In recent decades DNA minority governments have been the most common, if only because the nonsocialist government coalitions that are their main alternative have tended to break up over internal differences.

Norwegian Governments since 1945

In Office Date (M/Y)	Prime Minister (Party)	#M	Parties in Cabinet
11/45	Gerhardsen, E. (DNA)	14	DNA
10/49	Gerhardsen, E. (DNA)	14	DNA
11/51	Torp, O. (DNA)	13	DNA
10/53	Torp, O. (DNA)	13	DNA
01/55	Gerhardsen, E. (DNA)	13	DNA
10/57	Gerhardsen, E. (DNA)	15	DNA

continued

Norwegian Governments since 1945 *Continued*

In Office Date (M/Y)	Prime Minister (Party)	#M	Parties in Cabinet
10/61	Gerhardsen, E. (DNA)	15	DNA
08/63	Lyng, J. (H)	15	H Sp KrF V
09/63	Gerhardsen, E. (DNA)	15	DNA
10/65	Borten, P. (Sp)	15	H KrF Sp V
09/69	Borten, P. (Sp)	15	H KrF Sp V
03/71	Brattelli, T. (DNA)	15	DNA
10/72	Korvald, L. (KrF)	15	Sp V KrF
10/73	Brattelli, T. (DNA)	15	DNA
01/76	Nordli, O. (DNA)	16	DNA
09/77	Nordli, O. (DNA)	16	DNA
02/81	Brundtland, G.H. (DNA)	17	DNA
10/81	Willoch, K. (H)	18	H
06/83	Willoch, K. (H)	18	H KrF Sp
09/85	Willoch, K. (H)	18	H KrF Sp
05/86	Brundtland, G. H. (DNA)	18	DNA
10/89	Syse, J. (H)	18	H Sp KrF
11/90	Brundtland, G. H. (DNA)	19	DNA
10/93	Brundtland, G. H. (DNA)	19	DNA
10/96	Jagland, T. (DNA)	19	DNA
10/97	Bondevik, K. M. (KrF)	19	KrF Sp V

ACRONYMS

DLF	Liberal People's Party
DNA	Norwegian Labour Party
FP	Progress Party
H	Conservative Party
KrF	Christian People's Party
SF	Socialist People's Party
SP	Center Party
SV	Socialist Left Party
V	Liberal Party

REFERENCES

Strøm, Kaare, and Jørn Y. Leipart. (1989). "Ideology, Strategy, and Party Competition in Postwar Norway," *European Journal of Political Research* 17, 263–288.

Strøm, Kaare, and Lars Svåsand, eds. (1997). *Challenges to Political Parties: The Case of Norway.* Ann Arbor: University of Michigan Press.

Poland

SUMMARY OF PARTY SYSTEMS

1991	extreme multiparty system with a balance among the parties
1993	extreme multiparty system with two main parties (SLD and PSL)
(1997–)	moderate multiparty system with two main parties (AWS and SLD)

HISTORY

Poland reappeared on the map after World War I. A short period of largely democratic government until 1926 gave way to military rule and semidemocracy until the German conquest of 1939. Falling into the Soviet camp, the Poles proved especially stubborn and resistant, and were allowed private farms as well as autonomy for the Catholic Church. The Solidarity trade union formed in 1981 was quickly banned, but would prove instrumental in achieving Poland's transition to democracy. As a result of the brutal German occupation and the forced westward shift of Poland's borders by Stalin, a heterogenous interwar society is now one of Europe's most homogeneous.

ELECTORAL SYSTEM

Poland has fifty-two multimember (three to seventeen seats) district constituencies, and one multimember (sixty-nine seats) national constituency. The 391 of the 460 deputies elected in the districts are elected by proportional representation, with the distribution of seats being effected on the basis of the d'Hondt method; parties win seats according to the aggregate vote for their candidates in a given district and then allocate them to those with the highest individual totals. The remaining sixty-nine seats are allocated proportionately on the basis of the d'Hondt method according to votes cast for national lists (correlated with local lists of candidates) of parties that are eligible; seats are allotted to individual candidates on the basis of their order within each list. Only those constituency lists of candidates for deputies that obtain at least 5 percent of the national vote are taken into account when allocating the seats (8 percent when the list is submitted by an election coalition). Similarly, in order to participate in the allocation of the sixty-nine seats at the national level, the constituency lists of a party or coalition must have obtained at least 7 percent of the national vote. These thresholds were adopted in an electoral law that was passed in May 1993. Previously, the 5 percent threshold only applied to the sixty-nine seats decided by a national list of parties. Parties could also make it onto the national list if they had won 5 or more seats of the 391 decided through thirty-seven electoral districts. Vacancies arising between general elections are filled by the individual who is "next in line" on the list of the party that formerly held the seat.

POLITICAL PARTIES AND CLEAVAGES

The former Polish communists reformed into the **Social Democracy of the Polish Republic (SdRP)**, and along with other left-wing and communist elements first formed the **Democratic Left Alliance (SLD)** for the 1991 elections. It advocates a larger role for the state in the economy, and stresses the importance of state ownership of industry, state-sponsored welfare, and state control of market forces. The party is also committed to reducing the Church's influence in politics and everyday life.

The **Polish Peasant Party (PSL)** is the largest party representing Poland's present population. The PSL argues for state intervention to ensure protection of Polish agricultural goods from foreign products. In 1991 it ran as the **Polish Peasants' Party-Programmatic Alliance (PSL-SP)**, but became simply the PSL in 1993 and 1997.

The **Democratic Union (UD)** was formed in 1991 by the merger of two smaller parties in advance of the upcoming Sejm elections. These two parties—the **Citizens Movement for Democratic Action Party (ROAD)** and the **Democratic Social Movement (RDS)**—were themselves not more than a year old at the time of the merger. The UD, at its inception, contained a number of elements, including a social-democratic faction that advocated a humane form of capitalism, a laissez-faire faction, and a faction that argued for a limited role for the church in political life. Gradually, however, the party developed more of single mind, which was for the continuation of reforms begun in 1989, and was anti-populist and anti-demagogic. The party contains many intellectuals and dissidents from the communist era.

In 1994 the UD formed an electoral alliance with the **Liberal Democratic Congress (KLD)**. The KLD is pro-market and pro-enterprise and favors a quicker pace to reforms. While winning seats in 1991, the party failed to make the 5 percent threshold in 1993. The alliance formed by the KLD and the UD is now called the **Freedom Union (UW)**. Before 1993, the KLD had been together with the **Polish Economic Program (PPG)** in a parliamentary alliance called the **Polish Liberal Program Coalition (PPL)**.

The **Christian Democratic Party (PChD)** and the **Peasant Christian Alliance (SLCh)**, two small right-of-center, pro-Catholic peasant parties, won representation in 1991 and found themselves a part of the 1992 government. However, the largest of the Catholic parties has been the **Christian National Union (ZChN)**. Formed in 1989 the ZChN is both anti-Communist and nationalist. The party was the principle element behind first the **Catholic Election Action (WAK)** alliance that contested the 1991 elections, and then the **Catholic Electoral Action—"Fatherland"** alliance in 1993. The party supports protectionist measures against the import of foreign goods, and believes in a strong place for the Catholic Church in everyday life. The party's base of support is Poland's rural population. Despite WAK having won the third highest number of seats in the 1991 elections, the Fatherland alliance failed to make it over the new 8 percent threshold for coalitions, and therefore failed to win representation in 1993. The **Peasant Alliance (PL)** is another right-of-center party appealing to Poland's rural voters. It was in the Fatherland alliance, as well, and, like the ZChN, was in the 1992 government. The **Confederation for an Independent Poland (KPN)** is a nationalist populist party that appeals to the most disgruntled members of Polish society. While it won seats in both 1991 and 1993, it was seen as too extreme to enter government.

For the 1993 elections, then-President Lech Walesa formed the **Non-Party Bloc in Support of Reforms (BBWR)** as a group to appeal to voters fed up with the traditional parties. The **Center Alliance (PC)**, an earlier Walesa-inspired creation, would lose half its support in 1993.

The **Labor Union (UP)** was formed after the 1991 elections and was successful in winning seats in 1993, but it fell below the 5 percent threshold in 1997. The party promotes economic interventionism and a slow pace of reforms, and it is anti-clerical while emphasizing its noncommunist roots. Poland's powerful trade unions were represented directly in the 1991 and 1993 elections by the **Solidarity** Trade Union. Although its vote share dropped only fractionally in 1993, this was enough to push Solidarity just below the 5 percent threshold for seats. It was thus one of the many center-right forces which fell victim in 1993 to the new electoral law. To forestall a similar fate in the next elections, in May 1996 Solidarity presided over the creation of an umbrella organization, called the **Solidarity Electoral Alliance (AWS)**, that would go on to win the plurality of seats in the 1997 elections. Besides Solidarity itself, the AWS contains the ZChN, the PL, the KPN, the BBWR, and the PC. Indeed, the AWS in fact is comprised of no less than thirty-six parties!

The Polish party system can best be conceived in a two-dimensional manner, with the main parties or blocs represented:

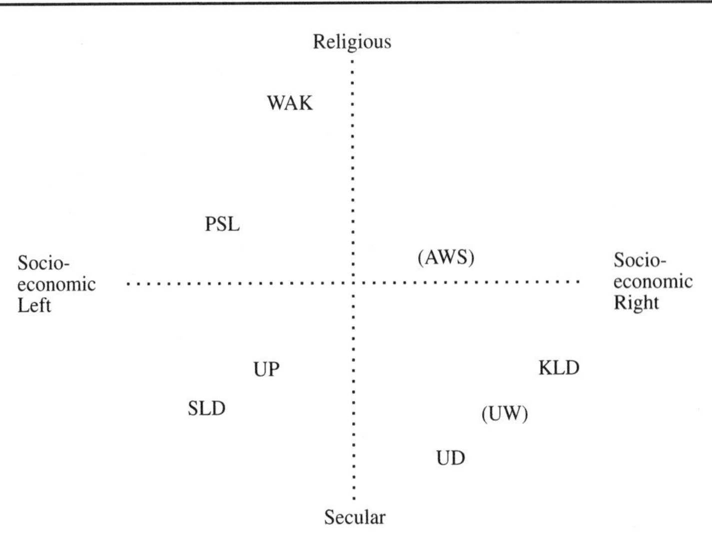

ELECTIONS

The elections held on 27 October 1991 were the first properly democratic elections held in Poland since 1928. Over ninety parties competed for the 391 seats at stake in the thirty-seven electoral districts. Since a threshold only applied to the sixty-nine seats decided by the national lists, a huge number of parties managed to gain representation in the Sejm, including the humorous **Polish Beer Lovers' Party (PPPP)**. Turnout reflected the general disillusionment felt by Poles with respect to the transition from the communist economic system. Only 43 percent of Poles cast ballots in 1991. A comment made, as a result, was that "Poland lost the elections."

Elections in Poland

	1991		1993			1997	
	%V	#S	%V	#S		%V	#S
SLD	12.0	60	20.4	171		27.1	164
PSL	8.7	48	15.4	132		7.3	27
UD	12.3	62	10.6	74	}		
KLD	7.5	37	4.0	0	}		
UW					}	13.4	60
WAK/Fatherland	8.7	49	6.4	0		(core into AWS)	
PL	5.5	28	2.4	0		(into AWS)	
KPN	7.5	46	5.8	22		(into AWS)	
PC	8.7	44	4.4	0		(into AWS)	
Solidarity	5.1	27	4.9	0		(into AWS)	
PPPP	3.3	16	0.1	0		—	—
UP	—	—	7.3	41		4.7	0
BBWR	—	—	5.4	16		(into AWS)	
ROP	—	—	—	—		5.6	6
AWS	—	—	—	—		33.8	201
pensioners parties	—	—	—	—		3.8	0
German minority	1.2	7	0.7	4		0.4	2
others	19.5	36	12.2	0		3.9	0
TOTAL SEATS		460		460			460

Indeed, no less than eighteen parties held the thirty-six seats that went to "other" parties in 1991. The left-wing parties did better in 1991 than opinion polls suggested they would. The campaign focused on issues regarding the place religion should have in public life, and pace at which economic reforms should continue. The Catholic Church involved itself in the campaign by openly supporting certain parties and candidates.

The elections of 1993, conducted under the new electoral law, saw few parties gain representation, and a huge number of votes wasted on the fragmented center-right of the spectrum. The elections were held as a result of the collapse of the coalition government that was formed in

1992. During the period since the 1991 elections the growth rate of the Polish economy was impressively high but so too was the unemployment rate, which reached 14.4 percent in 1993. These were among the pressing issues facing the electorate. Unlike in 1991, the church did not get heavily involved in the 1993 campaign.

The SLD was the most successful of the parties and campaigned with slogans such as: "things do not have to be like this," and "let reforms serve the people." The PSL gained the farm vote, promising trade protectionism from foreign agricultural goods. The UD, which had won the plurality of seats in 1991, finished behind both the SLD and the PSL. The party was blamed for being unaware of the economic hardships of ordinary people. The newly formed BBWR was successful in gaining the votes of those disillusioned with the traditional parties.

The 1997 elections held on 21 September saw over 20 parties, or coalitions, and a total of some 6,400 contestants for the 460 Diet seats. The SLD and the newly formed AWS, the right-wing opposition bloc gathered around the Solidarity trade union, proved to be the main contenders in the elections.

These two groups had similar campaign platforms: both favored pro-market economic policies and, in foreign affairs, supported integration with the European Union and NATO. The AWS, however, put greater emphasis on traditional, Christian values and, among other things, opposed abortion. The Freedom Union (UW), regarded as the architect of Poland's economic reforms in the 1990s (which had led to a current annual growth rate of 6 percent), finished a distant third. The campaign as a whole was generally calm.

The Peasant Party (PSL), partner in the outgoing governing coalition with the SLD, lost more than one hundred seats, falling to fourth place. Only one other group—the **Movement for the Reconstruction of Poland (ROP)**, which was formed in 1995—crossed the 5 percent threshold needed for Diet representation.

GOVERNMENTS

There have been six Polish governments since the country democratized. The first two governments formed were large coalition governments, because so many parties gained representation following 1991. The 1992 government collapsed in the wake of a scandal involving the existence of files containing the names of secret police collaborators of the communist era. The government was defeated in May 1993 by one vote in a vote of nonconfidence. The post-1993 governments have had the luxury of being composed of only two parties (or blocs) and of having the support of a majority of parliamentarians in the Sejm.

Polish Governments since 1991

In Office Date (M/Y)	Prime Minister (Party)	#M(I)	Parties in Cabinet
12/91	Olszewski, J. (PC)	17(8)	PC ZChN PL
07/92	Suchocka, H. (UD)	25(4)	UD ZChN KLD PL PChD SLCh PPG
10/93	Pawlak, W. (PSL)	20(7)	PSL SLD
03/95	Oleksy, J. (SLD)	21(6)	SLD PSL
02/96	Cimoszewicz, W. (SLD)	21(6)	PSL SLD
10/97	Buzek, J. (AWS)	24(6)	AWS UW

ACRONYMS

AWS	Solidarity Electoral Alliance
BBWR	Non-Party Bloc in Support of Reforms
KLD	Liberal Democratic Congress
KPN	Confederation for an Independent Poland
PC	Center Alliance
PChD	Christian Democratic Party
PL	Peasant Alliance
PPG	Polish Economic Program
PPL	Polish Liberal Program Coalition
PPPP	Polish Beer Lovers' Party
PSL	Polish Peasant Party
PSL-SP	Polish Peasants' Party–Programmatic Alliance
RDS	Democratic Social Movement
ROAD	Citizens Movement for Democratic Action Party
ROP	Movement for the Reconstruction of Poland
SdRP	Social Democracy of the Polish Republic
SLCh	Peasant Christian Alliance
SLD	Democratic Left Alliance

UD	Democratic Union
UP	Labour Union
UW	Freedom Union
WAK	Christian Electoral Action
ZChN	Christian National Union

REFERENCES

Taras, Ray. (1999). "Politics in Poland," pp. 364–420, in Gabriel A. Almond, Russell J. Dalton, and G. Bingham Powell Jr., eds. *European Politics Today.* New York: Longman.

Tworzecki, Hubert. (1996). *Parties and Politics in Post–1989 Poland.* Boulder: Westview Press.

Portugal

SUMMARY OF PARTY SYSTEMS

1975–85	moderate multiparty system with a balance among the parties
1987–91	moderate multiparty system with one dominant party (PSD)
1995–(99)	two-and-a-half-party system

HISTORY

Portugal has been a geographically cohesive polity since the eleventh century. The longstanding monarchy was overthrow in 1910, ushering in a highly unstable and centrifugal parliamentary system that in turn was overthrown by the army in 1926. The finance minister of the new regime, Dr. Antonio Salazar, consolidated his personal position as dictator by 1932 and then proceeded to establish a state-corporatist *Estado Novo* as of the 1932 constitution. Salazar remained as prime minister until 1968, then passed the position on to Dr. Marcello Caetano. Caetano tried to rule as a liberal authoritarian, but social tensions grew rapidly, in part over the cost of maintaining Portugal's empire in Africa. The armed forces overthrew Caetano in 1974, but then they quickly divided between moderates and left-wingers. Finally moderate armed-forces personnel and politicians negotiated a transition in which a general would be the first president and a military-dominated "Council of the Revolution" would play an overseeing role. Constitutional changes in 1982 would eliminate the military's role, and further changes in 1989 would eliminate the constitutional commitment to state ownership.

Portugal is thus a semipresidential system, although one in which the presidency has grown weaker with each decade. The Socialists have held the presidency since 1986.

ELECTORAL SYSTEM

Portugal uses a party-list, proportional-representation electoral system and the d'Hondt method. There are twenty-two multimember constituencies.

POLITICAL PARTIES AND CLEAVAGES

It should be noted at the start that when many of the democratic political parties were founded in Portugal, they described themselves as left of center or socialist in order to distance themselves from the country's pre-1975 political history regardless of whether or not this was a true representation of the party's ideology. Not all parties have bothered to "correct" their names.

The **Social Democratic Party (PSD)** was founded in 1974 as the **Popular Democratic Party (PPD)**. As with other political parties, the PPD proclaimed itself a socialist party and was therefore highly critical of the capitalist system, calling for the nationalization of key industries. In 1976 the party changed its name to the PSD, and through the late 1970s it became more clear that the party was less committed to socialism than it once professed. The PSD has a fairly fluid ideology and, as a result, has espoused a broad range of policies. The party has, however, been fairly consistent in supporting a more liberal economic policy and has been very supportive of Portugal's membership in the EU. In the 1979 and 1980 elections the party formed the **Democratic Alliance (AD)** with the more conservative CDS and PPM. The party has a very broad voter base, but gets its strongest support from outside the more densely populated urban areas.

The **Popular Party (PP)** was founded in 1977 as the **Social Democratic Center (CDS)**. It is a self-described centrist party, which means that it is, in fact, the most conservative of the mainstream parties in Portugal. The party espouses Christian-democratic values and has called for lower taxes, smaller government, and more privatization. Since the 1980s it has been rather nationalistic and opposed to further European integration.

The **Popular Monarchist Party (PPM)** was a party that was founded in support of the return of the monarchy to Portugal. The party attacked both communism and liberalism, as it felt that neither gives adequate protection to the environment. The PPM participated in the Democratic Alliance in 1979 and 1980 but then failed to win representation on its own.

On the actual left of the spectrum, the **Portuguese Socialist Party (PSP)** was reestablished in 1973 as the modern continuation of the country's historic socialist party. The party is more dedicated to socialist policies than is the PSD. The PSP is, however, reformist rather than Marxist in ideology. The party wants a role for government in the economy but argues for smaller bureaucracy and less centralized planning. The PSP supports Portugal's EU and NATO membership. Like the PSD, the PSP enjoys a fairly broad base of support and, in the 1990s, became rather "catch-all."

The **Portuguese Communist Party (PCP)** was originally founded in 1921. The party has been described as the "most Stalinist" of the West European communist parties. It opposed Portugal's entry into the European Community, does not support NATO, and has formed several electoral coalitions with smaller far-left parties. These coalitions have including the 1976 **United People's Electoral Front (FEPU)** with the **Popular Democratic Movement (MDP)**, the **United People's Alliance (APU)** from 1979 to 1985 with the MDP, and the **United Democratic Coalition (CDU)** with the **Greens** since 1987. Despite these changes, the Communist-led electoral coalitions have lost support in each of the last four national elections.

The **Democratic Renewal Party (PRD)** was founded in 1985 and was the popular political vehicle of the then president of Portugal, President Eanes. The PRD campaigned for the return of honesty and higher moral and ethical standards in government and rejected traditional ideologies. Once the president left office, however, the party ceased being a political force and lost most of its prominent members.

Elections in Portugal

	1975		**1976**		**1979**		**1980**		**1983**	
	%V	**#S**	**%V**	**#S**	**%V**	**#S**	**%V**	**#S**	**%V**	**#S**
PSD	28.4	81	25.2	73	(part of AD)				27.8	75
CDS/PP	8.1	16	16.7	42	(part of AD)				12.7	30
AD	—	—	—	—	46.3	128	48.3	134	—	—
PSP	40.7	116	36.7	107	28.2	74	28.7	74	37.3	101
PCP/FEPU/ APU	13.4	30	15.3	40	19.5	47	17.4	41	18.7	44
others	9.3	7	5.9	1	5.8	1	5.6	1	3.5	0
TOTAL SEATS		250		263		250		250		250

	1985		1987		1991		1995		1999	
	%V	#S	%V	#S	%V	#S	%V	#S	%V	#S
PSD	30.6	88	51.3	148	50.4	135	34.0	88	33.0	81
PP	10.0	22	4.4	4	4.4	5	9.1	15	8.6	15
PSP	21.4	57	22.8	60	30.0	72	43.9	112	44.9	115
APU/CDU	16.0	38	12.5	31	8.8	17	8.6	15	9.2	17
PRD	18.5	45	5.0	7	—	—	—	—	—	—
others	3.5	0	4.0	0	6.4	1	4.4	0	4.3	2
TOTAL SEATS		250		250		230		230		230

SELECTED ELECTIONS

The 1979 and 1980 elections were dominated by the newly formed Democratic Alliance, led by the PSD. In 1979 the PSD-led AD campaigned to revise the constitution and to remove references to ensuring a transition to socialism. In these elections the main issue of the campaign was the alleged fraud of the PSD leader and prime minister, with the PSP calling for his removal. The elections also featured tension between the president and the leader of the PSD, with the latter accusing the president of showing favoritism to the left-leaning parties.

In the 1985 elections the newly formed Party of Democratic Renewal won the third-highest number of votes and seats. This success was largely the result of the popularity of the then president and leader of the party. The party however only managed to hold on to seven of these seats in the following elections.

The only single party to have won a majority of seats (and also votes) is the PSD, which did so in both the 1987 and 1991 elections. The success of the party during these elections was in part due to the populist campaign run by the PSD, and the party's effective use of the state-monopolized TV. In both campaigns the party argued that a PSD-majority government would bring the most stability to the country. The popular PSD leader also threatened to resign if the party did not win a majority.

In the 1995 elections, one of the major issues was the country's participation in the European Union. Both major parties were supportive of Portugal's continued full participation in the EU and of preparing the country for the upcoming monetary union. The results ended a ten-year trend of a government and president from different parties, as both are now in the hands of the PSP.

In the 1999 elections, Portugal's most recent, the Socialists aimed to win their first-ever single-party majority, which would have required a gain of only 2 to 3 percent of the vote, and certainly not an actual majority of votes. Such a gain seemed within their reach according to the opinion polls, and given the popularity of Prime Minister Guterres. The opposition PSD, with its third leader in four years, did not pretend that it could actually win the elections. Instead, the PSD, along with the smaller parties, campaigned heavily against the possibility of a PSP majority; as the PSD noted, with the presidency in Socialist hands, a Socialist parliamentary majority would have led to more of a concentration of power in one party than anywhere else in Europe. In the end, the PSP gained only 1.0 percent of the vote and three seats to tie the combined opposition, thus leaving the Socialists still one seat short of an absolute majority. Overall, there was a clear swing to the left, as the only other relative winners were the CDU and a new far-left coalition.

GOVERNMENTS

In the unstable early years of Portuguese democracy, governments themselves were unstable, and at times the president set up the government directly. With the rise of the PSD to majority status in the late 1980s, the system changes to one of stable governments with no presidential interference. As of 1995, single-party government has remained under the PSP (which in fact has twice come just short of a majority).

Portuguese Governments since 1976

In Office Date (M/Y)	Prime Minister (Party)	#M(I)	Parties in Cabinet
07/76	Soares, M. (PSP)	20(6)	PSP
01/78	Soares, M. (PSP)	11(2)	PSP CDS
08/78	Nobre da Costa, A. (Ind)	(15)	
11/78	Mota Pinto, C. (Ind)	(17)	
07/79	Pintassilgo, M. (Ind)	(21)	
01/80	Sá Carneiro, F. (PSD)	15(1)	PSD CDS PPM

In Office Date (M/Y)	Prime Minister (Party)	#M(I)	Parties in Cabinet
01/81	Pinto Balsemão, F. (PSD)	18(2)	PSD CDS PPM
09/81	Pinto Balsemão, F. (PSD)	15(1)	PSD CDS PPM
06/83	Soares, M. (PSP)	17(1)	PSP PSD
11/85	Cavaco Silva, A. (PSD)	16(3)	PSD
08/87	Cavaco Silva, A. (PSD)	18(3)	PSD
10/91	Cavaco Silva, A. (PSD)	19(2)	PSD
10/95	Guterres, A. (PSP)	18(4)	PSP
10/99	Guterres, A. (PSP)		PSP

ACRONYMS

AD	Democratic Alliance
APU	United People's Alliance
CDS	Social Democratic Center
CDU	United Democratic Coalition
FEPU	United People's Electoral Front
MDP	Popular Democratic Movement
PCP	Portuguese Communist Party
PP	Popular Party
PPD	Popular Democratic Party
PPM	Popular Monarchist Party
PRD	Democratic Renewal Party
PSD	Social Democratic Party
PSP	Portuguese Socialist Party

REFERENCE

Magone, José M. (1999). "Portugal: Party System Installation and Consolidation," in David Broughton and Mark Donovan, eds., *Changing Party Systems in Western Europe.* London: Pinter, pp. 232–254.

Romania

SUMMARY OF PARTY SYSTEM

1992–(96) extreme multiparty system with two main parties (FDSN/PDSR and CDR)

Note: Because of the unfairness of the 1990 elections, classification of Romania's party system begins in 1992.

HISTORY

Romania was recognized as independent at the Berlin Congress in 1879. It made large territorial gains following World War I but lost substantial areas to Hungary, the Soviet Union, and Bulgaria in 1940. Transylvania was returned from Hungary after the Second World War, and Romania continues to have a significant Hungarian minority. King Michael used the entry of Soviet troops in 1944 to dismiss a pro-German regime and switch to the Allied side. The king was forced to accept a Communist government in 1945, and abdicated in 1947. In 1965 Nicolae Ceauşescu took over and began a policy of independence from the Soviet Union. Romania's transition from communism was relatively violent and brutal, culminating in the 25 December 1989 execution of Ceauşescu and his wife.

ELECTORAL SYSTEM

Romania uses proportional representation in forty-two multimember (four to twenty-nine seats) constituencies; there is one deputy for every seventy thousand inhabitants. There is a 3 percent threshold for individual parties; for alliances this 3 percent goes up 1 percent for each additional party, up to a maximum of 8 percent. That is, for an alliance of two parties, the threshold is 4 percent, for three parties the threshold is 5 percent, and so forth. In addition to the 328 seats now elected "nationally," there are fifteen seats reserved for minorities (this was thirteen in 1992).

POLITICAL PARTIES AND CLEAVAGES

In general, Romanian parties are not sharply defined, nor are the party programs well crystallized. However, most Romanian politicians do refer to themselves as belonging to the center, the center left, or the center right.

Two of Romania's main parties descend directly from the former **National Salvation Front (FSN)** group, which took power away from the ruling communist party and formed the transitional government before the 1990 elections. The first of these is the **Social Democracy Party of Romania (PDSR)**, which, prior to a 1993 name change and absorption of a smaller socialist-democratic party and a republican party, was known as the **Democratic National Salvation Front (FDSN)**. The FDSN split from its forerunner, the FSN, in 1992 as the breakaway **FSN-22 December Group**. This is the party of Ion Iliescu, the popularly elected president in both 1990 and 1992. The party lost support and popularity during the years leading to its defeat in the 1996 elections. The PDSR would position itself on the center left of the Romanian political spectrum. Its 1995 government coalition with extremist and nationalist parties further increased questions over the PDSR's commitment to democracy and created strife within the party.

The second party to descend from the FSN group is the **Democratic Party-National Salvation Front (PD-FSN)**, also known just as the **Democratic Party (PD)**. This was the FSN rump group that remained after Iliescu split with his group in 1992. The FSN grouping that remained renamed itself prior to the 1996 elections to encompass the Democratic Party rubric. For the 1996 elections the party created the **Social Democratic Union (USD)** along with one of Romania's smaller social democratic parties, which had won one seat in the 1990 elections. The spilt in the FSN that created the PD-FSN and the PDSR was not an ideological one; instead, it was caused by a personal conflict between Iliescu and the PD-FSN leader and former prime minister Pete Roman. Therefore the PD-FSN can be said to sit on the center left of the Romanian political spectrum as well.

The main group that emerged in opposition to the FSN and its later splinter parties is the **Democratic Convention of Romania (CDR)**. Formed for the 1992 elections, the center-right CDR is a grouping of several parties, some of which gained seats in the 1990 elections. The most prominent party within the CDR is the **National Peasant and Christian Democratic Party (PNT-CD)** which is a continuation of one of Romania's historic political parties—the Peasant Party—which was active in the prewar period and was subsequently banned by the communists. It was revived in 1990. Another historical party represented in the CDR is the **National Liberal Party (PNL)**, which existed in its historical form from 1869 to 1947 and was revived in 1990. In addition to Christian Democrats and liberals, the CDR also encompasses Green groups including the **Romanian Ecological Party (PER)** and Eastern Europe's largest environmental group, the **Romanian Ecological Movement (MER)**. The PER and MER, both founded in 1990, together won over 5 percent of the seats in the 1990 elections.

Romania also has its share of nationalist parties. The **Party of Romanian National Unity (PUNR)**, founded in 1990, was at its most successful in the early 1990s, gaining thirty seats in the 1992 elections, the third-highest total after the three big parties mentioned. However, its popularity has slipped since, as has its performance in elections. Relying solely on its nationalist identity, the party has failed to develop a clear position on economic policy or Romania's foreign relations with Western Europe, two areas of importance to Romanian voters. The only area in which the PUNR has been consistent is in its position that Hungarian groups in Romania and in Hungary itself present a threat to Romania's national and territorial sovereignty.

The **Greater Romania Party (PRM)**, formed in 1992, shares many of the PUNR's ideas on minorities within Romania and on neighboring countries but is even more extreme in its nationalistic program. Despite this fact, the PDSR relied on support from the PRM and the PUNR for its 1994 coalition government.

In response to the PRM and the PUNR, there exists the **Hungarian Democratic Union of Romania (UDMR)**. Formed in 1990, the UDMR represents the interests of the Hungarian population in Romania. The UDMR has attempted to guarantee the rights of Hungarians to education, culture, and protection of language and local government. Many of the UDMR's policies have therefore fueled even greater nationalistic rhetoric on the part of the PMR and the PUNR.

The former hard-line communists are still represented in Romanian politics by the neocommunist **Socialist Labor Party (PSM)**. The PSM, which is considered the main successor to the ruling communist party, was able to win thirteen seats in the 1992 elections, but was unable to win any in 1996.

The Romanian party system can best be conceived in this two-dimensional manner:

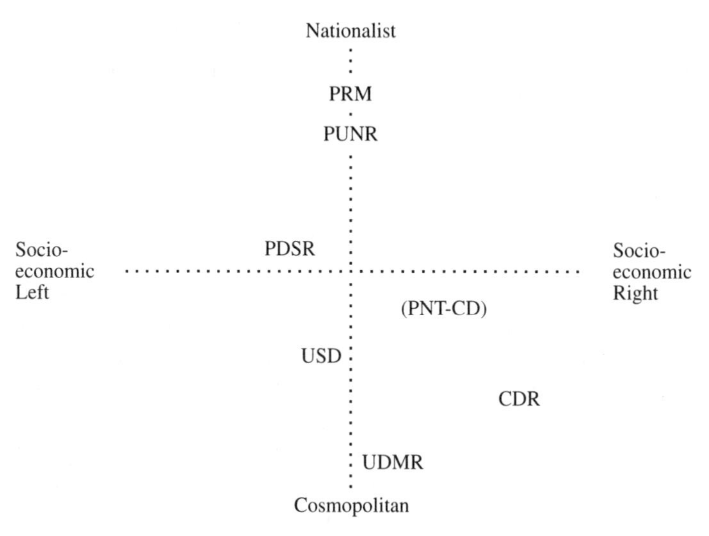

ELECTIONS

On 20 May 1990 the first multiparty elections were held in Romania since 1937. However, international observers stopped short of calling them completely fair or free. PR was used to determine the then-387 elected seats in the Chamber of Deputies but there was no threshold for representation. The short period between the fall of the Ceauşescu regime and the elections gave little time for parties to develop a clear platform to present to voters. This, coupled with the fact that the FSN represented the moderate change that voters preferred, resulted in an overwhelming FSN victory.

The September 1992 elections were thus the first basically free and fair elections held in Romania since 1937. They saw 88 parties, out of 144 registered ones, field candidates for the 328 elected seats in the Chamber of Deputies. Only twelve parties managed to get more than 3 percent, six of which belonged to the CDR coalition. The CDR's performance in the elections was in large part due to the split that had occurred in the FSN. With eighty-two seats the CDR secured its position as the largest opposition force in Romanian politics. Over half of these eighty-two seats were won by the PNT-CD. Alarming for the prospects of Romanian democracy at the time were the number of seats gained by the two nationalist parties and the neocommunists. Together the PUNR, the PRM, and the PSM received close to 15 percent of the seats in the Chamber of Deputies.

With the popularity of the FDSN dwindling and the chance of a CDR victory increasing, many feared that the 1996 elections would be marred by fraud and irregularities. In actuality, the biggest problems were organizational, mainly getting an exact voters list. In Bucharest the voters list included 100,000 deceased residents in place of a few neighborhoods of living residents. The PDSR did conduct a campaign of misinformation against the CDR, claiming, among other things, that the CDR was preparing to cede territory to Hungary and that the CDR supported a return to a monarchy. The campaign was also marked by an attempt by many candidates to display religious feeling in order to match the growing religiosity among the general population. The main issues of the campaign for the CDR were the poor performance of the previous FDSN government and the restructuring of the agricultural sector. The rural population was targeted heavily for support by the CDR, who issued a "Contract with Romania" (perhaps inspired by Newt Gingrich and the Republican Party in the United States), which focused on the rural population. The PDSR tried to counter its poor performance record with the recent talks of getting Romania into NATO.

In all, "only" forty-eight parties ran in the elections, forty less than in the previous elections, and only six parties got over the 3 percent threshold. Of the 327 elected seats, 103 were acquired by the process of redistribution of those parties that did not clear 3 percent. The two nationalist parties lost seats and the PSM failed to win any.

Elections in Romania

	1990*		**1992**		**1996**	
	%V	**#S**	**%V**	**#S**	**%V**	**#S**
FSN	66.3	263	10.2	43	—	—
USD	—	—	—	—	12.9	53
FDSN/PDSR	—	—	27.7	117	21.5	91
PNL	6.4	29	(into CDR)			
PNT-CD	2.6	12	(into CDR)			

	1990*		1992		1996	
	%V	#S	%V	#S	%V	#S
PER	1.7	8	(into CDR)			
MER	2.6	12	(into CDR)			
CDR	—	—	20.0	82	30.2	122
PUNR	2.1	9	7.7	30	4.4	18
UDMR	7.2	29	7.5	27	6.6	25
PRM	—	—	3.9	16	4.5	19
PSM	—	—	3.0	13	—	—
others	11.1	21	19.8	0	19.9	0
Elected Total		383		328		328
Minorities		13		13		15
TOTAL SEATS		396		341		343

*1990 elections were not completely free or fair.

GOVERNMENTS

The FDSN government of 1992 was headed by a technocrat because the FDSN fell well short of a strong minority government. If the FSN had not split, the party would have been easily able to form a government based on the 40 percent of the seats that the FDSN and the FSN each received independently. But with the acrimony that existed between the two parties' leaders, Iliescu and Roman, no cooperation was possible. The FDSN was forced to form an informal alliance with the nationalist PRM and PUNR in order to maintain the government. This alliance was formalized in the PDSR government of 1994, which gave some ministerial posts to the PUNR and formally relied on the support of the PSM and PRM. Following the CDR's victory in the 1996 elections, it was able to form the government. With its coalition partners, the USD and the UDMR, the government controlled just over 58 percent of the seats.

Romanian Governments since 1992

In Office Date (M/Y)	Prime Minister (Party)	#M(I)	Parties in Cabinet	Supporting Parties
11/92	Vacaroiu, N. (I)	22(6)	FDSN	
08/94	Vacaroiu, N. (I)	25(6)	PDSR PUNR	PSM PRM
as of 10/95:				PSM
12/96	Ciorbea, V. (CDR*)	28	CDR USD UDMR	
04/98	Vasile, R. (CDR*)	..	CDR USD UDMR	

*Both of the Christian Democrat National Peasant Party (PNT-CD).

ACRONYMS

CDR	Democratic Convention of Romania
FDSN	Democratic National Salvation Front
MER	Romanian Ecological Movement
PD-FSN	Democratic Party–National Salvation Front
PDSR	Social Democracy Party of Romania
PER	Romanian Ecological Party
PRM	Greater Romania Party
PNL	National Liberal Party
PNT-CD	National Peasant and Christian Democratic Party
PSM	Socialist Labor Party
PUNR	Party of Romanian National Unity
UDMR	Hungarian Democratic Union of Romania
USD	Social Democratic Union

REFERENCES

Mihut, Lilian. (1994). "The Emergence of Political Pluralism in Romania." *Communist and Post-Communist Studies,* Vol. 27, pp. 411–22.

Popescu, Lilian. (1997). "A Change of Power in Romania: The Results and Significance of the November 1996 Elections." *Government and Opposition,* Vol. 32, pp. 172–86.

Stan, Lavinia, ed. (1997). *Romania in Transition.* Aldershot, England: Dartmouth.

Russia

SUMMARY OF PARTY SYSTEMS

1993	extreme multiparty system with a balance among the parties
(1995–)	moderate multiparty system with one dominant party (KPRF)

HISTORY

Russia's first Duma was created in 1905 by Tsar Nicholas II as a concession to his detractors, who felt he was too powerful. Following the 1917 revolution, Russia came under Bolshevik rule. In the late 1980s, reforms were brought about by Gorbachev. In the early 1990s Yeltsin became president and Russia began to more fully embrace democratic competition. The Soviet Union itself was dissolved at the end of 1991.

ELECTORAL SYSTEM

There are a total of 450 members elected to the Russian State Duma: 225 seats are elected by a simple plurality system, with the average size of districts being 470,000 voters (the largest is 738,000 and the smallest just 13,800), and the remaining 225 seats are elected separately by party list proportional representation, with a 5 percent national threshold. For a single-member district election to be valid, turnout in the constituency must be at least 25 percent. Results from the single-member districts have no effect on the allocation of the PR seats. Finally, the party list ballot specifically allows a voter to cast a ballot "against all lists."

POLITICAL PARTIES AND CLEAVAGES

In Russian politics, the main division has been between pro-government and opposition parties. The latter category can be divided into three different subtypes: nationalist opposition parties, left-wing opposition parties, and pro-reform opposition parties, with a residual group of centrist deputies.

In analyzing Russia, an initial distinction needs to be made between parties and parliamentary groups. In the Russian Duma, the minimum number of deputies required for a parliamentary faction is thirty-five; members outside of a faction have very little influence. Consequently, after an election most independents organize themselves into parliamentary groups so as to qualify as factions, while a minority join actual parties. After the 1993 elections, three such groups were formed; after the 1995 elections, there was but one main parliamentary group.

After the 1993 elections, the main pro-government party was **Russia's Democratic Choice (DVR)**. It was the second most successful party in these elections. Many, but not all, of its members would go on to form a new pro-government party for the 1995 elections, causing the DVR to fall to only nine seats in 1995. The new and now most important pro-government party is **Our Home Is Russia (NDR)**. This is the party led by Victor Chernomyrdin, Yeltsin's prime minister for many years. The NDR is virtually the state party. It has at its disposal the resources of the state, which it can use in its campaign efforts. As is stressed by Urban and Gelman (1997: 206), the NDR is Russia's "premier power bloc, comprising a complex web of government offices, private capital and state-private conglomerates (chief among which would be the energy sector's Gazprom, the world's largest profit-making organization) decked out as a political party."

Among the opposition parties, the left-wing parties hold the most seats in parliament. The strongest of these parties is the **Communist Party of the Russian Federation (KPRF)**. The KPRF was founded in 1990, banned in 1991 by Boris Yelstin following the coup attempt in August of that year, but legalized again for the 1993 elections. The party is the largest of the six or so parties that claim to be the sole legitimate heir to the **Communist Party of the Soviet Union (CPSU)**. The party is in favor of a high degree of state control and stresses the priority of restoring state order. The party is critical of aspects of the communist past such as the authoritarianism and antireligiousness of the former ruling party. The KPRF nevertheless likes to stress the importance of heroes of the Soviet period, like Yury Gagarin and Marshal Zhukov among others. It has become increasingly nationalistic.

The second largest of the left-wing parties is the **Agrarian Party of Russia (APR)**. The APR is the political arm of the state and of collective farms. The party included many former members of the KPRF when it was banned in 1991. It has concentrated on two goals: first, to prevent the legalization of a market in the agricultural sector, and second, to secure generous subsidies to the agro-industrial sector. The party has been highly successful in accomplishing these goals by allying itself with the KPRF to bloc government reform policies.

Also on the left after the 1993 elections was the parliamentary group **Russia's Path (RP)**. For the 1995 elections, Russia's Path became an actual new party called **Power to the People (VN)**. The party, which labels itself a "left-patriotic" party, advocated a platform of reinstituting Soviet-era social policies, reunifying the Soviet Union, and increasing state involvement in industry. The VN wanted to create a coalition of forces on the left encompassing both the KPRF and the APR. This idea was turned down by the leadership of the KPRF.

The pro-reform bloc of opposition parties and parliamentary groups is currently the second largest in the Duma and can be seen as on the moderate right. The key party here is the **Yavlinsky-Boldyrec-Lukin Bloc**, more commonly known as **Yabloko**. Yabloko has stressed the importance of the demonopolization of state industries and has advocated a foreign policy that has a clear conception of Russia's national interests. Another party in the pro-reform bloc is the **Party of Russian Unity and Accord (PRES)**. PRES did well in 1993 but only managed to win one seat in 1995. The key parliamentary groups formed from reformist deputies have been the **Liberal-Democratic Union of December 12 (Dec 12)**, formed after the 1993 elections, and the **Regions of Russia (RR)**, formed after the 1995 elections.

The third bloc represented in parliament, the nationalist bloc, is headed by the **Liberal Democratic Party (LDPR)**. The LDPR is led by Vladimir Zhirinovsky. The LDPR, which was founded in 1990, claims to be dedicated to the idea of a state based on law and a market economy. In reality, however, the party calls for the reestablishment of the Russian state within the boundaries of the USSR or, better yet, the boundaries of 1865, which would incorporate Alaska and large portions of Poland, including its capital of Warsaw. The party is neither liberal nor democratic, but rather xenophobic, anti-Western, and supportive of harsh measures against crime.

For the 1995 elections, two other nationalist parties appeared. The first was the **Congress of Russian Communities (KRO)**, which backs the popular General (and 1996 presidential candidate) Alexander Lebed'. Perhaps not surprisingly, it did disproportionately well among military voters. The second new nationalist party was the **Derzhava**

(Great Power) **Party** formed by former Vice President Alexander Rutskoi. Neither party was able to win any PR seats, however.

Centrist parties and groups that are not part of any of the aforementioned blocs, but have won seats, include the feminist **Women of Russia (ZR)**, which won seats in both 1993 and 1995, and the **Democratic Party of Russia (DPR)** won fifteen seats in 1995 but did not contest the 1995 elections. After the 1993 elections, a parliamentary group was formed in the center called **New Regional Policy (NRP)**, consisting of deputies with close ties to state industry. Overall, though, these centrist elements have effectively ceased to exist.

Although left and right are certainly applicable terms in Russia, it may make more sense to focus specifically on how quickly parties wish to move to a (fully) capitalist economy. This can be combined with their sense of nationalism or cosmopolitanism. Consequently, the Russian party system can usefully be conceived of in this two-dimensional manner, with the main parties represented:

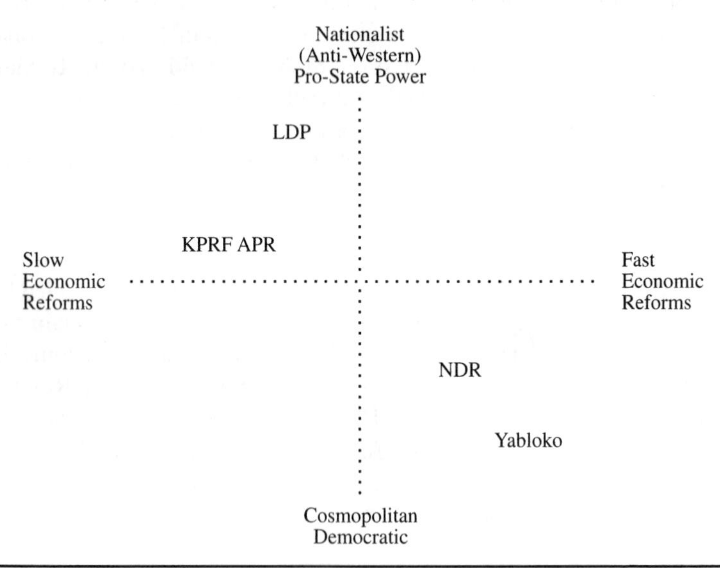

To stress again, the economically anticapitalist parties are also anti-Western and nationalist to varying degrees; in contrast, the NDR and, even more, Yabloko are liberal *and* democratic.

ELECTIONS

The Russian elections of 1993 were held when Yeltsin dissolved parliament. The situation in Russia was rather chaotic, with the civil war that had occurred in Moscow in the previous weeks. The forces that fought against Yeltsin were supported by the LDPR during the election campaign. The campaign itself was rather low key and was fought largely through television. In this area the parties representing the government apparatus, particularly the DVR, had the biggest advantage. Coverage on state TV overwhelmingly went to the DVR. This fact and other elements of the campaign led many to doubt that the elections would indeed be fair. During the campaign, polls showed that only 55 percent of voters thought that the election would be free and fair. However, following the elections this number increased to 77 percent, and among the KPRF's supporters, who were very doubtful about the fairness of the elections, this number increased from 66 percent to 95 percent after the elections.

The 1995 elections were conducted in a fairly well-defined legal environment. However, as in 1993, the provisions regulating campaign expenditure and media coverage were widely abused. Pro-government parties were again able to acquire significantly larger amounts of airtime on TV than opposition parties. The campaign featured a lot of cooperation on the part of the political parties on the left. The KPRF, the APR, and the newer and smaller VN agreed to not run candidates against one another in certain districts and instead to just run one candidate from one of the three parties in order to avoid dividing the support for the left. Despite fighting for the same constituency, the VN refused to attack the KPRF. This type of cooperation, however, was not exhibited by the democratic parties contesting the elections.

Elections in Russia and Postelection Parliamentary Situations

	Elections Dec 1993		April 1994	Elections Dec 1995		Jan 1996
	%V	#S	#S	%V	#S	#S
Votes against All Lists	4.3			2.8		

continued

Elections in Russia . . . *Continued*

	Elections Dec 1993 %V	Elections Dec 1993 #S	April 1994 #S	Elections Dec 1995 %V	Elections Dec 1995 #S	Jan 1996 #S
Pro-Government Parties						
DVR	15.5	70	73	3.9	9	—
NDR	—	—	—	10.3	55	65
Pro-Reform Opposition Parties and Groups						
Yabloko	7.9	23	28	7.0	45	46
PRES	6.7	19	30	0.4	1	—
Dec 12 *	—	—	26	—	—	—
RR *	—	—	—	—	—	41
Centrist Opposition Parties and Groups						
ZR	8.1	23	23	4.6	3	—
DPR	5.5	15	15	—	—	—
NRP *	—	—	66	—	—	—
Leftist Opposition Parties and Groups						
KPRF	12.4	48	45	22.7	157	149
APR	8.0	33	55	3.8	20	35
RP*/VN	—	—	14	1.6	9	37
Nationalist Opposition Parties						
LDPR	22.9	64	64	11.4	51	51
KRO	—	—	—	4.4	5	5
Derzhava	—	—	—	2.6	0	—

	Elections Dec 1993 %V	#S		April 1994 #S	Elections Dec 1995 %V	#S		Jan 1996 #S
All Other Parties								
	8.7	8	}		24.5	18	}	
			}				}	
Independents		141	}	5		77	}	21
Unfilled Seats		6		6				
TOTAL SEATS		450		450		450		450

*Parliamentary group formed after the elections by independents elected in single-member districts.

Note: Vote percentages refer to the national lists.

The drop in seats suffered by ZR can be attributed to the fact that in 1993 it was the only party that was discussing the problems of the family and Russia's social-welfare policy, whereas in 1995 several other parties had this very same platform.

In general, the big cities voted overwhelmingly for the democratic and reformist parties, while poorer rural voters tended to vote for the left.

GOVERNMENTS

The governments in Russia are chosen by the president and therefore do not necessarily contain party representatives. This is especially true in the makeup of the cabinet, wherein the prime minister, as in Victor Chernomyrdin's case, may come from a specific party though he or she does not necessarily represent that party. Since 1992 there have been eight different governments and six different prime ministers.

Russian Governments since 1992

In Office Date (M/Y)	Prime Minister
06/92	Gaidar, Y.
12/92	Chernomyrdin, V.

continued

Russian Governments since 1992 *Continued*

In Office Date (M/Y)	Prime Minister
01/94	Chernomyrdin, V.
01/96	Chernomyrdin, V.
04/98	Kiriyenko, S.
09/98	Primakov, Y.
05/99	Stepashin, S.
08/99	Putin, V.

ACRONYMS

APR	Agrarian Party of Russia
Dec 12	Liberal-Democratic Union of December 12
Derzhava	Great Power
DPR	Democratic Party of Russia
DVR	Russia's Democratic Choice
KRO	Congress of Russian Communities
KPRF	Communist Party of the Russian Federation
LDPR	Liberal Democratic Party of Russia
NDR	Our Home Is Russia
NRP	New Regional Policy
PRES	Party of Russian Unity and Accord
RP	Russia's Path
RR	Russia's Regions
VN	Power to the People
Yabloko	Yavlinsky-Boldyrev-Lukin Bloc
ZR	Women of Russia

REFERENCES

Belin, Laura, and Robert W. Orttung. (1997). *The Russian Parliamentary Elections of 1995: The Battle for the Duma.* New York: M. E. Sharpe.

Löwenhardt, John, ed. (1998). *Party Politics in Postcommunist Russia.* London: Frank Cass.

Remington, Thomas F. (1999). *Politics in Russia.* New York: Longman.

Urban, Michael, and Vladimir Gelman. (1997). "The Development of Political Parties in Russia," pp. 175–219, in Karen Dawisha and Bruce Parrott, eds. *Democratic Changes and Authoritarian Reactions in Russia, Ukraine, Belarus, and Moldova.* Cambridge, England: Cambridge University Press.

White, Stephen, Richard Rose, and Ian McAllister. (1997). *How Russia Votes.* Chatham, N.J.: Chatham House.

Wyman, Matthew, Stephen White, and Sarah Oates, eds. (1998). *Elections and Voters in Postcommunist Russia.* Cheltenham: Edward Elgar.

Slovakia

SUMMARY OF PARTY SYSTEMS

1990	extreme multiparty system with a balance among the parties
1992–94	extreme multiparty system with one dominant party (HZDS)
(1998–)	extreme multiparty system with two main parties (HZDS and SDK)

HISTORY

Slovakia was part of the Austro-Hungarian Empire, and thus after 1867 under Hungarian rule. In 1918 the Czechoslovak Republic was formed, including the Czechs as well as a sizable number of German and Hungarian minorities. Slovaks have seen the interwar government as an instrument of Czech hegemony. A Slovak state was created in 1939 as a puppet regime of Nazi Germany. Reunited Czechoslovakia was under communist rule from 1948. There were mass protests and demonstrations in 1989, with the Public against Violence movement playing a role similar to that of the Civic Forum in Czech lands. Czechoslovakia itself was peacefully dissolved by the leaders of the Czech Republic and Slovakia at the end of 1992—in what was called the "velvet divorce." What follows pertains to Slovakia only from 1990.

ELECTORAL SYSTEM

Slovakia has four multimember districts, returning from twelve to fifty deputies each. Deputies are elected pursuant to a party-list, proportional-representation system that involves the Hagenbach-Bischoff method and second distribution of seats by the greatest-remainder rule. Each elector votes for the party list of his or her choice and can also cast four preferential votes for individual candidates on the list. Each political group obtaining at least 5 percent of the valid votes cast (7 percent in the case of a coalition of two or three parties, 10 percent for a coalition of four or more parties) gains National Council representation, the mandates being divided proportionally for each of the four regions. Leftover mandates are awarded to candidates who were unsuccessful in the initial distribution. Vacancies arising between general elections are filled by substitutes chosen at the same time as deputies.

POLITICAL PARTIES AND PARTY CLEAVAGES

As Abraham (1995: 96) has noted, the "[m]ain political actors in Slovakia are divided more according to their former political status or their different interpretation of Slovakia's history than according to the ideological banners they presently carry." Specifically, the main point of contention is between those who defend the fascist Slovak state of World War II and those who praise the antifascist Slovak National Uprising of 1944.

Like its Czech counterpart, the **Public against Violence (VPN)** was the main opposition movement to the ruling communist government in Slovakia. And like its Czech counterpart, the VPN largely disintegrated into several factions following the first elections in 1990. The movement's direct successor, the **Civic Democratic Union (ODU)**, formed in 1991, lasted only one year. The major political party to form from the VPN was the **Movement for a Democratic Slovakia (HZDS)**. Headed until recently by Vladimir Mečiar, the HZDS was at first only mildly nationalistic but developed into a more nationalistic party that has combined leftist economic and social policies with symbols and an appeal to national sentiments more typical of radical right-wing parties. The HZDS has contested all elections in alliance with the small **Farmer's Party of Slovakia (RSS)**, which was founded in 1990 and merged with the even smaller **Slovak Farmer's Movement (HPS)** in 1997 to form the **New Agrarian Party (NAS)**.

The HZDS was weakened by defections of its own. In 1994 the HZDS government was brought down when members of the party left to form the **Alternative of Political Realism (APR)**, which was subsequently renamed the **Democratic Union of Slovakia (DUS)**. The DUS, a centrist party in orientation, later absorbed two smaller like-minded parties—the **Alliance of Democrats of the Slovak Republic (ADSR)** in late 1994, and the **National Democratic Party–New Alternative (NDS)** in 1995. Both of these parties had a single minister in the short-lived DUS government of 1994.

Parties closely allied with the HZDS include the **Slovak National Party (SNS)**, a party that dates back to the first republic. The SNS is both intensely nationalist and anti-Hungarian. It is a Catholic, conservative party that advocates cautious economic policies. In 1994 the party passed a resolution stating that only ethnic Slovaks could be party members.

The **Association of Workers of Slovakia (ZRS)**, which split away from the **Party of the Democratic Left (SDL)** in 1994 because the latter was moving closer to the center of the political spectrum, is another ally of the HZDS. The ZRS urges the protection of workers' rights and argues against Slovak membership in NATO. The SDL was formed in 1990 by former communists and reform communists as the **Communist Party of Slovakia (KSS)**. For the 1992 elections the party changed its name to the SDL to reflect the party's ideological shift toward the center of the political spectrum. The SDL aims to be a modern social-democratic party.

The main center-left forces grouped together for the 1994 election in the **Common Choice (SU)** alliance. The alliance included the SDL, the **Social Democratic Party of Slovakia (SDSS)**, and the **Green Party of Slovakia (SZS)**. In 1997 a new center-left party was formed, the **Party of Civic Understanding (SOP)**, seeking to lessen the polarization in Slovak politics.

Parties representing the Hungarian minority in Slovakia also formed an alliance for the 1994 elections. The **Hungarian Coalition (SMK)** grouped together two Hungarian parties that had previously won representation as an alliance: the **Hungarian Christian Democratic Movement (MKdH)** and **Coexistence (ESWS)**, as well as several smaller Hungarian parties that had previously failed to win any representation.

The other (relatively) longstanding center party in Slovakia is the **Christian Democratic Movement (KDH)**. Founded in 1990 the KDH has strong links to the Catholic Church and seeks to be a mainstream European Christian Democratic party that supports privatization and smallholders. The party was originally in opposition to independence for Slovakia. The KDH leader Jan Carnogursky served as prime minister in the April 1991 government. The party returned to the government coalition that ousted Mečiar, if only temporarily, in 1994. In late 1996 the KDH formed the "Blue" opposition alliance with the DUS and the smaller **Democratic Party (DS)**, which had failed to win representation in 1994—the "Blue" represents the parties' pro-European position.

One can visualize the Slovak party system after the 1994 elections in two dimensions:

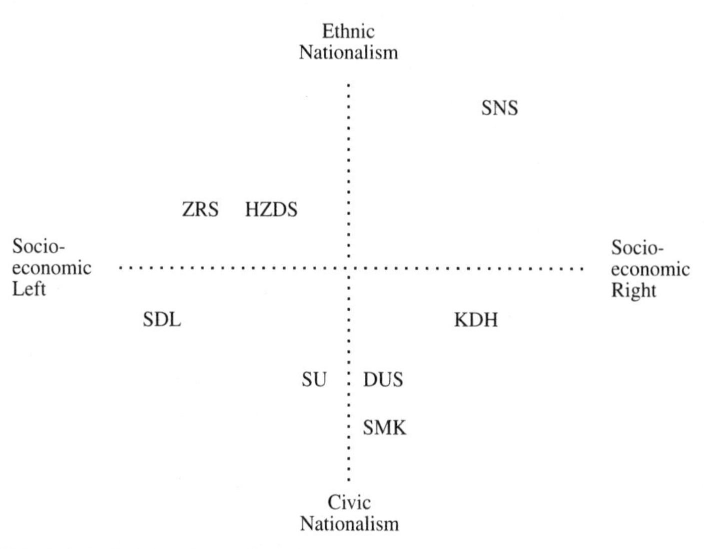

ELECTIONS

The 1990 elections, held when Czechoslovakia was still united, saw victory for the VPN, as similar elections in the Czech lands saw victory for the Civic Forum. The elections were used by the new leaders of Czechoslovakia to validate the changes that had taken place in government since the fall of the communist regime. At this time the threshold for representation was only 3 percent in the Slovak National Council. This would be increased to 5 percent in 1992. Seven parties gained representation in the National Council thanks to the low threshold. Turnout was very high at 95.4 percent of eligible voters.

The 1992 elections saw the emergence of the HZDS as the main successor party to the VPN. But, as in 1990, no party was able to win a majority of seats. The ODU successor to the VPN failed to get over the new 5 percent threshold and therefore failed to win representation. The SDL, the recently renamed and more centrist Communist Party, won the second-largest number of seats—thirty-nine—representing an increase from their showing in 1990.

The 1994 elections were the first elections of the fully independent Slovakia. The elections were called early as a result of the ouster of the

Mečiar government in April of that year and the subsequent failure of the new government to maintain confidence in parliament. The elections saw the formation of coalitions to compete against the HZDS. The Common Choice alliance argued for improved relations with Hungary and Romania as well as a more open media and cultural policy. In order to perform well the SU coalition partners attempted to minimize the differences between one another. The HZDS and the SNS tried to remind voters of the SU's communist background especially with respect to the SDL. The two nationalist parties also alluded to the SU's close alliance with the Hungarian parties. The ZRS advocated an antiprivatization and antimodernization platform. Conflicts emerged between the main partners of the SU alliance, the SDL, and the KDH concerning privatization and control over media issues, and this contributed to the poor performance of the SU alliance, which was at one point expected to receive 20 percent of the votes, but in fact got only half that. The anti-Mečiar parties were also hurt by the radical position adopted by the Hungarian parties' alliance. Reaction to the results of the election was pessimistic regarding the fate of democracy in Slovakia. The elections were seen as a turning point between moving toward consolidated democracy and continuing with Mečiar's semidemocracy.

The 1998 elections were largely a replay of 1994, in that the parties were clearly lined up in pro- and anti-HZDS camps. Within the anti-Mečiar camp, the SDL ran separately this time. Meanwhile, the KDH joined in a center-right electoral alliance with the DUS and the remnants of the SU. This new **Slovak Democratic Coalition (SDK)** polled just over a quarter of the vote. In contrast, the HZDS dropped to barely hang on to first place, and its ally, the ZRS, was eliminated from the parliament. Consequently, Mečiar stepped down peacefully. The four anti-Mečiar forces—the SDK, SDL, SMK, and SOP—together won 93 of the 150 seats, and proceeded to form a coalition government.

Elections in Slovakia

	1990		1992		1994		1998	
	%V	#S	%V	#S	%V	#S	%V	#S
VPN	29.3	48	4.0	0	—	—	—	—
KDH	19.2	31	8.9	18	10.1	17	(into SDK)	
SNS	13.8	22	7.9	15	5.4	9	9.1	14
KSS/SDL	13.3	22	14.7	39	—	—	14.7	23

	1990		1992		1994		1998	
	%V	#S	%V	#S	%V	#S	%V	#S
ESWS-MKdH	8.7	14	7.4	14				
→ SMK					10.2	17	9.1	15
DS	4.4	7	—	—	3.4	0	—	—
SZS	3.5	6	—	—	—	—	—	—
HZDS	—	—	37.3	74	35.0	61	27.0	43
SU	—	—	—	—	10.4	18	(into SDK)	
DUS	—	—	—	—	8.6	15	(into SDK)	
ZRS	—	—	—	—	7.3	13	1.3	0
SDK	—	—	—	—	—	—	26.3	42
SOP	—	—	—	—	—	—	8.0	13
others	7.7	0	23.8	0	9.6	0	4.5	0
TOTAL SEATS		150		160		150		150

Note: The 1990 and 1992 elections were to the Slovak National Council within then-Czechoslovakia.

GOVERNMENTS

Of the six Slovak governments since 1990, Vladimir Mečiar has led three. The HZDS/SNS government fell in 1994 due to defections in the HZDS to form the ADSR and the NDS. The subsequent government that was formed contained, or was supported by a rainbow coalition of left, center, and center-right parties. The point of commonality among these groups was their dislike of Mečiar and the fear of the damage that continuation of his HZDS and SNS government might do to democracy in Slovakia. All these parties also were opposed to communism and the Slovak state. Additionally, all wanted good relations with their Czech and Hungarian neighbors. The earlier Carnogursky government of 1991–92 featured the KDH, which had been the second-strongest party behind the VPN, and the remaining elements of the VPN, which had not broken off to form the HZDS. In both the cases the end of the non-Mečiar governments brought about new elections. The current Drurinda government is quite broadly based and suffers internal contractions. Indeed, shared opposition to the return of Vladimir Mečiar seems to be the main thing holding it together.

Slovakian Governments since 1990

In Office Date (M/Y)	Prime Minister (Party)	#M(I)	Parties in Cabinet	Supporting Parties
06/90	Mečiar, V. (PAV)	23	PAV KDH DS	
04/91	Carnogursky, J. (KDH)	?	KDH and parts of VPN	
06/92	Mečiar, V. (HZDS)	14	HZDS SNS	
03/94	Moravčik, J. (DUS)	14(8)	SDL DUS	MKdH
12/94	Mečiar, V. (HZDS)	18	HZDS ZRS SNS	
10/98	Dzurinda, M. (SDK)	20	SDK SDL SMK SOP	

ACRONYMS

ADSR	Alliance of Democrats of the Slovak Republic
APR	Alternative of Political Realism
DS	Democratic Party
DUS	Democratic Union of Slovakia
ESWS	Coexistence
HPS	Slovak Farmers' Movement
HZDS	Movement for a Democratic Slovakia
KDH	Christian Democratic Movement
KSS	Communist Party of Slovakia
MKdH	Hungarian Christian Democratic Party
NAS	New Agrarian Party
NDS	National Democratic Party–New Alternative
ODU	Civic Democratic Union
RSS	Farmers' Party of Slovakia
SDK	Slovak Democratic Coalition
SDL	Party of the Democratic Left
SDSS	Social Democratic Party of Slovakia
SMK	Hungarian Coalition Party
SNS	Slovak National Party
SOP	Party of Civic Understanding
SU	Common Choice

SZS	Green Party of Slovakia
ZRS	Association of Workers of Slovakia
VPN	Public Against Violence

REFERENCES AND FURTHER READINGS

Abraham, Samuel. (1995). "Early Elections in Slovakia: A State of Deadlock." *Government and Opposition,* Vol. 30: 1, pp. 86–100.

Wolchik, Sharon L. (1997). "Democratization and Political Participation in Slovakia," pp. 197–244, in Karen Dawisha and Bruce Parrott, eds. *The Consolidation of Democracy in East-Central Europe.* Cambridge, England: Cambridge University Press.

Slovenia

SUMMARY OF PARTY SYSTEM

1992–(96) extreme multiparty system with a balance among the parties

HISTORY

Historically, Slovenia was territory consisting of a number of Austrian crown lands, then it was part of Kingdom of the Serbs, Croats, and Slovenes, which was later, in October 1929, renamed Yugoslavia. During World War II Slovenia was divided between Germany, Hungary, and Italy. In 1945 Slovenia became a constituent republic of the Yugoslavian Federation; this was followed by forty-five years of Communist one-party rule. In the spring of 1990 the Democratic United Opposition (DEMOS) obtained a majority of legislative seats in the tricameral Slovene Assembly in the first multiparty elections to take place in the Yugoslav Federation since the Second World War. On 2 July 1990 the Slovene parliament accepted a Declaration on the Sovereignty of the Republic of Slovenia. In February 1991 the Slovene assembly resolved to disassociate from Yugoslavia. This was followed by a brief war with Federal Yugoslav forces after which the federal government accepted Slovene independence.

ELECTORAL SYSTEM

Slovenia has ninety MPs, almost all of which are elected in eight multi-member constituencies, each with eleven seats. The last two seats are single-member constituencies, with one each for the (small) Hungarian and Italian minorities in the country. Proportional representation using the simple quotient and the preferential system is used, with a 3 percent threshold for representation. Each voter votes for a party list with an indication of his or her choice among the candidates, or for an individual candidate. Any remaining seats are distributed at the national level using the d'Hondt method, with deputies selected from those lists with the highest remainders. A simple majority preferential vote is used for the two deputies representing the Italian and Hungarian communities. Vacancies arising between general elections are filled by the candidate who would have been elected by the same party had not the original candidate won. If no candidate can be identified in this manner, or if a vacancy occurs within six months after the beginning of the term, a by-election is held. No by-election is held if the vacancy arises less than six months before the end of the term.

POLITICAL PARTIES AND CLEAVAGES

Post-communist-party politics in Slovenia began with a bipolar structure of anticommunists versus reformed communists, then moved to a multi-polar structure based on left-right ideology and religiosity. To this has now been added a division of old versus new political parties. This being said, nearly all the parties tend to present themselves as center parties.

The **Liberal Democracy of Slovenia (LDS)**, formerly the **Liberal Democratic Party (LDS)**, founded in 1990, has been Slovenia's most successful party in the two elections following independence in 1991. The party has held the post of prime minister in every postindependence government. The party adopted the Liberal Democracy rubric in 1994 when the LDS merged with the small left-center **Socialist Party of Slovenia (SSS)** and a splinter faction of the Democratic Party. The original LDS was descended from the former League of Socialist Youth of Slovenia—the youth wing of the ruling communist party. When the question of independence was raised, the LDS supported an independent nation-state, but argued that the decision should be made democratically by the people of Slovenia. Having discarded its former communist leanings, the party describes itself as more or less a traditional liberal party locating itself in the center of the political spectrum.

The **Slovene Christian Democrats (SKD)** won the second largest number of seats in the 1992 elections and were the largest component of the **Democratic Opposition of Slovenia (DEMOS)**, which took the majority of seats in the pre-independence elections of 1990 but formally dissolved in 1991. Formed in 1990 by a group of "nonclerical Catholic intellectuals," the SKD was a member of both the 1993 and

1994 governments. The SKD is a Western-style Christian-democratic party that supports the social market and traditional conservative and religious values. It strongly supports both EU and NATO membership for Slovenia. For the 1996 elections the SKD formed the **Slovene Spring Alliance (SP)** with the People's Party and the Social Democrats. However, of these parties only the SLS was invited into the government that subsequently was formed.

The other members of the SP include **the Slovene People's Party (SLS)**, which like the SKD (and almost every other party in Slovenia) describes itself as of the center although recently the SLS has alluded to being (maybe) just slightly to the right of center. The SLS, a conservative-values party, claims to descend from the prewar party of the same name. The SLS has reservations about EU membership. The party calls for greater protection of farmers and believes in greater decentralization in local government. The modern SLS was reformed in 1988 as the nonpolitical **Slovene Peasant League (SKZ)** and registered itself formally as a party in 1990, becoming a member of the DEMOS grouping. It adopted the SLS rubric prior to the 1992 elections.

The third member of the SP alliance is the **Social Democratic Party of Slovenia (SDS)**. This self-described "social-democratic party in the traditions of European democracy and the social state" was founded in 1989 and narrowly won representation in the 1992 elections but nevertheless found its way into the coalition government of 1993—despite its social-democratic name and the party's claims, the SDS is in reality on the right of the political spectrum and was expelled from the Socialist International. The party is anti-Communist and relatively populist.

One of the few parties not to position itself in the crowded center of Slovene politics is the **Party of Democratic Reform (SDR)**, successor to the former **League of Communists of Slovenia (ZKS)**. The ZKS, in its time, was Eurocommunist in orientation and was committed to internal democracy. As the ZKS, the party contested the 1992 elections as part of the **United List of Social Democrats (ZLSD)**, but left that alliance to compete as an independent party in 1996. The SDR places itself in the tradition of "European-left" parties. It favors EU membership, but it also advocates neutrality as an alternative to NATO membership. The party won nine seats in the 1996 elections, competing on its own.

The **Slovene National Party (SNS)** is located on the far right. The SNS supports a militarily strong Slovenia and advocates the preservation and restoration of Slovene culture and heritage. The party believes that the family is the basic unity of society. Following its success in the 1992 elections, however, the SNS began to flounder due to party disunity. Contributing to this were revelations that its leader had been named as a federal Yugoslav agent and that other prominent members were informers during the Communist era. The SNS subsequently lost eight of the twelve seats it held in the Slovene Assembly to the formation of two splinter groups and to members becoming independents. The SNS barely managed to meet the 3 percent threshold in the 1996 elections.

Finally, there is an interest-based party in the form of the **Democratic Party of Pensioners of Slovenia (DeSUS)**. The DeSUS is also known as the "Grey Panthers" because of the constituency from which it draws its support. Another party that has won seats in the past but is currently not represented is the **Democratic Party of Slovenia (DSS)**. The DSS was formed in 1990 as **the Slovene League of Democrats (SDZ)** and was one of the strongest supporters of secession. In the spring 1990 elections it competed as a part of the DEMOS group before adopting its current name and contesting the 1992 elections on its own. The party was unable to hold on to its seats after the 1996 election. The other party to win seats in 1992 but not in 1996 is the **Greens of Slovenia (ZS)**. The ZS describes itself as a "holistic party" that cannot be conceived of in left-right terms. The ZS had been an active nonpolitical group long before it registered as an official party in 1989.

ELECTIONS

The elections of 6 December 1992 were the first since Slovenia's independence. Turnout was 76 percent of an approximate electorate of 1.5 million. No less than thirty-three parties and/or coalitions competed for the eighty-eight elected seats. Seventeen-point-five percent of the vote went to parties not making the threshold for representation.

The election of 10 November 1996 saw a slight drop in turnout from its 1992 level to 74 percent. The number of parties competing also dropped from thirty-three to twenty-four. In general, all the principal parties were in agreement on the main issue of the campaign with regard to Slovenia joining NATO and the EU. The differences emerged with respect to the pace for seeking membership in these organizations. Other issues included low salaries in industry; employment; and health and education costs.

The ZLSD was again the one party that campaigned against NATO membership, arguing instead that Slovenia should adopt a neutral position. The LDS once again came out with a plurality of seats, increasing both the percentage of votes and the number of seats that it had won in the 1992 elections.

The SP alliance parties argued for a rapid completion of the economic reform process and finished in the second, third, and fourth spots with a combined total of forty-five seats, while the United List of Social Democrats only won back nine of the fourteen seats it had had in 1992 due to its transformation from an alliance to a single party no longer encompassing the DeSUS or the SDR. The SNS saw its seat total drop by eight from the twelve it held after the 1992 elections. The total vote going to parties not gaining representation also dropped considerably, down over half to 6.9 percent in 1996. Both the DSS and ZS failed to reach the 3 percent threshold and therefore did not hang on to the seats they had won in 1992.

Elections in Slovenia

	1992		1996	
	%V	#S	%V	#S
LDS	23.7	22	27.0	25
SKD	14.5	15	9.6	10
SLS	8.8	10	19.4	19
SDS	3.3	4	16.1	16
ZLSD	13.6	14	9.0	9
DeSUS	—	—	4.3	5
SNS	9.9	12	3.2	4
ZS	3.7	5	1.8	0
DSS	5.0	6	2.7	0
others	17.5	0	11.3	0
total elected from party lists		88		88
ethnic minorities		2		2
TOTAL SEATS		90		90

GOVERNMENTS

All the Slovene governments have been headed by the LDS, and the only changes have been with regards to which parties (so far always plural) the LDS has decided to choose as allies. With the two largest parties failing to win a majority of seats in the 1992 election, a government alliance of five parties encompassing sixty seats of the ninety-seat assembly was formed. The 1997 government formed between the LDS, SLS, and DeSUS was a little surprising considering the strong performance of the SP electoral alliance, which won exactly half of the seats. However, the LDS was able to entice the SLS into forming a coalition with it and not with SLS's alliance partners. The SLS was thereby rewarded with more cabinet seats than the LDS. Along with the seats brought in by DeSUS, the governing coalition controlled forty-nine of the ninety seats in the Slovene Assembly.

Slovene Governments since 1993

In Office Date (M/Y)	Prime Minister (Party)	#M(I)	Parties in Cabinet
01/93	Drnovsek, J. (LDS)	16	LDS SKD ZLSD SDS ZS
03/94	Drnovsek, J. (LDS)	17(2)	LDS ZLSD SKD
02/97	Drnovsek, J. (LDS)	19(1)	SLS LDS DeSUS

ACRONYMS

DEMOS	Democratic Party of Slovenia
DeSUS	Democratic Party of Pensioners of Slovenia
DSS	Democratic Party of Slovenia
LDS	Liberal Democratic Party
LDS	Liberal Democracy of Slovenia
SDR	Party of Democratic Reform
SDS	Social Democratic Party of Slovenia
SKD	Slovene Christian Democrats
SKZ	Slovene Peasant League
SLS	Slovene People's Party
SNS	Slovene National Party

continued

ACRONYMS *Continued*

SP	Slovene Spring Alliance
SSS	Socialist Party of Slovenia
ZKS	League of Communists of Slovenia
ZLSD	United List of Social Democrats
ZS	Greens of Slovenia

REFERENCES

Fink-Hafner, Danica and John R. Robbins, eds. (1997). *Making a New Nation: The Formation of Slovenia.* Aldershot: Dartmouth.

Spain

SUMMARY OF PARTY SYSTEMS

1977–79	two-and-a-half-party system
1982–89	moderate multiparty system with one dominant party (PSOE)
1993–(96)	two-and-a-half-party system

HISTORY

Once a great European power, Spain went into comparative decline in the seventeenth century. By the nineteenth century patterns of political instability had set in. Ideologically Spain was highly polarized among monarchical nationalists, liberal republicans, regionalists, and later, socialists and anarchists. The Second Republic of 1931–36 was Spain's first true democracy. This republic was both highly fragmented and very polarized, and divisions and mistrust between secular republicans and Catholic conservatives eventually set the stage for a military rebellion and consequent civil war. Victorious in the civil war, General Francisco Franco established an authoritarian regime that was strongly centralist. Franco remained in power for decades; toward the end of his rule, he decided that after his death the monarchy would be restored. However, unforeseen by Franco, the new king, Juan Carlos, initiated democratization. All parties, including the Communists, were allowed to compete, and elections were held in 1977. A new constitution, which included varying elements of regional government, was approved by 87 percent of the voters in a 1978 referendum. Elements of the military made a last ditch, somewhat farcical attempt to overthrow the regime in 1981, but most of the army stayed loyal to the king, who actively opposed the uprising.

ELECTORAL SYSTEM

Spain uses a proportional representation system with multimember districts. However, its 350 deputies are elected through no less than fifty-two districts. Two of these are single-member districts for the African enclaves of Ceuta and Melilla, and the rest of the electoral districts are Spain's fifty provinces (not to be confused with the Autonomous Communities, where regional power lies). Every province, no matter how small, is entitled to a minimum of three deputies. Conversely, only in Barcelona and Madrid are the districts large enough to be truly proportional. There are no national compensatory seats. Consequently, the system is rather disproportional; but this has aided in lessening fragmentation.

PARTIES AND CLEAVAGES

Post–Franco Spain has had relatively few national parties, but many regional ones. Of the national parties, the most consistent force since 1977 has been the **Spanish Socialist Workers' Party (PSOE)**, which dates back to 1879. During the Franco years, party leaders were either underground or in exile in France. Felipe González became the PSOE secretary-general in 1974, just in time to lead it in democratic elections. After coming a respectable second in the 1977 elections, the PSOE shed its Marxism and became a moderate social-democratic party. Indeed, after coming to power in 1982 the party often governed in a right-of-center way, especially concerning economic restructuring and foreign policy (where it reversed its traditional opposition to NATO). Yet it made clear contributions to democratic deepening and political decentralization. The PSOE is supported by workers, but particularly by state employees and pensioners.

Its historic rival on the left was the **Spanish Communist Party (PCE)**, which was founded in 1921 and, as noted above, legalized in 1977. Traditionally Leninist, the party moderated its ideology somewhat in 1978 and also accepted the new democratic order, including the monarchy. Despite these changes, in the 1977 and 1979 elections the PCE got only around 10 percent of the vote, much less than in other Latin European countries, as the Socialists were able to dominate the left. Furthermore, the autocratic leadership style of PCE General Secretary Santiago Carrillo led to internal conflict and a drop in support in the early 1980s. Risking marginalization, the party responded after the 1986 elections by forming a broader front with other small leftist parties such as the **Socialist Action Party (PASOC)**, which had been founded in 1983. This new front has been known since 1989 as the **United Left (IU)** and has regained the 10 percent or so of Spanish voters who had backed the PCE in the late 1970s.

In Spanish politics, however, the key initial force after Franco's death was that of the **Union of the Democratic Center (UCD)**. Adolfo Suárez had been picked by King Juan Carlos in 1976 to establish democracy, and Suárez needed an organization to contest the 1977 elections. He thus created the UCD from above, bringing together some thirteen parties from the center left to the moderate right. As its name implies, the party stressed its democratic credentials and its centrism. Victorious in both the 1977 and 1979 elections, the UCD was nevertheless largely held together by the cohesion of government and Suárez's personality. With Suárez's sudden resignation as prime minister in 1981, and his subsequent departure from the party, the UCD fragmented and collapsed. It was dissolved in 1983.

Suárez, himself, founded another center party, the **Democratic and Social Center (CDS)**, in 1982. The CDS peaked in 1986, when it became the third-largest party in Spain. However, like the UCD, the CDS could not survive Suárez's departure from politics in the early 1990s. After failing to win any seats in the 1993 elections, the CDS was dissolved.

With the collapse of the UCD, and the failure of the CDS to recapture the broad center, the main opposition to the PSOE became, almost by default, the **Popular Alliance (AP)**. The AP was founded in 1977 as a home for conservatives and ultraconservatives, including many former Franco officials. Indeed, it was the former minister of information and tourism under Franco, Manuel Fraga, who founded and initially led the AP. Although popular in his home region of Galicia, Fraga's democratic credentials were questioned by most Spaniards. Consequently, although the party got a quarter of the vote in the 1982 elections after the collapse of the UCD (and the transfer of many UCD voters), it remained stuck at that level throughout the 1990s, well behind the Socialists who were clearly a dominant party. With a name change to the **Popular Party (PP)** in 1989 and, more important, changes in leadership, the party has finally been able to position itself on the moderate right and has thus become "acceptable." Its current leader, José Maria Aznar, was able to take the PP above a third of the votes in 1993, and finally to a plurality of votes and seats in 1996. The party is favored to stay in office after the 2000 elections. The PP has established a fairly standard conservative voting base of free-market-oriented business people and social conservatives, including religious Spaniards. It remains weak, however, in the more nationalistic regions of Spain, where there are local center-right parties and where the historic centrism of the Spanish right is looked at quite unfavorably.

All of the aforementioned are national, or what the Spanish call "state-wide" parties, in that they run candidates throughout the country. Spain also has, however, various regional or "nonstatewide" parties in most of its "autonomous communities," as they are known. There are thus literally dozens of regional parties in Spain, and these are collectively strongest in the Basque Country and Catalonia, both in national and regional elections. Indeed, party politics in these two regions is analyzed in subsequent chapters. This being said, three of Spain's regional parties are worth noting for their impact on national politics in terms of determining governments. The parties are the **Basque Nationalist Party (PNV)**, founded in 1985; the Catalan **Convergence and Union (CiU)**, founded in 1979; and the **Canarian Coalition (CC)** in the Canary Islands, founded as a merger of local parties in 1993, of which the most important group was and is the **Association of Canary Islands Independents (AIC)**. The PNV, CiU, and CC are all center-right parties in a socioeconomic sense, therefore one might assume that they have been close to the PP. This would be a false assumption, however. Because the Socialists have been more open to decentralization than the conservatives, and because the PSOE governments have been, if anything, right of center on economics, the PNV and especially the CiU were willing to support the PSOE after it was cut down to a minority in 1993. Indeed, these main regional parties have been quite adept at using the balance of power to extract concessions from the main national parties.

KEY ELECTIONS

The first democratic elections, those of 1977, were obviously important in the transition to democracy and in giving Suárez and the UCD a working plurality of seats. However, in terms of party politics, the 1982 elections were crucial, in that they saw the PSOE coast to a landslide majority, the UCD be marginalized, and the AP become the main opposition. Indeed, given that turnout jumped almost 12 percent in 1982 (to a record 79.8 percent), the Spanish elections of 1982 have been one of the few postwar European elections that can be considered realigning in the American sense of the term. The 1993 elections saw the return of a hung parliament, which also occurred in 1996. In both cases the Socialists suffered from a slowing economy, problems of corruption, and the general sense that they had been in office too long. However, the PSOE still had popular prime minister Felipe González. Yet even he could not stop the PSOE slipping into second place in 1996.

Elections in Spain

	1977		1979		1982		1986	
	%V	#S	%V	#S	%V	#S	%V	#S
PSOE	30.3	118	30.5	121	48.4	202	44.3	184
PCE	9.3	20	10.8	23	4.1	4	3.8	7
UCD	34.8	165	35.0	168	6.8	12	—	—
AP	8.4	16	6.5	9	26.5	106	26.1	105
CiU	2.8	11	2.7	8	3.7	12	5.1	18
PNV	1.7	8	1.7	7	1.9	8	1.5	6
CDS	—	—	—	—	2.9	2	9.2	19
others	12.7	12	12.8	14	5.7	4	10.0	11
TOTAL SEATS		350		350		350		350

	1989		1993		1996	
	%V	#S	%V	#S	%V	#S
PSOE	39.6	175	38.7	159	37.5	141
IU	9.2	17	9.6	18	10.6	21
PP	25.4	107	34.8	141	38.9	156
CiU	5.3	18	5.0	17	4.6	16
PNV	1.3	5	1.2	5	1.3	5
CDS	7.8	14	1.8	0	—	—
AIC/CC	0.3	1	0.9	4	0.9	4
others	11.1	13	8.0	6	6.2	7
TOTAL SEATS		350		350		350

GOVERNMENTS

Spanish governments have always been single-party affairs, despite the use of positive parliamentarianism. In the 1980s, of course, the Socialists won three straight majority governments, making any coalition unnecessary. However, the bias in the electoral system has ensured that even if the lead party does not win a majority, it is not that far short of this (by around only ten to twenty seats). Thus the UCD in the 1970s, the PSOE in 1993, and the PP in 1996 were all able to form stable minority governments, although in the 1990s this was at the price of concessions to the regional parties. In 1996, the negotiations between the PP and the main regional parties were difficult, and it took some two months for PP leader Aznar to get their agreement.

Spanish Governments since 1977

In Office Date (M/Y)	Prime Minister (Party)	#M(I)	Parties in Cabinet	Supporting Parties
07/77	Suárez, A. (UCD)	20(1)	UCD	
03/79	Suárez, A. (UCD)	24(2)	UCD	
02/81	Calvo Sotelo, L. (UCD)	19	UCD	
12/82	González, F. (PSOE)	17	PSOE	
07/86	González, F. (PSOE)	17	PSOE	
12/89	González, F. (PSOE)	19(3)	PSOE	AIC
as of 10/90:				CiU CDS PNV AIC
06/93	González, F. (PSOE)	18(6)	PSOE	CiU PNV
05/96	Aznar, J.M. (PP)	15(3)	PP	CiU PNV CC

ACRONYMS

AIC	Association of Canary Islands Independents
AP	Popular Alliance
CC	Canarian Coalition
CDS	Democratic and Social Center
CiU	Convergence and Union (Catalonia)
IU	United Left
PASOC	Socialist Action Party
PCE	Spanish Communist Party
PNV	Basque Nationalist Party
PP	Popular Party
PSOE	Spanish Socialist Workers' Party
UCD	Union of the Democratic Center

REFERENCES

Gunther, Richard, Giacomo Sani, and Golden Shabad. (1988). *Spain after Franco: The Making of a Competitive Party System.* Berkeley: University of California Press.

Heywood, Paul. (1995). *The Government and Politics of Spain.* Basingstoke, England: Macmillan.

Hopkin, Jonathan (1999). "Spain: Political Parties in a Young Democracy," in David Broughton and Mark Donovan, eds., *Changing Party Systems in Western Europe.* London: Pinter, pp. 207–231.

Newton, Michael T., and Peter J. Donaghy. (1997). *Institutions of Modern Spain: A Political and Economic Guide.* New York: Cambridge University Press.

The Basque Country

SUMMARY OF PARTY SYSTEMS

1980–84	extreme multiparty system with one dominant party (PNV)
1986–(98)	extreme multiparty system with a balance among the parties

HISTORY

As a people, the Basques go back to the eighth century. The Basque language is quite unique and distinct from its neighbors'. The three historic Basque provinces were incorporated into Castile (Spain) in 1200. Due to conflicts arising from the succession to the Spanish throne in 1700, the Basque provinces were largely unique in Spain in being allowed to maintain their charters and institutions, including taxation powers. The non-tax powers were, however, eliminated in the 1870s, and the tax powers were limited to two of the three provinces. Nevertheless, this institutional legacy has combined with linguistic distinctiveness to produce a strong sense of Basque identity.

The three Basque provinces were set up as an Autonomous Community of contemporary democratic Spain in 1979. However, the Basque deputies never signed the 1977 Spanish constitution. Of the seventeen

Autonomous Communities in Spain, the Basque Country is the only one plagued with nationalist violence, that of ETA (the "Basque Liberty and Homeland" movement). Overall, the Basque Country remains the most (sub-)nationalistic region in Spain.

ELECTORAL SYSTEM

Elections in the Basque Country use proportional representation. Since the 1984 elections there have been seventy-five seats that are divided equally into twenty-five seats for each of the three Basque provinces (Alava, Guipúzcoa, and Vizcaya). A party must win 5 percent of the vote in one province to qualify for representation. However, since just over half the population lives in Vizcaya, compared to about one-third in Guipúzcoa, and only about 13 percent in Alava, this equal treatment of provinces introduces an obvious bias. It is perhaps not coincidental that the only province with its own party is Alava.

PARTIES AND CLEAVAGES

The Basque Country has quite a fragmented party system, which is first and foremost divided into Basque and national (Spanish-wide) parties. Collectively, the Basque parties have always had a majority of seats. Of the Basque-specific parties, the largest has been the **Basque Nationalist Party (PNV)**, which dates back to 1895. It does best in the province of Vizcaya, including the Basque capital, Bilbao. The PNV combines Basque nationalism with a basic semiloyalty to Spain. In socioeconomic matters it is moderately conservative. Overall, the PNV should be seen as a "catchall" party for the Basques.

A bad showing for the PNV in the Spanish national elections of June 1986 led to a split within the PNV, with the former *lehendakari* (premier), Garaikoetxea, presiding over the creation later that year of **Basque Solidarity (EA)**. EA shared the same moderate nationalism of the PNV, but was slightly left of center. This combination thus put it in the same space as the **Basque Left (EE)**, which was founded in 1977. The Basque Left would merge with the Socialists in 1993.

A much harder sense of Basque nationalism, as well as of leftism, has been offered by **Herri Batasuna (HB–United People)**, formed in 1978. This party is closely linked to the terrorist organization ETA and obviously is supported only by the most nationalistic Basques. It also has a younger demographic than the PNV. For the 1998 elections, HB reformulated itself as **Euskal Herritarrok (EH–Basque Citizens)**, with a somewhat softer image.

Running in the various Basque elections have been the key national Spanish parties—the PSOE (socialists), the communists, the centrists of the UCD and later the CDS, and the conservatives (AP/PP). Until recently, of these parties only the socialists were relatively successful. The conservative AP/PP, for its part, was initially seen very negatively as a Madrid-oriented centralist force. However, with time it was seen as more acceptable, and it has grown in support in each of the last three Basque elections. Finally, there is a subregional party in the form of the **Unidad Alavesa (UA–Alevesan Unity)**, a 1986 split-off from the AP in rural Aleva, the province in which the AP had traditionally done best. The AP has never received more than 18 percent of the Alevesan vote, but its share is magnified by the disproportional number of seats in Aleva.

In summary, national orientation is the first key cleavage in the Basque Country, followed by the left-right ideological distinction. Using data from the Spanish Centro de Investigaciones Sociológicas, Llera Ramo (1995: 289) thus outlines these two main divisions in the Basque Country as of the early 1990s:

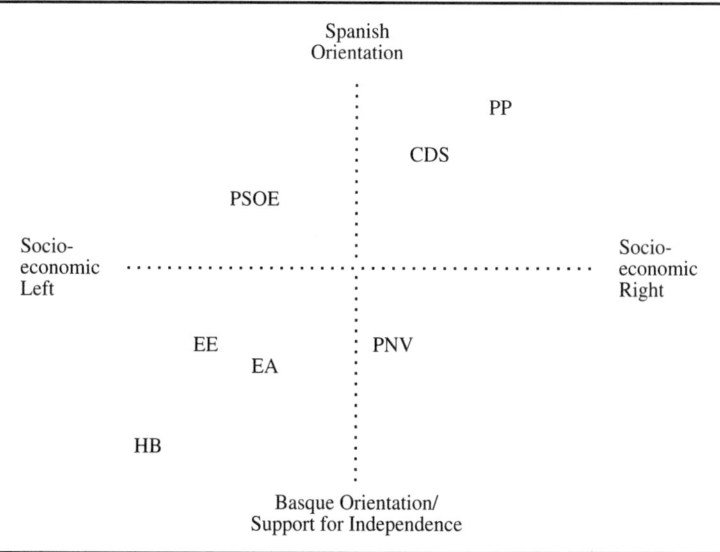

RECENT ELECTIONS

The 1993 merger of EE into the PSOE would make the latter somewhat less Spanish and more nationalistic than its place in the diagram. It was hoped that this broader party might become the largest one. This hardly happened, however, as this combined force lost almost half its seats in the 1994 elections. Indeed, most of the support for the former EE went into a reinvigorated IU.

In 1998, with a cease-fire announced by Eta and hopes of some sort of peace settlement (paralleling what happened that year in Northern Ireland), greater attention was paid to the Basque election of that year, and turnout did increase by 11.1 percent. For its part, the strong nationalists of the EH were able to win a record fourteen seats. Overall, there was not much volatility, although the workings of the electoral system caused the United Left (IU) to lose most of its seats.

Autonomous Elections in the Basque Country

	1980		**1984**		**1986**		**1990**	
	%V	**#S**	**%V**	**#S**	**%V**	**#S**	**%V**	**#S**
PSOE	14.2	9	23.4	19	22.0	19	19.9	16
PNV	38.0	25	42.7	32	23.7	17	28.5	22
AP/PP	4.8	2	9.5	7	4.8	2	8.2	6
EE	9.8	6	8.1	6	10.9	9	7.8	6
PSOE-EE	—	—	—	—	—	—	—	—
PCE/IU	4.0	1	1.4	0	—	—	1.4	0
UCD	8.5	6	—	—	—	—	—	—
HB/EH	16.6	11	14.9	11	17.5	13	18.4	13
CDS	—	—	—	—	3.5	2	0.6	0
EA	—	—	—	—	15.8	13	11.4	9
UA	—	—	—	—	—	—	1.4	3
others	4.1	0	0.0	0	1.8	0	2.4	0
TOTAL SEATS		60		75		75		75

	1994		1998	
	%V	#S	%V	#S
PSOE	(merged)			
PNV	29.8	22	27.9	21
AP/PP	14.4	11	20.1	16
EE	(merged)			
PSOE-EE	17.1	12	17.5	14
PCE/IU	9.1	6	5.6	2
UCD	—	—	—	—
HB/EH	16.2	11	17.9	14
CDS	—	—	—	—
EA	10.3	8	8.7	6
UA	2.7	5	1.2	2
others	0.4	0	1.1	0
TOTAL SEATS		75		75

GOVERNMENTS

All Basque governments have been based around the PNV, which has monopolized the position of *lehendakari*. Nevertheless, coalition negotiations have usually been difficult and time consuming. The PNV-led governments have often involved coalitions with the Socialists, as the second strongest party. However, the current 1999 government indicates a very clear Basque orientation, in that it comprises the PNV and EA, supported by EH.

Basque Governments since 1980

In Office Date (M/Y)	*Lehendakari* (Party)	#M	Parties in Cabinet
04/80	Garaicoetxea, C. (PNV)	?	PNV
04/84	Garaicoetxea, C. (PNV)	11	PNV

continued

Basque Governments since 1980 *Continued*

01/85	Ardanza, J. A. (PNV)	10	PNV
02/87	Ardanza, J. A. (PNV)	10	PNV PSOE
01/91	Ardanza, J. A. (PNV)	13	PNV EA EE
09/91	Ardanza, J. A. (PNV)	15	PNV PSOE EE
			(PSOE and EE merge in 1993)
12/94	Ardanza, J. A. (PNV)	11	PNV PSOE-EE EA
06/98	Ardanza, J. A. (PNV)	?	PNV EA
01/99	Ibarretxe, J. J. (PNV)	10	PNV EA supported by EH

BASQUE ACRONYMS

EA	Basque Solidarity
EE	Basque Left
EH	Basque Citizens
HB	United People
PNV	Basque Nationalist Party

REFERENCE

Llera Ramo, Francisco José. (1995). "La construcción del pluralismo polarizado vasco," in Pilar del Castillo, ed. *Comportamiento político y electoral,* 2d. ed. Madrid: Centro de Investigaciones Sociológicas, pp. 275–295.

Catalonia

SUMMARY OF PARTY SYSTEMS

1980	moderate multiparty system with a balance among the parties
1984–95	moderate multiparty system with one dominant party (CiU)
(1999–)	moderate multiparty system with two main parties (CiU and PSC)

HISTORY

Despite being under the Spanish crown in the fifteenth and sixteenth centuries, Catalonia retained its own official language, currency, taxes, and its independent institutions. However, Philip V would abolish all of these in 1716 and institute direct, repressive control from Madrid. Since then Catalans have struggled for (the return of) their autonomy within Spain. The stillborn First Republic of Spain 1873–74 would have granted Catalonia autonomy, and the Second Republic did in fact do so in 1932. Catalonia was a strong supporter of Republican Spain in the civil war, so the entry of Franco's troops into the region in 1938 ended all autonomy. With the return to democracy, autonomous status was returned to Catalonia, this status being confirmed by the Catalan people in the referendum of 25 October 1979.

ELECTORAL SYSTEM

Elections in Catalonia use party-list, proportional representation. The territory is divided into four constituencies, which range quite a bit in size, that is, from fifteen to eighty-five seats. The cutoff for representation is only 3 percent in one constituency.

POLITICAL PARTIES AND CLEAVAGES

Catalan nationalism structures its party system, along with left-right ideology. The former forces us to distinguish between Catalan and "Spanish" parties, that is, between parties that only exist in Catalonia, and the national Spanish parties that also compete in the community. The main

Catalan party is the **Convergence and Union (CiU)**. It was created in 1979 as a merger of centrists from the **Democratic Convergence of Catalonia (CDC)**, moderates from the **Democratic Left of Catalonia (EDC)**, and the Christian-Democratic **Democratic Union of Catlonia (UDC)**. The name "Convergence and Union" reflects the sense in which the CiU is a merger and the Christian-Democratic wing in particular retains a clear identity. Initially social democratic in its economic orientation, the party quickly shifted to the moderate right. It has a clear "catch-all" vocation.

Left-wing Catalan nationalists thus would support either the **Republican Left of Catalonia (ERC)** or the **Initiative for Catalonia (IC)**. The ERC was the governing party of Catalonia during the pre-Franco republican period. Reformed in 1975, and allied with small Maoist groups, it did not do very well in the first Catalan elections of 1980. Its subsequent choice to support the CiU minority government led to a further loss of supporters directly to the CiU. The Initiative for Catalonia was formed in 1987, as the successor to the **Unified Socialist Party of Catalonia (PSUC)**. The PSUC had been formed in 1936 as an autonomous communist party, and after the return to democracy, the party reestablished its autonomy from the national PCE (now IU). The PSUC came in a strong third in the 1980 elections, but thereafter slumped as a result of internal ideological divisions. The IC formation, with its nonleftist name, thus seeks to establish a broader base of support for the party; nevertheless, its appeal is largely limited to the industrial belt around Barcelona.

The two main national parties—the Socialists and the Popular Party—also compete in Catalan elections, as did initially the UCD and later the CDS. In the case of the Socialists, there is in fact an autonomous Catalan party, the **Socialist Party of Catalonia (PSC)**, founded in 1978. The PSC is nevertheless an integrated part of the PSOE in a way in which the IC is not vis-à-vis the national IU. Consequently the official party label of the Catalan socialists is "PSC-PSOE." As for the Popular Party, it does not have any special autonomous Catalan (or Basque) wing. The PP has been limited in Catalonia both by its (until recently) highly centralist image and by the reality that most of its theoretically natural supporters (moderate conservatives, shopkeepers, etc.) are loyal to the CiU.

Using data from the Spanish Centro de Investigaciones Sociológicas, Pallarés and Font (1995: 245) outline the two main cleavages in Catalonia:

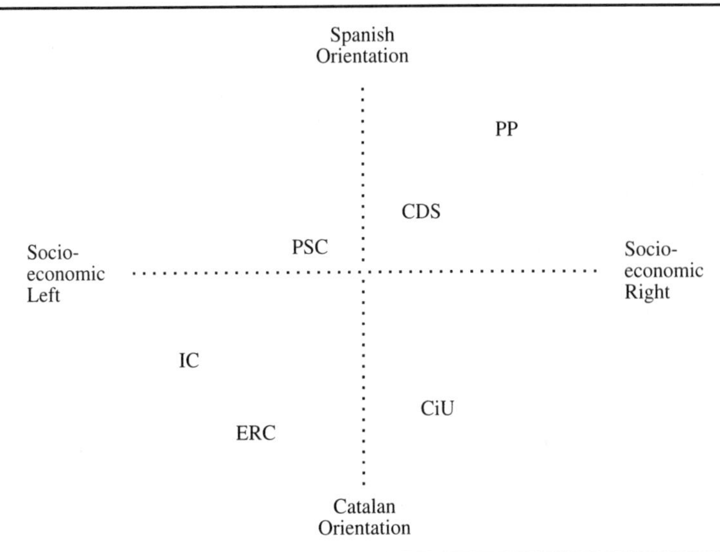

It should also be noted that geography overlaps somewhat with this distinction. Specifically, the PSC-PSOE does best in Barcelona, and worst in medium and smaller centers such as Gerona. For the CiU and the ERC, the situation is essentially the reverse, as Catalan nationalism is stronger in the "provinces" than in the capital. Support for the PP is, however, relatively equal across Catalonia and, as noted above, the IC does fight with the PSC-PSOE for the votes of Barcelona's industrial workers.

ELECTIONS

The first elections in Catalonia, those of 1980, were its most fragmented. However, as the plurality party, the CiU was able to form the government, and its moderate nationalist policies proved so popular that it won a majority in 1984. This majority held in 1988 and 1992. The CiU opted for early elections in late 1995 to get these out of the way before the national elections that were expected, and did occur, the following year. However, 1995 saw a modest breakthrough for the PP that cost the CiU enough support to deny the latter a majority.

In the 1999 elections the CiU was defending, or in another sense was burdened by, a record of almost two decades in office. By this time 69 years old, its leader Jordi Pujol indicated this would be his last campaign. Facing him for the socialists was their strongest candidate to date, Pasqual Maragall, age 58, who until 1997 was the long-serving mayor of Barcelona. Moreover, the socialists formed an electoral alliance with the Greens in the three constituencies outside of Barcelona, so as to maximize their joint seats. Maragall was able to lead the socialists to victory in the Barcelona constituency (a first), and with its allies to a slight lead in the popular vote. However, the CiU strength in the over-represented rural areas causes it to remain on top in terms of seats. Nevertheless, the CiU has lost its dominance within the system.

Autonomous Elections in Catalonia

	1980		1984		1988		1992	
	%V	#S	%V	#S	%V	#S	#V	#S
ERC	8.9	14	4.4	5	4.1	6	7.9	11
AP/PP	2.3	0	7.7	11	5.3	6	5.9	7
UCD	10.5	18	—	—	—	—	—	—
PSUC/IC	18.7	25	5.6	6	7.7	9	6.5	7
PSC-PSOE*	22.3	33	30.0	41	29.6	42	27.4	40
CiU	27.7	43	46.6	72	45.5	69	46.0	70
CDS	—	—	—	—	3.8	3	0.9	0
IC+Greens **	—	—	—	—	—	—	—	—
others	9.6	2	5.7	0	4.0	0	5.4	0
TOTAL SEATS		135		135		135		135

*In 1999, includes IC and green votes in the Tarragona, Lleida, and Girona constituencies.

**Refers only to the separate IC-Green list in the Barcelona constituency.

CATALAN ACRONYMS

CDC	Democratic Convergence of Catalonia
CiU	Convergence and Union
EDC	Democratic Left of Catalonia
ERC	Republican Left of Catalonia
IC	Initiative for Catalonia
PSC	Socialist Party of Catalonia
PSUC	Unified Socialist Party of Catalonia
UDC	Democratic Union of Catalonia

1995		1999		
%V	#S	%V	#S	
9.6	13	8.8	12	ERC
13.2	17	9.6	12	AP/PP
—	—	—	—	UCD
9.8	11	—	—	PSUC/IC
25.1	34	38.2	52	PSC-PSOE*
41.3	60	38.0	56	CiU
—	—	—	—	CDS
—	—	2.5	3	IC+Greens**
0.9	0	2.8	0	Others
	135		135	TOTAL SEATS

GOVERNMENTS

In contrast to the Basque Country with its shifting coalitions, Catalonia has always been governed by the CiU, and indeed with the same premier since 1980. However, since losing its absolute majority in 1995, the CiU has come to rely on either the PP or the ERC to support government policy. Specifically, the CiU has sought, and normally received, support from the PP on economic matters, and from the ERC on nationalist matters. In 1999, the PP went so far as to vote for Pujol's investiture.

Catalan Governments since 1980

In Office Date (M/Y)	Premier (Party)	#M(I)	Parties in Cabinet	Supporting Parties
05/80	Pujol, J. (CiU)	13(5)	CiU ERC	
05/84	Pujol, J. (CiU)	?	CiU	
06/88	Pujol, J. (CiU)	?	CiU	
04/92	Pujol, J. (CiU)	?	CiU	
12/95	Pujol, J. (CiU)	?	CiU	
11/99	Pujol, J. (CiU)		CiU	PP

REFERENCE

Pallarés, Francesc and Joan Font. (1995). "Las elecciones autonómicas en Cataluña (1980–1992)," in Pilar del Castillo, ed. *Comportamiento político y electoral,* 2d. ed. Madrid: Centro de Investigaciones Sociológicas, pp. 221–273.

Sweden

SUMMARY OF PARTY SYSTEMS

1948–85	moderate multiparty system with one dominant party (SAP)
1988–(98)	extreme multiparty system with one dominant party (SAP)

HISTORY

Sweden established a national monarchy and political independence from Denmark in 1523 and would become a European power in the seventeenth century. Since 1814, however, the country has pursued a policy of neutrality. The first modern constitution, that of 1809, gave the monarch full executive power and provided for a parliament *(Riksdag),* elected from four estates. A bicameral parliament was established in 1866, but fully responsible government did not come until 1917. The struggle for responsible government had pitted Liberals and later Social Democrats against conservatives, thereby shaping the pre–World War I party system. Full democratization, and thus universal suffrage, saw the Social Democrats quickly become the largest party.

The upper house of parliament was abolished in 1970. Prior to this, it had been elected by the regional and city councils using an eight-year rotation system. Further constitutional changes in 1975 made the monarch a pure figurehead, to the extent that it is the speaker of the Riksdag who appoints the prime minister.

ELECTORAL SYSTEM

Sweden introduced proportional representation with the Saint Laguë formula in 1917. Until 1970 there was no national threshold, but the smallness of various constituencies discriminated somewhat against smaller parties and gave a slight bonus to the Social Democrats. In 1970 a unicameral Riksdag of 350 seats was established, but after the 1973 elections produced a dead-even tie (175 to 175) between the socialist and nonsocialist blocs, this was changed to 349. The electoral system for the unicameral Riksdag has two main changes. First, in addition to the 310 members elected in multimember districts, a further thirty-nine seats were distributed at the national level to ensure overall proportionality. Second, a legal threshold for seats was established, this being 4 percent of the national vote. Otherwise, if a party wins at least 12 percent of the vote in a given constituency, it wins seats in that constituency. Given the lack of regional parties in Sweden, this second point is rarely relevant.

The lower house of the Riksdag had a four-year term, but the term for the unicameral Riksdag from 1970 was only three years. This changed back to four years as of the 1994 elections.

POLITICAL PARTIES AND TRADITIONAL CLEAVAGES

Sweden is a largely homogeneous country. Thus, for much of this century the main divide was the class cleavage, although there was also a rural-urban cleavage. From the 1920s to the 1980s, the same five parties monopolized the parliament. Of these, the dominant one has been the **Social Democratic Workers' Party** (**SAP**, or in recent years just **S**), which was founded in 1889. The party has been Sweden's largest for decades, but has won outright majorities only in 1940 and 1968. Its forty-four straight years of power from 1932 to 1976 set a record in democratic Europe. The party has never stressed nationalization, but in power it has built up a major welfare state. The SAP has dominated the blue-collar vote, aided by Europe's highest level of unionization and the SAP's close ties to the Swedish Confederation of Trade Unions (LO). However, the SAP has also done well with lower- and middle-class white-collar workers, especially in the public sector.

Social Democratic internal cohesion was aided by the fact that more left-wing elements broke off in 1917 to form the **Left Social Democratic Party (VSdP)**, most of which in 1921 became the **Communist Party (KP)**. Essentially autonomous in relation to the Soviet Union, the party changed its name in 1967 to the **Left Party Communists (VPK)** and again in 1990, after the collapse of communism in eastern Europe, simply to the **Left Party** (**VP**, or just **V**). The name changes to VPK and now VP symbolized a change in its voting base, from one largely of older blue-collar workers to now a postmaterialist base of students and public-sector workers.

On the nonsocialist or "bourgeois" side of the spectrum, the parties most in opposition to the Social Democrats are Sweden's conservatives, formed in 1904 as the **Right Party (HP)**. With right-wing politics proving to have limited appeal in a social-democratic country, the party changed its name in 1969 to the **Moderate Coalition Party** (**MSP**, or just **M**). The party clearly favors smaller government and a more market-oriented society. Since 1979 it has been the largest of the nonsocialist parties.

Less clear in its postwar ideology has been the **Liberal People's Party (FP)**, which was founded in 1902 and split for a time, between the wars, into prohibitionist and nonprohibitionist parties. The liberals are right of center, but not as clearly laissez-faire as the conservatives. The FP voting base, too, has been somewhat unfocused, but it has been based largely on urban white-collar workers.

As noted, in addition to social-class divisions, Sweden has had a historic rural-urban cleavage. This found expression in the **Agrarian Party (BF)**, dating back to 1910. Although the Agrarians were a nonsocialist party, they were open to reform and suspicious of urban elites. Consequently, from the 1930s onward they cooperated with the Social Democrats, ultimately becoming a junior coalition partner in the 1950s. As the rural population declined, the party decide to target centrist voters in the cities as well, and thus changed its name in 1957 to the **Center Party** (**CP**, or just **C**). Somewhat overlapping the rural-urban cleavage has been a very modest religiosity cleavage that led in 1964 to the creation of the **Christian Democratic Society Party** (**KDS** or just **KD**). For many years the party barely registered a presence at the national level. In 1985 and 1988 it ran in alliance with the Center Party, winning one seat in the first case. In 1991, its support suddenly jumped, enabling it to clear the 4 percent threshold.

Selected Elections in Sweden

	1948		1956		1968		1970		1976	
	%V	#S	%V	#S	%V	#S	#V	#S	%V	#S
SAP	46.1	112	44.6	106	50.1	125	45.3	163	42.7	152
FP	22.7	57	23.8	58	14.3	34	16.2	58	11.1	39
HP/MSP	12.3	23	17.1	42	12.9	32	11.5	41	15.6	55
BF/CP	12.4	30	9.5	19	15.7	39	19.9	71	24.1	86

continued

Selected Elections in Sweden *Continued*

	1948		1956		1968		1970		1976	
	%V	#S	%V	#S	%V	#S	#V	#S	%V	#S
KP/VPK	6.3	8	5.0	6	3.0	3	4.8	17	4.8	17
KDS	—	—	—	—	—	—	—	—	1.4	0
TOTAL SEATS		230		231		233		350		349

	1982		1988		1991		1994		1998	
	%V	#S	%V	#S	%V	#S	#V	#S	%V	#S
SAP	45.6	166	43.2	156	37.7	138	45.3	161	36.4	131
FP	5.9	21	12.2	44	9.1	33	7.2	26	4.7	17
MSP	23.6	86	18.3	66	21.9	80	22.4	80	22.9	82
CP	15.5	56	11.3	42	8.5	31	7.7	27	5.1	18
VPK/VP	5.6	20	5.9	21	4.5	16	6.2	22	12.0	43
KDS	1.9	0	2.9	0	7.1	26	4.1	15	11.8	42
MpG	1.6	0	5.5	20	3.4	0	5.0	18	4.5	16
NyD	—	—	—	—	6.7	25	1.2	0	—	—
TOTAL SEATS		349		349		349		349		349

Note: Lower chamber of parliament through 1968, unicameral Riksdag since 1970.

REALIGNMENT AND A NEW DIVISION

The left-right ideological division has remained key in Swedish politics. As noted, through the 1950s at least, there was also an important urban-rural cleavage. Since perhaps the late 1960s, however, the second line of conflict in Swedish party politics has been one of materialism versus postmaterialism. The first major focus for this division was the issue of nuclear power in the 1970s, this being opposed by the VPK and the CP, and supported to varying degrees by the SAP, the MSP, and the FP. The nuclear power issue also led to the establishment in 1981 of a specific

Green Party, the **Environmentalist Party–the Greens** (**MpG**, or just **MP**). In addition to being against nuclear power, the party has stressed gender equality, decentralization, and direct democracy. Initially, the Swedish Greens rejected the left-right continuum, and were indeed more centrist than, say, the German Greens. However, in the 1990s the party openly placed itself on the left of center.

Although the nuclear-power issue is an ongoing one in Sweden, in the 1990s it was displaced, or more precisely reinforced, by the issue of Swedish membership in the European Union. After decades of saying that neutral Sweden had no need to be part of European integration, the ruling Social Democrats changed their tune, and, after a national referendum, Sweden joined the EU as of the beginning of 1995. Sweden's joining, and now continued membership, has, however, been strongly opposed by the Left Party, the Greens, and most of the Center Party, all of whom see dangers to Swedish democracy, values, and the environment in being ruled from Brussels. In contrast, the Social Democrats, Liberals, and Moderates stress the economic benefits of membership.

In short, one can view contemporary Swedish party politics as existing on the following two dimensions:

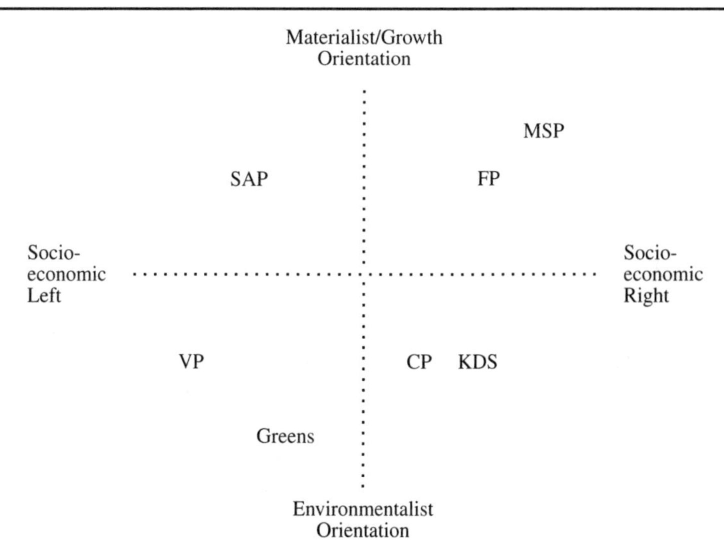

RECENT ELECTIONS

Given various problems in the Swedish economy, especially high unemployment in a country traditionally known for full employment, the elections of the 1990s have gone less well for the Social Democrats than in previous decades. In 1991 they fell below 40 percent of the vote for the first time since 1928, with losses going in various directions including to a new—and short-lived—far-right protest party called **New Democracy (NyD)**. After these elections, the four center-right parties—MDS, FP, CP, and KDS—formed a minority nonsocialist coalition. Dissatisfaction with welfare cuts by this government led to a swing back to the Social Democrats in 1994, when New Democracy also disappeared from parliament. The Social Democrats formed a minority government, eventually supported by the Center Party in return for the promise to decommission some nuclear reactors. The main event during this government, however, was Sweden's entry into the European Union. With the public still split over this policy, the Social Democrats hit another new (relative) low in the 1998 elections, with most of their losses going to the Left Party. On the center right, the KDS was able to continue their growth at the expense of the Center and Liberal parties, so that the KDS is now clearly the second-largest nonsocialist party. Also worth noting is that due to voter disillusionment, turnout in 1998 was the lowest since 1958.

GOVERNMENTS

With the exception of 1976–82 and 1991–94, all postwar Swedish governments have been formed, or led, by the SAP. The first nonsocialist governments were unstable due to strong divisions among the nonsocialist parties, especially over nuclear energy. In contrast, the four-party nonsocialist coalition formed in 1991 survived its full term. As for the Social Democrats, they have generally formed minority governments supported by the Center Party and occasionally the Liberals, but after 1998 turned to the Left Party and the Greens—thus reinforcing Sweden's traditional left-right divide.

Swedish Governments since 1946

In Office Date (M/Y)	Prime Minister (Party)	#M(I)	Parties in Cabinet	Supporting Parties
10/46	Erlander, T. (SAP)	16(2)	SAP	
10/48	Erlander, T. (SAP)	19(3)	SAP	
09/51	Erlander, T. (SAP)	16(3)	SAP AF	
09/52	Erlander, T. (SAP)	16(3)	SAP AF	
09/56	Erlander, T. (SAP)	17(4)	SAP AF	
10/57	Erlander, T. (SAP)	15(2)	SAP	
06/58	Erlander, T. (SAP)	15(1)	SAP	
10/60	Erlander, T. (SAP)	15(1)	SAP	
10/64	Erlander, T. (SAP)	16	SAP	
09/68	Erlander, T. (SAP)	17	SAP	
10/69	Palme, O. (SAP)	19	SAP	
09/70	Palme, O. (SAP)	19	SAP	VPK
10/73	Palme, O. (SAP)	18	SAP	VPK
10/76	Fälldin, T. (CP)	20(1)	CP FP MSP	
10/78	Ullsten, O. (FP)	18(1)	FP	
10/79	Fälldin, T. (CP)	21(1)	CP MSP FP	
05/81	Fälldin, T. (CP)	18(1)	CP FP	
10/82	Palme, O. (SAP)	20	SAP	VPK
10/85	Palme, O. (SAP)	21	SAP	VPK
03/86	Carlsson, I. (SAP)	20	SAP	VPK
09/88	Carlsson, I. (SAP)	21	SAP	VPK
02/90	Carlsson, I. (SAP)	22	SAP	
10/91	Bildt, C. (MSP)	21(3)	MSP CP FP KdS	
10/94	Carlsson, I. (SAP)	22	SAP	VP
as of 05/95:				CP
03/96	Persson, G. (SAP)	21	SAP	CP
09/98	Persson, G. (SAP)	20	SAP	VP Greens

ACRONYMS

BF	Agrarian Party
CP or C	Center Party
FP	Liberal People's Party
HP	Right Party
KDS or KD	Christian Democratic Society Party
KP	Communist Party
MpG or MP	Environmentalist Party–the Greens
MSP or M	Moderate Coalition Party
NyD	New Democracy
SAP or S	Social Democratic Workers' Party
VP or V	Left Party
VPK	Left Party Communists
VSdP	Left Social Democratic Party

REFERENCES

Arter, David (1999). "Sweden: A Mild Case of 'Electoral Instability Syndrome'," in David Broughton and Mark Donovan, eds., *Changing Party Systems in Western Europe.* London: Pinter, pp. 143–162.

Lane, Jan-Erik, ed. (1991). *Understanding the Swedish Model.* London: Frank Cass.

Misgeld, Klaus, Karl Molin, and Klas Åmark, eds. (1992). *Creating Social Democracy: A Century of the Social-Democratic Labor Party in Sweden.* University Park, Pa.: The Pennsylvania State University Press.

Switzerland

SUMMARY OF PARTY SYSTEM

1947–(99)	moderate multiparty system with a balance among the parties

HISTORY

Switzerland dates back to 1291, when a treaty of alliance was signed between three independent cantons. The number of cantons grew over time, reaching twenty-two by 1815. However, Switzerland as a polity remained confederal. Divisions over increasing central control (opposed by Catholic mountain cantons) led to a brief civil war in 1847. The following year a federal constitution was drawn up and passed by almost seven-to-one in a referendum. Federal power was further strengthened in 1874. Switzerland is strongly bicameral, and the now twenty-six Swiss cantons have considerable autonomy. Some of these are divided into half cantons. The Swiss population, through either initiatives or referenda, has a considerable influence over public policy. As such, elections are but one part of the political process rather than key events per se. Women did not receive the right to vote until 1971.

ELECTORAL SYSTEM

Switzerland elects its 200-member National Council through a system of proportional representation with the cantons (or half-cantons) serving as the electoral districts. However, five of these—Uri, Obwalden, Nidwalden, Glarus, and Appenzell-Inner Rhoden—are so small as to only have one deputy each. Elections in these five are, thus, effectively by single-member plurality. In the remaining districts, PR with the d'Hondt highest-average formula is used. Since there are a relatively high number of districts, and no national compensation seats, the system is not perfectly proportional and it occasionally happens that the second-place party in terms of votes comes first in seats.

POLITICAL PARTIES AND CLEAVAGES

Despite there being four official languages in Switzerland, religiosity, religion, social class, and region have all mattered as much or more than language in terms of electoral cleavages. In the case of Switzerland, it is also useful to distinguish between the four parties of government and the remaining, smaller parties. The first of these parties of government is the **Radical Party** (**FDP** in German, **PRD in French**), which monopolized power in Switzerland from the civil war of 1848 to the introduction of proportional representation in 1917. The Radicals are radical in the nineteenth-century continental sense of being strongly secular. It is largely an urban party, supported by the Swiss bourgeoisie, but also by the farmers in French Protestant areas.

The **Social Democratic Party of Switzerland** (**SPS** in German, **PSS** in French) was founded in 1870, and it is the only major left-wing party in Switzerland. It is strongest among workers in the Protestant industrial areas of the country. Never very doctrinaire (as it could not be in such a bourgeois country), the SPS/PSS has, since the 1980s, added environmental issues to its platform.

The **Christian Democratic People's Party** (**CVP** in German, **PDC** in French) was formed in 1912. Although intended as a party for all Christians, its support is disproportionately Catholic. Like most European Christian-democratic parties, the CVP/PDC supports moderate state intervention and sees itself as a bridge between social classes and, in the Swiss case, between the mountainous and the more urbanized areas. The party suffers from an aging electorate and has been in decline in recent elections.

The fourth traditional party of government was until 1971 the **Party of Farmers, Traders, and Citizens (BGB)**, founded in 1917 and essentially restricted to German-speaking Protestant areas. In 1971 the BGB merged with the small **Swiss Democratic Party (SDP)**, formed in 1942, to create the **Swiss People's Party** (**SVP** in German, **UDC** in French). The SVP emphasized agricultural policy, and thus was particularly strong among farmers, but, again, only in the German-speaking Protestant areas. As Switzerland considered closer relations with the European

Union in the 1990s, the SVP adopted a more militant protectionist and isolationist stance. Such a populist stance has allowed it to expand in recent years into German-speaking *Catholic* mountainous areas, largely at the expense of the CVP.

Beyond these four parties, there is quite a range of smaller parties. Of these, the following are of note: the **Liberal Party of Switzerland** (**PLS** in French, **LPS** in German) is a long-standing essentially French bourgeois party, particularly strong in Geneva. Meanwhile, the French working class, especially in Geneva, has been the voter base for the historically communist **Swiss Workers' Party** (**PdT** in French, **PdA** in German). The PdT and especially the PLS have tended to enjoy a positive seat bias due to the regional concentration of their support. The **Alliance of Independents** (**LdU** in German, **AdI** in French) was formed in 1936 as an outgrowth of the cooperative movement. It is middle-of-the-road and has allied with both left and right. Strongest in Zurich, it is perhaps most unique in its close ties to a large supermarket chain! The **Evangelical People's Party** (**EVP** in German, **PEP** in French) dates back to 1917; it is a party of churchgoing German Protestants, and has been close to the LdU. On the far right, the **National Action for People and Homeland (NA)** was formed in 1961 and became the **Swiss Democrats (SD)** in 1991. The party is nationalistic and isolationist, and in particular seeks to reduce the numbers of foreigners living and working in Switzerland. It is strongest in the major cities and tends to support environmental initiatives as well.

A more focused pro-environment outlook has recently come from the **Green Party of Switzerland** (**GPS** in German, **PES** in French), formed in 1983. Like other European Green parties, its support comes disproportionately from young, urban voters, but it also does best in the German-speaking cities. Switzerland is obviously not unique in having a Green Party, but it may well be in having an explicitly "anti-Green" party. The **Swiss Motorists' Party (SAP)** was formed in 1985, and in 1994 became the **Freedom Party of Switzerland (FPS)**. Its original name indicates its orientation, namely private automobile users, and its key policies, such as lower gasoline taxes. The FPS would lose all of its seats in 1999, however.

ELECTORAL TRENDS

The Swiss party system has been extremely stable throughout the postwar period. With a full range of parties speaking to many cleavages, and with the possibility of referenda down the road, elections have rarely hinged on issues. The 1995 elections were somewhat different, however, in that the Socialist Party ran in part on an explicitly pro–European Union platform. In contrast (and in response), the Swiss People's Party stepped up its anti-European rhetoric. The two other main parties, the Radicals and the Christian Democrats, were less clear-cut. The voters seemed to favor clarity, though, as both the Socialists and the Swiss People's Party gained support. In 1999 the SPS stabilized, but the SVP surged forward on a wave of anti-EU and anti-foreigner sentiment. The SVP, which had always been the fourth largest of the four governing parties, jumped to a very narrow first place in votes and second place in seats. In part, SVP gains came at the expense of the even-more populist FPS, which was wiped out. The European issue is likely to remain important for some time to come.

Selected Elections in Switzerland

	1951		**1971**		**1987**		**1991**	
	%V	**#S**	**%V**	**#S**	**%V**	**#S**	**%V**	**#S**
FDP/PRD	24.0	51	21.7	49	22.9	51	21.0	44
SPS/PSS	26.0	49	22.9	46	18.4	41	18.5	41
CVP/PDC	22.5	48	20.7	44	20.0	42	18.3	36
BGB	12.6	23	(merged into SVP/UDC)					
SDP	2.2	4	(merged into SVP/UDC)					
SVP/UDC	—	—	11.0	23	1..0	25	11.9	25
EVP/PEP	1.0	1	2.1	3	1.9	3	1.9	3
PLS/LPS	2.6	5	2.2	6	2.7	9	3.0	10
LdU/AdI	5.1	10	7.6	13	4.2	8	2.8	5
PdT/PdA	2.7	5	2.5	5	0.9	1	0.8	2
NA/SD	—	—	3.2	4	3.0	3	3.0	5
GPS/PES	—	—	—	—	5.0	9	6.2	14
SAP/FPS	—	—	—	—	2.6	2	5.1	8
others	1.3	4	6.1	7	7.4	6	7.5	7
TOTAL SEATS 200		200		200		200		200

	1995		1999	
	%V	#S	%V	#S
FDP/PRD	20.2	45	20.4	43
SPS/PSS	21.9	54	23.0	51
CVP/PDC	17.0	34	16.1	35
BGB				
SDP				
SVP/UDC	14.9	29	23.1	44
EVP/PEP	1.8	2	1.9	3
PLS/LPS	2.7	7	2.3	6
LdU/AdI	1.8	3	0.8	1
PdT/PdA	1.2	3	1.0	2
NA/SD	3.1	3	1.9	1
GPS/PES	5.0	9	5.1	9
SAP/FPS	4.0	7	0.9	0
others	6.4	4	3.6	5
TOTAL SEATS		200		200

GOVERNMENTS

In 1959, the so-called "magic formula" was achieved, wherein the Radicals, Socialists, and Catholic People's Party each got two of the seven seats on the Federal Council (cabinet), and the BGB, and then SVP, got the last one. It should be noted that once voted in by parliament, the Swiss cabinet is not subject to nonconfidence votes. Hence governments almost invariably last the four-year term.

Swiss Governments since 1947

In Office Date (M/Y)	#M	Parties in Cabinet
12/47	7	FDP CVP SPS BGB
12/51	7	FDP CVP SPS BGB

continued

Swiss Governments since 1947 *Continued*

In Office Date (M/Y)	#M	Parties in Cabinet
12/53	7	FDP CVP BGB
12/55	7	FDP CVP BGB
12/59	7	FDP CVP SPS BGB
12/63	7	FDP CVP SPS BGB
12/67	7	FDP CVP SPS BGB
12/71	7	FDP CVP SPS SVP
12/75	7	FDP CVP SPS SVP
12/79	7	FDP CVP SPS SVP
12/83	7	FDP CVP SPS SVP
12/87	7	FDP CVP SPS SVP
12/91	7	FDP CVP SPS SVP
12/95	7	FDP CVP SPS SVP
12/99	7	FDP CVP SPS SVP

Notes: Switzerland has no prime minister. Only the German-language acronyms are given.

ACRONYMS (ORIGINAL LANGUAGE)

AdI	(French)	Alliance of Independents
BGB	(German)	Party of Farmers, Traders, and Citizens
CVP	(German)	Christian Democratic People's Party
EVP	(German)	Evangelical People's Party
FDP	(German)	Radical Party
FPS	(German)	Freedom Party of Switzerland
GPS	(German)	Green Party of Switzerland
LdU	(German)	Alliance of Independents
LPS	(German)	Liberal Party of Switzerland
NA	(German)	National Action for People and Homeland
PdA	(German)	Swiss Workers' Party
PDC	(French)	Christian Democratic People's Party
PdT	(French)	Swiss Workers' Party
PEP	(French)	Evangelical People's Party

PES	(French)	Green Party of Switzerland
PLS	(French)	Liberal Party of Switzerland
PRD	(French)	Radical Party
PSS	(French)	Socialist Party of Switzerland
SAP	(German)	Swiss Motorists' Party
SD	(German)	Swiss Democrats
SDP	(German)	Swiss Democratic Party
SPS	(German)	Socialist Party of Switzerland
SVP	(German)	Swiss People's Party
UDC	(French)	Swiss People's Party

REFERENCES

Church, Clive. (1996). "The Swiss Elections of 1995: Real Victors and Real Losers at Last?" *West European Politics,* Vol. 19, pp. 641–48.

Geissbühler, Simon. (1999). "Catholicism, Political Attitudes and Party Attachment in Switzerland, 1970–1995," *West European Politics,* Vol. 22, No. 3, pp. 223–240.

Kerr, Henry R. (1987). "The Swiss Party System: Steadfast and Changing," in Hans Daalder, ed. *Party Systems in Denmark, Austria, Switzerland, the Netherlands, and Belgium.* London: Frances Pinter, pp. 107–92.

Linder, Wolf. (1998). *Swiss Democracy: Possible Solutions to Conflict in Multicultural Societies,* 2d. edition. Basingstoke, England: Macmillan.

Turkey

SUMMARY OF PARTY SYSTEMS

1950–57	two-party system (CHP and DP)
1961–77	two-and-a-half-party system (AP and CHP the two main parties)
1983–87	moderate multiparty system with one dominant party (ANAP)
1991–(99)	moderate multiparty system with a balance among the parties

HISTORY

The Ottoman Empire once ruled the Balkans, the Mideast, and North Africa. By the nineteenth century, however, the Ottoman Empire was seen as "the sick man of Europe." After defeat in the First World War, Mustapha Kemal Atatürk proclaimed Turkey a republic in 1923, and established a secular, nationalistic legacy. Democracy was introduced in 1946, and the first truly competitive election was in 1950. The doctrine of "Kemalism" has been used no less than four times in the post-1945 period to justify military intervention. The first three interventions (1960, 1971, 1980) were actual military coups followed by short authoritarian regimes and constitutional changes. Of these, the 1980–83 period of military rule was the longest lasting and the most fundamental, in that all previous parties and most political leaders were banned for a further five years. The last instance of military intervention, that of 1997, was called a "soft coup," which involved the military forcing the Islamist prime minister out of office.

ELECTORAL SYSTEM

In the 1950s Turkey used a majoritarian electoral system in which the party with the plurality of votes in a given province won all of that province's seats. This led, not surprisingly, to some very lopsided victories. Moreover, since this victories meant defeats for the elite's preferred party, the CHP, in the 1961 constitution the electoral system was changed to proportional representation with d'Hondt quota, with the seats still calculated within each of the sixty-seven provinces, but now proportionally. In an attempt to limit the fragmentation caused by such a system, the coup administration introduced a very high threshold for electoral representation: 10 percent of the national vote. Furthermore, a party must also have a functioning organization in at least half of the provinces and in at least one-third of the districts affiliated with those provinces to win any seats. Finally, within each province there are bonuses for the largest party (these vary depending on the province).

CLEAVAGES, IDEOLOGIES, POLITICAL PARTIES, AND ELECTORAL HISTORY

There have been three main overlapping divisions in Turkish society: traditional versus secular/universal values, rural versus urban, and left versus right. All of these have arisen out of opposition to or support for the Kemalist view of Turkey, and the location of people with one set of beliefs or the other. "Kemalism" holds to the principles of republicanism, secularism, statism, national solidarity, Westernization, and (but) also Turkish nationalism. In short, "Kemalism" is situated on the secular left. Atatürk himself felt that traditional, Islamic Turkey needed to be modernized, and in many ways this meant adopting Western values. The original Kemalist party was the **Republican People's Party (CHP)**, founded by Atatürk in 1923 and the sole political party in Turkey until 1946. Unfortunately for the party, the ideals of "Kemalism" were strongly supported only by urban elites, so the party was rarely successful in electoral competition. In the 1960s it stressed its leftism somewhat more and targeted urban industrial workers. After being banned in 1980, the CHP split into two: the **Democratic Left Party (DSP)**, formed in 1984, and the **Social Democratic Peoples' Party (SHP)**, formed in 1985. Until the 1995 elections, the SHP was the stronger of the two. For those elections, the SHP changed its name back to the Republican People's Party.

If the CHP and its successors have been the party of the dominant elites (although not the dominant number of voters) in Turkish society, then the **Democratic Party (DP)** and its successors have been, until recently, the party or parties of the rural periphery in opposition to the secular, bureaucratic elite. The DP, formed in 1946, won all three of the elections in the 1950s, in the first two cases with a majority of the vote as well. In its policies it did not actually deviate much from the official "Kemalist" secularism and statism. Nevertheless, the DP was liquidated by the military after the 1960 coup. The party then reconstituted itself in 1961 as the **Justice Party (AP)**, which positioned itself moderately right of center. The AP was at its strongest in the mid-to-late 1960s, winning outright majorities in 1965 and 1969. It was supported by urban business people, farmers, and moderate Islamists.

In the most recent period, two parties have claimed the legacy of the DP/AP. The first of these is the **Motherland Party (ANAP)**, formed in 1983 for the elections of that year. Deemed the "acceptable" right-of-center party by the military, and benefiting from the bias in the electoral system, ANAP was able to win majorities in 1983 and 1987. From the mid-1980s onward, the party became both explicitly secular and more laissez-faire in its economics. In doing so, it has become the preferred party of urban, Westernized, private-sector voters. The other party claiming the DP/AP legacy is the **True Path Party (DYP)**, formed after the 1983 elections. The DYP has a less clear ideology, in that it wants to appeal to urban entrepreneurs but also hold on to the traditional DP/AP rural vote. Nevertheless, there is not a significant difference between the views of the DYP and the ANAP, and the main reason for the persistence of two major right-of-center parties (as opposed to just one) is the personal animosity between the party leaders.

Beyond these principal parties, there have been other, smaller parties, some of which got into government as junior coalition partners in the 1960s and 1970s. Many of these smaller parties arose as splits from either the CHP or the DP/AP. Thus the **Republican Reliance Party (GCP)**, existing from 1973 to 1980, was a right-of-center but elitist party, and the **New Turkey Party (YTP)**, existing from 1961 to 1970, was a less free-market version of the AP. However, there was also on the extreme left the **Turkish Workers Party (TIP)**, formed in 1961, and on the far right the **Nation Party (MP)** and the **Republican Peasants' National Party (RPNP)**, which in 1969 merged along with other far-right forces into the more clearly fascistic **National Action Party (MHP)**. These more extreme parties tended to act as centrifugal forces in the 1960s

(TIP) and 1970s (NAP), contributing to the polarization that led to military intervention in 1971 and 1980. In 1997, Devlet Bahceli took over as leader of the MHP and removed its extremist and violent fringes, allowing the party to enter, or at least approach, the political mainstream.

Last but certainly not least have been the Islamist parties in Turkey. The first of these was the **National Salvation Party (MSP)** of the 1970s, which was able to get itself into government under both the CHP and the AP. The MSP was essentially reformed in 1983 (after the last period of military rule) as the **Welfare Party** (**Refah**, or **RP**), which gained steadily in both the 1991 and 1995 elections. The growth in Refah support should not be seen primarily as reflecting a growth in religious-conservative Muslims, for these in fact have accounted for less than half its support in recent years. Rather, Refah quickly established itself as a successful protest party, particularly for the large and growing number of urban migrants, that is, those poorer rural Turks who have moved to the main urban areas, as opposed to traditional urban residents who have tended to support "Kemalism." In 1996 Refah formed a coalition with True Path. In 1997, however, worried about Refah's Islamist orientation and attempts to "desecularize" Turkey, the military forced Refah leader Necmettin Erbakan out of the prime minister's office in June. The party itself was soon dissolved and Erbakan himself banned from politics. Nevertheless, the party simply reconstituted itself that December as the **Virtue Party (FP)**.

Selected Elections in Turkey

	1950		**1965**		**1969**		**1977**	
	%V	**#S**	**%V**	**#S**	**%V**	**#S**	**%V**	**#S**
CHP	40.0	69	28.7	134	27.4	143	41.4	213
DP/AP	53.5	408	52.7	240	46.5	256	36.9	189
YTP	—	—	3.7	19	2.2	6	—	—
TIP	—	—	3.0	15	2.7	2	0.1	0
MP	—	—	6.3	31	3.2	6	(merged into MHP)	
RPNP	—	—	2.2	11	1.0	1	(merged into MHP)	
MHP	—	—	—	—	—	—	6.4	16
GCP	—	—	—	—	6.6	15	1.9	3
MSP	—	—	—	—	—	—	8.6	24
others	6.5	7	3.4	0	10.4	21	4.7	5
TOTAL SEATS		484		450		450		450

continued

Selected Elections in Turkey *Continued*

	1987		1991		1995		1999	
	%V	#S	%V	#S	%V	#S	%V	#S
ANAP	36.3	292	24.0	115	19.7	132	13.2	86
DYP	19.1	59	27.0	178	19.2	135	12.0	85
SHP/CHP	24.7	99	20.8	88	10.7	49	8.7	0
DSP	8.5	0	10.8	7	14.7	76	22.2	136
Refah/FP	7.1	0	16.9	62	21.4	158	15.4	111
MHP	—	—	—	—	8.2	0	18.0	129
others	4.3	0	0.5	0	6.1	0	10.3	3
TOTAL SEATS		450		450		550		550

RECENT ELECTIONS

Both the 1991 and 1995 elections were dominated by issues of the economy (high inflation and interest rates, and the national debt), and by criticisms of political corruption in the traditional parties. Nevertheless, the politicians often focused more on personalities than on the issues, this being especially true of the leaders of the two center-right parties, Ms. Tansu Çiller (DYP) and Mr. Mesut Yilmaz (ANAP), vis-à-vis each other. In the 1991 elections, DYP did well chiefly because ANAP had been the government. In both 1991 and 1995, however, the pro-Islamic Refah made major gains, so that by 1995 it was the largest party in Turkey. In the campaigns, Refah stressed social justice and opposition to corruption more than explicit religious themes. Nevertheless, after 1995 the four major secular parties (DYP, ANAP, CHP, and DSP) all vowed to keep Refah out of office. A DYP-ANAP government was eventually formed, but then quickly collapsed. Thereafter, the DYP "broke ranks," agreeing to share power with Refah, Refah initially having the prime ministership with the understanding that this would come back to the DYP. As noted, the Turkish military soon forced Refah out of office, and opposition to this government within the DYP led to many of its MPs quitting the party to either sit as independents or in new (and ultimately temporary) small parties such as the **Democratic Turkey Party (DTP)**.

Thus, in the run-up to the 1999 elections, Turkey was governed by a minority DSP government under Mr. Bulent Ecevit, who had been prime minister in the 1970s. He had clear democratic and leftist credentials, but also nationalist ones. Consequently, when Turkey captured the Kurdish leader Abdullah Ocalan, this greatly increased the popularity of Ecevit and the DSP. In what turned out to be a rather nationalistic outpouring, the other big winner was the far-right MHP. Indeed, the MHP was able to replace Refah/Virtue as the party of protest. The mainline center-right parties, ANAP and DYP, plagued as they were with scandals, both lost heavily. The CHP did not lose much, but enough to fall below the 10 percent hurdle and lose all its seats, thus completely marginalizing the namesake of Atatürk's original party.

GOVERNMENTS

Governments in Turkey have tended to be led by one of the two main parties in a given period. There have been many single-party majorities, but with the exception of the 1950s, this pattern has not been sustainable over the long haul. Thus there is often space for smaller parties to maneuver themselves into a few cabinet seats. Since 1991, moreover, a new pattern seems to have been established in which, rather than a larger party forming the government with a smaller party or parties, two larger parties (ANAP, DYP, SHP, Refah, and/or now DSP) get together in government. Such governments have required protracted negotiations and have tended to be unstable. The May 1999 Ecevit government is in fact composed of three reasonably sized parties, which may or may not make it even less stable.

Turkish Governments since 1950

In Office Date (M/Y)	Prime Minister (Party)	#M(I)	Parties in Cabinet	Supporting Parties
First Republic				
05/50	Menderes, A. (DP)	18	DP	
05/54	Menderes, A. (DP)	18	DP	
10/57	Menderes, A. (DP)	20(1)	DP	

[military coup in 1960]

continued

Turkish Governments since 1950 *Continued*

In Office Date (M/Y)	Prime Minister (Party)	#M(I)	Parties in Cabinet	Supporting Parties
Second Republic				
11/61	Inönü, I. (CHP)	22	CHP AP	
06/62	Inönü, I. (CHP)	23	CHP NTP RPNP	
12/63	Inönü, I. (CHP)	23(3)	CHP	
10/65	Demirel, S. (AP)	23	AP	
11/69	Demirel, S. (AP)	25	AP	
03/70	Demirel, S. (AP)	25	AP	
[military coup in 1971]				
01/74	Ecevit, B. (CHP)	25	CHP MSP	
11/74	Irmak, Y. (Ind)	..	(caretaker government)	
03/75	Demirel, S. (AP)	30	AP MSP CGP MHP	
06/77	Ecevit, B. (CHP)	16(1)	CHP	
08/77	Demirel, S. (AP)	29	AP MSP MHP	
01/78	Ecevit, B. (CHP)	25	CHP CGP DP	
11/79	Demirel, S. (AP)	29	AP	MSP MHP
[military coup in 1980]				
Third Republic				
12/83	Ozal, T. (ANAP)	22(2)	ANAP	
12/87	Ozal, T. (ANAP)	25	ANAP	
11/89	Akbulut, Y. (ANAP)	31	ANAP	
06/91	Yilmaz, M. (ANAP)	30	ANAP	
10/91	Demirel, S. (DYP)	32	DYP SHP	
06/93	Çiller, T. (DYP)	32	DYP SHP	
03/96	Yilmaz, M. (ANAP)	33	DYP ANAP	
06/96	Erbakan, N. (Refah)	18	Refah DYP	
06/97	Yilmaz, M. (ANAP)	19(1)	ANAP DSP DTP	CHP
01/99	Ecevit, B. (DSP)	25(3)	DSP	ANAP DYP
05/99	Ecevit, B. (DSP)	35	DSP MHP ANAP	

ACRONYMS

ANAP	Motherland Party
AP	Justice Party
CHP	Republican Peoples' Party
DP	Democratic Party
DSP	Democratic Left Party
DTP	Democratic Turkey Party
DYP	True Path Party
FP	Virtue Party
GCP	Republican Reliance Party
MHP	National Action Party
MP	National Party
MSP	National Salvation Party
Refah	Welfare Party
RPNP	Republican Peasants' National Party
SHP	Social Democratic Peoples' Party
TIP	Turkish Workers Party
YTP	New Turkey Party

REFERENCES

Çarkoglu, Ali. (1998). "The Turkish Party System in Transition: Party Performance and Agenda Change." *Political Studies,* Vol. 46, pp. 544–71.

Heper, Metin. (1997). "Islam and Democracy in Turkey: Toward a Reconciliation?" *Middle East Journal,* Vol. 51, pp. 32–45.

Heper, Metin, and Jacob Landau, eds. (1991). *Political Parties and Democracy in Turkey.* New York: IB Taris and Company.

Ukraine

SUMMARY OF PARTY SYSTEMS

1994	moderate multiparty system with one dominant party (KPU)
(1998–)	extreme multiparty system with one dominant party (KPU)

HISTORY

Ukraine was under Polish rule in the sixteenth century and then was briefly independent in the seventeenth century. It came under Russian control in the eighteenth century. In 1917 Ukraine became briefly independent once again, but then it was forcibly incorporated into the USSR in 1922. In July 1990 the Ukraine Supreme Soviet issued a sovereignty declaration, followed in August 1991 by a formal declaration of independence.

ELECTORAL SYSTEM

The electoral system used in the 1994 Ukrainian elections was adopted in November 1993. Under this system, 450 deputies were elected—all in single-member constituencies elected on a majority basis. If there was no clear winner after the second ballot, then a new election was held between the top two candidates. In addition, turnout had to be 50 percent in a constituency for the election to be valid. Failing this, a further election was held with the hopes of higher turnout, sometimes months later.

In October 1997 a new electoral law was passed that was then used in the 1998 elections. Under this new system, which is similar to that of Russian law, 225 deputies—that is, exactly one-half—are (still) elected in single-member constituencies by majority vote. The turnout requirement has been eliminated, however. The other 225 deputies are elected in one nationwide constituency by a party-list proportional-representation system, the calculation of which does not take into account the results from the single-member seats. Parties must pass a 4 percent vote threshold to gain party-list representation. As in Russia, the party list ballot specifically allows a voter to cast a ballot "against all lists".

POLITICAL PARTIES AND CLEAVAGES

Ukraine does not have a very well-established party system. In 1994 the party affiliations of candidates were not even listed on the ballots. Following the March/April 1994 elections, independents were by far the largest single group represented in parliament, holding just over half of the seats! While in 1998 this figure dropped to 28 percent, independents still remained the second-largest grouping in parliament. After elections many independents clearly drift into one bloc or another; however, they are not officially a member of any party.

The actual parties in Ukraine can be divided into four blocs. The left bloc in parliament includes communists, socialists, and a peasant party, as well as smaller socialist parties. The **Ukrainian Communist Party (KPU)** was founded in 1993 with no legal claims to the Communist Party that ruled the Ukraine and was banned in 1991 for allegedly supporting the coup in August 1991. The KPU's main base of support is retirees, embittered workers, and others nostalgic for the Soviet past. The **Socialist Party of Ukraine (SPU)** was founded in 1991 by rank and file members of the ruling Communist Party, and the party did avoid recruiting any former high-ranking Communists. The SPU is pro-Russian and anti-Ukrainization, advocating legal status for the Russian language, and dual citizenship. The third party in the left bloc is the **Peasants' Party of Ukraine (SePU)**. Because both the SPU and the SePU rely on support from the rural population, the two parties presented a joint list for the 1998 elections. On the far left in parliament is the **Progressive Socialist Party (PSP)**, which was formed in 1996 by two members who were expelled from the SPU after having criticized the leadership of the party. The Progressive Socialist Party won sixteen seats in 1998.

The center bloc of parties is the second strongest in the Ukrainian parliament. The larger parties in this bloc include the pro-reform **People's Democratic Party of Ukraine (NDPU)**, which was formed in 1996 by a merger of two other, smaller centrist parties—the **Party for Democratic Revival (or Renewal) of Ukraine (PDVU)** and the **Labor Congress of Ukraine (TKU)**. The NDPU is the main government party and is supported by pro-government business. The other big party in the center is the **United Social-Democratic Party (OSDPU)**. The OSDPU draws on support from Ukrainians who agree with the government's policies but do no like the personalities or parties associated with these policies. The center bloc also included three new parties for the 1998 elections. The first, **Hromada**, gained most of its support from businessmen eager for state subsidies, and managed to win twenty-three seats. Also new in the center is the **Party of Greens of Ukraine (PZU)**, who chose the center as the most reformist bloc. Finally, the **Agrarian Party of Ukraine (APU)** is supported by collective farm directors.

The moderate right bloc is the second weakest in parliament but does contain the party that received the second largest number of votes in the 1998 elections, **Rukh**, formally the **Ukrainian Popular Movement**. Rukh, founded in 1989, was originally a broad-based democratic coalition similar to the popular fronts of the Baltic states. In the early 1990s, however, Rukh began to suffer from an identity crisis and began to support a moderately nationalist program. It is now clearly the vehicle of the nationalist western Ukraine. In the 1998 elections, small liberal parties also won single-member seats in parliament. Finally, the far-right bloc in Ukraine is made up of ultranationalist parties such as the **Congress of Ukrainian Nationalists (KUN)**.

ELECTIONS

The 1994 elections were the first since the Ukraine gained independence in 1991. In August 1991 over 90 percent of the population had supported independence in a referendum. Since 1991, however, the people of Ukraine were no longer as heavily in support of independence. Many in the predominantly Russian-speaking eastern part of the country had suffered the most from the cessation of the Soviet economic system. Therefore, parties like those of the communists and socialists gained support there. The campaign featured regional polarization and lack of party affiliation. As mentioned, party affiliation of candidates was not listed on the ballot sheets. Also, despite 150 of the sitting 450 members of parliament running for reelection, only 57 of these were successful. Clearly the people of the Ukraine wanted a change from the parliament that had been sitting since 1991. In fact, elections were not supposed to be held until 1995 but pressure from the public and opposition parties resulted in early elections.

The main issues of the 1994 campaign turned out to be the economy and the foreign policy of the Ukraine, particularly with respect to Ukraine-Russian relations. Crime was also an issue. There were some reports of irregularities, and charges of coercion, miscounting, and multiple ballots. Party-based candidates only won half of the filled seats.

Because of poor turnout in the second round of elections in April 1994, 112 seats were not filled. Repeat elections were held in July/August 1994, in November/December 1994, and a year later in December 1995 in order to fill these seats. After the December 1995 repeat elections, thirty-one seats still remained unfilled. This number increased to thirty-two shortly after, when one of the elected candidates died. These seats remained unfilled until the 1998 elections, and their electorates were thus disenfranchized—or perhaps more accurately "self-disenfranchized"—due to low turnout.

During 1994 and 1995 most independents joined centrist parties or formed new centrist groupings. Some other deputies also shifted to the center, in particular a breakaway faction of the Agrarians who became the **Agrarians for Reform**.

The 29 March 1998 elections were held for all the seats in parliament at the normal (four-year) end of the parliamentary term of office, based on the first election date of March 1994. As noted, based on the experience of the 1994 elections, which after two years of repeat elections still did not see all the seats in parliament filled, the Electoral Law was modified in October 1997 to provide for a mixed electoral system.

In the campaign, parties on the left, like the Communists and Socialists, criticized the president's reform program in the economic sector. The ultraleft Progressive Socialists managed to win moderate support in regions traditionally favoring the Communists and Socialists. Led by an outspoken husband-and-wife team, Natalya Vitrenko and Volodymyr Marchenko, the party took 21 percent of the vote in the northeastern Sumy Region and also got more than 4 percent in eight other regions sharing a border with Russia. Vitrenko and Marchenko traveled extensively during the campaign, attacking both the government and its main opponents, lashing out at democrats and more moderate leftists alike.

Altogether, over six thousand candidates vied for the 225 district and 225 party-list seats, with some thirty parties or blocs competing in the latter category. As in 1994, independents captured half of the majority mandates; many of these were reportedly centrist businessmen.

Ukrainian Election Results and Parliamentary Evolution

	March/ April 1994 Elections %V	#S	As of December 1994 #S	As of December 1995 #S	1998 Elections %V*	#S
total left	*18.5*	*118*	*145*	*136*	*42.7*	*173*
of which KPU	12.7	86			25.4	122
SPU	3.1	14		}		
SePU	2.7	18		}	8.8	34
PSP	—	—			4.1	16
total center	*1.8*	*11*	*86*	*183*	*29.2*	*98*
of which NDPU					5.2	29
OSDPU					4.1	17
Hromada					4.8	23
PZU					5.6	19
APU	—	—			3.8	8
total moderate right	*9.1*	*31*	*83*	*61*	*16.1*	*53*
of which Rukh	5.1	20			9.7	46
total far right	*2.1*	*8*	— —	— —	*3.9*	*6*
other parties	*1.9*	*0*	— —	— —	*2.6*	*4*
against all lists		—	— —	— —	*5.4*	—
independents	*66.5*	*170*	*89*	*38*		*116*
TOTAL DEPUTIES		338	403	418		450
unfilled seats		112	47	32		0

*1998 vote percentages are for the national lists only (share of valid votes).

GOVERNMENTS

Seven governments have been formed in the Ukraine since 1994, but only one prime minister has been associated with a party. This is largely due to the nature of government formation in the Ukraine, which rests largely on the whims of the president and contains many technocrats and nonparty individuals.

Ukrainian Governments since 1994

In Office Date (M/Y)	Prime Minister (Party)
06/94	Masol, V.
03/95	Marchuk, Y.
04/95	Marchuk, Y.
05/96	Lazarenko, P.
08/96	Lazarenko, P.
07/97	Pustovoitenko, V. (NDPU)
05/98	Pustovoitenko, V. (NDPU)

ACRONYMS

APU	Agrarian Party of Ukraine
KPU	Communist Party of Ukraine
NDPU	People's (or Popular) Democratic Party of Ukraine
OSDPU	United Social Democratic Party of Ukraine
PDVU	Party for Democratic Revival of Ukraine
PZU	Party of Greens of Ukraine
SePU	Peasants' Party of Ukraine
SPU	Socialist Party of Ukraine
TKU	Labor Congress of Ukraine

REFERENCES

Birch, Sarah. (1995). "The Ukrainian Parliamentary and Presidential Elections of 1994." *Electoral Studies,* Vol. 14, pp. 93–99.

Birch, Sarah, and Andrew Wilson. (1999). "The Ukrainian parliamentary elections of 1998." *Electoral Studies,* Vol. 18, pp. 276–282.

Dawisha, Karen, and Bruce Parrott, eds. (1997). *Democratic Changes and Authoritarian Reactions in Russia, Ukraine, Belarus, and Moldova.* Cambridge, England: Cambridge University Press.

Kuzio, Taras, ed. (1997). *Ukraine under Kuchma.* Basingstoke, England: MacMillan Press.

United Kingdom

SUMMARY OF PARTY SYSTEMS

1945–79	two-party system (Conservatives and Labour)
1983–87	moderate multiparty system with one dominant party (Conservatives)
1992	two-and-a-half-party system
(1997–)	moderate multiparty system with one dominant party (Labour)

HISTORY

The United Kingdom has at its core England, to which Wales was formally joined in 1536 and Scotland in 1707—these three nations forming Great Britain. The island of Ireland was under British rule for centuries, but in 1921 the Catholic south broke away, leaving only Northern Ireland within the United Kingdom.

Internally, British political developments evolved slowly, sparing the country the turmoil that occurred in most of Europe. Parliamentary government was achieved by the 1830s, but the suffrage was extended over a century. Britain has also not been invaded for centuries, leading to an insular outlook, especially in England.

ELECTORAL SYSTEM

The United Kingdom uses a straightforward single-member-plurality electoral system. It was not until 1948, however, that extra votes for business people and certain university graduates were eliminated, as were the special university seats.

POLITICAL PARTIES AND CLEAVAGES

The **Labour Party** was formed in the early 1900s as a grouping of socialist intellectuals and members of the trade-unionist movement. The party has battled throughout its history with the conflict of adhering to the socialist doctrine on which the party was founded on the one hand, and electoral viability on the other. The party platform has therefore swung between espousing more far-left and center-left policies. In the early 1980s the party was on the far left arguing for nuclear disarmament, more socialist economic polices, and the withdrawal of the United Kingdom from the European Community. This swing left was counteracted by a shift to the right in the late 1980s and early 1990s, culminating in the "New Labour" movement championed by Tony Blair, which has included calls for budget constraint and welfare reform. The party has been consistent in its support of devolution of powers with regard to Scotland and Wales.

The **Conservative Party** (or Tory Party) is the United Kingdom's oldest modern party, whose lineage some have dated back as far as the seventeenth century. The party has never had a very firm ideology and has therefore espoused a variety of policies throughout its history. In recent decades, though, the party has been most closely associated with economic liberalism. The party has also consistently been suspicious of (or outright opposed to) the devolution of powers to British territories. The party's main bases of support have been business, the middle class, and farmers.

The **Liberal Democratic Party** was formed by the merger of the historic Liberal Party and the newer Social Democratic Party. The **Liberal Party** was formed in 1859 and was the major rival to the Tories prior to Labour's rise to prominence in the 1920s. The **Social Democratic Party** was created by moderate Labour members who split from the party in 1981 over opposition to the party's anti-EC stance and far-left policy swing. The two parties first got together in 1982 to form an electoral alliance that competed in the 1983 and 1987 elections. The Liberal Democrats then competed in subsequent elections as a unified party. The party has concentrated on issues such as the protection of the environment and support for the European Union.

Among the smaller parties, those of note include Britain's two nationalist parties, representing the Scottish and Welsh minorities. The **Scottish National Party (SNP)** was formed in 1934 and advocates an independent Scotland. **Plaid Cymru**, the Welsh Nationalist Party was founded in 1925 and has long advocated democratic-socialist self-government for Wales. Plaid Cymru was initially solely concerned with the Welsh speakers of Wales but in recent years has attempted to broaden its appeal to all the population of Wales. The party has also run in alliance with the **Greens** in recent years. These nationalist parties were jointly most successful in the October 1974 elections, when the SNP won eleven seats in the House of Commons, and Plaid Cymru won three. They were then able to pressure the Labour government to hold referenda on devolving powers to their regions. From 1979 onward, however, both parties have won very few seats in the House of Commons and thus have had a very marginal national influence. The creation of regional parliaments in Scotland and Wales has provided both the SNP and Plaid Cymru with a more successful forum.

In contrast to the Scottish and Welsh regional parties, most if not all of the parties discussed in the Northern Ireland section have, since 1974, contested and won seats in the House of Commons. The most significant of these are the **Ulster Unionist Party (UUP),** which since 1974 has been the fourth-largest party in the British House of Commons, and the Catholic **Social Democratic and Labour Party (SDLP)**. Indeed, the principal British parties no longer run candidates in Northern Ireland.

Selected Elections in the United Kingdom

	1945		**1950**		**1951**	
	%V	**#S**	**%V**	**#S**	**%V**	**#S**
Conservatives	39.8	213	43.5	299	48.0	321
Labour	48.3	393	46.1	315	48.8	295
Liberals	9.1	12	9.1	9	2.6	6
SNP	0.1	0	0.1	0	0.0	0
Plaid Cymru	0.1	0	0.0	0	0.0	0
others	2.6	22	1.2	2	0.6	3
TOTAL SEATS		640		625		625

	1959		**1964**		**1970**	
	%V	**#S**	**%V**	**#S**	**%V**	**#S**
Conservatives	49.4	365	43.4	304	46.4	330
Labour	43.8	258	44.1	317	43.1	288
Liberals	5.9	6	11.2	9	7.5	6
SNP	0.1	0	0.2	0	1.1	1
Plaid Cymru	0.3	0	0.3	0	0.6	0

	1959		1964		1970	
	%V	**#S**	**%V**	**#S**	**%V**	**#S**
others	0.5	1	0.8	0	1.3	5
TOTAL SEATS		630		630		630

	Feb 1974		Oct 1974		1979	
	%V	**#S**	**%V**	**#S**	**%V**	**#S**
Conservatives	37.9	297	35.8	277	43.9	339
Labour	37.2	301	39.3	319	36.9	269
Liberals	19.3	14	18.3	13	13.8	11
SNP	2.0	7	2.9	11	1.6	2
Plaid Cymru	0.5	2	0.6	3	0.4	2
UUP	1.5	11	1.5	10	1.3	10
SDLP	0.5	1	0.5	1	0.4	1
others	1.1	2	1.1	1	1.7	1
TOTAL SEATS		635		635		635

	1983		1992		1997	
	%V	**#S**	**%V**	**#S**	**%V**	**#S**
Conservatives	42.4	397	41.9	336	30.7	165
Labour	27.6	209	34.4	271	43.2	418
Liberal Democrats *	25.4	23	17.9	20	16.8	46
SNP	1.1	2	1.9	3	2.0	6
Plaid Cymru	0.4	2	0.5	4	0.5	4
UUP	1.4	15	0.8	9	0.8	10
SDLP	0.4	1	0.6	4	0.6	3
others	1.3	1	2.0	4	5.4	7
TOTAL TOTAL SEATS		650		651		659

Note: In 1983 and 1987 the Liberals and Social Democrats maintained separate identities but competed in an alliance, then in 1992 and 1997 competed as one party, the Liberal Democrats.

RECENT ELECTIONS

The 1983 elections were significant for the highs and lows reached by many of the parties competing. For Labour, 27.6 percent of the vote and 209 seats represented the party's lowest vote total since before the 1923 election, and the lowest seat total since 1931. This election marked the low point of a slide the party had been experiencing since the mid-1960s. In large part, these disastrous results experienced by Labour can be attributed to the more far-left policies the party was espousing at the time. In terms of popular vote, the party was nearly overtaken by the electoral alliance formed by the Liberals and Social Democrats who had split from Labour in response to the party's shift leftward. Despite winning only 1.8 percent less of the vote than Labour, the Liberal and Social Democrats did place a distant third in terms of share of seats, finishing 186 behind Labour due to the electoral system. The election also saw the Ulster Unionists win an impressive fifteen seats on only 1.4 percent of the popular vote. This result still represents the high-water mark of the party's showing in British general elections.

The 1992 election campaign was dominated by the issue of taxation. The Tories attacked Labour for its plan to increase the personal income taxation rate of higher-income earners. The Liberal Democrats, competing for the first time as a unified party, campaigned to raise the basic tax rate across the board so as to have more revenue to invest in education. Labour also campaigned on improving the health care provided through the National Health Service. The issue of greater powers for Scotland also featured prominently in the campaign, with both Labour and the Liberal Democrats arguing for the creation of a separate Scottish parliament. The SNP called for "independence within Europe," while the Tories opposed any devolution of powers.

The results gave the Conservative Party an overall majority of seats but the margin over Labour had decreased from the previous 1987 elections, in which the Tories had won 376 seats to Labour's 229. The Liberal Democrats continued to see their share of the popular vote decrease from the high the party had reached in 1983.

The most recent elections, held in 1997, saw Labour return to majority-party status in parliament after twenty-five years in opposition. No single issue dominated the campaign; instead, several issues shared prominence, including: the state of the economy, the country's future relationship with Europe; education; health care; and constitutional reform. The issue that proved most problematic for the Tory Party was Europe. The party was very divided over the issue, as Euro-skeptics within the party were ardently opposed to the European EMU. The Conservatives were also hurt by low public confidence in the national economy (which was actually showing signs of improvement), for which the Tories got most of the blame. Labour proved popular with its platform of "New Labour," which, among other things, promised no increase in personal taxes. The Liberal Democrats, while seeing their share of votes drop for the third straight election, did manage to double their share of seats—their best result since 1929 when the Liberals had won fifty-nine. This success was in large part due to the utter collapse of the Conservatives. In terms of number of seats won, it was the Tories' worst showing in over seventy-five years.

GOVERNMENTS

Since 1945, governments in the United Kingdom have always been single-party affairs, either of the Conservatives or the Labour Party. Although the February 1974 elections were the only elections to return a hung parliament, by 1977 the Labour majority elected in October 1974 had become a minority, dependent on the Liberals. Likewise, at the end of the 1992–97 Major government, divisions within the Conservative Party over European integration forced the government to rely on the votes of the Ulster Unionists.

United Kingdom Governments since 1945

In Office Date (M/Y)	Prime Minister (Party)	#M	Parties in Cabinet
07/45	Attlee, C. (Labour)	21	Labour Party
02/50	Attlee, C. (Labour)	18	Labour Party
11/51	Churchill, W. (Cons)	16	Conservative Party
04/55	Eden, A. (Cons)	18	Conservative Party
05/55	Eden, A. (Cons)	18	Conservative Party
01/57	Macmillan, H. (Cons)	19	Conservative Party
10/59	Macmillan, H. (Cons)	20	Conservative Party
10/63	Douglas-Home, A. (Cons)	22	Conservative Party
10/64	Wilson, H. (Labour)	22	Labour Party
04/66	Wilson, H. (Labour)	22	Labour Party

continued

United Kingdom Governments since 1945 *Continued*

In Office Date (M/Y)	Prime Minister (Party)	#M	Parties in Cabinet
06/70	Heath, E. (Cons)	18	Conservative Party
03/74	Wilson, H. (Labour)	21	Labour Party
10/74	Wilson, H. (Labour)	23	Labour Party
04/76	Callaghan, J. (Labour)	23	Labour Party
[from 1977 onward supported by the Liberal Party]			
05/79	Thatcher, M. (Cons)	22	Conservative Party
06/83	Thatcher, M. (Cons)	21	Conservative Party
06/87	Thatcher, M. (Cons)	21	Conservative Party
11/90	Major, J. (Cons)	22	Conservative Party
04/92	Major, J. (Cons)	22	Conservative Party
04/97	Blair, T. (Labour)	22	Labour Party

ACRONYMS

SDLP Social Democratic and Labour Party (Northern Ireland)
SDP Social Democratic Party
SNP Scottish Nationalist Party
UUP Ulster Unionist Party (Northern Ireland)

REFERENCES

Garner, Robert, and Richard Kelly (1998). *British Political Parties Today,* 2d. ed. Manchester: Manchester University Press.

King, Anthony, et al. (1998). *New Labour Triumphs: Britain at the Polls.* Chatham, N.J., Chatham House.

Peele, Gillian. (1995). *Governing the United Kingdom,* 3rd. ed. Oxford/Cambridge, Mass.: Blackwell.

Robins, Lynton, Hilary Blackmore, and Robert Piper, eds. (1994). *Britain's Changing Party System.* London: Leicester University Press.

Webb, Paul, and Justin Fisher (1999). "The Changing British Party System: Two-Party Equilibrium or the Emergence of Moderate Pluralism?," in David Broughton and Mark Donovan, eds., *Changing Party Systems in Western Europe.* London: Pinter, pp. 8–29.

Northern Ireland

SUMMARY OF PARTY SYSTEM

1996–(98) extreme multiparty system with a balance among the parties

HISTORY

From 1921 to 1972 a regional parliament existed in Northern Ireland, the elections for which were always won by the Ulster Unionist Party. Catholic frustration at this outcome led to violence and finally suspension of the parliament (considered part of the "problem") by the British government, which had retained full sovereignty. A tentative peace settlement in the 1990s led to elections for a constitutional forum and then the creation of a new Northern Irish Assembly. However, disagreements over the decommissioning of weapons led to repeated delays in forming an actual government for Northern Ireland. This finally occurred in November 1999, with power then devolved from London.

ELECTORAL SYSTEM

Northern Ireland uses the single-transferable-vote system of proportional representation, with eighteen districts electing six members each. STV has always been used for local and European elections in the region.

POLITICAL PARTIES AND CLEAVAGES

In Northern Ireland the main cleavage is overwhelmingly religion, between Protestant-unionist and Catholic-nationalist/republican parties. There is, however, a third group of parties that is nonsectarian.

The largest of the unionist parties is the **Ulster Unionist Party (UUP)**. The UUP (also known as the Official Ulster Unionist Party–OUUP), led by David Trimble, has as the main goals of its official party platform "the maintenance of Northern Ireland's position as an integral part of the United Kingdom" and the requirement of "the immediate unilateral withdrawal of the Irish Republic's territorial claim over Northern Ireland." It has, however, been far less rigid in this position than other unionist parties by showing its willingness to tolerate North-South Irish intergovernmental bodies as long as they have no executive powers. While the party leadership was a full supporter of the peace process and the Good Friday Agreement, segments of the party membership remain opposed. The party enjoys a broad base of support but is especially strong among the Protestant establishment. Despite having reservations about the EU, the party is a limited supporter of it.

The **Democratic Unionist Party (DUP)** was created in 1971 by the more radical members of the unionist movement. The DUP has a smaller base of support compared to that of the UUP. The party's support initially came primarily from members of the Free Presbyterian Church, which was organized by the Reverend Ian Paisley, leader of the DUP. Today, however, the party enjoys support from segments of the working class as well. Openly anti-Catholic (Rev. Paisley has denounced the pope regularly) and anti-Dublin, the party has also been a harsh critic of the European Union, as it is seen as a threat to national sovereignty. The party attracts the Protestant protest vote and is opposed to the Good Friday Agreement.

Other unionist parties include: the **UK Unionist Party (UKUP)**, which is opposed to the peace agreement and has called for closer links with Britain; the **Ulster Democratic Party (UDP)** and **Progressive Unionist Party (PUP)**, which both signed the Good Friday Agreement but were critical of what they saw as too many concessions to republican/nationalist parties. The latter two of these parties are also significant because they have strong links with different loyalist paramilitary groups; the UDP is associated with the Ulster Defence Association (UDA), and the PUP is linked with the Ulster Freedom Force (UFF).

On the nationalist side of the political spectrum, the largest party is the left-of-center **Social Democratic and Labour Party (SDLP)**, led by John Hume. Formed in 1970, the party is largely Catholic and has argued that popular consent should determine reunification with the Republic of Ireland. It has been instrumental in getting the peace process underway. The party has rejected violence as a means by which to attain political goals. The party is a strong supporter of the EU.

The nationalist party perhaps more well known than the SDLP, but with less electoral support, is **Sinn Féin**. The party, whose name means "We Ourselves," is an Irish-wide party that has argued for an end of partition, and for the reunification of the country. The party is led by Gerry Adams and is a Catholic and working-class party. The party is famous (or infamous) for its connection to the Irish Republican Army (IRA).

The **Alliance Party** is the largest of the truly communal political parties in Northern Ireland. The party, which was founded in 1970, is a nonsectarian, centrist party supported by both Protestants and Catholics. The Alliance Party has made a priority of giving support to those elements of Northern Ireland's political system that have been most inclusive to all interests. It supports the concept of a strong Northern Ireland Assembly with a high degree of devolved powers similar to Scotland. The party also espouses a liberal economic policy and is strongly pro-EU. The **Northern Ireland Women's Coalition (NIWC)** is another communal party. The NIWC was formed in the spring of 1996 on a nonsectarian platform that sought to raise the profile of women in politics in Northern Ireland.

Finally, the three independent Unionists elected in 1998 formed the **United Unionist Assembly Party** that September.

ELECTIONS

The 1996 elections were held to elect a 110-member constitutional forum from which parties would choose negotiating teams for the all-party talks that were to take place. The ten most successful parties were automatically granted (a minimum of) two seats.

The 1998 elections, held on 25 June, were the first to the newly created Northern Irish Assembly, which was established as a result of the all-party talks. The parties campaigned largely on whether or not they supported the agreement and the new assembly, and it was generally understood that the results of the election would be key to the success or failure of a historic peace agreement. In general, the results were a big success for the parties that supported the agreement (in particular for the SDLP and the UUP) and they left supporters of the province's peace deal in a strong position to put their provisions in place. The SDLP actually won the largest percent of the popular vote but, due to the electoral system, ended with four fewer seats than the UUP. The more hard-line unionist position, represented by parties such as the DUP, PUP, and UDP, also saw its share of the vote drop from the levels reached in 1996.

Elections in Northern Ireland

	1996		1998	
	%V	#S	%V	#S
UUP	24.2	30	21.3	28
SDLP	21.4	21	22.0	24
DUP	18.8	24	18.0	20
Sinn Féin	15.5	17	17.7	18
Alliance Party	6.5	7	6.5	6
UKUP	3.7	3	4.5	5
PUP	3.5	2	2.6	2
NIWC	1.0	2	1.6	2
UDP	2.2	2	1.1	0
Labour Party	0.9	2	0.3	0
Independent Unionists	—	—	—	3
others	2.4	0	4.4	0
TOTAL SEATS		110		108

GOVERNMENT

Disagreements over the timing of the decommissioning of Irish Republican Army weapons prevented a Northern Irish government from being formed until November 1999. Under the peace accord, the new government in Northern Ireland was to reflect the results of the 1998 elections, but in a consociational way. Thus, as the leader of the largest party, David Trimble of the UUP became first minister. Likewise, a member of the second largest party, the SDLP, became deputy first minister. Ten additional cabinet members (the number being fixed) responsible for specific ministries were assigned based on the d'Hondt version of proportional representation. Consequently, using this formula, the UUP got three cabinet seats (beyond that of the first minister), as did the SDLP (beyond that of the deputy first minister), while the hardline Protestant DUP and Sinn Féin each got two cabinet seats. The Northern Irish government can thus be described as an "involuntary coalition."

Governments in Northern Ireland since 1999

In Office Date (M/Y)	Prime Minister (Party)	#M	Parties in Cabinet
11/99	Trimble, D. (UUP)	12	UUP SDLP DUP Sinn Féin

ACRONYMS

DUP Democratic Unionist Party
NIWC Northern Ireland Women's Coalition
PUP Progressive Unionist Party
SDLP Social Democratic and Labour Party
UDP Ulster Democratic Party
UKUP United Kingdom Unionist Party
UUP Ulster Unionist Party

REFERENCE

Mitchell, Paul, and Rick Wilford (1999), eds. *Politics in Northern Ireland.* Boulder, Colorado: Westview.

Scotland

SUMMARY OF PARTY SYSTEM

(1999–) moderate multiparty system with one dominant party (Labour)

HISTORY

The monarchies of England and Scotland were united in 1603, but it was not until 1707 that Queen Anne finally "forced" Scotland into the United Kingdom, despite objections in Scotland. Prior to this unification, Scotland had been independent for centuries and had had a parliament since 1326. The 1707 Treaty of Union thus ended the separate Scottish parliament, but Scotland retained its separate church, educational, and legal systems. In the decades before World War I, the Liberal Party made various unsuccessful attempts to introduce "home rule" for Scotland. However, a separate administrative office, the Scottish Office, was created, and the secretary of state for Scotland would become a cabinet position in 1926.

In the first post–World War II decades, the British parties showed little interest in further changes for Scotland. However, a 1967 by-election victory by the Scottish National Party led to various reports and ultimately to modifications of opinion in the British parties. What was now called "devolution" concerned the transfer of powers to a new Scottish parliament. In 1977, in a minority situation, and under pressure from the SNP and Plaid Cymru, the Labour government introduced legislation to allow for referenda on devolution in Scotland and Wales. However, an amendment opposed by the government but passed by the House of Commons required that the vote not only be positive but that the "yes" vote represent at least 40 percent of the electorate. Thus, although in the referendum of March 1979 the Scots did vote 52 percent to 48 percent in favor of devolution, the yes votes were only 32.9 percent of the electorate. Consequently, the vote failed, and the Labour government was soon replaced by the Conservatives under Margaret Thatcher.

Prime Minister Thatcher was opposed to devolution, but the unpopularity of her party and its policies, in Scotland, led eventually to an upturn in popular support for Scottish devolution. This was formalized in the Scottish Constitutional Convention established in 1989, largely an alliance of Labour and Liberal Democrats. The victorious Labour government of 1997 was thus much more enthusiastic about devolution than it had been in the late 1970s and quickly introduced legislation for another referendum. This vote, held in September 1997, asked first about devolving powers to a Scottish parliament and then, in a second question, asked whether this parliament should have modest powers to raise income taxes. Both questions received a decisive yes vote (74.3 percent and 63.5 percent, respectively). No specific share(s) of the electorate were required. The Scottish Parliament thus came into existence in 1999. It has full powers over such things as agriculture, economic development, education, the environment, health, and policing.

ELECTORAL SYSTEM

Most of the seats in the Scottish Parliament (73 of 129) are elected by single-member plurality. The remaining fifty-six seats are assigned to "top up" the results in each district so as to make the district results as proportional as possible. There are eight districts, each of which has seven top-up seats. Once these seven seats are awarded, that is the end of the process, even if not every party has been fully equalized. (In other words, there is no possibility of expanding the Parliament as in Germany or New Zealand.) It is also important to stress that the calculation is done within each district, rather than for Scotland overall (which would be more proportional). Although there is no legal threshold to receive top-up seats, the effective threshold in a region is 5 to 6 percent.

POLITICAL PARTIES AND CLEAVAGES

The three principal British parties—Conservatives, Liberal Democrats, and Labour—contest the elections to the Scottish Parliament. Labour is strongest in the Glasgow area and in central Scotland, and correspondingly both the Conservatives and the Liberal Democrats are weakest in those areas. The Green Party also competes in Scotland. There are also various Scotland-specific parties. The most important of these is the **Scottish National Party (SNP)**. Founded in 1934, it won its first seat in the U.K. House of Commons in a by-election in April 1945, but quickly lost it in the general elections of June of that year. It was not until 1970 that it won a seat in a British general election. The SNP has long campaigned for Scottish independence and is also clearly a left-of-center party. Support for the party relates inversely to age. Its regional support is strongest in the northeast of Scotland and in the Highlands and Islands. Two other leftist parties have formed in recent years, in part as a reaction to the moderate policies of the Labour Party under Tony Blair. These are the **Scottish Socialist Party (SSP)**, formed in 1998, and the **Socialist Labour Party**. The SSP is concentrated in Glasgow.

There are thus two main cleavages in Scotland. The first is the traditional left-right cleavage, which overlaps with the distinction between the industrial and nonindustrial areas. The second main cleavage is the national one, that is, whether Scotland should become independent or remain part of the United Kingdom. This cleavage essentially separates the SNP from the other parties.

ELECTIONS

In the 1999 elections the Labour Party enjoyed the position of the traditional dominant party in Scotland. It also benefited from the personal popularity of Prime Minister Blair. However, Labour's middle-of-the-road policies meant that it wound up being relatively right wing in terms of the major parties. In particular, Labour opposed the wish, most strongly expressed by the Liberal Democrats and the SNP, to abolish university tuition.

As predicted, Labour came comfortably first, winning most of the single-member seats. Perhaps the clearest result of the elections was the lower-than-expected performance of the SNP. In part this can be attributed to party leader Alex Salmond's criticism of NATO's ongoing bombing campaign in Yugoslavia.

The 1999 Scottish Elections

			Of which	
	%V	**#S**	**Single-Member Seats**	**Regional Top-Up Seats**
Labour	33.6	56	53	3
SNP	27.3	35	7	28
Conservatives	15.3	18	0	18
Liberal Democrats	12.4	17	12	5
Greens	3.6	1	0	1
Socialist Labour	2.4	0	0	0
SSP	2.0	1	0	1
others	3.4	1	1	0
TOTAL SEATS		129	73	56

Note: Vote percentage refers to the total party list vote.

GOVERNMENT

As was expected, after the elections Labour and the Liberal Democrats formed a coalition government. This marked the first postwar coalition in Britain. The divisive issue of tuition fees was passed on to an inquiry.

Governments in Scotland since 1999

In Office Date (M/Y)	First Minister (Party)	#M	Parties in Cabinet
05/99	Dewar, D. (Labour)	11	Labour Party Liberal Democrats

ACRONYMS

SNP Scottish National Party
SSP Scottish Socialist Party

REFERENCES

Kellas, James G. (1990). "Scottish and Welsh Nationalist Parties Since 1945." In Anthony Seldon, ed. *United Kingdom Political Parties since 1945*. Hemel Hempstead: Philip Allan, pp. 122–37.

Newell, James L. (1994). "The Scottish National Party: An Overview," in Lieven de Winter, ed. *Non-Statewide Parties in Europe*. Barcelona: ICPS, pp. 71–96.

Wales

SUMMARY OF PARTY SYSTEM

(1999–) moderate multiparty system with one dominant party (Labour)

HISTORY

Wales was finally conquered by England in 1283. Acts of Union were passed in 1536 and 1543 that phased out all Welsh laws and administrative systems, replacing these with English ones. The only surviving element of Welsh identity was the Welsh language, but this too would face inroads by the English over the next centuries. (Today, less than 20 percent of the Welsh population, mainly in the northwest, speaks Welsh.)

Overall, Welsh demands for autonomy have always been less than those of Scotland. It was not until the 1960s that a Welsh Office and a secretary of state for Wales were established.

A referendum on devolution was held in 1979, on the same day as and similar to the one in Scotland. Only 20 percent of the Welsh voters voted yes to devolution. Facing uncertain support, the pro-devolution Labour government of 1997 held a referendum vote in Wales a week after the vote in Scotland, in hopes of a domino effect. Even with this added boost, the vote for devolution in Wales only passed by 50.3 percent to 49.7 percent.

Devolution has given the Wales an Assembly, as in Northern Ireland, as opposed to the Parliament in Scotland. The nomenclature is important, as the Assembly has less power in two senses. First of all, the National Assembly for Wales will have no power over taxation. Secondly, although it will deal with largely the same areas as the Scottish Parliament (agriculture, economic development, education, the environment, health, and also the Welsh language), the National Assembly for Wales has only powers of secondary legislation in these areas. That is, primary or framework legislation (which applies everywhere but Scotland) must first be passed by the House of Commons in London. Then the Welsh assembly will have the power to "fill in the details."

ELECTORAL SYSTEM

Two-thirds of the seats in the National Assembly for Wales (forty out of sixty) are elected by single-member plurality. The remaining twenty seats are assigned to top up the results in each district so as to make the district results as proportional as possible. There are five districts, each of which has, thus, only four top-up seats. Once these four seats are awarded, that is the end of the process even if not every party has been fully equalized. (In other words, there is no possibility of expanding the Assembly, as in Germany or New Zealand.) It is also important to stress that the calculation is done within each district, rather than for Wales overall (which would be more proportional). Although there is no legal threshold to receive top-up seats, the effective threshold in a region is 7 to 8 percent.

POLITICAL PARTIES AND CLEAVAGES

The three principal British parties—Conservatives, Liberal Democrats, and Labour—contest the elections to the Welsh assembly. Labour has traditionally been the strongest party in Wales, often winning mining constituencies with huge majorities. The Green Party also competes in Wales. However, the main indigenous party is the Welsh National Party, **Plaid Cymru**. Founded in 1925, it did not gain its first seat in the U.K. House of Commons until a by-election in July 1966. It won its first seat in a British general election in February 1974. Plaid Cymru has always stressed self-government for Wales rather than outright independence. Its support has traditionally been limited to rural Wales, especially the Welsh-speaking northwest. Even if nationalistic, non–Welsh speakers have been somewhat suspicious of it. There is thus a clear ethnic/linguistic cleavage in Wales in addition to the overall left-right divide.

ELECTIONS

In the 1999 elections to the National Assembly, the Labour Party started from the position of the traditional dominant party in Wales and hoped for an absolute majority. However, the imposition of the party leader (and prospective "first secretary" or premier) by the party leadership in London, overriding a more popular but also more independent local personality, proved to be a liability. Labour thus failed to win the overall majority that seemed within its grasp in the months leading up to the vote. In contrast, Plaid Cymru was able to make a major breakthrough, winning constituencies in the mining areas of the South Wales valleys. The party stressed that it should no longer be seen just as a party for Welsh speakers and referred to itself with the bilingual label "Plaid Cymru—The Party of Wales." Plaid Cymru was still unsuccessful in urban areas, however.

The 1999 Welsh Elections

			Of which	
	%V	**#S**	**Single-Member Seats**	**Regional Top-Up Seats**
Labour	35.4	28	27	1
Plaid Cymru	30.5	17	9	8
Conservatives	16.5	9	1	8

continued

The 1999 Welsh Elections *Continued*

	%V	#S	*Of which* Single-Member Seats	*Of which* Regional Top-Up Seats
Liberal Democrats	12.5	6	3	3
Greens	2.5	0	0	0
others	2.6	0	0	0
TOTAL SEATS		60	40	20

Note: Vote percentage refers to the total party list vote.

GOVERNMENT

Although Prime Minister Blair favored a Labour–Liberal Democrat coalition in Wales to parallel the one developed in Scotland, the Labour first secretary (or premier), Alun Michael, chose to form a minority administration. This pleased Plaid Cymru, sensing it would have greater influence in a minority situation.

Governments in Wales since 1999

In Office Date (M/Y)	First Secretary (Party)	#M	Parties in Cabinet
05/99	Michael, A. (Labour)	9	Labour Party

REFERENCE

Kellas, James G. (1990). "Scottish and Welsh Nationalist Parties Since 1945," in Anthony Seldon, ed. *U.K. Political Parties since 1945*. Hemel Hempstead: Philip Allan, pp. 122–37.